WOMAN'S BODY

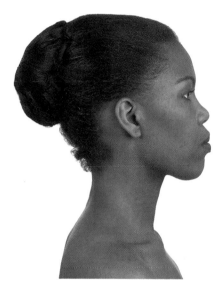

CONTRIBUTORS AND CONSULTANTS

◆

Jennifer Altman, PhD
Research consultant and writer specializing in the neurosciences

James A Bee, PhD
Senior lecturer in veterinary anatomy

Gillian Bendelow, PhD, SRN, RMN
Doctor of medical sociology specializing in women's issues

Nigel Brown, PhD
Consultant in fetal development

Felicity Challoner, MB, BS, MRCGP, DCH, DROG
General practitioner specializing in women's health and fertility

Susie Dinan, Cert Ed, Post Grad Dip
*Exercise educator and assistant director of development
at London Central YMCA*

Linda Ficker, MB, FRCS, FC, Ophth
Ophthalmic consultant, lecturer, and surgeon

Jill Gaskel, BSc (Hons)
Exercise educator and director of development at London Central YMCA

Sami Girling, MCSP, SRP, PGDSP
Physiotherapist

Diane Jakobson, PhD
Consultant and writer in medical sciences

Molly Jennings, MCSP, Chartered ACPOG
Consultant in women's health

Valerie J Lund, MS, FRCS
Reader in rhinology and honorary consultant ENT surgeon

Jessica Mann
Lecturer and consultant in cardiovascular pathology

Lesley H Rees, MDDSc, FRCP, FRCPath
Professor of chemical endocrinology

Ann Sandison, MPhil, MBChB
Consultant and assistant lecturer in histopathology

John Schetrumpf, FRCS Ed
Cosmetic surgeon

Linda Shaw, BDS, PhD (Lond), FDSRCS
Consultant and senior lecturer in dentistry

Mary Sheppard, MD, MRCPath
Senior lecturer in lung pathology

Nicholas Siddle, MB, ChB, MRCOG
Consultant in obstetrics and gynecology

Robert Whittle, MB, BS
Medical editor and writer

◆

CANADIAN MEDICAL ASSOCIATION

WOMAN'S BODY

Contributing Editors
Miriam Stoppard, MD, MRCP ◆ Catherine Younger-Lewis, MD, CCFP

The Reader's Digest Association (Canada) Ltd.
MONTREAL

A DORLING KINDERSLEY BOOK

Created and Produced by
CARROLL & BROWN LIMITED
5 Lonsdale Road
London NW6 6RA

Editorial Director   Amy Carroll
Senior Editor   Claire Burdett
Editor   Stella Vayne
Assistant Editor   Alison MacTier

Design Director   Denise Brown
Art Editor   Heather Johnston
Designer   Hazel Taylor
Assistant Designers   Carmel O'Neill, Lucy De Rosa
Mac Artworkers   Kevin Barrett, Mike Dyer

Photographers   Debi Treloar, Jules Selmes
Assisted by Steve Head

Production Consultant   Lorraine Baird
Production Editor   Wendy Rogers
Production Assistant   Amanda Mackie

CANADIAN MEDICAL ASSOCIATION
President   Bruno L'Heureux, MD
Secretary General   Léo-Paul Landry
Executive Director   Barbara E. Drew
Director of Publications   Stephen Prudhomme
Editor-in-Chief   Bruce P. Squires, MD, PhD
Associate Editor-in-Chief   Patricia Huston, MD, MPH
Medical Editor   Catherine Younger-Lewis, MD, CCFP
Assistant Director of Publications, Operations   Leesa D. Bruce

READER'S DIGEST
Editor   Sandy Shepherd
Researchers   Wadad Bashour, Anita Winterberg

Published in Canada in 1995 by
The Reader's Digest Association (Canada) Ltd.
215 Redfern Avenue
Westmount, Quebec H3Z2V9

CANADIAN CATALOGUING IN PUBLICATION DATA
Main entry under title:
Woman's body
Includes index.
ISBN 0–88850–246–X
1. Women – Health and hygiene. 2. Women –
Physiology. I. Stoppard, Miriam II. Younger-Lewis,
Catherine III. Reader's Digest Association (Canada)
RA778.W65 1995   613'.0424   C94–900667–X

Reproduced by Colourscan, Singapore
Printed in Italy by New Interlitho Spa, Milan
95 96 97 98 99/5 4 3 2 1

CONTENTS

Throughout the book, words have been set in small capital letters to indicate that this subject matter is discussed more fully elsewhere. Refer to the index for the relevant page(s). As you would expect, woman, rather than man, has been used as the name of the species.

INTRODUCTION

Woman's Body has been written for women of all ages and from all cultural backgrounds. It is a book of discovery – for teenagers and eighty-year-olds alike. All too often, women's bodies are written about, and judged, through the eyes of men. But here you can read about and celebrate women's bodies through the eyes of women. The following eight chapters uncover, in illuminating detail and clear illustrations, your physical and mental characteristics, the fascinating way your body changes and develops from birth to the post-menopausal years, and the enormous range of women's experiences and achievements, as well as customs and perceptions of women around the world.

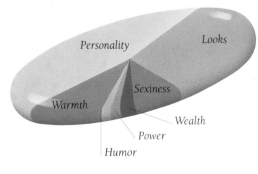

Negroid mesomorph

THE PHYSICAL WOMAN

Millions of years of evolution have made you, a woman, into one of the most complex, intelligent, and sensual of all living creatures. But women's bodies are not all the same. They differ from each other in shape and racial type. Compare your shape with those in this book, and read about some of the typical behaviors and beliefs of various cultures concerning different parts of a woman's body. Detailed diagrams also enable you to explore your intricate anatomy. Look at how your muscles work, and discover the science of movement. Inform yourself about some of the problems and diseases that can afflict you, and make comparisons between women and men, and women and other animal species, to discover some similarities – and differences.

Personality

Looks

Sexiness

Warmth

Wealth

Power

Humor

Statistics on what men find attractive about women

THE INNER WOMAN

The history of women's psychology and how your personality may be shaped by your beliefs and culture is laid out here in intriguing detail.

Skeletal muscles

You are depicted in your various roles – as worker, thinker, leader, mother, and lover. Examples of amazing women in history will inspire and entertain you. Knowing about other women's achievements will expand your horizons and help you to reach your potential; understanding yourself is key to realizing it.

THE SEXUAL WOMAN

A woman's sexuality is a potent blend of emotional and physical drives. You will find in this book the exciting, complex range of female sexual behavior – from fantasies to understanding and achieving orgasm. Various positions for sexual activity are shown here, masturbation is described, and safer sex techniques are discussed. Discover how to deal with some common sexual problems and how sexually transmitted diseases can be avoided.

Performing breast massage

THE HEALTHY WOMAN

Motivating yourself to stay fit and in good health takes some work, but your efforts will go a long way to ensure that you get the most out of your life. A well-balanced diet is essential to staying healthy and is not difficult to achieve once you know the basics of good nutrition – the major food groups, and what vitamins and minerals can do for you. Learn about eating disorders, such as anorexia nervosa and bulimia, so that you can avoid them. Keeping fit does not mean you have to be an athlete – hiking, ballroom dancing, and other activities will maintain your stamina and muscle tone, and challenge you at the same time. Suggestions on skin care, massage, health checks, and alternative therapies will help you take the best care of your body.

The cilia inside the fallopian tube

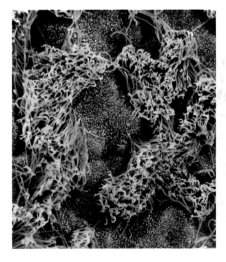

Reflex points on the sole of the foot

THE FERTILE WOMAN

The ability to create new life is one of the amazing potentials of all females, whether human or of other animal species. Find out about the voyage an ovum makes each month in your body, and the subtle signs that occur when this happens. Learn how genes work, and what kinds of contraception may be best for you. We discuss infertility and what tests can be done to determine the cause.

Bonding between mother and child

THE PREGNANT WOMAN

Pregnancy may be natural, but it is not always easy. Consider the effect pregnancy can have on your emotions and lifestyle, and how your body changes both inside and out. Our explanations tell you how to care for yourself during pregnancy, and after the birth, and give you tips on how to deal with some of the difficulties. You can also compare your experiences with those of other cultures, and their views on conception, pregnancy, and birth.

THE OLDER WOMAN

Menopause can be a time of accomplishment. You are likely to be free of young children, financially more stable than before, and you will probably have more energy to take advantage of the many years that stretch ahead of you. In Canada, many older women stay fit and maintain a vibrant role in their community. Find out how to minimize the risks of osteoporosis, and learn the latest on hormone replacement therapy. The more you know about the physical and psychological aspects of aging, the more likely you will feel confident in dealing with them.

THE EMERGING WOMAN

The milestones in the development of girls, from the womb to toddlerhood and school age are laid out here one by one. They are rarely the same for each girl, however – girls change into women at different times, and both early and late bloomers are normal. Look at the way girls grew up in the past, and how girls are regarded in other cultures. Read about a girl genius, see images of girls throughout the ages, and find out what school is like for girls in different cultures.

Post-menopausal woman

This book is ideal for browsing. A large team of people have worked to create in this book an image of women's bodies that will help women understand, celebrate, and care for their bodies more than they have before, as well as gaining a deeper appreciation of women worldwide. If after reading this book you are more knowledgeable and enthusiastic about what it means to be a woman, then the book's goal will have been realized.

Patricia Huston MD, MPH
Associate Editor-in-chief,
Canadian Medical Association Publications

8

THE PHYSICAL WOMAN

PHYSIQUE

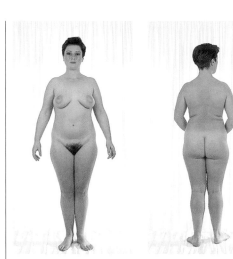

Medium-build endomorph. Caucasoid.

Medium-build mesomorph. Negroid.

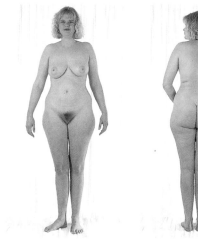

Large-build mesomorph. Caucasoid.

Medium-build ectomorph. Caucasoid.

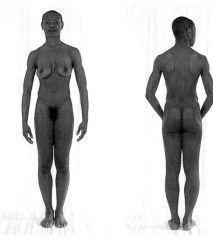

Large-build ectomorph. Negroid.

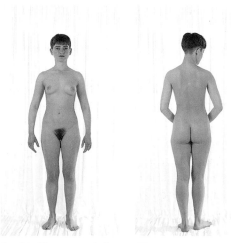

Small-build mesomorph. Caucasoid.

A woman's body

Shapes and sizes of women's bodies vary tremendously. Whatever her build, a woman's body falls into one of three body types: endomorph (apple-shaped), mesomorph (pear-shaped), or ectomorph (beanpole-shaped). These are described more fully on page 17. The world racial types, to one of which each woman belongs, are discussed on page 19. Our feature shot (above) is a medium-build Caucasoid–Mongoloid mesomorphic woman.

10

WOMAN'S SKELETON

The average woman's skeleton contains 206 bones; it provides her body with a protective and supportive framework for the muscles and surrounding soft tissues. Compared to the average man's skeleton, the average woman's skeleton is smaller and lighter. Relative to her height and build, the average woman has narrower shoulders, a shorter thorax (ribcage), and a broader pelvis than the average man.

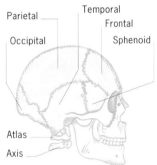

Parietal
Temporal
Frontal
Occipital
Sphenoid
Atlas
Axis

Skull

Twenty-nine flat, fused bones make up the skull. These protect the brain and delicate sensory organs. The spine's top vertebra, called the atlas, rotates around the second vertebra (the axis), enabling a woman to move her head to locate sensory stimuli.

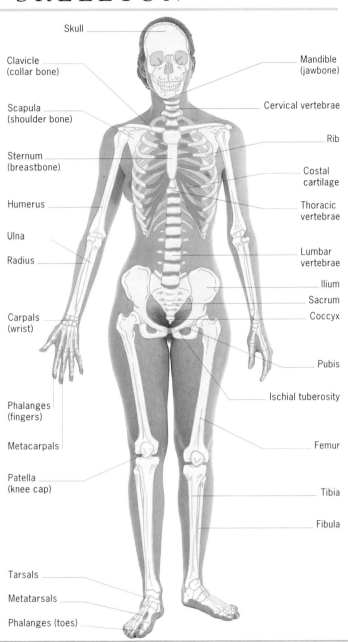

Skull

Clavicle (collar bone)

Scapula (shoulder bone)

Sternum (breastbone)

Humerus

Ulna

Radius

Carpals (wrist)

Phalanges (fingers)

Metacarpals

Patella (knee cap)

Tarsals

Metatarsals

Phalanges (toes)

Mandible (jawbone)

Cervical vertebrae

Rib

Costal cartilage

Thoracic vertebrae

Lumbar vertebrae

Ilium

Sacrum

Coccyx

Pubis

Ischial tuberosity

Femur

Tibia

Fibula

JOINTS

Rigid bones meet at joints, which allow flexible movement where needed. Fixed joints, present in the skull, are firmly secured; cartilaginous joints, like those in the pelvis, provide some elastic movement; synovial joints are freely movable.

MOBILE JOINTS

The surfaces of synovial joints are coated with cartilage to reduce friction during movement. The joint cavities are filled with synovial (lubricating) fluid.

Ball-and-socket joints
Found in the hips and shoulders, these permit a range of movement in all directions.

Saddle joints
As in the thumb, these can move back and forth.

Hinge joints
Elbows, knees, and other joints are hinged and can bend in a single plane.

Gliding joints
The intercarpal joints in the hands move back and forth and side to side.

WOMAN VS. ANIMAL

All mammals share the same basic skeletal plan. A woman's neck, for example, contains the same number of vertebrae as that of a giraffe, despite the size difference.

BONE

The outer layer of bone is the hard periosteum. Beneath this are cells called osteocytes embedded in the mineralized lamella. The internal surface of bone is the endosteum, which surrounds the marrow cavity in which blood cells and PLATELETS form.

Endosteum

Lamella

Periosteum

The shape of the pelvis differs noticeably between the sexes, reflecting their different functions.

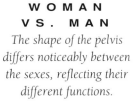

Pubic arch

Ischial spine

A woman's pelvis is tilted forward with a broad, shallow cavity. The bones are thinner and less dense than a man's. The upper "false" pelvis (hipbones) and the lower "true" pelvis are usually wider than a man's, and the pubic arch is broader (over 90°) and more rounded. The ISCHIAL SPINES are only significant during childbirth.

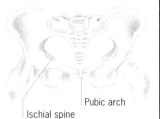

Pubic arch

A man's pelvis is also tilted forward but, unlike a woman's pelvis, which has evolved to accommodate childbirth, it has a narrow, deep cavity. This allows support for heavier muscles and for bones that are heavier, denser, and thicker than a woman's bones. A man's pelvis is usually narrower than that of a woman, and the angle of the pubic arch is very acute (less than 90°).

LIGAMENTS

These tough bands of white, fibrous, slightly elastic tissue are important components of joints. They bind together the bone ends and prevent excessive movement of the joint. They also support various body organs, including the uterus, bladder, and breasts.

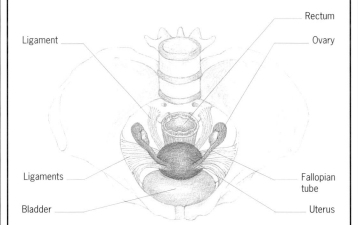

Ligament

Rectum

Ovary

Ligaments

Fallopian tube

Bladder

Uterus

SPINAL COLUMN

Twenty-four vertebrae (bones), roughly cylindrical, end in the fused vertebrae of the sacrum, and the tiny bones of the tail-like coccyx, to form a column that supports the body's trunk and head. Tough, fibrous intervertebral discs, with a jellylike core, cushion the cartilage-coated vertebrae. The spinal column also forms a protective enclosure for the spinal cord, consisting of inner gray matter and outer white matter. Gray matter contains NERVE BODY cells, BLOOD VESSELS, and glial (glue) cells. White matter contains axons (extensions of nerve cells), whose cell bodies are in the brain and the spinal cord. These axons convey messages between the spinal cord and the brain.

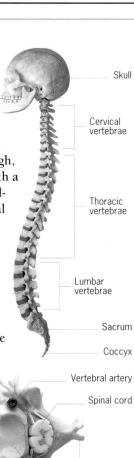

Skull

Cervical vertebrae

Thoracic vertebrae

Lumbar vertebrae

Sacrum

Coccyx

Vertebral artery

Spinal cord

Vertebra

Vertebral body

Movable bony protection
The individual vertebrae protect the spinal cord, support the body, and make the spine flexible.

POSTURE

A woman's SPINAL COLUMN (below) resembles an elongated S: in a normal spine the lumbar vertebrae curve forward, while the thoracic vertebrae and sacrum curve backward. This allows the spine to absorb shocks that would otherwise reach the vulnerable brain.

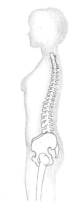

Standing
The head, shoulders, and hips are all in line when a woman's posture is good. Bad posture puts the body under strain.

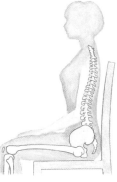

Sitting
Shoulders should be in line with the hips when posture is good.

Wearing high heels
A woman wearing high heels is tilted forward; she sticks out her bottom to compensate.

WOMAN'S STATURE

The average Western woman is 1.62m (5ft 4in) tall (right). By contrast, most of the female members of the Tutsi tribe of Rwanda and Burundi stand 1.78m (5ft 10in) tall (right), while most female members of the Mbuti of Zaire are approximately 1.35m (4ft 5in) tall (right). While two individual women can have as much as a 60cm (2ft) difference in height between them, only about 7.5–12.5cm (3–5in) separates the average woman from the average man. This small difference has made a crucial contribution to the age-old ideas of "femaleness" and "maleness." Being small is perceived as super-feminine, while being very tall is seen as super-masculine. Many women, therefore, have an inherent preference for mates who are at least slightly taller than they are. For the same reason, very tall women are often seen as unfeminine.

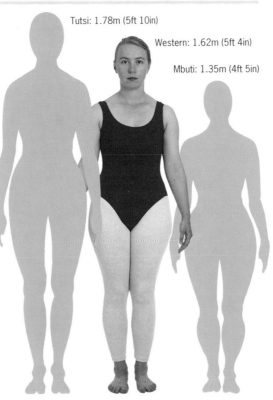

Tutsi: 1.78m (5ft 10in)

Western: 1.62m (5ft 4in)

Mbuti: 1.35m (4ft 5in)

SHORTEST/TALLEST

Pauline Musters (1876–95) measured 61cm (24in) in height (above) and was the shortest human being ever recorded. Zeng Jinlian (1964–82) was the tallest woman at 2.47m (8ft 1¾in).

FAT DISTRIBUTION

About 20–25% of a woman's weight consists of fat (compared to 15–20% for a man). Fat deposits are essential for female FERTILITY. To be fertile, a woman's body must carry at least 16% fat to maintain the necessary hormone production. Fat is distributed mainly over a woman's thighs, buttocks, breasts, upper arms, and abdomen, which results in the typically curvaceous female figure. Despite the Western enthusiasm for extreme female slenderness, most men are instinctively attracted to the curvaceous female figure because it signals fertility. Once a woman experiences MENOPAUSE, her fat deposits mirror those of a man and fat accumulates over her waist, rather than hips and thighs.

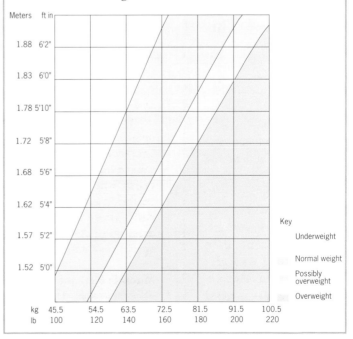

Fat distribution
The areas colored blue represent large fat deposits on the female body.

WEIGHT AND HEIGHT

The Body Mass Index (BMI), although only based on average build, can gauge ideal weight. An ectomorphic woman with large bone structure may weigh more, but be thinner, than an endomorphic woman of the same height with small bone structure.

Meters	ft in
1.88	6'2"
1.83	6'0"
1.78	5'10"
1.72	5'8"
1.68	5'6"
1.62	5'4"
1.57	5'2"
1.52	5'0"

Key

Underweight

Normal weight

Possibly overweight

Overweight

kg	45.5	54.5	63.5	72.5	81.5	91.5	100.5
lb	100	120	140	160	180	200	220

MORE WOMAN TO LOVE

Contrary to the Duchess of Windsor's fabled remark that "one can never be too thin," many cultures worldwide find well-endowed women extremely attractive. In some societies, such as the Waririke tribe of Nigeria, women approaching marriage are given the best food to fatten them up and make them more desirable.

FAT LOSS IN BODYBUILDING

One of the aims of bodybuilding is to convert fat into muscle and so produce a lean shape. In women bodybuilders, this is most noticeable on the chest, where, in many cases, the breasts are nearly, or completely, lost. The thighs and buttocks also become very muscular and toned. In the most extreme forms, the body may acquire an asexual appearance. A professional female bodybuilder may lose the ability to OVULATE and MENSTRUATE if her body has insufficient fat for adequate hormone production.

MUSCULAR STRUCTURE

A woman's body contains more than 600 muscles, and these account for about 40% of her body weight. There are three TYPES OF MUSCLE in the body: skeletal, smooth, and cardiac. The majority are voluntary muscles or under conscious control (skeletal), the rest are partly (smooth) or completely involuntary (cardiac).

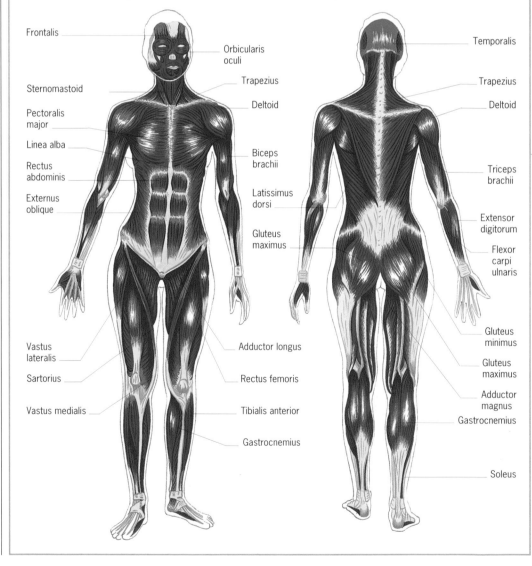

Frontalis
Orbicularis oculi
Sternomastoid
Trapezius
Pectoralis major
Deltoid
Linea alba
Biceps brachii
Rectus abdominis
Latissimus dorsi
Externus oblique
Gluteus maximus
Vastus lateralis
Adductor longus
Sartorius
Rectus femoris
Vastus medialis
Tibialis anterior
Gastrocnemius

Temporalis
Trapezius
Deltoid
Triceps brachii
Extensor digitorum
Flexor carpi ulnaris
Gluteus minimus
Gluteus maximus
Adductor magnus
Gastrocnemius
Soleus

STEATOPYGIA

Certain races, such as the San (Bushmen) of Southern Africa, have extra deposits of fat on their buttocks and thighs. This is known as steatopygia. In times of famine, the fat acts as an energy store. Some authorities believe that ancient woman was endowed similarly to the modern San woman.

TYPES OF MUSCLES

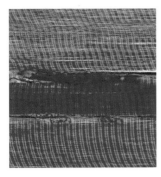

Skeletal muscles

Extensors open out joints, flexors close them; adductors draw body parts inward, abductors move them outward; rotators turn inward or outward; sphincters (constrictors) surround and close orifices.

Skeletal muscle consists of bundles of muscle fibers that appear striped.

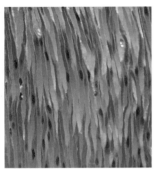

Smooth muscles

These line the walls of the internal body organs and help them function. For example, smooth muscles enable the digestive organs to process food and waste products and the uterus to expel a baby during labor.

Smooth muscle is composed of long, spindle-shaped cells arranged in bundles.

Cardiac muscle

Found solely in the heart, cardiac muscle works unceasingly to propel blood through the CIRCULATORY SYSTEM by contracting and relaxing rhythmically. This happens more than 100,000 times per day. Cardiac muscle contains many short, branching cells (pink), divided by intercellular junctions (blue).

THE LARGE MUSCLES

The *gluteus maximus*, which forms the buttock, is normally the bulkiest muscle in a woman's body. It extends from the lower backbone to the upper thighbone and moves the thigh. The uterus increases by about 35 times during pregnancy, so that by term it weighs over 1kg (2lb), making it the largest muscle.

MOVING SKELETAL MUSCLES

Skeletal muscles are usually arranged in pairs on each side of every joint, so that as one contracts the other slowly relaxes to give a smooth, controlled movement. Muscles gently pull against each other all the time, creating muscle tone.

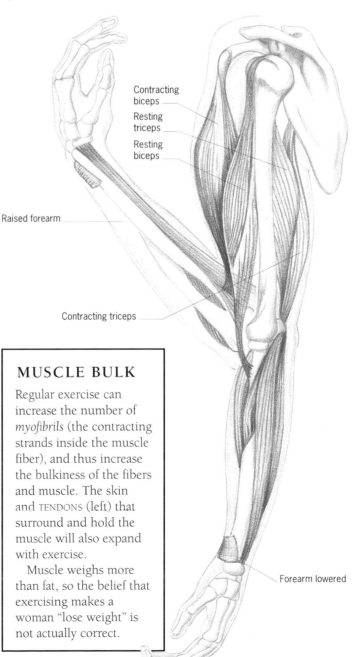

Contracting biceps

Resting triceps

Resting biceps

Raised forearm

Contracting triceps

Forearm lowered

TENDONS

These fibrous cords convey the power of locomotion from muscle to bone. They are strong and flexible, but relatively inelastic, and are made up principally of bundles of collagen (fibers with high tensile strength) and some blood vessels. Large tendons have a nerve supply. Where they may be subject to excessive friction, tendons are enclosed in fibrous capsules and bathed in a lubricating fluid.

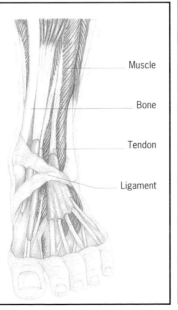

Muscle

Bone

Tendon

Ligament

MUSCLE BULK

Regular exercise can increase the number of *myofibrils* (the contracting strands inside the muscle fiber), and thus increase the bulkiness of the fibers and muscle. The skin and TENDONS (left) that surround and hold the muscle will also expand with exercise.

Muscle weighs more than fat, so the belief that exercising makes a woman "lose weight" is not actually correct.

TENNIS ELBOW

Although known as tennis elbow, pain and tenderness at the outer side of the elbow and in the back of the forearm may result from activities other than tennis, where there is overuse of the muscles that straighten the wrist and fingers. Tennis elbow occurs when a woman repeatedly bends her elbow while gripping tightly – when lifting a toddler frequently, for example.

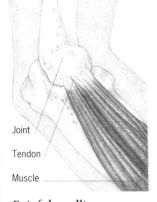

Joint

Tendon

Muscle

Painful swelling
Constant tugging of the tendons at the point of attachment results in inflammation.

MUSCLE FIBERS

The ratio of fast fibers (those that burn glucose as fuel) and slow fibers (those that burn fat as fuel) found in muscles, varies from woman to woman. Some women have more fast fibers and this is thought to cause their muscles to burn up less fat. Women are born with their fiber types fixed, and can only change some fast fibers to slow fibers with endurance training. Women with "fast" muscles are usually sprinters and weightlifters; those women with slow fibers are distance runners.

ATHLETIC PROWESS

Current record-holders demonstrate remarkable abilities. One notable example is Hilda Lorna Johnstone, who competed in the equestrian dressage test in the 1972 Olympic games, when she was aged 70 years and 5 days.

Young athletic talent
In 1990, Jennifer Capriati of the USA became the youngest-ever winner at Wimbledon. She was 14 years and 86 days old.

SPEED
Delorez Florence Griffith Joyner, aged 28 years, of the USA, achieved a top speed of 39.56km (24$^{1}/_{2}$ miles) per hr in the 100m (329ft) race in 1988.

STAMINA
The triathlon (swimming 3.8km/2.4 miles, cycling 180km/112 miles, and running 42.195km/26 miles 385yd) was completed by Paula Newby-Fraser of Zimbabwe in 9hr 56sec on October 15, 1989. This was only 40 seconds longer than the male winner.

The fastest 42.195km (26 miles 385yd) marathon race ever was run by Ingrid Kristiansen of Norway. She completed the London Marathon in 2hr 21min 6sec on April 21,1985.

The fastest-ever swim across the English Channel (7hr 40min) was by Penny Dean of the USA on July 29, 1978.

JUMPING
A record 7.52m (24ft 8$^{1}/_{4}$in) long jump was made by Galina Chistyakova (from the former USSR) on June 11, 1988.

Stefka Kostadinova of Bulgaria jumped a record 2.09m (6ft 10$^{1}/_{4}$in) in the high jump on June 11, 1987.

LIFTING STRENGTH
A record of 115kg (253$^{1}/_{2}$lb) in the "snatch" and 150kg (330$^{1}/_{2}$ lb) in the "jerk" (a total of 265kg/584lb), was achieved by Li Yajuan of China on May 24, 1992.

TENNIS
The greatest number of Wimbledon tennis championships was won by Billie Jean King of the USA in the period 1961–79. She won 20 in total: six singles, ten women's doubles, and four mixed doubles.

Martina Navrátilová of the USA won a record nine Wimbledon tennis singles championships between 1978 and 1990.

WOMAN'S MUSCLE STRENGTH

Traditionally, women are not considered to be as strong as men in terms of muscle strength, but any continuing discrepancy in modern times centers on the upper body because men have proportionally larger lungs and bigger ribcages than women. Where lower body muscle strength is concerned, the abilities of men and women have drawn much closer. Differences in strength began to disappear in the second half of the 20th century as women dramatically improved their abilities, while men have made only moderate gains over the same period.

NECK STRETCHING

The Paduang tribe of Burma artificially elongates the necks of its young girls. At the age of five, metal rings are put around a girl's neck and additional rings are added as she grows. These depress the shoulders and make the neck appear longer. The custom leaves the woman with a weak neck, so that if the rings were to be removed, her neck would be unable to support her head.

FIGURE MANIPULATION

Whalebone corsets, foundation garments, and even surgical removal of one or more ribs were devices used by Victorian women to achieve hourglass figures. In the Edwardian period, hip pads and bustles were used to accentuate women's hips and buttocks in emulation of a mature figure. Many modern women exercise and follow low-calorie DIETS in pursuit of waiflike thinness.

HEAD BINDING

Several Native American tribes and the Maya of Central America bound the heads of their babies with boards to produce a flattened, elongated skull. They considered this to be very beautiful.

The head was bound from birth.

WEIGHT TRAINING

MUSCLE BULK is increased by stimulating protein production. Although it is dangerous, some athletes take anabolic steroids to mimic the muscle-enhancing properties of TESTOSTERONE.

WOMAN'S BODY TYPES

Women's shapes vary in many ways, which makes the classification of body type a less than exact science. All women, however, have a tendency toward one of the three body types, and the extremes are easily identifiable. The basic body structure is always discernible, even though its contours can be altered by MANIPULATION (above), illness, starvation, DIETING, WEIGHT TRAINING (left), BODYBUILDING, or plastic surgery.

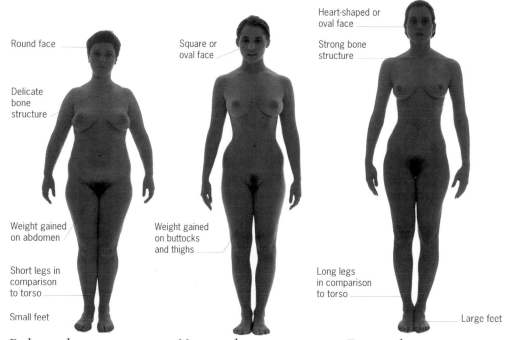

Round face

Delicate bone structure

Weight gained on abdomen

Short legs in comparison to torso

Small feet

Square or oval face

Weight gained on buttocks and thighs

Heart-shaped or oval face

Strong bone structure

Long legs in comparison to torso

Large feet

Endomorph

If plump, endomorphs tend to be apple-shaped because they gain weight mainly on their abdomens. Their legs are shorter than their torsos, and their breasts tend to be larger than average. Endomorphs have light bone structures and generally gain weight very easily.

Mesomorph

Pear-shaped mesomorphs are the most typically female in shape. Their hips are larger than their shoulders, and their legs are about the same length as their torsos. Mesomorphs gain weight first on the thighs, and then on the hips and buttocks.

Ectomorph

If thin, ectomorphs tend to be beanpole-shaped. They have long legs in proportion to their torsos and strong bone structures. Ectomorphs tend not to gain weight easily. If they do so, it is usually distributed evenly over the body, rather than in one place.

WOMAN'S CHANGING SHAPE

Throughout history, the "ideal" woman's body has altered according to changing perceptions of beauty. In the West, the 20th century alone has produced a wide range of different "ideally" beautiful bodies.

1970s Earth mother
During the flower-power era, long hair and generous proportions – amply illustrated by Mama Cass of "The Mamas and the Papas" – were widely fêted.

1920s Flapper
In the Jazz Age, the preferred shape was slender, elegant, and boyish, with no waistline and shingled hair.

1950s Venus
Marilyn Monroe was the archetypal hour glass, with a large bust, small waist, and womanly hips.

1990s Gladiatorial
The ideal woman of the 1990s is seen as strong, physically fit, and confidently sensual.

1960s Sex kitten
Jane Fonda in the film Barbarella personified the prototypical, futuristic sex kitten – slim, curvy, and long-haired, with pouting lips.

WORLD RACIAL TYPES

If not of mixed race, a woman will belong to one of four ethnic groups. These are distinguished by certain features – some are readily discernible and others are identified by specialized tests. Within each ethnic type, the three BODY TYPES can occur.

Caucasoid
This most varied group includes tall, blonde Nordic women, shorter, darker Mediterranean women, and fine-boned, dark-skinned Indians and Arabs.

Caucasoids 49%

Mongoloid
Resilient and well adapted to adverse climates, particularly extreme cold, Mongoloid women vary in shape from the stocky Inuit to the taller Tartars.

Mongoloids 28%

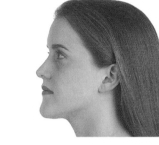

Negroid
Women in this group vary from the tall Tutsi, whose average height is 1.78m (5ft 10in), to the diminutive Mbuti, whose average height is 1.35m (4ft 5in).

Negroids 12%

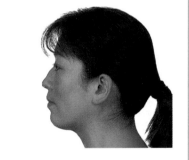

Mixed racial types
Varying widely in appearance, these women usually evince a blend of their inherited racial characteristics. Our model is Caucasoid–Mongoloid.

Mixed race 9%

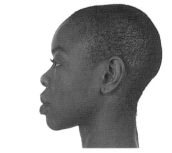

THE OTHER 2%
The remaining 2% of the world's population is made up of groups that do not readily fit into the four main types (left). They include the Australian Aborigines, the Khoisan of southern Africa, and the Pacific Islanders (below).

CLIMATIC INFLUENCES
As human beings evolved, environment may have helped shape their physical character-istics. Migrating away from the equator, they experienced decreasing hours of sunlight, which meant they produced less VITAMIN D. Some groups may have evolved lighter skin and hair to adapt to fewer daylight hours. MONGOLOID women, such as the Inuit, below, may have developed extra facial fat as an adapta-tion to the cold, and retained the epicanthic fold (a skin crease on the upper eyelid) to protect against snow glare.

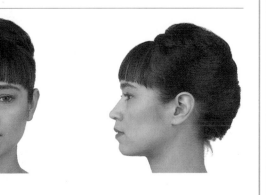

BRAIN & NERVES

WOMAN VS. MAN

A man's brain tends to be larger and heavier than a woman's, just as the average man is larger and heavier than the average woman. Proportionally, a woman's brain is both larger and heavier – about 2% of her body weight, while a man's brain forms 1% of his body weight. The size, shape, and form of the brain's individual parts differ slightly between the sexes. For example, women have a proportionally larger forebrain than men.

◆

In most people, the left cerebral hemisphere, the DOMINANT HEMISPHERE, organizes language and logical thought. It is larger than the right hemisphere, which is involved in spatial and global processes. The difference between the right and left hemispheres seems to develop later in girls than in boys, and many women appear to have less separation of global and logical functions than men. Such differences may result from conditioning and are not considered by scientists to be reliable evidence that brain structure is sexually determined.

ANATOMY OF WOMAN'S BRAIN

The brain controls all our actions, whether the actions are conscious, subconscious, or involuntary. It is the seat of a woman's personality, and its makeup determines her intelligence and skills. It uses 20% of the body's available oxygen and energy.

The cerebrum (forebrain) is the brain's management center and is concerned with consciousness. It consists of two large cerebral hemispheres, which have a deeply folded cortex, or outer layer, of gray matter. The cortex enables us to perceive, understand, communicate, and make controlled movements. The two hemispheres are connected by the *corpus callosum*, a "bridge" that contains over 200 million nerve fibers. The hippocampus and the amygdala are parts of the limbic system, which controls our emotions and feelings and is involved in storing new memories. The basal ganglia help organize complex motor responses and feelings of pleasure. The diencephalon contains the thalamus, an information distribution center, and the hypothalamus and pituitary gland, which make up the ENDOCRINE control center.

The midbrain and the hindbrain form the brain stem, which relays information to and from the spinal cord, and is responsible for functions such as sleep, arousal, and breathing. The cerebellum is the area of the brain that fine-tunes a woman's movements.

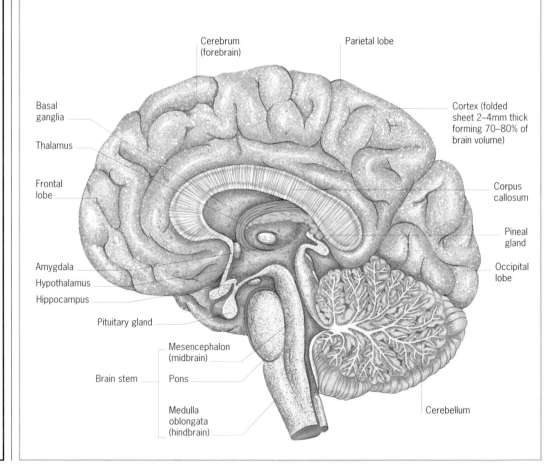

NEURONS AND SYNAPSES

The brain contains about 100 billion neurons (nerve cells). Each neuron has an axon and several branches called dendrites. The axon of one neuron branches to connect with the dendrites of other neurons at junctions that are called synapses. The brain contains more than 100,000 billion synapses.

Electrical pulses run down the axons and release chemicals from small packets, called vesicles, in the synaptic axon terminal. The chemical crosses a small gap to the dendrite, which it may either activate (excite) or depress (inhibit). Synapses become stronger with repeated use, thus establishing MEMORY.

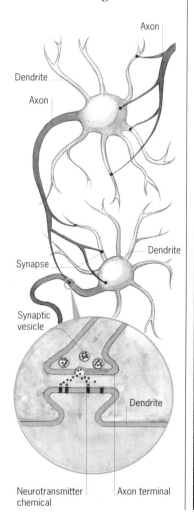

Axon

Dendrite

Axon

Dendrite

Synapse

Synaptic vesicle

Dendrite

Neurotransmitter chemical

Axon terminal

MAP OF THE BRAIN

Specific areas of the brain's cerebral cortex perform particular functions. In areas dealing with sensory stimuli (vision, hearing) and with MOTOR CONTROL, each area contains a "map" of the body. Different aspects of stimuli, such as the color, shape, and movement of a ball, are "seen" in different parts of the visual cortex.

The various aspects are brought together in the association areas of the parietal, temporal, and frontal lobes.

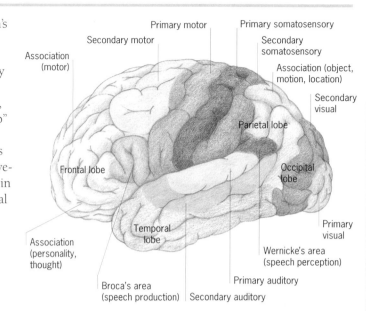

Association (motor)

Secondary motor

Primary motor

Primary somatosensory

Secondary somatosensory

Association (object, motion, location)

Secondary visual

Parietal lobe

Frontal lobe

Occipital lobe

Temporal lobe

Primary visual

Association (personality, thought)

Wernicke's area (speech perception)

Broca's area (speech production)

Secondary auditory

Primary auditory

LANGUAGE CENTERS

The information content of speech is dealt with by the left hemisphere of the brain. Wernicke's area in the posterior (or back) of the cortex is the center for speech comprehension, and Broca's area in the anterior (or front) of the cortex deals with speech production. Strokes or tumors can cause aphasia or specific language problems: after damage in Wernicke's area, the ability to understand speech is destroyed; when Broca's area is damaged, the ability to speak in a comprehensive manner is lost. The right hemisphere of the brain deals with the emotional content of speech, and damage to the equivalents of Wernicke's and Broca's areas destroys the individual's ability either to appreciate, or produce, emotional color in speech.

Speech therapy is designed to help people suffering from a variety of communication problems. Any woman with a disturbance of language or a disorder of articulation, voice production, or fluency of speech may be helped by speech therapy. In some circumstances, these problems may occur as part of a broader problem, such as a physical handicap, a learning disability, or hearing loss.

Treatment usually has two quite distinct parts. First a program of exercises is undertaken to improve a specific aspect of language ability or speech performance (such as a technique to improve speech fluency). Second, the therapist works with the people most involved with the patient on a day-to-day basis (family, teachers, or friends), and explains to them the nature of the difficulties being faced, and the ways in which they can help. The aim is to create a climate that will provide maximum opportunities for more effective communication in the future.

SIDES OF THE BRAIN

Information from one side of the body crosses over in the brain to the other side; the left hemisphere of the brain senses and controls the right side of the body and vice versa. The hemispheres are specialized for different tasks.

The left side, for example, controls the information content of speech, logical and serial analysis, and learned musical skills (pitch, rhythm, analysis of melody). The right side controls the emotional content of speech, musical appreciation, spatial and global appreciation, and artistic and musical ability.

The left hemisphere is dominant in most right-handers and many left-handers. These left-handers, however, may have less marked asymmetry between the two hemispheres. In other left-handers, the right hemisphere is dominant. Left-handers are also more prone to suffer from dyslexia (impaired reading ability). Dyslexia is less common in women than men.

MOTOR CONTROL

The nervous system
The brain sends signals to the spinal cord, which is responsible for telling the muscles when to contract and relax.

Spinal cord

Sensory root

Spinal nerve

Motor root

Vertebra

Sympathetic ganglia of autonomic nervous system

Most bodily movements are generated by the motor cortex in response to sensory inputs from the environment and the whole body. From the cortex, signals run through a loop of NEURONS through the BASAL GANGLIA and back to the cortex. This feedback loop regulates the motor signals the cortex sends to the body. The neural centers involved in the loop have two distinct functions: some "turn up the volume," while others "turn it down." A second loop of neurons between the cortex and the CEREBELLUM fine-tunes the movement and regulates timing.

MOTOR MEMORIES

Rapid, skilled movements, such as writing, playing a musical instrument, or typing, are stored by the cortex. As a woman practices and repeats the same movements over and over again, a "motor memory" forms. The cerebellum also helps in learning these motor skills. Once a motor memory has been formed, the conscious part of the brain no longer needs to be involved and the action can be performed on "remote control." Complicated patterns of movements, such as those in a piece of music, are also remembered in this way.

Head, trunk, and limbs

Hands and fingers

Face and mouth

Tongue and throat

Motor map
The motor cortex is divided into areas, each of which controls the movements of one part of the body. The larger the area of cortex that controls a body part, the more complicated and precise are the movements that can be performed.

THE POWER OF TOUCH

The somatosensory cortex (below) deals with information from the sensory receptors for touch in different parts of the body. The larger the size of the controlling area of the cortex, the more sensitive the area. The proportions of the homunculus (bottom) reflect the sensory importance of the parts of a woman's body.

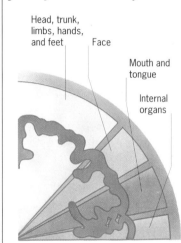

Head, trunk, limbs, hands, and feet

Face

Mouth and tongue

Internal organs

Sensory map
The somatosensory cortex monitors sensory importance.

PAIN MECHANISM

This is a protective mechanism that alerts the body to tissue injury or damage. The damaged tissue produces chemicals that stimulate the sensory nerve endings in the area to send pain signals to the brain through the spinal cord (right).

The body is able to reduce the amount of pain that is felt by producing endorphins. These are chemicals that block the transmission of signals at SYNAPSES in the pain pathways. Morphine and related drugs work by mimicking the action of endorphins at the same synapses.

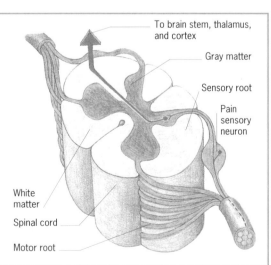

To brain stem, thalamus, and cortex

Gray matter

Sensory root

Pain sensory neuron

White matter

Spinal cord

Motor root

Homunculus
Body part size indicates the proportion of the cortex that controls it.

VIEWING THE BRAIN

Before the development of imaging techniques that measure the activity of the living brain, neurologists compared perceivable differences in behavior and ability between normal and brain-damaged patients with anatomical findings at autopsy. They also used invasive tests on monkeys. Now the living brain can be imaged noninvasively using magnetic resonance imaging (MRI), which shows anatomical details, and positron emission tomography (PET), which estimates activity in specific areas by measuring the blood flow through them and is used to assess function.

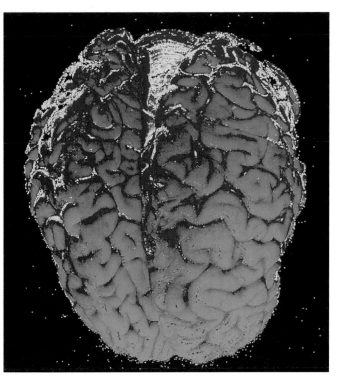

MEMORY

Memories are stored in the cortex by coded patterns of electrical activity between NEURONS. A small fragment of the coded patterns will usually activate the recall of the entire memory. Working memory enables us to hold material while doing complex tasks. Declarative memory states knowledge about the world and includes language. Associative memory links actions and results. Each type uses circuits in different centers in the FOREBRAIN.

PROTECTING THE BRAIN

The skull provides a protective armor, while the leathery meningeal dura mater anchors the brain and prevents movement. The cerebrospinal fluid helps cushion the brain, maintains a constant environment for the NEURONS, and removes toxic substances produced in the brain. A blood–brain barrier layer in the blood vessels prevents TOXINS from entering the brain, but allows oxygen and nutrients to enter.

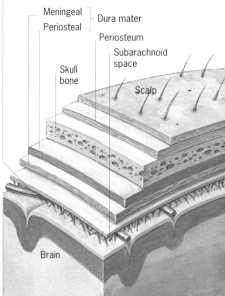

Arachnoid membrane
Meningeal
Periosteal
Dura mater
Periosteum
Subarachnoid space
Skull bone
Scalp
Brain

THE ACTIVE BRAIN

The female fetal brain develops faster than that of the male, and all female systems are fully formed by the eighth month following conception. From this point onward, connections between NEURONS increase and are refined until a woman reaches her mid-twenties, after which they slowly begin to decline.

In middle age, the neurons begin to die, but surviving neurons may compensate by growing new branches and synapses. Neurons in a brain damaged by accident or STROKE do not regenerate branches, because the supporting cells produce a protein that inhibits growth. Some recovery of function is possible, however, as undamaged surrounding areas take on control of the lost function.

BRAIN POWER

A woman's brain is six times larger than that of most mammals (in relation to body size – see below). In addition to size, brain power depends on the density of neural wiring and coordination of the electrical activity patterns. The cerebral cortex, responsible for conscious thought, is unique to mammals and is very large in humans.

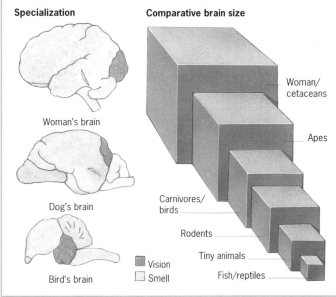

Specialization

Woman's brain

Dog's brain

Bird's brain

Comparative brain size

Woman/cetaceans

Apes

Carnivores/birds

Rodents

Tiny animals

Fish/reptiles

☐ Vision
☐ Smell

WOMAN AND SLEEP

Adult women need up to 9½ hours of sleep each night (compared with an average of 8 hours for men), and may spend approximately a third of their lives asleep. A new-born baby needs 16 hours of sleep, a teenager 10–11 hours, and an older woman 4–6 hours (below).

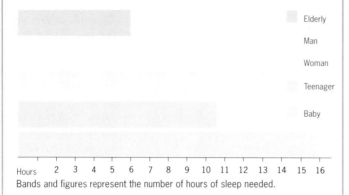

Elderly

Man

Woman

Teenager

Baby

Hours   2   3   4   5   6   7   8   9   10   11   12   13   14   15   16
Bands and figures represent the number of hours of sleep needed.

PHYSICAL CHANGES DURING SLEEP

During sleep, the blood pressure falls, the pulse rate and body temperature drop, respiration slows, peripheral blood circulation increases, the digestive tract is active, muscles relax, and the METABOLIC RATE drops by 20%. As sleep becomes deeper, the brain becomes increasingly less responsive to external stimuli.

FACTOR S

Otherwise known as muramyl peptide, factor S is composed of the remains of bacteria after they have been digested by the digestive tract. It is incorporated into the body's chemistry and may play a part in triggering sleep. Factor S interacts with the neurotransmitter SEROTONIN, which is very important in regulating the sleep state.

MOVEMENTS DURING SLEEP

The sleeping position changes during the night. In NREM (non-rapid eye movement) sleep, the sleeper makes major movements at least every 20 minutes and smaller ones about every five minutes. In contrast, REM (rapid eye movement) sleep is marked by cessation of all regular movements except for those of the eye: REM eye movements are characterized by slow rolling with bursts of rapid movement superimposed. The body is motionless and the muscles slack, apart from the occasional twitch.

INSOMNIA

An inability to sleep has many causes, including emotional disturbance, DEPRESSION, and changes in normal daily rhythm. Insomniacs often do sleep, but their pattern of sleep is abnormal and so unrefreshing. Certain drugs can help to break a pattern of insomnia, but many can become addictive if used regularly.

BRAIN WAVES

Five brain wave patterns occur during a night's sleep. They are the four stages of NREM (non-rapid eye movement) sleep and the single stage of REM (rapid eye movement) sleep. These stages are repeated in cycles of about 60–90 minutes. The levels of sleep are deepest at the beginning of the night and become progressively lighter. The last cycles will not usually include stages 3 or 4.

REM (RAPID EYE MOVEMENT) SLEEP

This occurs in each cycle, the first instance being about 60–70 minutes after a woman falls asleep. REM sleep accounts for about 25% of the total night's sleep.

NREM (NON-RAPID EYE MOVEMENT) SLEEP

Stage 1 of NREM sleep is the transition period between wakefulness and true sleep. It accounts for 5% of the total.

Stage 2 is a deeper state of sleep, and it is known as "true sleep." It makes up 50% of the night's sleep.

Stage 3 is another transition phase, between stages 2 and 4. It accounts for 7% of the total sleeping time.

Stage 4 is the deepest level of sleep and accounts for up to 13% of the total in young adults. This stage decreases in duration with age until it is almost totally absent from the sleep of the elderly.

Sleeping brain wave patterns

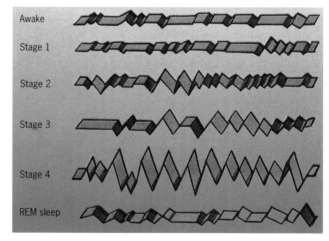

Awake

Stage 1

Stage 2

Stage 3

Stage 4

REM sleep

DREAMING

Everyone dreams during REM sleep, but not all dreams are remembered upon waking. Dreams are not just the brain's filing process or a selection of random messages; they also incorporate stimuli that occur during sleep. They may assist the transition of memories from short- to long-term storage. Problems that are set before sleep can be solved in dreams, and many believe that dreams reveal emotional conflicts.

DISORDERS OF THE BRAIN

ALZHEIMER'S DISEASE

Recent studies suggest that one person in five is affected with Alzheimer's disease by the age of 80. Sufferers have a reduced activity in the parietal and temporal regions of the CORTEX. They are unable to store new memories and become confused and disoriented; some become paranoid and aggressive. Alzheimer's disease is characterized by an increase in the deposit of amyloid proteins and accumulation of abnormal proteins in the NEURONS, causing neuron death.

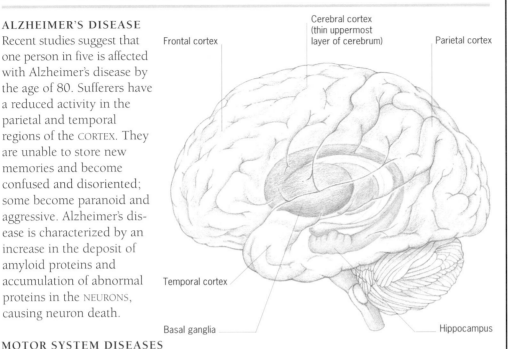

Frontal cortex

Cerebral cortex (thin uppermost layer of cerebrum)

Parietal cortex

Temporal cortex

Basal ganglia

Hippocampus

MOTOR SYSTEM DISEASES

Parkinson's and Huntington's diseases are disorders where coordinated movement is lost owing to the gradual degeneration of particular cells in the BASAL GANGLIA. This disturbs the balance in the cortex–basal ganglia motor loop; the slow movements of Parkinson's disease are due to too little stimulation; the jerky movements of Huntington's disease are due to excessive stimulation. Both diseases are progressive. Huntington's disease is clearly inherited; the causes of Parkinson's disease are not so clear cut, although there does appear to be a genetic link.

STROKES

Occurring most frequently after the age of 45, strokes are caused by a BLOOD CLOT or by bleeding that cuts off the blood supply to a part of the brain. It is thought that NEURONS are starved of oxygen, become activated, and release excess glutamate, a transmitter chemical. This overstimulates the neurons, causing receptor channels to open and calcium to flood in. The influx activates enzymes that disrupt cell structure and lead to the release of highly active free radicals that cause more damage. The damaged neurons lose their ability to transmit messages, and the functions of the damaged area are lost.

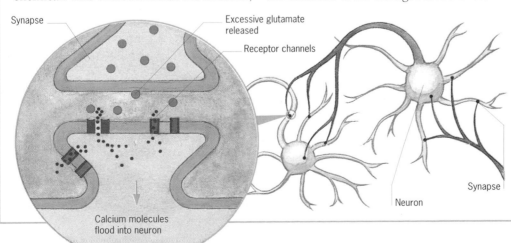

Synapse

Excessive glutamate released

Receptor channels

Calcium molecules flood into neuron

Neuron

Synapse

EPILEPSY

Affecting one person in 200, epilepsy ranges from a momentary loss of consciousness to *grand mal* seizures (convulsions). Some people have an "aura" (a smell, sound, or heavy feeling) before a seizure; others experience no warning at all. During a seizure, the inhibition to cortical NEURONS is reduced, resulting in hundreds of neurons firing rhythmically together. This produces the jerky movements of a seizure.

Some people have only a few seizures throughout their lives, while others have many in a day. One person in 20 suffers an isolated seizure at some point in her life. Most serious cases of epilepsy can be controlled by drugs.

DEPRESSION

An imbalance of transmitter chemicals in the brain may be responsible for depressive and manic-depressive illnesses, although social pressures may also play a part. Some depressed patients also have altered levels of certain HORMONES. Some depressive illness has a strong genetic basis.

Lack of sunlight can also cause depression; this is known as SEASONAL AFFECTIVE DISORDER (SAD). Drugs that alter transmitter production, release, and removal are used to treat depression.

SCHIZOPHRENIA

Usually beginning between the ages of 15 and 25, schizophrenia generally tends to appear up to five years later in females than it does in males. It often begins insidiously, with sufferers becoming more withdrawn and introverted, and increasingly sensitive to STRESS. *As the disease takes hold, the sufferer loses touch with reality, may become paranoid, and experiences delusions and hallucinations, of which hearing voices is the most common type.*

Schizophrenia has a worldwide incidence of just under 1%, and there is a genetic influence. The disease can be treated with psychotropic drugs.

BRAIN SURGERY

Great strides forward in knowledge, equipment, and techniques for brain surgery have been made during the last decades of the 20th century.

Brain surgery is normally performed following accidents that cause head injuries or for cancer of the brain tissue. Surgeons now know more about how the brain works and have increasingly sophisticated equipment, such as magnetic resonance imaging (MRI), and positron emission tomography (PET) scanners, to give a view of the living brain. Lasers are also at their disposal. Such aids increase the abilities of doctors to pinpoint brain injuries and to diagnose disease, as well as improving their chances of being able to effect cures.

The brain, however, like the lower depths of the oceans, remains mainly uncharted, and many of the techniques are still at a relatively early stage of development. Laser treatment of cancer of the BRAIN STEM, for example, is currently performed by only a tiny percentage of surgeons.

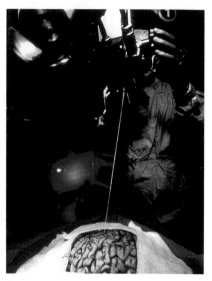

Laser treatment
The precision of the laser is invaluable in performing surgery to destroy cancerous tissue in the brain.

BRAIN GRAFTS

Unlike other organs in the body, the brain has very little ability to repair itself. There are also mechanisms in the brain to prevent unwanted nerve cell growth; these stop repair when axons are damaged. Some success in repairing damage has been achieved by grafting healthy human fetal brain tissue into animals with brain damage or disease, and into a few patients with PARKINSON'S DISEASE. There are ethical, moral, and practical dilemmas, however, about the use of fetal tissue. Consequently, biologists are working to produce genetically engineered skin cells to supply brain chemicals missing because neurons have died (right).

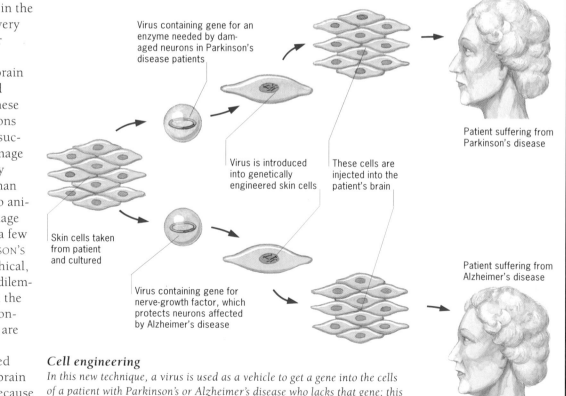

Virus containing gene for an enzyme needed by damaged neurons in Parkinson's disease patients

Virus is introduced into genetically engineered skin cells

These cells are injected into the patient's brain

Patient suffering from Parkinson's disease

Skin cells taken from patient and cultured

Virus containing gene for nerve-growth factor, which protects neurons affected by Alzheimer's disease

Patient suffering from Alzheimer's disease

Cell engineering
In this new technique, a virus is used as a vehicle to get a gene into the cells of a patient with Parkinson's or Alzheimer's disease who lacks that gene; this will enable the patient's cells to make the missing substances.

SKIN

SKIN STRUCTURE

Skin covers the entire surface of a woman's body, protecting her internal organs from the environment. It varies in texture and structure in different parts of the body.

There are two types of skin – hairy and glabrous (hairless). Most skin is hairy, the most hairy being the scalp; the least hairy parts are the face, the backs of the hands, and the tops of the feet. Glabrous skin occurs on the palms of the hands, the soles of the feet, and the lips. Skin is made up of three main components – the epidermis, comprising KERATINOCYTES (living epidermal cells) and the corneal layer (the protective outermost layer of dead keratinocytes); the dermis, made up of skin appendages, such as sweat glands and hair follicles, surrounded by fibrous supporting tissue and collagen; and the subcutis, a layer of fibrous tissue and subcutaneous fat. Keratinocytes originate in the basal or germinative layer of the epidermis and slowly reach the top of the epidermis as the dead outer layers are shed. This life cycle of the skin is about 28 days in length. The hair and nails are extensions of the skin and are made up mainly of keratin, the chief constituent of the corneal layer of the epidermis.

IT'S A FACT

The surface area of a woman's skin is between 1.5–2.0sq m (15–20sq ft) and weighs about 4kg (8lb). The skin can vary in thickness from 0.5–4mm or more, depending on its location on the body.

It has been calculated that, on average, every 6.5sq cm (1sq in) of a woman's skin contains 4.5m (15ft) of blood vessels, 3.75m (12ft) of nerves, 1,500 sensory receptors, 650 sudoriferous (sweat) glands, 100 sebaceous (oil) glands, and over 3 million cells; 90% of household dust is made up of dead skin.

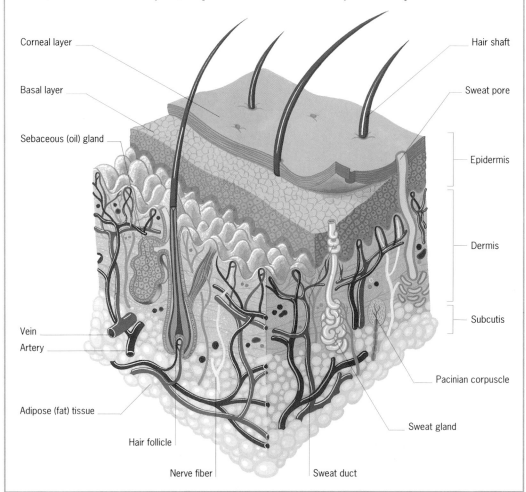

Corneal layer

Basal layer

Sebaceous (oil) gland

Vein

Artery

Adipose (fat) tissue

Hair follicle

Nerve fiber

Sweat duct

Hair shaft

Sweat pore

Epidermis

Dermis

Subcutis

Pacinian corpuscle

Sweat gland

27

EPIDERMIS

Skin thickness varies, depending on its location on the body – it is thickest on the soles of the feet and thinnest on the eyelids. The epidermis forms the upper, protective barrier of the skin and is the strongest layer. The corneal layer, the outermost part of the epidermis, is composed of dead cells, which look very similar to paving stones when viewed under a microscope (right). Many millions of dead epidermal cells are shed each day, and they are continuously replaced by cells budding off from the single layer of basal epidermal cells. These keratinocytes (living epidermal cells) are packed with keratin (structural protein) and become progressively flattened as they grow upward from the basal layer to the corneal layer.

MELANOCYTES, among the basal cells of the epidermis, produce the protective pigment MELANIN, which is responsible for skin color. In exposure to sunlight, the melanocytes are stimulated to produce more melanin to defend the body against UV rays. The epidermis is also the component of the skin in which vitamin D is formed from cholesterol under the influence of daylight.

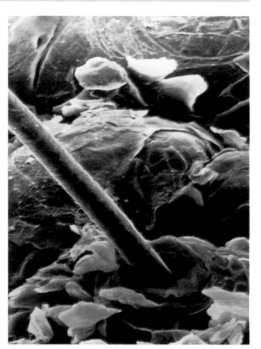

Electron scanning of a woman's arm
This microscopic view of the skin on the arm shows the keratinized corneal layer of the epidermis and a hair shaft. Millions of dead cells like these are shed each day and replaced continuously.

FUNCTIONS OF THE SKIN

The skin acts as a physical and immunological barrier against the outside world, protecting a woman's body from external injury by TOXINS and bacteria. The skin also plays an important role in regulation of a woman's body temperature (right).

Receptors for touch, pain, pressure, warmth, and cold are also contained within the skin's layers. Here, too, are found important secondary structures, such as hair and sweat glands, which are involved in maintaining core body temperature, and nails on the hands and feet. Nails enhance a woman's perception of touch, as well as her ability to perform delicate tasks with her fingers.

DERMIS

The bulk of the skin consists of the dermis, which is made up of a fibrous protein, collagen, and connective tissue. Embedded in the dermis are blood vessels, NERVES and sensory receptors, LYMPH VESSELS, sweat glands, oil glands, and HAIR FOLLICLES with their muscles. (The glands and hair follicles are formed from specialized EPIDERMAL CELLS that project into the dermis.) The SEBACEOUS GLANDS secrete SEBUM (the skin's natural oil). APOCRINE SWEAT GLANDS are mainly in the armpit and pubic areas, while ECCRINE SWEAT GLANDS are distributed over the entire skin surface. These glands maintain the skin's pH balance, remove dirt and oil from the pores, and help regulate body temperature.

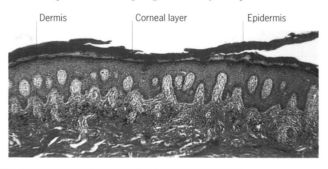

Dermis   Corneal layer   Epidermis

TEMPERATURE CONTROL

The skin plays an important role in keeping the body temperature constant, at a norm of 37°C (98.6°F). When the body becomes hotter than normal, the ECCRINE SWEAT GLANDS secrete sweat. This cools the body as it evaporates. For additional cooling, blood vessels in the DERMIS (below) dilate to dissipate heat. If the body becomes colder than normal, the blood vessels constrict, which conserves body heat, and the erector muscles in the HAIR FOLLICLES cause the hairs to rise in an attempt to trap a warm layer of air against the skin's surface. As body hair is too sparse to fulfill this aim, the action instead produces "goose bumps."

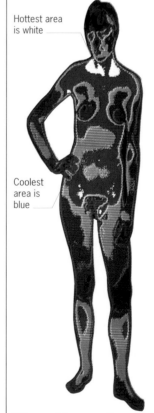

Hottest area is white

Coolest area is blue

Thermal image of a woman
This shows differences in temperature over various parts of her body.

WOMAN'S SKIN SENSITIVITY

The skin contains several receptors for sensing touch, pressure, pain, warmth, and cold. Different parts of the body experience different levels of sensation. The skin of the clitoris, lips, and fingertips, for example, is much more sensitive to touch than that of the back.

The sensitivity of the skin can be measured by finding out at what distance apart on the skin surface two simultaneously applied stimuli (for example, pencil points) have to be before they are perceived as two separate stimuli rather than as one stimulus. The less distance there is between the stimuli, the more sensitive is the skin.

Gauging skin sensitivity

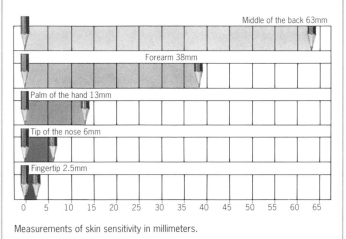

Middle of the back 63mm
Forearm 38mm
Palm of the hand 13mm
Tip of the nose 6mm
Fingertip 2.5mm

| 0 | 5 | 10 | 15 | 20 | 25 | 30 | 35 | 40 | 45 | 50 | 55 | 60 | 65 |

Measurements of skin sensitivity in millimeters.

DEFENDER OF THE BODY

Skin is a strong physical barrier against injury to a woman's body. SEBUM (oil) is secreted by SEBACEOUS GLANDS in the skin, and this creates a protective antibacterial layer over the body, which discourages the growth of bacteria. The skin also has its own immune system, known as SALT (which stands for skin-associated lymphoid tissue). SALT comprises a network of immune cells, which are able to recognize and destroy any foreign substances in the skin, such as TOXINS and bacteria. The "front-line" cells in this immune system are Langerhans cells, which are derived from the bone marrow. These cells react first to any foreign substances and then attract the WHITE BLOOD CELLS ("killer cells"), such as LYMPHOCYTES and MACROPHAGES, from the bloodstream to the site of injury or infection.

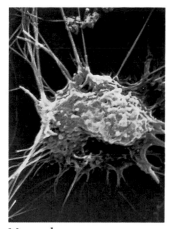

Macrophage
In its active state, when it is needed to remove bacteria, this scavenging white blood cell engulfs foreign bodies, including bacteria.

SKIN PATTERNS

PRINTS
The skin ridges and grooves on the fingers and palms of the hands, and on the toes and soles of the feet, evolved to give a good grip. The fingertips are well supplied with blood capillaries and with receptors for touch and pain. Each woman has her personal, unique inherited pattern of finger- and toeprints.

CLEAVAGE LINES
These run longitudinally in the skin of the limbs and in circular patterns in the neck and trunk. They are caused by bundles of interlocking COLLAGEN fibers in the skin's DERMIS. Surgical incisions made along these lines will heal better than cuts made across them.

FLEXURE LINES
Where the SUBCUTIS and dermis are attached to the underlying fascia and cannot stretch or slide over the tissues, flexure lines occur.

Fingerprints (above)
In the keratinized corneal layer of the epidermis, minute ridges form distinctive patterns, unique to each individual woman.

The palmist's view (right)
Cleavage lines in the palm are said by palmists to denote character, chart past events, and predict a woman's future.

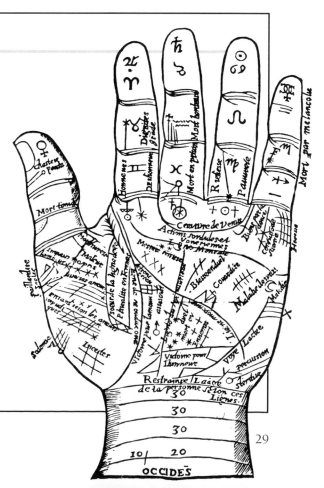

WOMAN'S SKIN COLOR

MELANOCYTES, which produce granules of the skin pigment MELANIN, make up 10% of the cells in the basal layer of the EPIDERMIS. These cells pass the melanin to the other cells in the epidermis through connecting tendril-like branches. Melanin granules accumulate in the epidermal cells and protect a woman's skin from the harmful ultraviolet rays in sunlight. The amount and distribution of melanin in the epidermis determines the color of the skin. Ebony-skinned NEGROID women produce the greatest amounts of melanin, while red-haired, pink-skinned Celtic CAUCASOID women produce the least. The pinkish skin coloring of many Northern Caucasoid women is the result of HEMOGLOBIN (contained in red blood cells), showing through. Carotene, an orange pigment that accumulates in the epidermis and in the underlying layers, is abundant in the skin of MONGOLOID and Southern Caucasoid women (those women of Mediterranean, Indian, and Arabian origin). An excess of foodstuffs that contain high levels of carotene, such as carrots, can cause yellow discoloration in the skin of Northern Caucasoid women.

Negroid skin | Caucasoid skin | Mongoloid skin

BEAUTY SPOTS

Freckles are small flat spots of skin pigment. Moles are larger accumulations of MELANOCYTES. *Aesthetically placed moles have often been thought beautiful (below) and, in Georgian England, women resorted to false beauty spots.*

CHANGEABLE SKIN COLOR

Fluctuations in a woman's skin color can communicate information about her emotional state, as well as indicate underlying medical conditions.

BLUSHING
The red flush of the blush is caused by the dilation of the blood capillaries in the DERMIS. Blushing can be caused by an emotional reaction, or it may be a physical response to overheating.

HEIGHTENED COLOR
Reddish skin most commonly occurs as a physiological reaction, but it may also indicate a skin disease, such as ECZEMA or ROSACEA. In rare cases, a systemic disease, such as HEART DISEASE, HYPERTENSION, or fever, may be the cause.

BLANCHING AND PALLOR
A transitory whitening of the skin can be an emotional response to fright or anger, or a physical response to cold, caused by contraction of the blood capillaries in the dermis. Pale skin can also indicate ANEMIA.

CYANOSIS
This blue discoloration of the skin is due to insufficient oxygen reaching the blood capillaries in the skin tissues.

BIRTHMARKS

Many babies are born with skin blemishes, but only a few birthmarks persist into adulthood. Makeup can be used to camouflage many minor marks, while plastic surgery or laser treatment can remove more prominent birthmarks.

HEMANGIOMA
This is the medical term for a reddish purple birthmark, which can be raised or flat. Raised hemangiomas are usually caused by a collection of dilated blood vessels; these are normally bright red and protuberant and are known as strawberry marks. In some instances, they may be tinged with blue, owing to the presence of deoxygenated blood from a vein. Flat hemangiomas are purple-red marks known as port-wine stains. They may sometimes be faded by a laser or removed by cryosurgery (freezing).

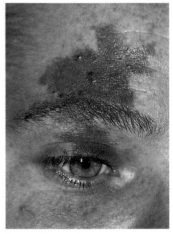

Port-wine stain
This is an area of purplish red skin, which can be disfiguring and may persist throughout life.

CAFE AU LAIT SPOTS
These brownish blemishes are caused by discrete (distinct) areas of increased pigment. Cafe au lait spots persist into adulthood and can usually be camouflaged using makeup.

SKIN CARE PRODUCTS

The main benefit to the user of commercial skin preparations is the feeling of relaxation and pampered luxury obtained from their application. Often perfume is added to increase this effect. Since the outer layers of the skin are dead, such products have little lasting effect on the skin structure although, unlike soap and water, they do not strip the skin of essential oils and moisture. Skin care products can also protect the skin from excessive sun and wind damage.

CLEANSERS

The oils in cleansing creams and lotions loosen dirt and layers of makeup from the facial skin, which can then be wiped away. Microscopic particles, such as those in crushed apricot kernels or aduki beans, can aid removal of dead skin cells, and are often added to make a gentle facial scrub.

TONERS

Skin fresheners and toners contain alcohol or similar substances that evaporate quickly, producing a slight tingling sensation and tightening of the pores of the skin.

MOISTURIZERS

These creams and lotions leave a thin layer of oil on the surface of the skin, making it feel smooth and soft. Moisturizers contain oils (such as lanolin, the sebum of sheep), paraffin, water, perfume, and preservatives.

Some moisturizers are advertised as containing the proteins COLLAGEN, reticulin, and elastin. These substances are all formed in the living cells of the basal layer of the EPIDERMIS and are found in healthy skin, so they are of little benefit when applied externally on the dead cells of the corneal (outermost) layer of the skin's epidermis.

WRINKLES

As a woman's skin ages, the COLLAGEN in the DERMIS of the skin loses water, causing the loss of much of the skin's firmness and flexibility. This process is exacerbated by the slowing down of the activity of the oil-producing SEBACEOUS GLANDS and water-producing sweat glands, and also by the loss of fat in the SUBCUTIS. The formation of wrinkles and blemishes that results is often aggravated by damage from wind and, more importantly, the sun.

Moisturizing creams and lotions cannot mend a damaged complexion, but they can reduce deterioration by providing the skin with a protective coating against the elements.

SKIN LOTIONS

In Canada, women spend millions every year on skin-care products and makeup. Most moisturizing creams and lotions are based on emulsions of oil and water. The first recorded use of such "cold creams" was in the 2nd century, when lotions were based on water, beeswax, and olive oil. By the early 20th century, vegetable oils had been largely replaced with mineral oils, although vegetable oils have recently become popular with buyers once again.

Commercial creams and lotions have become increasingly lighter and less greasy. The lightest are emulsions of fatty acid, glycerol, and water.

LABELING COSMETICS

Up to 8,000 ingredients have been used in cosmetics, including oils, waxes, alcohols, perfumes, pigments, minerals, and preservatives. Listing of ingredients on cosmetics packaging (including active and, in some cases, inactive ingredients) is not mandatory in Canada, although it is in many other countries.

Most cosmetic ingredients have a history of safe use, but skin-lightening soaps and creams have been found to contain some banned substances, such as mercury and monobenzylether hydroquinone, which are highly toxic.

"Hypoallergenic" is a term used by manufacturers of cosmetics to imply that ingredients are not known to cause allergic reactions. However, the term is not defined by government regulations.

Older skin
Weather damage, combined with the aging process, causes the skin on the face to wrinkle.

SKIN PEELS

When they are applied to the skin, face masks absorb surface grease, dirt, and the top layer of skin debris, leaving a clean layer of skin. Prepared face masks can be gel-like substances that are peeled off, or claylike substances that dry out and then have to be washed off or rubbed away.

The more drastic medical procedure of chemical skin peeling uses either an enzyme or an abrasive agent in order to remove several layers of the EPIDERMIS at once. It is used to thin the skin temporarily, thus making it look younger. It is essential that chemical skin peeling be supervised only by a qualified practitioner, who is preferably a dermatologist, and that it be performed very infrequently because the damage to the skin can become excessive. Chemical skin peeling can be useful for the treatment of scars resulting from acne.

MAKEUP

Cosmetics is a multimillion-dollar industry. Makeup is used to soak up grease, to hide blemishes (such as open pores, pimples, and scars), and to give a smooth texture to the skin. It can be applied either as a powder, usually over a foundation, or as a cream. Face powders can be colored or translucent, and usually contain talcum powder and kaolin (clay). Blush and bronzing powder add color to the skin and help enhance bone structure.

Blusher applicator brush

Tinted face powder

Bronzing beads

Cream blusher

DANGERS OF MAKEUP

The modern science of cosmetology has identified many substances and practices associated with cosmetic products that are harmful to health. Makeup can irritate the skin or trigger allergic reactions. Even products labeled hypoallergenic simply reduce, not eliminate, the risk of allergic reactions. Use only fresh makeup; discard any that has changed color or has an off odor.

Carelessly applied mascara or eye liner can produce a scratched cornea. Hair spray squirted in the wrong direction can also damage eyes. All types of makeup, including foundation, liquid blush, and other products used on the delicate skin of the face, can produce allergic reactions. Some skin and hair treatments can burn the skin chemically. Facial powders, if inhaled, can cause breathing difficulties. Perfumes can irritate mucous membranes.

Preservatives that are used in makeup to prevent bacterial growth once a product has been opened have also been found to irritate the skin of some women. There is a trend to reduce their use in skin makeup, but this introduces the risk that a product will become contaminated with bacteria, which can cause infections when applied to the skin.

LUMINESCENT SKIN GLOWS

Powdered silk, mother-of-pearl, or artificial agents are added to sophisticated types of skin makeup (particularly face makeup) to reflect light and give an attractive glow or sheen to the skin.

DERMABRASION

This technique, performed by a cosmetic surgeon, is usually used to lighten the skin or make it look younger. The outer layers of the skin are rubbed away, with the result that the skin is thinner and looks younger. Abraded skin is also more vulnerable to tearing and other damage, as well as to scarring.

TATTOOING

Elaborate patterns and images can be produced on the skin, and some tattoo fanatics cover most of their bodies with patterns. To create a design, an insoluble dye is injected into the DERMIS. The use of carbon is common, but different colored dyes can also be used, although they will normally fade with time. The effect of dyes that have been injected into the skin is unknown – traces have been found in LYMPH GLANDS in the armpits and groin.

Tattooing is practiced in many cultures. Veil-like markings are sometimes tattooed on women's faces upon reaching womanhood. In Western society women mainly use tattoos as a fashion statement.

Tattoos are difficult and painful to remove because the procedure involves removing the skin's dermis as well as the EPIDERMIS; more success has been achieved recently using lasers. Many doctors discourage tattooing because it involves puncturing the skin, and contaminated needles could transmit AIDS or HEPATITIS.

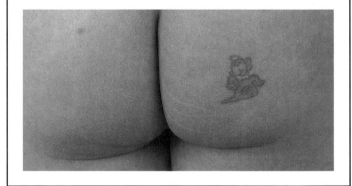

ARTIFICIAL TANS

Self-tanning lotions are dyes that color the skin in shades from honey to bronze. Emollients are added to lotions so that the dyes spread evenly and are quickly absorbed into the skin. Some lotions stay on the skin's surface and can be washed off. Others permeate the skin and are semipermanent, fading only when new cells replace the corneal layer of the EPIDERMIS.

SUN AND WOMAN'S SKIN

Sunlight contains visible rays, infrared rays, and ultraviolet rays. It is the ultraviolet rays that are predominantly responsible for tanning and skin damage. The ultraviolet rays in sunlight can be split into three types: UVA, UVB, and UVC. UVA are longer, tanning rays, and UVB are shorter, burning rays. Both of these UV rays easily injure the DNA of cells and the pigment-forming MELANOCYTES, causing skin damage and SKIN CANCER (below). At the present time, very little of the UVC radiation, which is potentially extremely dangerous, reaches earth because it is filtered out by the ozone layer of the atmosphere; the development of holes in this layer is of increasing concern. UV rays can also damage the LANGERHANS CELLS in the skin's EPIDERMIS that scavenge for invading bacteria or cancerous cells.

NATURAL PROTECTION

When a woman's skin is exposed to sunlight, the melanocytes of the epidermis are stimulated to produce more MELANIN. This results in a darker skin color, which is the body's first line of defense against ultraviolet (UV) rays. A second defense mechanism is provided by the skin's ability to thicken, by increasing the rate at which new skin cells are formed. This can result in the leathery skin that is often seen in older women who have spent a lot of time outdoors.

ARTIFICIAL PROTECTION

Most sunblocks protect only against harmful UVB rays (the higher the "factor," the greater the degree of protection), although some also protect against UVA rays. Despite the dangers of overexposure to the sun, many women still do not use sunblocks.

Skin tone	Peel	Burn	Tan
Pink	☉☉☉	☉☉☉	
White	☉☉☉	☉☉☉	☉
Cream	☉	☉☉	☉☉
Yellow	☉	☉☉	☉☉
Tan	☉	☉	☉☉☉
Brown		☉	☉☉☉
Black			☉☉☉☉

The number of "suns" indicates the likelihood of occurrence.

INCREASES IN SKIN CANCER

If caught early, most cases of SKIN CANCER (below) can be treated successfully through surgical excision, although some can prove fatal. It is cause for dismay that skin cancers have increased by 7% in fair-skinned women worldwide over the past ten years. Factors that may increase a woman's risk of developing skin cancer include having fair skin (particularly pink or white skin) that burns easily; skin that has a tendency toward freckling; skin that has many moles; a family history of MALIGNANT MELANOMA (below); one (or more) attack of severe sunburn during childhood; age over 30 years; the thinning of the ozone layer above her place of residence (such as in parts of Australia, southern South America and northern North America); and years of exposure to strong sunlight.

TYPES OF SKIN CANCER

BASAL CELL CARCINOMA

This is the most common skin cancer in fair-skinned CAUCASOID women. Basal cell carcinoma may originate from hair follicles and forms as a pearly colored, hard-edged, often dimpled lump, usually on the face, head, or neck. The lump then breaks down into an ulcerous crater that bleeds. Although basal cell carcinomas often cause considerable local tissue damage, this type of skin cancer generally spreads only to surrounding tissues. Consequently, secondary cancers usually do not form elsewhere in the body, and basal cell carcinomas are therefore regarded as almost completely harmless, provided they are treated.

SQUAMOUS CELL CARCINOMA

This skin cancer usually affects women over 60, and originates in the EPIDERMIS. Crusted and wartlike, it appears on exposed areas of the skin, such as the hands, face, neck, or ears. Secondary tumors rarely occur if it is treated early.

MALIGNANT MELANOMA

Although the incidence is increasing annually, malignant melanomas are not very common. They are tumors composed of cancerous MELANOCYTES (skin pigment cells). A melanoma can occur at any age. If it is removed early, when it is thin, secondary cancer is unlikely to develop.

Diagnosing skin cancer
Because skin cancers are easy to see, doctors can often diagnose them immediately. Treatment is by surgical excision under local anaesthetic. Malignant melanoma is the most dangerous skin cancer, and may be fatal if medical attention is delayed.

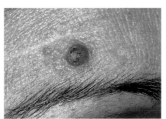
Basal cell carcinoma

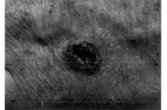
Squamous cell carcinoma

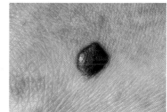
Malignant melanoma

WOMAN VS. ANIMAL

The basic structure of skin is similar in most animals; the differences between species reflect specialized functions. In birds, and in furry and spiny mammals, the skin tends to be relatively thin because the feathers, fur, or spines protect the skin. In species that evolved in an aquatic environment, however, the skin thickened to provide protective strength as hair was lost. Other animals have skin that evolved into natural "armor-plating."

Pigs
Evolving originally as swamp dwellers, pigs have thick skin and relatively sparse hair.

Leopard
Furry mammals, like the cats, rely on their dense fur to protect their thin skin.

Alligator
Extremely thick skin has evolved in some animals, such as the rhino and the alligator.

BURNS

The severity of burns is categorized (according to the depth of skin affected) as first degree (EPIDERMIS), second degree (epidermis and DERMIS), or third degree (epidermis, dermis, and SUBCUTIS). Third-degree burns result in massive infection and, sometimes, death, depending on age and the percentage of skin burned (below).

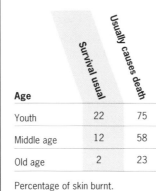

- Head 7%
- Neck 2.5%
- Upper Arm 4%
- Torso 26%
- Forearm 3%
- Hand 3%
- Buttocks 5%
- Thigh 9.5%
- Calf 7%
- Foot 3.5%

Approximate percentages of total skin area for each body part (above).

Age	Survival usual	Usually causes death
Youth	22	75
Middle age	12	58
Old age	2	23

Percentage of skin burnt.

BROKEN BLOOD VESSELS

Commonly known as broken veins, these are usually the natural result of the loss of the supporting tissues in the skin, owing to aging and to sun and wind damage. They may also be a part of the skin disease rosacea, in which the skin on the cheeks and nose becomes permanently flushed.

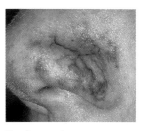

Broken veins
Unsightly broken veins sometimes can be treated using an electric current or laser.

SWEATING

Eccrine glands are distributed over the skin's surface and are responsible for temperature control. Apocrine (scent) glands are located in the groin and armpits and around the nipples. Both types produce a milky sweat that contains fats and proteins. Sweating is a natural process for controlling body temperature; it increases with OBESITY, MENSTRUATION, MENOPAUSE, anxiety, infection, and fever. Alcohol, drugs, or low blood glucose levels may also cause excessive sweating.

BODY ODOR
Sweat itself has little odor, but if it lies on the skin for a few hours, bacterial activity reacts with the sweat and this, in an enclosed space, such as within clothing, produces body odor.

Sweat glands also have a minor excretory function; chemicals in food, such as strong spices and garlic, are excreted through the glands in sweat.

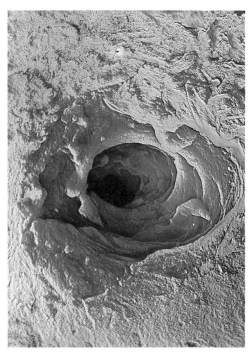

Sweat pore
Under the microscope, the minute sweat pores appear as depressions tunneling into the ridges in the skin.

TYPES OF DERMATITIS

IRRITANT
The most common form of dermatitis, this is caused by continual use of substances containing chemicals that inflame the skin. These include harsh detergents.

ALLERGIC CONTACT
This can arise in a susceptible woman when her skin comes in contact with a substance that causes an allergic reaction. The skin recovers once the allergen is removed.

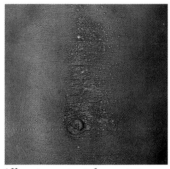

Allergic contact dermatitis
The skin on this woman's abdomen reacted with the metal in a zipper.

SEBORRHEIC
Red, flaky patches develop on the skin where SEBACEOUS glands are most numerous (face, scalp). It is a common cause of severe dandruff.

VARICOSE
The skin becomes fragile and susceptible to bruises and abrasions. This affects older women with VARICOSE VEINS or those who have suffered a deep-vein thrombosis.

ECZEMA
The skin becomes inflamed and itchy. Small blisters may appear, and when these burst the skin can easily become infected. Eventually the skin becomes thickened and the outer layer will flake away as scales.

MINOR SKIN PROBLEMS

BRUISING
Bruising is caused by blood escaping from blood vessels into surrounding tissue to form hematomas (clots). The structure of blood in the hematoma is altered by a chain of chemical reactions, resulting in the yellow, black, and blue marks of bruises. Excessive bruising can result from a lack of vitamin C in the diet or may be a symptom of a bleeding disorder.

HIVES
An allergic reaction, hives produces a rash. Certain foods, such as strawberries, shellfish, or mushrooms, can produce an allergic reaction in some women. Heat and allergy to ultraviolet rays may also cause hives; in this instance they are known as heat rash.

COLD SORES
Caused by the herpes simplex virus, cold sores are caught from other people. Once in a woman's body, the virus can be triggered to "come out" as cold sores – usually when a woman's immune system is suppressed by an illness, or when she experiences sudden climatic change, like exposure to strong sunlight or cold weather. Cold sores are common on the lips and in the nasal passages, although they can occur on the genital tract if passed on during sex.

ACNE
This is the blockage of HAIR FOLLICLES by excessive SEBUM secretion and KERATIN. It is usually associated with a change in HORMONE LEVELS, such as occurs during PUBERTY. Acne causes blackheads, raised red pustules, and fluid-filled cysts. It can be painful and may lead to scarring.

BOILS
Heavily infected hair follicles that become filled with pus, boils can be lanced to release the pus, after which they will heal.

WARTS
The result of a virus that invades the EPIDERMIS, warts are highly contagious. The virus stimulates rapid skin-cell division and abnormal elevation of the skin. Warts on the feet are known as plantar warts.

RINGWORM
This is a fungal infection of the skin, which forms red circles of scaly, itchy skin and is very contagious. Fungal infections may also occur in the nails and hair.

ATHLETE'S FOOT
The skin between the toes is the usual host to this fungal infection, but it can affect other areas of moist skin, such as in the groin.

PSORIASIS
Typically, red scaly patches develop on the limbs and trunk in this fluctuating and chronic disease. One person in 50 has psoriasis, and there is a genetic link.

CAUCASOID women tend to be affected far more by psoriasis than NEGROID or MONGOLOID women. Exposure to ultraviolet light can reduce the psoriasis; medication helps reduce the growth rate of the skin cells.

SHINGLES
The varicella zoster virus infects nerves in certain areas of the skin and results in a very painful rash. It also causes chicken pox. Following an infection, some of the viral organisms can survive and lie dormant in the ganglia (part of the nerve root as it enters the spine). If the immune system later becomes stressed, the virus may multiply, pass along the nerves, and cause painful blisters to erupt. Shingles (also called herpes zoster) is very common in individuals whose immune systems are weak; three people in 100 are likely to suffer from shingles, and it mostly affects those over 50. Complications depend on the area of the body that is infected. They can include muscle wasting, temporary bowel and urinary INCONTINENCE, paralysis of the face, and deafness. It is common, however, for shingles to lead to continual pain: one person in 10 suffers neuralgia, and this increases to one in two in sufferers over 60 years of age.

HAIR

A head of hair

There are approximately 100,000 hairs on the scalp alone, and at six months the human fetus has developed its full quota of hair follicles. Blonds have more follicles than brunettes, who have more follicles than redheads.

WOMAN VS. MAN

Women appear less hairy than men, although both sexes have the same number of hair follicles. Men usually have more noticeable hair on the face and chest. They lose hair on their heads due to the action of testosterone; women can lose their hair after pregnancy or after MENOPAUSE.

Wavy blonde. Caucasoid.

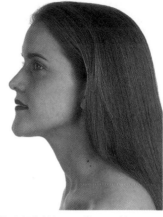

Straight light brown. Caucasoid.

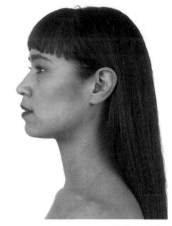

Straight dark brown. Caucasoid-Mongoloid.

Curly black. Straight ponytail extension. Negroid.

Curly red. Caucasoid.

Curly black. Negroid.

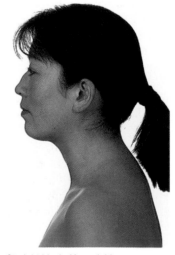

Straight black. Mongoloid.

Wavy blonde. Caucasoid.

Early human females were hairy like their ape cousins. The theory of an AQUATIC PERIOD suggests that it led to the development of a layer of subcutaneous fat for warmth and to increasingly sparse body hair. The lie of the hair also evolved to give the least resistance to water as it flowed over the body. This can still be seen clearly in the lie of fetal LANUGO hair (below).

STRUCTURE OF HAIR

Each hair is a flexible filament, which grows out of a HAIR FOLLICLE – a specialized part of the skin's EPIDERMIS. The shaft of the hair projects from the surface of the skin, and the root of the hair is embedded in the skin in a pocketlike follicle. The outer surface of each hair consists of layers of flattened overlapping scales that together form the CUTICLE. Beneath the cuticle is a middle layer, the CORTEX, which is made up of several layers of flattened cells. The MEDULLA (central core) is made up of large cells that are separated by air spaces. Hair cells contain large deposits of the fibrous protein, KERATIN. Cuticle cells are little more than tough, dead, keratin-filled scales.

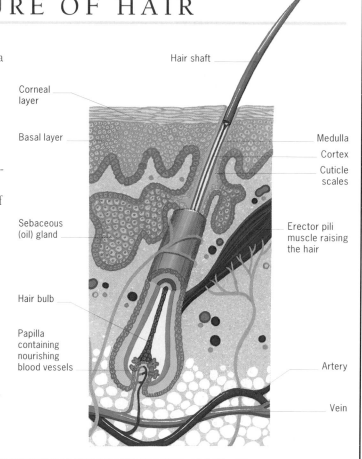

Hair shaft

Corneal layer

Basal layer

Sebaceous (oil) gland

Hair bulb

Papilla containing nourishing blood vessels

Medulla

Cortex

Cuticle scales

Erector pili muscle raising the hair

Artery

Vein

HAIR COLOR

Hair color is determined by a range of MELANIN (below) pigments produced by specialized cells. These pigments, combined in varying quantities and deposited in different parts of the hair shaft, give rise to hair colors ranging from shades of blond, red, and brown, to black. The appearance of gray hair is a complicated process and results partly from failure to produce pigments and partly from altered refraction of light on the hair shaft. Hair color may be changed by sunlight (bleached) or severe physical illness (reduced pigment production), but other agents, such as pollution and drugs, are unlikely to make substantial differences in hair color.

MELANIN

This is produced as minute granules by specialized cells, called melanocytes, at the base of the HAIR FOLLICLE. These pigment granules are then transferred to the cells of the cortex and medulla (central core) in the hair shaft (right). Differing sizes and densities of melanin granules produce different hair colors. In blonde women, the pigment is pale and is confined to the cortex, while in raven-haired women, the pigment is dark and found in the medulla as well as in the cortex of the hair shaft.

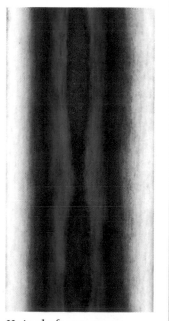

Hair shaft structure
The medulla is enclosed in the cortex (blue in this micrograph image) and the cuticle (white).

GRAY HAIR

The speed with which a woman's hair becomes gray depends on her genetic makeup. If her parents went gray at a certain age, then she is likely to follow suit. The average CAUCASOID woman has gray hairs at 34 years of age, while the average black woman does not display any until she is 44 years of age. White hairs show up more against dark hairs, but blondes are likely to end up with more gray hairs, and eventually become totally gray. Only 28% of women end up with pure white hair.

STRESS, disease, DIABETES, MALNUTRITION, ANEMIA, and emotional or physical trauma can all lead to the appearance of gray hair.

WOMAN'S HAIR FORM

Peppercorn hair
The extreme form of spiraling hair, with visible gaps between the curls, is known as "peppercorn" hair. It is mainly found among the Hottentots (shown above) and the San of Southern Africa, the Aborigines of Australia, and the Pacific Islanders as well as in Negroid women.

Numerous GENES control hair form. The gene for straight, coarse hair, common in MONGOLOID women, is dominant over the one producing tightly curled hair, while fine, straight hair, common in CAUCASOID women, is always carried by a recessive gene.

The rare occurrence of "woolly" hair in some (usually blonde) Northern Caucasoid women probably originated as a mutation. Such hair is fuzzy and brittle and is very different from the tightly curled hair of NEGROID women.

Tightly curled hair grows in two forms. In the helical form, the loops are of constant diameter. In the spiral form, the diameter of the loops diminishes from the scalp outward. Tight curls are thought to have a protective function in strong sun. In areas of rain forest, tight spiral curls are common; their more open structure is thought to allow sweating and help heat regulation to be more efficient.

WHORLS AND PEAKS

On the top of the scalp, toward the back of the head, everyone has a whorl of hair, which can twirl in either a clockwise or counterclockwise direction. The majority of women have hair whorls that go counterclockwise, although some have double whorls and, occasionally, three or four whorls, each of which may twist in a different direction. Some women have a whorl of hair at the front of the scalp, when it is known as a "widow's peak."

HAIR LOSS

Women's hair loss tends to be genetically inherited, although a temporary shedding of hair can be due to changes in hormone levels, such as those that occur after the end of pregnancy. Hair can also fall out as a result of alopecia areata, an immune disorder.

STRESS, fever, starvation, and some drugs (particularly those used to treat CANCER) can also interfere with hair growth and cause a woman's hair to fall out. Once the cause is removed, new hair growth usually appears.

Some steroids used by bodybuilders, however, can cause complete hair loss, and the hair may not grow back once the drug ceases to be taken. An excess of vitamin A in the diet, and protein-deficient diets, may also slow hair growth.

WOMAN'S HAIR GROWTH AND TEXTURE

Hair growth varies according to the position of the hair on the body, as well as a person's sex and age. Hair growth is usually 0.5–1.5mm per week, and the fastest growth occurs between the teens and forties. After the age of 50, hair growth begins to slow down. Thinning occurs when growth is not fast enough to match the rate at which hairs are shed.

GROWTH CYCLES

In women, the HAIR FOLLICLES on the head are active for about six years, compared to three years in men. Hair length is determined by cell cycle and hair growth rate. The active period of all hair follicles is followed by a resting phase when the follicle shrinks. Between three to six months later, the follicle is reactivated to produce a new hair that, while growing, pushes out the old hair, which is then shed. About 100 scalp hairs are shed each day, and the cycle of hair growth determines the length of the hair. Women's hair has been known to grow as long as 3.65m (12ft 2in); but usually their hair length is limited to 0.6–1m (2–3ft).

CURLS, KINKS, AND TEXTURE

Hair follicles are angled so that each hair lies in a particular direction. The lie of the hair is a legacy from the AQUATIC PERIOD, and follows the way in which water flows over the head while a woman is swimming. The thickness and shape of the hair follicle also determines the texture; a flattened, ribbon-shaped follicle produces kinky hair; an oval follicle, wavy hair; and a perfectly round follicle, straight hair.

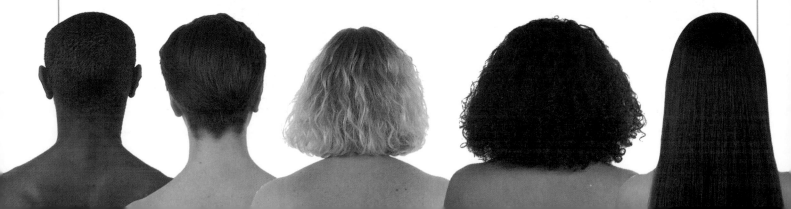

HAIR THROUGH THE AGES

A woman's hair has always been a focus of attention and sexual attraction. Throughout the centuries, lengths and styles have veered from flamboyant to demure, romantic to reactionary, complicated to simple, reflecting fashion and women's changing roles. At the end of the 20th century, individual choice dictates hairstyle.

16th century (left)
During the reign of Queen Elizabeth I, hair was curled with hot tongs and arranged over pads on top of and on either side of the head.

18th century (right)
Hair was frizzed, curled, and piled up and backward to accommodate a hat. False hair was often added to achieve the required bulk.

1920s
Hair was bobbed (cut short) or shingled (cut close to the head in layers). The ends were often curled or put in ringlets so that they would peep out from beneath a fashionable cloche hat.

1950s
Permed hair was worn piled high (above); an extreme style was the permed and backcombed "beehive."

1960s
The close-cropped "gamine" look was very popular in the "swinging" sixties.

HAIR MANIPULATION

PERMING

Using a chemical process, all perms (also called permanent waves) swell the hair shaft, and some add thickness by coating the hair with an elastic film. Perms can give curl, lift, bounce, and texture to the hair fiber.

There are two different types of perms. Alkaline perms break the molecular bonds in the hair fiber and then reset them into a new form. These perms are long-lasting but cause structural damage. Acid perms have a gentler action and do not restructure the hair fiber. They last only six to eight weeks.

TEMPORARY CURLING

Rollers, curling irons, and benders can be used to create temporary curls and styles, particularly for straight or wavy hair that is of fine to medium texture.

When using rollers, it is best to put setting lotion or mousse on the hair first (whether wet or dry) and then brush it through; this gives more body to the style and makes it last longer. Next, working from the front of the scalp, wrap even (2.5–5cm/1–2in) sections of hair smoothly around each of the rollers. The larger the roller, the looser the resulting curls.

If wet hair is wrapped around rollers, it can be left to dry naturally or can be dried using a hair dryer; in the latter instance, the hair should be allowed to cool before the rollers are removed. The lowest rollers should be removed first. By varying the direction and size of the rollers, many different temporary hairstyles can be achieved.

Curling irons can be used to create a new look instantly, although straight medium to long hair benefits most from the regular, crinkled look that results.

Dramatic hair
By experimenting with hair coloring and cuts, individual styles can be achieved to suit a woman's lifestyle and particular occasions.

HAIR STRAIGHTENING

Curly hair can be straightened using perming solutions that work by breaking down the links shaping the hair shaft. This is a fairly harsh treatment, however, and leaves the hair very brittle.

HAIR COLORING

The porousness of the hair shaft determines how each woman's hair responds to artificial colorants, both when it initially takes up the dye and as the dye is leached (and so fades) from the hair. Hair colorants tend to lift the scales on the surface of each hair, making the hair more brittle and porous.

WIGS AND HAIRPIECES

To cover thinning hair or to create more elaborate styles, women make use of additional human or artificial hair. Wigs cover the whole head; hairpieces and extensions are attached to the ends of the natural hair.

HIRSUTISM

In this condition, hair on the female body follows the male pattern of growth; there is coarse, excess hair on various parts of the body (below). Hirsutism does not usually signify any underlying disorder, although polycystic ovary syndrome (imbalance of hormones, usually resulting in multiple OVARIAN CYSTS) and adrenal hyperplasia (over-production of ANDROGENS) may result in hirsutism.

Many women think they have excessive hair growth, particularly on the legs, and they spend a great deal of money on removing hair. Techniques for dealing with unwanted body hair include shaving, bleaching, waxing, depilatory creams, plucking, and electrolysis.

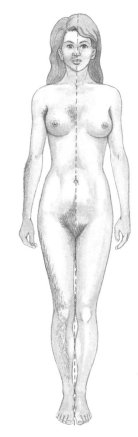

Excessive hair growth
The picture above shows normal female hair growth on the right, and full hirsutism on the left.

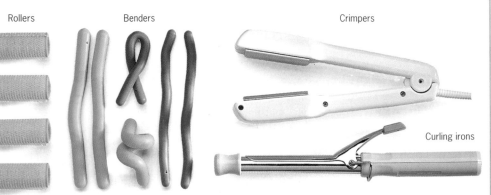

Rollers   Benders   Crimpers

Curling irons

HAIR CARE

Hair can vary in texture from fine and "flyaway" to thick, coarse, or frizzy. The appearance of hair is due to its structure as well as to its condition.

Coarse, curly hair does not reflect light as easily as straight, fine hair. As a result, fine hair can appear to have more luster. Fine hair, however, is more affected by static than coarse hair, so it is more "flyaway." Scales on each hair shaft lie flat in healthy hair (right). When hair has been damaged by styling, drying, brushing, or untangling, split ends result (below).

WASHING

Shampoo is basically a detergent that removes grease, dirt, skin scales, and any residues from styling products from the hair. The detergent improves the cleansing action and helps the removal of grease. Different shampoos contain different strengths of detergent – those for greasy hair contain more than those for dry hair. The constant use of strong detergent shampoos can result in the scalp compensating for the removal of grease by secreting more sebum (natural oil).

CONDITIONERS

The hair shaft projecting from the surface of the skin is largely a dead structure that cannot be fed or nourished in the usual sense. Conditioners can only soften and swell the dead fiber, strengthen it, or coat its surface.

BRUSHING AND BLOWDRYING

Brushing hair helps untangle it and to spread sebum along the hair shaft. Blowdrying can dry out the scalp, and the heat can damage the hair structure. Blow-dry creams protect the structure.

STYLING PRODUCTS

There is a huge variety of products on the market aimed at controlling women's hair and enhancing its appearance. Products such as setting lotion and styling mousse are usually applied to wet hair before styling and help prolong a hairstyle; hair sprays are used after the hair is dry to hold the style in place. Most of these products come in a variety of different "strengths," depending on the firmness of hold required.

Healthy hair
These hair shafts are rounded and healthy. The scales on the surface of each hair lie flat against the shaft.

Unhealthy hair
Under the microscope, split ends look frayed. Split ends occur when the hair is damaged by styling, brushing, rubbing hair dry, and untangling knots.

DANDRUFF

Scales of dead skin shed from the scalp can appear on the hair surface as white flakes, known as dandruff. It is usually caused by SEBORRHEIC DERMATITIS, **a form of** ECZEMA, **but may also be seen in other skin conditions, including** PSORIASIS.

HAIR LICE

NITS

Head lice are minute insects whose flattened and elongated shape enables them to slip between hairs; they then cling to the hair scales with their specially adapted legs. The lice attach their eggs to the base of hair shafts. As the hair grows, the eggs are lifted from the scalp and become visible as small, pale nits attached to the hair shaft. They are often first seen around the nape of the neck where the hair grows most rapidly.

Head lice can be caught by anyone; contrary to belief, lice prefer clean hair to dirty. The first indication of infection is an itchy scalp that cannot be relieved by shampooing. The usual treatment is to wash the hair with a shampoo that contains a safe insecticide.

CRABS

Pubic lice, commonly known as crabs, are larger than head lice. Crabs are mainly transmitted during sexual intercourse. The chief symptom is intense itching in the pubic region. A lotion to kill the lice can be obtained from a pharmacist. Bedding and clothing will need to be washed thoroughly to avoid the danger of reinfection.

EYES

A woman's eyes

Like other primates, women are heavily reliant on their front-facing eyes; it is estimated that as much as 80% of all information about the outside world is relayed to the brain via vision. Most women have brown eyes, although Northern Caucasoid women often have paler eye coloring, such as blue, gray, green, hazel, or violet. Mongoloid women have eyes that look slanted because of the presence of the epicanthic fold, a crease of skin on the upper eyelid that overlaps the inner and outer corners of the eye. All fetuses have the epicanthic fold, but it is retained after birth only by Mongoloid women and children with Down's syndrome.

WOMAN VS. MAN

The female eye is slightly smaller than that of the male and shows a higher proportion of sclera (the white of the eye). In many cultures, the TEAR GLANDS are more active in females than in males.

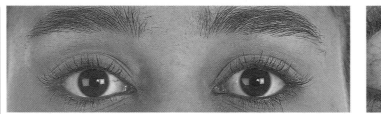
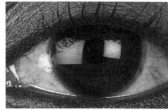
Caucasoid–Negroid. Color: light brown. Shape: round.

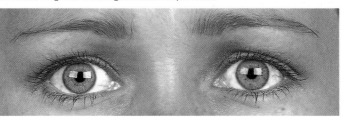

Caucasoid. Color: blue. Shape: round.

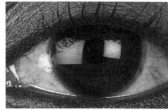
Negroid. Color: dark brown. Shape: almond.

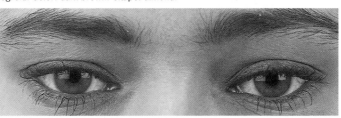
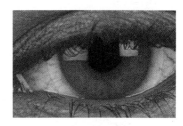
Caucasoid–Mongoloid. Color: green. Shape: almond, slanted.

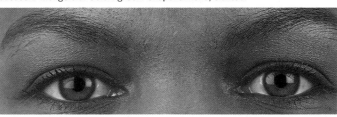
Negroid. Color: brown. Shape: almond.

Caucasoid. Color: hazel/gray. Shape: round.

EYEBROWS

Plucked eyebrows.

Shaped and colored eyebrows.

Eyebrows are used to signal mood changes, and they evolved so that they stand out in the face. Male eyebrows are bushier than those of females and the femininity of women's brows has often been emphasized by techniques such as plucking, shaving, and coloring.

Artificial eyebrows (made of mouse fur) were fashionable in the 17th century. From the middle of the 20th century, strong female eyebrows, as epitomized by Sophia Loren (left), have gained in popularity.

EYELASHES

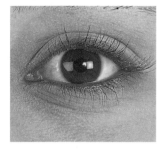

Each eye is protected by a fringe of about 200 lashes – more on the upper eyelid than on the lower. Each lash lasts for three to four months. Eyelashes do not lose their pigment unless affected by certain diseases, which happens very rarely.

EYE COLOR

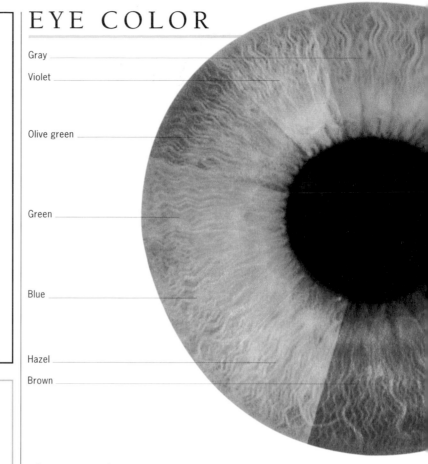

Gray

Violet

Olive green

Green

Blue

Hazel

Brown

The amount of MELANIN pigment in the iris determines eye color. Dark brown eyes are the consequence of a generous amount of pigment in the front layers of the iris. If pigment is largely confined to the deeper layers of the iris, the eyes will be paler, ranging from hazel or green to gray or blue as the pigment content decreases. Violet eyes are the result of blood showing through thin pigment.

GAZE BEHAVIOR

When a woman looks closely at another face for any length of time, her gaze does not remain focused on one particular feature; her eyes scan the face but concentrate mostly on the eyes, nose, and mouth (left).

Gazing
Pink tracery indicates the gaze's direction and intensity.

While women are engaged in conversation, their gaze will shift in a remarkably predictable way. The speaker will glance at her companion as she starts to speak, then look away until she is nearing the end of her comment, when she will glance back to check the effect of her words on her companion. This process also occurs if she is talking for a long time and needs to see her companion's response.

While the speaker is talking, the listener will keep her eyes on the speaker's face, and may nod or give verbal encouragement when their eyes meet. Women listeners generally give far more encouragement to the speaker than men do; men tend to nod only if they agree with what is being said.

As the listener takes over the conversation, she looks away in turn as her words gain momentum, glancing back only to check on the effect of what she is saying.

EYE ANATOMY

The sensory cells of the eye are an extension of the brain, budding out from the brain during FETAL DEVELOPMENT. The eye shows less growth than any other organ between birth and adulthood.

The eye is sensitive to light, which is focused through the cornea and the lens onto the retina at the back of the eye. The eye's retina contains 137 million cells, of which 130 million are rod-shaped and used for black and white vision and sensing movement in poor light, while seven million are cone-shaped and used to sense color and pattern in bright light. Cones are concentrated in the *macula*. The *fovea centralis* (central depression) is rod-free. A network of nerve cells on the surface of the retina changes the light signals into electrical nerve impulses and then

relays them to the brain via the optic nerve. The eye contains 70% of the body's sensors and can deal with one and a half million simultaneous messages. The pupils automatically dilate or contract to control the amount of light that falls on the retina.

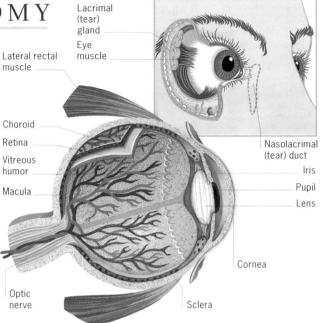

Lacrimal (tear) gland
Eye muscle
Lateral rectal muscle
Choroid
Retina
Vitreous humor
Macula
Optic nerve
Nasolacrimal (tear) duct
Iris
Pupil
Lens
Cornea
Sclera

TEARS

The lacrimal (tear) gland is positioned above and toward the outer edge of the eyeball. It releases a saline fluid that contains lysozymes (protective anti-bacterial substances). When a woman blinks, this fluid lubricates the surface of the eye and then drains away through the naso-lacrimal duct. Anxiety, strong emotion, or eye irritation will usually result in tears.

COLOR BLINDNESS

This doesn't usually affect all three color pigments, so color blindness normally involves a failure to differentiate between two major colors. Red/green color blindness is the most common, and is a gender-linked GENETIC DISORDER. It is much rarer in women than it is in men.

Test pattern
Those with complete color vision can distinguish the 57 in the pattern.

COLOR VISION

In common with other primates, humans sense only part of the electromagnetic spectrum. The color pigments we perceive are blue, green, and red. Color is registered by the cones in the *macula* and the *fovea centralis*. Each cone has a sensitivity curve that has maximum sensitivity for blue, green, or red, and intermediate sensitivity to the rest

of the color spectrum. These curves overlap so that wavelengths other than blue, green, or red also trigger color perceptions: for example, where light hits an overlapping curve of red and blue, the color purple is "seen." Humans can see color only in bright light and must look directly at the image so that light is focused on the *macula*.

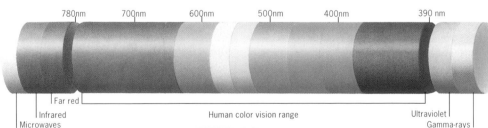

780nm   700nm   600nm   500nm   400nm   390 nm

Far red
Infrared
Microwaves
Human color vision range
Ultraviolet
Gamma-rays

Spectrum wavelengths
Measured in nanometers (one is equal to a thousand-millionth of a meter), the color energy band that a woman is able to perceive is only a small portion of the total electromagnetic spectrum (above).

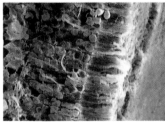

Light-sensitive retina
False-color scanning electron micrograph (SEM) of the retina (left) shows layers of light-sensitive cells. Light first strikes the surface cells (white) and is then detected by the rods and cones behind them (purple).

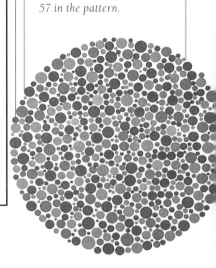

FOCUSING AND SIGHT

A woman's eye is more efficient at accommodation (ability to resolve fine detail) than the eyes of most other mammals. Light enters the eye through the pupil, which dilates or contracts according to lighting conditions, lens adjustment, and emotions. The lens then focuses the light on the retina by changing shape. When focusing over long distances (over 7m/20ft), the lens is at its flattest and thinnest. When focusing on objects that are nearby, the lens becomes rounder and thicker. The closest point at which the eye can focus varies with age, from 7cm (2¾in) in infancy to only 40cm (16in) in old age. The lens focuses an image upside down on the retina (below); the con-

scious mind interprets the image and "sees" it in its true position. A child's eye has a range of about 14 diopters (a diopter is the unit used to measure the refracting power of the lens), although this range progressively decreases with age to one diopter.

The eye's strength of accommodation is determined by the number of light receptors (divided into rods and cones) present and how closely they are packed together. A woman has 200,000 receptors per sq mm, giving excellent resolution as long as vision during infancy has not been impeded in any way. Some creatures need even higher resolution – the buzzard's retina, for example, contains one million receptors per sq mm.

FIELD OF VISION

FIELD OF VISION

Women have eyes that are placed on the front of the head, giving binocular and peripheral vision. Peripheral vision means that a woman can see 180° without moving her head, with an overlap of 90° between the right and left visual fields. This enables her to judge distances and pick out detail and improves sensitivity in poor light.

☐ Monocular vision
☐ Panoramic monocular vision
☐ Binocular vision

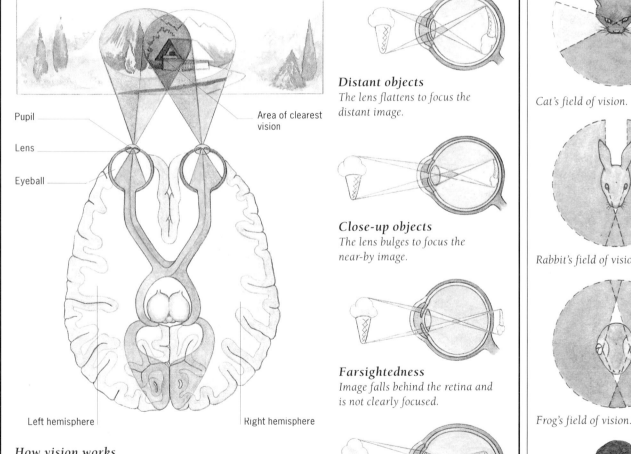

Pupil
Lens
Eyeball

Area of clearest vision

Left hemisphere   Right hemisphere

How vision works
The left side of the brain "sees" the right visual field of each of the eyes, while the right side of the brain "sees" the left visual field. The overlap of the fields of vision is the area in which a woman sees most clearly.

Distant objects
The lens flattens to focus the distant image.

Close-up objects
The lens bulges to focus the near-by image.

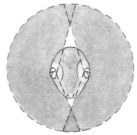

Farsightedness
Image falls behind the retina and is not clearly focused.

Nearsightedness
Image falls in front of the retina and appears blurred.

Cat's field of vision.

Rabbit's field of vision.

Frog's field of vision.

Woman's field of vision.

EYE MANIPULATION

Women emphasize their eyes in various ways to increase their sexual attractiveness and to exaggerate the social signals that they make with their eyes. Makeup was used by the ancient Egyptians and has remained popular to the present day.

False eyelashes are used to increase the length and thickness of the natural eyelashes; mascara or eyelash tinting is used to darken the lashes and make them look thicker; eyedrops are used to enhance the natural whiteness of the eye; and tinted contact lenses can be used to change eye color. Eyeliner is a popular method of emphasizing the shape and size of the eye, and some women's eyes are permanently "made up" by being tattooed.

Colored contact lenses

THE CULTURAL EYE

Women who live in a very male-dominated society are often required to cover their heads totally when in public. The ability to communicate is only retained through the powerful social signals that are conveyed by their eyes.

Cover-up (left)
Even when the face is fully masked, the eyes usually remain uncovered.

Eye enhancement
Softly blended eyelid makeup enhances the eye.

Eye statement
Punk makeup emphasizes the area surrounding the eye.

COSMETIC EYE SURGERY

Blepharoplasty is one of the most popular cosmetic surgical procedures and is performed on upper and lower eyelids that have sagged and become wrinkled. Some women have surgery on "hooded" upper eyelids.

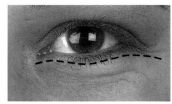

Upper eyelid
Skin is removed from the area between the dotted lines, and the edges are then sewn together.

Lower eyelid
The skin is cut below the eye, as shown, and is then pulled sideways before being rejoined.

THE LANGUAGE OF EYES

The size of the pupils is affected by the level of light and by stimuli. In low light levels and when a woman looks at something she finds pleasurable or exciting, her pupils dilate, while bright light and distasteful subjects make them contract. When women look at babies, whether they are mothers or not, their pupils dilate. When men look at babies, however, their pupils usually don't dilate unless they are fathers.

The sclera (whites) of a woman's eyes are larger than those of any other species' eyes; the theory of the AQUATIC PERIOD suggests they evolved to emphasize eye movements and aid communication. Staring at someone can be an indication of either strong attraction or aggression.

Love gazing
In the early stages of a relationship, lovers will often stare deeply into each other's eyes. They are unconsciously picking up and reacting to the dilation of each other's pupils, which increases the depth of the feelings they have for their partner.

VISION DISORDERS

A number of common eye disorders affect vision. Myopia (near-sightedness) is a result of the lens focusing the light at a point in front of, instead of on, the RETINA. This happens when the eyes have grown slightly larger than is appro-priate for the focusing distance between the retina and lens. Hypermetropia (far-sightedness) occurs when the lens focuses light behind the retina. This results from a rela-tively weak lens, which fails to focus an image on the retina. As the eye ages, the lens of the eye hardens and the ciliary muscle weakens, so that it is harder to focus on nearby objects. Known as PRESBYOPIA, this her-alds the need for reading glasses.

Some older women require one pair of eye-glasses for near focusing and another pair for distant focusing.

EYE DISORDERS

CATARACTS
Cloudiness in the lens of the eye, known as a cataract, is caused by the protein in the lens becoming opaque. Cataracts can be either present at birth, which is most common following maternal German measles during preg-nancy, or often develop after the age of 50. The effects of a cataract on the sight depend on the position and severity of the cataract; a cataract at the center of the lens will cause more problems than on the edge. Only one eye may be affected. Symptoms range from slight blurring of vision to reduction of sight to only awareness of light. Cataracts affect almost twice as many women as men. People with diabetes often develop cataracts earlier than normal.

STYES
During childhood and the teenage years, styes are the most common problem to affect the eyelids. Styes are caused by an infection at the root of an eyelash that results in a boil developing at the edge of the lid. The stye will be red, swollen, and uncomfortable. It may subside sponta-neously or come to a head and erupt. Styes are also more common in people with diabetes than in others.

CONJUNCTIVITIS
Inflammation of the conjunctiva (the mucous membrane that covers the eyeball and the under surface of the eyelid) causes redness, pain, and discharge. Usually, it is the result of infections or allergies (such as to mascara or HAY FEVER).

GLAUCOMA
Excessive pressure of the fluid in the eyeball results in compression and obstruction of the eye's tiny blood vessels and the OPTIC NERVE. Glaucoma can cause loss of vision.

GLASSES
Eyeglasses are worn to cor-rect poor eyesight, while sunglasses are worn to pro-tect the eyes from sunlight. Both change the face because the frames become part of the facial expression of the wearer. Generally speaking, a heavy upper rim (top) may make the wearer appear more dominant and aggressive, while circular frames (bot-tom) can make the wearer look wide-eyed, and hence surprised, young, or naive.

CONTACT LENSES

Contact lenses are very thin, concave transparent disks that fit onto the cornea to correct a visual defect; the curve of the contact lens changes the angle at which light enters the eye and so corrects the VISION DISORDER (above). Most sight defects for which glasses are prescribed can be corrected by contact lenses.

The most commonly worn contact lenses are hard and soft, although rigid gas-permeable, extended-wear, and dis-posable types are also used. Most contact lenses should be removed from the eyes and cleaned daily.

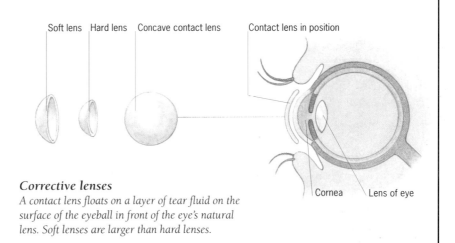

Corrective lenses
A contact lens floats on a layer of tear fluid on the surface of the eyeball in front of the eye's natural lens. Soft lenses are larger than hard lenses.

EARS

The individual ear

Each woman's ears are unique – no two pairs have an identical arrangement of ear folds on the pinna (external part of the ear); identifying criminals by their "ear maps" was once considered, but fingerprinting was chosen instead as the easier option. Earlobes also vary in size as well as in their degree of attachment – one woman in three has lobes that are smoothly attached, while two in three have freely hanging lobes. Curiously, the consistency of ear wax differs between the races – Negroid and most Caucasoid women produce a sticky wax, while some Caucasoid and all Mongoloid women have dry ear wax.

WOMAN VS. MAN

Women's ears tend to be smaller and have a neater shape than those of men, and the lobes are generally shorter (unless they have been artificially stretched).

Women are more likely than men to have ears that lie flat against the sides of the head, whereas men are more apt than women to have ears that stand away or that even stick out prominently.

An operation known as otoplasty can be performed to flatten protruding ears. Western women are more likely than men to have both earlobes pierced.

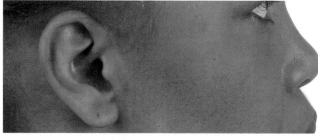
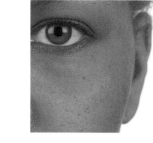

Rounded pinna; small hanging lobe. Negroid.

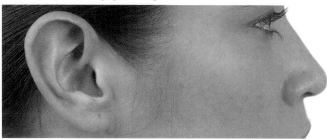

Sculpted pinna; smoothly attached lobe. Caucasoid–Mongoloid.

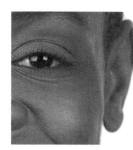

Sculpted pinna; fleshy hanging lobe. Negroid.

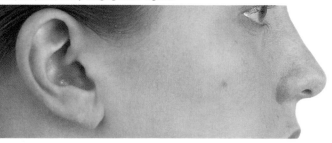

Fleshy pinna; pointed hanging lobe. Caucasoid.

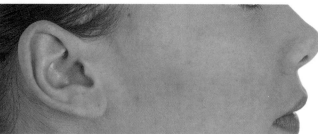
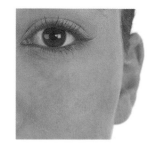

Angular fleshy pinna and lobe. Caucasoid–Negroid.

ANATOMY OF THE EAR

The ear is a highly efficient miniature sound system and is also responsible for the sense of BALANCE. The ear consists of the outer, middle, and inner ear. The PINNA (ear flap) is composed of a number of elastic pieces of cartilage. The pinna funnels sound into the 2.5cm (1in) long ear canal, which inclines upward toward the TYMPANIC MEMBRANE (eardrum); the lining of the inner two-thirds of ear canal contains 4,000 wax-secreting glands. The EUSTACHIAN TUBE, which runs from the throat to the middle ear, admits air, and this enables pressure to be equalized on either side of the tympanic membrane.

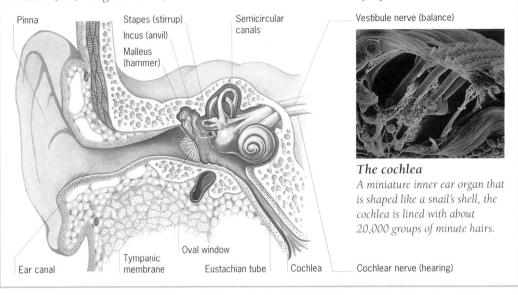

Pinna
Stapes (stirrup)
Incus (anvil)
Malleus (hammer)
Semicircular canals
Vestibule nerve (balance)
Ear canal
Tympanic membrane
Oval window
Eustachian tube
Cochlea
Cochlear nerve (hearing)

The cochlea
A miniature inner ear organ that is shaped like a snail's shell, the cochlea is lined with about 20,000 groups of minute hairs.

HOW SOUND REGISTERS IN THE EAR

Sound vibrations are channeled into the ear by the PINNA, travel up the ear canal, and strike the TYMPANIC MEMBRANE, displacing its surface. This is registered by the malleus, incus, and stapes. The pressure is amplified 22 times as it travels to the COCHLEA via the oval window; the amplified vibrations impinge upon some of the hair-like sensory cells in the cochlea. The impulses generated are relayed to the brain by the COCHLEAR NERVE.

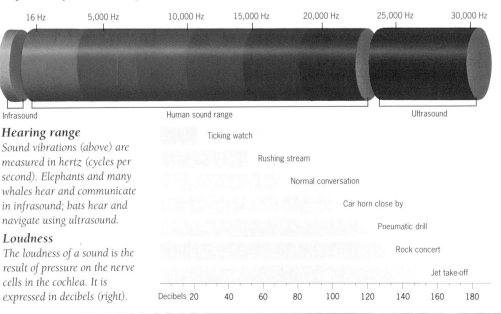

16 Hz   5,000 Hz   10,000 Hz   15,000 Hz   20,000 Hz   25,000 Hz   30,000 Hz

Infrasound   Human sound range   Ultrasound

Hearing range
Sound vibrations (above) are measured in hertz (cycles per second). Elephants and many whales hear and communicate in infrasound; bats hear and navigate using ultrasound.

Loudness
The loudness of a sound is the result of pressure on the nerve cells in the cochlea. It is expressed in decibels (right).

Ticking watch
Rushing stream
Normal conversation
Car horn close by
Pneumatic drill
Rock concert
Jet take-off

Decibels 20   40   60   80   100   120   140   160   180

Streamlined pinnae

Movable pinnae

Large, versatile pinnae

49

WOMAN'S BALANCE

The COCHLEA (a spiral tube forming part of the inner ear) and the inside of the SEMICIRCULAR CANALS (the part of the inner ear concerned with equilibrium) are fluid-filled and contain minute hair receptors. As the head moves, the fluid shifts and the hair cells bend, stimulating nerve impulses to the brain.

The semicircular canals maintain balance while the body is in motion; the cochlea is responsible for balance when the body is static. Ear infections can consequently cause dizziness. If the brain perceives that balance is being lost, it will signal some muscles to contract and others to relax in order to regain balance.

Balancing act
Tightrope walkers display a highly developed sense of balance.

The inner ear

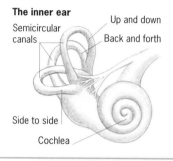

Semicircular canals

Up and down

Back and forth

Side to side

Cochlea

EAR DISORDERS

Earache occurs when either the middle or outer ear becomes inflamed or infected. This is usually the result of the viruses or bacteria that cause nose and throat infections traveling up the EUSTACHIAN TUBE into the middle ear.

Tinnitus is a fairly common condition in which the sufferer hears a constant ringing or buzzing sound in her ears. It can be extremely loud; this complaint is experienced more frequently by older women than younger ones.

Menière's disease is characterized by vertigo, tinnitus, and deafness. A sufferer is likely to experience fluctuating, rather than constant, levels of symptoms. There is no known cause, and Menière's disease can be totally debilitating. It is rare before the age of 50 years.

ADORNING THE EARS

The ears have been lavishly decorated for over 4,000 years; earrings were originally worn as lucky charms and have remained popular ornaments.

In some parts of Africa, long earlobes are seen as the ultimate standard of beauty, and a girl's earlobes are punctured and stretched systematically to increase her desirability.

In some cultures, it is thought that the ears are the seat of wisdom.

Multiple piercing is fashionable.

Ear piercing
Piercing and decorating the ears with such flamboyance demonstrates this woman's high status.

DEAFNESS

This is a condition that can be either congenital (present at birth) or progressive. There are two principal types of deafness – conductive, when something interferes with the transmission of sound vibrations to the inner ear, and sensorineural, when there is damage to the nerves that transmit messages from the ear to the brain. Conductive deafness is usually progressive and may be caused by an infection, a damaged eardrum, fluid in the middle ear, or otosclerosis (fixation of the stapes). Nerve deafness is often congenital, although it may be the result of a head injury.

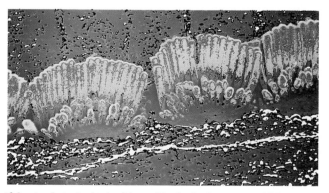

If the tiny hairs in this healthy cochlea broke, hearing would diminish.

NOSE

The adaptable nose

This remarkable air-conditioning organ warms and moistens air as well as filtering out dust and debris before it reaches the lungs. To function correctly, the lungs require warm, moist air. There is a theory that noses that evolved in cold and dry areas became longer and narrower to enable the nasal passages to produce the necessary moisture (99%) for air in its passage to the lungs. By contrast, noses that evolved in hot and moist areas became flatter and wider because they only needed to supply about 25% of the moisture that the lungs required. However, the noses of Mongoloid women, who are thought to have evolved in cold regions, tend to be flattened. And those of North African and Middle Eastern women, who live in hot areas, tend to be longer. The theory, therefore, is riddled with problems.

WOMAN VS. MAN

The nose of the average woman is smaller and flatter (and therefore more childlike) than that of the average man. This "childlike," feminine nose is thought to have evolved because it awakens the male's protective feelings. All adults evince a strongly positive reaction to small noses.

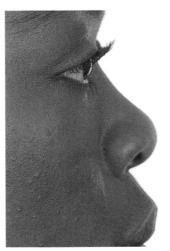

Medium flat. Negroid.

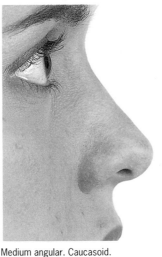

Medium angular. Caucasoid.

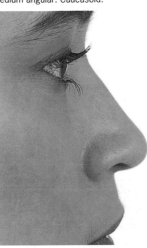

Angular. Caucasoid–Mongoloid.

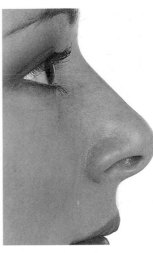

Large straight. Caucasoid.

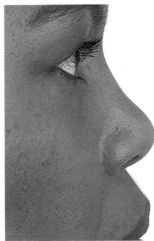

Small concave. Negroid.

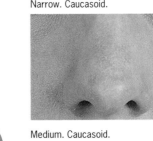

Small. Caucasoid–Negroid.

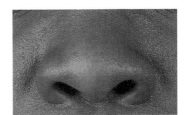

Broad. Negroid.

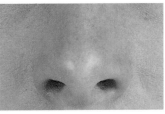

Narrow. Caucasoid.

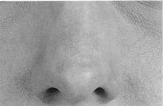

Medium. Caucasoid.

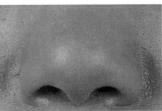

Medium. Negroid.

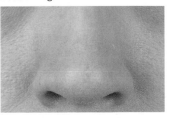

Narrow. Caucasoid–Mongoloid.

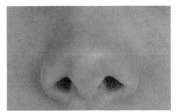

Snubbed. Caucasoid–Negroid.

WOMAN VS. ANIMAL

A woman's nose can identify a wide range of smells, and is an extremely efficient air-conditioning organ. The noses of other animals, however, are incredibly diverse in shape and function.

The elephant's trunk
Able to hit hard enough to kill a leopard, this nose can also pick a single blade of grass.

The camel's nose
The nostrils can deliberately be closed to prevent sand from entering the lungs.

The dolphin's blowhole
The single nostril emerges behind the head; it closes when the dolphin dives.

ANATOMY OF THE NOSE

The nose is the air conditioner for the respiratory system. The lungs require the air that enters them to be warm (35°C/95°F), moist (humidity of 95%), and clean (no dust and debris). Otherwise the vulnerable pulmonary membranes will become dried out or damaged. Lining the nasal cavities are blood vessels, which warm the air, and mucous membranes, which ensure air quality. The mucous membranes secrete 1 quart (1 liter) of mucus a day. Embedded in the membrane are millions of CILIA (minute hairs) that beat rhythmically about 12–15 times a second, shifting the mucus toward the throat at a rate of 1cm ($\frac{1}{2}$in) a minute. Dust and other debris are caught in the mucus, which is then swallowed. The cilia beat slower if a woman smokes, drinks alcohol, or is ill; the nose then works less efficiently.

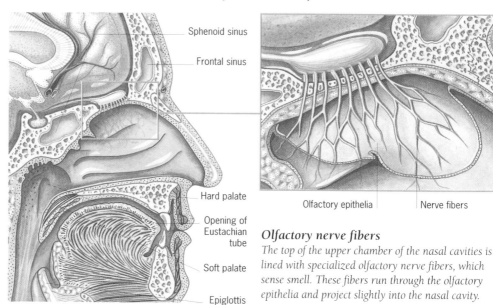

Sphenoid sinus

Frontal sinus

Hard palate

Opening of Eustachian tube

Soft palate

Epiglottis

Olfactory epithelia   Nerve fibers

Olfactory nerve fibers
The top of the upper chamber of the nasal cavities is lined with specialized olfactory nerve fibers, which sense smell. These fibers run through the olfactory epithelia and project slightly into the nasal cavity.

THE SENSE OF SMELL

The nose is the main organ of smell and taste (the tongue can detect only four basic flavors – sweet, sour, salty, and bitter; all other flavors are "tasted" by the nose). The nose accomplishes this via the olfactory epithelia, two postage-stamp-sized smell-receptor sites that are packed with five million yellowish hairlike fibers. To smell something properly, it is necessary to inhale deeply so that air swirls up over these olfactory nerve fibers (above). Odor must be in liquid form or must be dissolved in the mucus of the nose lining. The average woman is thought to be able to detect about 4,000 individual odors; an exceptional "nose" (such as possessed by perfumers and wine tasters) is capable of recognizing up to 10,000 different smells.

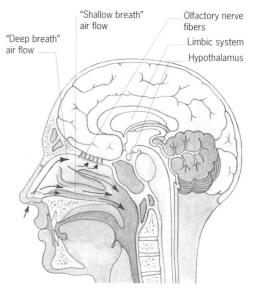

"Shallow breath" air flow

"Deep breath" air flow

Olfactory nerve fibers

Limbic system

Hypothalamus

Registering smell
Liquid scent stimulates olfactory nerve fibers; the limbic system and the hypothalamus register this.

BODY SCENTS

One of the most attractive, if subtle, signals that a woman's body sends out is her individual scent. The APOCRINE GLANDS in the armpits, VULVA, and vagina produce minute amounts of scent that contain copulins (female pheromones). These increase at OVULATION, and studies suggest that they have a powerful, unconscious, and arousing effect on men. So far, no successful imitation has been produced commercially, but there have been many attempts. The marketing potential of an identical copy would be immense.

A woman's hair color is thought to influence her body scent. Brunettes are said to exude a musky scent, redheads a sharp, sweet smell, and blondes a scent that is heady and flowery.

PERFUME

As long ago as 4,000 BC, wealthy women were using perfumed oils to anoint their bodies. The women of ancient Egypt and Rome were especially lavish with perfume – it was used in their hair and on their clothing and furnishings, as well as in baths.

Coco Chanel
The most famous and enduringly popular perfume in the world, Chanel No. 5, was named after couturier Coco Chanel.

Perfume usually has three levels, or "notes": – the top note, which conveys the first impression; the middle note, which makes up the "heart" of the scent; and the base note, which carries the perfume and makes it linger. Some modern scents, particularly the "power perfumes" of the 1980s, have minimal top and base notes and are known as "horizontals." There are three main perfume families – floral, oriental, and citrus green – although others, such as the synthetic aldehydic (one of the main ingredients of Chanel No. 5) and oceanic, also play an important part in many modern perfumes.

SINUSES

Air spaces in the skull, these decrease the weight of the skull and give the voice resonance. The sinuses are lined with a mucous membrane, which is similar to that lining the nose and throat. The nasal passage is linked to the sphenoid, maxillary, ethmoid, and frontal sinuses. Mucus produced by the sinuses supplements that from the nose. If the mucous membrane swells due to infection, drainage into the nose and throat is impaired and acute inflammation occurs, resulting in congestion and a classic sinus headache.

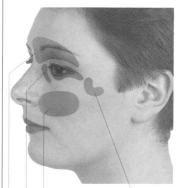

Maxillary sinus
Ethmoid sinus
Frontal sinus
Sphenoid sinus

NOSE TO NOSE

The nose has great significance in many different cultures, from "nose greeting" in Maori and Inuit societies (in which the noses merely touch, and are not rubbed together, as is commonly believed), to adornment with elaborate ornaments in many African, Asian, and American Indian (below left) cultures. Nose ornaments have also gained in popularity in the Western world, although their use is generally restricted to ethnic groups and some social subgroups, such as those of punks and bikers. The West has an obsession with the small, childlike female nose, and so rhinoplasty ("nose bobbing") is one of the most popular cosmetic operations.

Ideal nose
The "perfect" Western nose has a nasofacial angle (the angle the length of the nose makes with the front of the face) of between 36° and 40° and a columella angle (end of the nose to the upper lip) of between 90° and 120°. Grace Kelly had a "perfect" nose.

The decorated nose
A hole, or sometimes holes, are pierced in the lower part of the septum (the central partition between the nostrils) or in the fleshy side of the nostril.

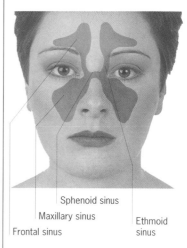

Sphenoid sinus
Maxillary sinus
Frontal sinus
Ethmoid sinus

Echo chambers
The exact size and position of the sinuses are crucial to the resonance and quality of a woman's voice.

MOUTH & TEETH

The versatile mouth

The mouth is the entrance to the digestive and respiratory systems. It is the instrument through which women produce sound and, therefore, language, using the tongue, teeth, lips, and palate. A woman's lips also have a sexual connotation, because they mimic the appearance of the labia (vulval lips), becoming swollen during sexual arousal. Attention is frequently drawn to the lips by the use of lipstick.

WOMAN VS. ANIMAL

Human beings are the only primates to have lips that are rolled outward so that part of the inner mucous membrane is exposed. This means that a woman's lips contrast strongly with her surrounding facial skin; and subtle facial expressions can be seen clearly from a distance.

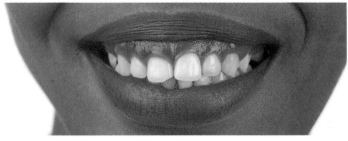

Medium-width mouth; full lips; white teeth. Negroid.

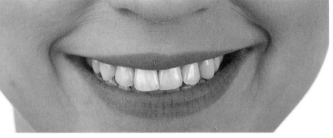

Narrow mouth; medium lips; pearly teeth. Caucasoid–Mongoloid.

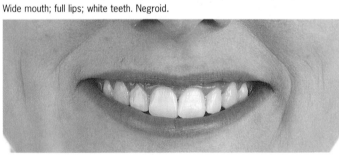
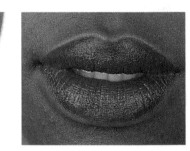

Wide mouth; full lips; white teeth. Negroid.

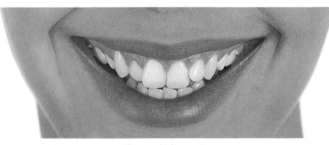
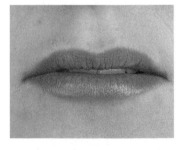

Medium-width mouth; thin lips; ivory teeth. Caucasoid.

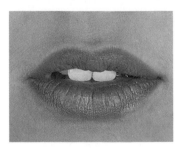

Wide mouth; full lips; ivory teeth. Caucasoid–Negroid.

ANATOMY OF THE MOUTH

The mouth and its surrounding lips form the entrance to a woman's digestive tract. The mouth interacts with food and other substances taken in from the outside world, and is extremely rich in sense organs for taste and touch. It contains the tongue, the teeth, and the openings of the SALIVARY GLANDS, all of which play a part in tasting, chewing, and swallowing food and drink, and in the process of SPEECH.

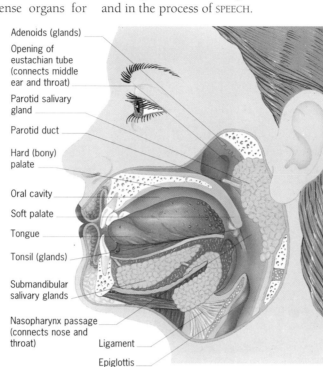

Tooth
Uvula
Hard palate
Tongue
Lip
Tonsil

Adenoids (glands)
Opening of eustachian tube (connects middle ear and throat)
Parotid salivary gland
Parotid duct
Hard (bony) palate
Oral cavity
Soft palate
Tongue
Tonsil (glands)
Submandibular salivary glands
Nasopharynx passage (connects nose and throat)
Ligament
Epiglottis

Primary digestive organ
Food digestion starts in the mouth. It is here that all the food that enters a woman's body begins to be broken down and is mixed to a wet, smooth paste that can be swallowed easily.

FLORA AND FAUNA

The mouth of a healthy woman may harbor more than 40 species of bacteria, as well as viruses, fungi, and protozoa. Each milliliter of SALIVA (below) can contain a billion streptococcal bacteria, and there are approximately 100 bacteria on every cell on the surface of the tongue.

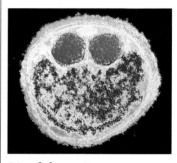

Mouth bacteria
This false-color micrograph shows a section through a Fusobacterium nucleatum, *a bacterium that occurs in gingival crevices in the gums.*

SALIVA

About 1 liter (1 quart) of saliva is secreted in a woman's mouth every day. Food greatly increases the production of saliva (resulting in a watering mouth), while fear and excitement reduce saliva production (resulting in a dry mouth). Saliva contains a digestive enzyme and mucus, lubricates the mouth, and allows the tasting and swallowing of food. It also acts as a buffer to acids in the mouth that are responsible for tooth decay, and it contains an epidermal growth factor that speeds the healing of cuts and abrasions of the skin. Saliva is produced by all mammals.

MOUTH AND FACIAL MUSCLES

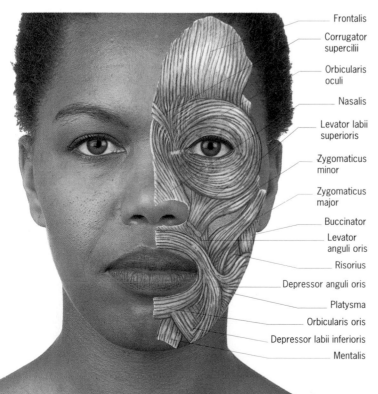

Frontalis
Corrugator supercilii
Orbicularis oculi
Nasalis
Levator labii superioris
Zygomaticus minor
Zygomaticus major
Buccinator
Levator anguli oris
Risorius
Depressor anguli oris
Platysma
Orbicularis oris
Depressor labii inferioris
Mentalis

A woman's mouth is the most expressive and mobile part of her face. It is controlled by the muscles surrounding the lips and those in the cheeks, chin, and jaw. There are several dozen muscles in the face (the illustration on the left shows only the main muscles), and these are responsible for the approximately 7,000 facial expressions that a woman can make. A woman's habitual expressions will eventually leave their mark permanently on her face in the form of lines and wrinkles. The facial muscles are directly connected to the skin that overlays them; therefore, facial exercises have the potential to improve skin tone.

KISSING

There are two types of kiss – the social kiss and the sexual kiss – and they are used almost universally. The social kiss can be used as a greeting, a mark of respect, or a gesture of affection. In the former instance, the status of the kisser, relative to the kissed, affects where the lips are applied. Women of equal status will exchange kisses on either the lips or the cheek. In unequal relationships, a woman of lower status will kiss areas that are increasingly far from the lips of the higher-ranking person. Such areas range from the hand to the ground in front of the person's feet. In the rarer instances where a woman of high status kisses someone of lower status, she usually bestows a kiss on the top of the head. The intimate sexual kiss is most certainly the older type of kiss, and it evolved from primitive feeding behavior. A mother would wean her child by using her tongue to transfer prechewed food from her mouth into the mouth of her child. Kisses, therefore, came to symbolize intimate care and love, and so became a deeply entrenched part of human culture.

High-status social kiss
The Pope kisses the head.

Sexual kiss
Open mouth-to-mouth kissing is a prelude to the most intimate sexual kisses, when lovers' tongues probe one another's mouths passionately.

Loving kiss
A mother's kiss expresses parental love.

ORAL PLEASURE

The pleasure and security that human infants experience when they suckle at the breast reverberate throughout life to a lesser or greater degree.

Children frequently suck their thumbs or a "security blanket," for reassurance, while adults experience oral pleasure and reassurance when smoking, eating (especially sweet foods), and sipping sweet, warm drinks. This partly explains why certain orally directed habits, such as nail-biting and smoking, are hard to break.

SMILING

A particularly human characteristic, smiling has a number of variants. The silent, closed-lip smile is the least expressive, and also tends to be practiced by those who feel self-conscious about their teeth.

A smile intensifies when the lips part, and this often results in a grin with the upper teeth exposed. If the smile becomes laughter, the mouth opens even wider.

When a woman "puts on a sunny face" and forces a smile, the corners of her mouth stay turned down during the smile.

If the eye muscles are not involved in the smile, then it isn't genuinely felt.

Full smile

Mild smile

ORAL CANCER

This is the commonly used term for cancer of the mouth, lip, and tongue. Two of the main causes are smoking and drinking alcohol, especially if in combination. (Chewing tobacco also increases the risk of oral cancer.) The first sign of cancer is usually the appearance of a painless lump, sore, or ulcer on the inside of the mouth, the lips, or on the tongue.

Oral cancer can affect a woman's speech and her ability to chew and swallow.

Usually, oral cancer can be treated successfully with surgery and radiation therapy, although treatment is frequently disfiguring and can cause lasting physical and personality problems.

ANATOMY OF THE TONGUE

This is a muscular, movable organ that is rooted to the base of the mouth. It is used for speaking, in swallowing, and for cleaning food particles from the teeth. On the surface of the tongue are three types of gustatory papillae (usually known as TASTE BUDS – below), and filiform papillae, a type associated with chewing. These latter are abrasive, conically shaped papillae and give the tongue its whitish color; they are found on the front two-thirds of the tongue. They give it a rough surface, which is useful for licking smooth food, such as ice cream. The fungiform (mushroom-shaped) papillae are numerous toward the front of the tongue; because they are well supplied with blood, they give the tongue its usual healthy red color.

Some women can extend their tongues out to touch their noses, while some have tongues that are so firmly attached to the floor of the mouth that their speech can be affected. Many people can roll their tongues into a tube shape, while a few can form a double tube. This is genetically determined.

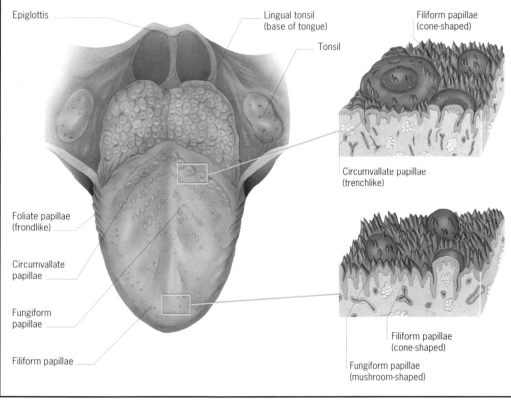

Epiglottis

Lingual tonsil (base of tongue)

Tonsil

Filiform papillae (cone-shaped)

Circumvallate papillae (trenchlike)

Foliate papillae (frondlike)

Circumvallate papillae

Fungiform papillae

Filiform papillae

Filiform papillae (cone-shaped)

Fungiform papillae (mushroom-shaped)

THE SENSE OF TASTE

A woman has about 5,000 gustatory papillae (taste buds), each of which are renewed every 24 hours. The taste buds are found throughout the mouth but the majority are found on the tongue. Generally, fungiform papillae, toward the front of the tongue, are most sensitive to sweet and salty tastes; foliate papillae, on the sides of the tongue, to sour tastes; and circumvallate papillae, (which are on the back of the tongue, and contain the highest proportion of taste buds), to bitter tastes. The sense of taste evolved because it was important for our ancestors to know if fruit was ripe (sweet) or unripe (sour), to identify potentially dangerous foods (sour or bitter), and also to maintain their bodies' correct chemical balance (salty). The ability of taste buds to distinguish flavors is actually quite crude; the refinement of the sense called taste is provided by the sense of SMELL. Some women have an extremely refined sense of taste, which may lead them into careers as "tasters" – of wine, beer, coffee, tea, or chocolate, for example.

SPEAKING TONGUE

The main ways in which a woman uses her tongue in visual gestures is based on the two ways in which the infant uses her tongue when suckling at the breast.

The sinuous tongue that originally sought the nipple, when transferred into an adult signal, invites sexually explorative behavior.

The protruding tongue, signifying the infant's rejection of the nipple when she has had enough milk, is employed by an adult in two contexts. When a woman is concentrating hard, she may push out the tip of her tongue, as if to convey to anyone who may want to interrupt a wish not to be disturbed. When she wants to make a strong gesture of rejection, she deliberately pokes out her tongue as a highly visible insult.

Occasionally, the tongue may also be used as a symbolic penis protruding between the lips, which are symbolic of the labia (vulval lips). The tongue is held stiffly in this position and is moved to mimic the thrusting action of copulation. This gesture appears to stem more from the way a woman's lips mimic the vulval lips than from infantile behavior.

WOMAN VS. ANIMAL

The abrasive filiform papillae in the middle of the tongue are rough in women, but not as rough as in some other mammals, such as cats. This is because cats' tongues are used for grooming fur and licking raw meat to soften it.

SETS OF TEETH

Women have two sets of teeth. Baby, or deciduous, teeth (only 20 in total) start to erupt at about the age of six months; permanent teeth (32) start to replace the deciduous teeth from about six years of age.

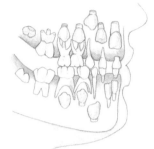

Deciduous teeth (seven years of age).

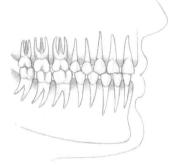

Permanent teeth (21 years of age).

TOOTH ANATOMY

A woman's tooth has three layers – enamel on the outside of the crown, the hard dentine below this, and the soft pulp at the center. Enamel is made up of hard, very dense, minerals (calcium and phosphorus). Capillaries and nerves fill the pulp; they reach it via the root canal. Cementum holds the root firm in the alveolar bone.

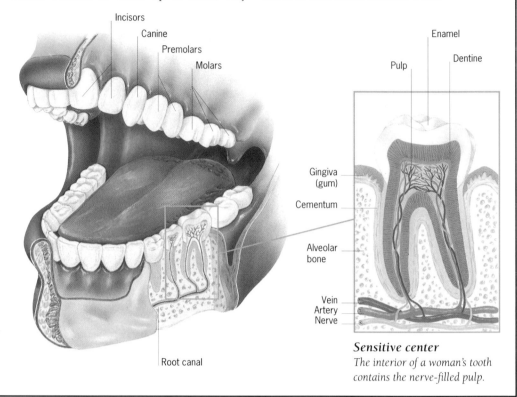

Incisors
Canine
Premolars
Molars

Enamel
Dentine
Pulp

Gingiva (gum)
Cementum
Alveolar bone
Vein
Artery
Nerve

Root canal

Sensitive center
The interior of a woman's tooth contains the nerve-filled pulp.

TOOTH DECAY

Dental caries (the medical term for cavities in the teeth) are caused by the bacteria in PLAQUE reacting with refined carbohydrates (sugar), which produces acid. This acidic plaque then eats away at the enamel surface of the teeth and, unless removed, causes dental caries. Women who do not eat refined carbohydrates, such as those who live in primitive societies or during wartime conditions when such foods are not available, generally have excellent teeth.

COSMETIC DENTISTRY

CROWNS
When part of a tooth has broken off above the root, the remaining section is sculpted into a peg, and an artificial porcelain crown is cemented on top.

COSMETIC SHIELDING
Thin plastic or porcelain covers are cemented to the front of teeth to close up spaces or shield discolored teeth.

BRIDGES
When a tooth at the front of the mouth is missing, an artificial one is put in the space. This can be attached to the back of the teeth on either side by light metal wires, or crowns, or screwed into the empty socket.

DENTURES
These artificial teeth are attached to a plastic plate that fits into the mouth. The plate is molded to fit snugly against the contours of the palate. Dentures usually last approximately five years.

GUM DISEASE

If PLAQUE (a bacteria-harboring mucus) is not removed from the teeth, calculus (tartar) may build up, and then cause marginal gingivitis (when the gum margins become inflamed). Gingivitis (infected and inflamed gums) may develop into periodontitis, a more severe form of gum disease where plaque and calculus affect the underlying bone. The gum may recede from the tooth and, in severe cases, can cause the tooth to loosen and fall out. The majority of women have mild gum trouble at times – only one person in 10 remains completely free from it, and one in seven is at risk of periodontitis.

NECK & THROAT

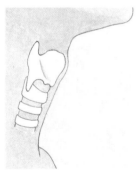
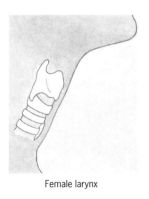
ANATOMY OF THE NECK

The complex muscles of the neck play a large part in the movements of the mouth and jaw, as well as those of the head. The neck is instrumental in the rotation, flexion, and extension of the head. It also houses major blood vessels leading to the brain, the VOCAL CORDS (below), and LARYNX (voice box). The position of the neck is the key to the body's posture. Restricted movement causes the neck muscles to be permanently contracted. The tension that results can be released by exercises to stretch the muscles.

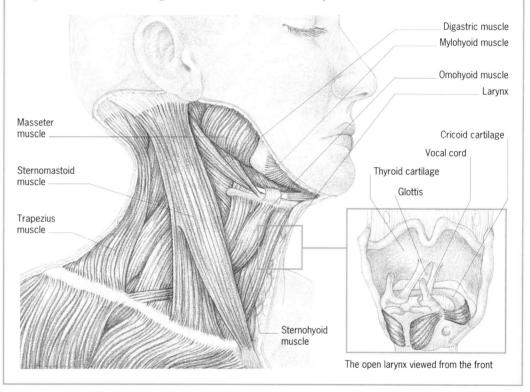

Masseter muscle

Sternomastoid muscle

Trapezius muscle

Sternohyoid muscle

Digastric muscle
Mylohyoid muscle
Omohyoid muscle
Larynx
Cricoid cartilage
Vocal cord
Thyroid cartilage
Glottis

The open larynx viewed from the front

VOCAL CORDS

Inside the LARYNX (voice box) are the VOCAL CORDS, which consist of two pairs of mucous membrane folds. These open and close to allow (or obstruct) air passing from the lungs through the larynx.

The GLOTTIS is the opening between the vocal cords. Air flow through the glottis causes the vocal cords to vibrate and produces waves of sound. The tautness of the vocal cords will determine whether the pitch of the voice is high or low. The precise degree of tautness will also produce a note when an individual is singing.

Anxiety makes the cords tense and contract, which is why a woman loses her voice or has a higher-pitched voice than normal when she is anxious or scared.

Breathing: larynx open.

Speaking or eating: larynx closed.

THE SEXUAL NECK

The neck has more nerve endings than many other parts of the body and is a particularly sensitive area. Its linking position between the mouth and breasts is also significant. As with other physical attributes that differ significantly between the sexes, women exploit the slenderness of their necks by exposing the throat or by drawing attention to the area with jewelry.

In the Western world, "love bites" or "hickeys," which are bruises caused by suction produced by the lips, are commonly seen on the necks of teenagers and some new lovers, where they act as a very public sign that the pair is sexually active.

During the 1940s and 50s, when sex before marriage was taboo in most parts of the Western world, the term "necking" was introduced to describe the passionate, if unconsummated, embraces of unmarried couples.

Some animals also concentrate on the neck during sexual displays or mating. Giraffes entwine necks during courtship, while tom cats and male lions grasp the scruff of a female's neck in their jaws during coitus.

Sensual zone
Kisses that are bestowed upon the neck feel particularly intimate, thrilling, and arousing.

A WOMAN'S VOICE

Unlike the majority of other animals, which rely mainly on nonverbal communication, women use vocalization as the main vehicle of information, and they have evolved complex patterns of sound – speech. This shift from using body language to using oral language is said to have occurred during the AQUATIC PERIOD because body language would have been very difficult to interpret when the bottom half of the body would usually have been hidden by water.

Although the LARNYX (voice box), VOCAL CORDS, tongue, teeth, lips, and cheeks can produce many different phonemes (sounds), individual languages use only some of them. This exclusivity gives each language its unique quality. In the Western world, the average woman's voice is pitched at about 230–255 cycles per second, while that of the average male voice is a deeper 130–145 cycles per second. Recent research, however, suggests that the average female voice is becoming deeper. Each voice is unique.

Sustained song depends on drawing a full breath.

SINGING

Musical notes are formed in the same way as normal speech, but air is expelled from the lungs forcefully, as in shouting. Babies and opera singers drop their diaphragms before drawing in a lungful of air, which results in crying or sustained song. This unconscious ability is lost in childhood, so it has to be relearned by opera singers (above).

WHISPERING

Rigid vocal cords result in whispering rather than normal speech. Inflamed vocal cords cause involuntary whispering, but a woman who chooses to whisper will consciously tighten her vocal cords so that they do not vibrate. Mouth, tongue, and lips then shape the lightly exhaled air into whispered speech that is independent of the vocal cords.

SHOUTING

The loudness of the voice depends on how fast and forcefully the air is expelled through the glottis (the opening between the vocal cords); the more violently air is released, the louder a shout will be. Men tend to speak and shout louder than women because they usually have bigger lungs within a larger chest.

SCREAMING

A primitive pain and FEAR response, screaming is widespread in many animal species. Screaming involves a similar process to shouting, but the vocal cords are held more tightly. Women and children may scream in situations of "safe panic."

Languages of officialdom
The map (left) gives a general view of the dominant language families worldwide. Most of the world's languages of government belong to one of seven language families.

■ Indian	■ African
■ Semitic	■ Anglo-German
■ Baltic	■ Latin
■ Asian	■ Others

NECKLACES

In many primitive human societies, the soul was believed to reside in the base of the neck. This led to the widespread use of neck adornments to protect this part of the body from the "evil eye." The protective function was forgotten in time, and necklaces became purely decorative (below). In some societies, the lack of a neck adornment emphasizes that a girl is a virgin, while in others, a special necklace indicates the same thing.

NECK AND THROAT PROBLEMS

Problems to do with the neck or the throat can be either internal, such as laryngitis, or external, such as a stiff neck.

SORE THROAT

An inflamed throat usually indicates that the body is fighting an infection, such as a COLD or INFLUENZA.

LARYNGITIS

Inflammation of the LARYNX (voice box) may occur because of a disease or infection, or because the larynx has been overused or strained, during excessive shouting, screaming, or singing, for instance. Speaking or shouting puts more of a strain on the larynx than does singing.

STIFF NECK

Also known as torticollis, a stiff neck results when the muscles in the neck go into spasm, causing intense pain. It is usually caused by bad posture, especially when working for extended periods at a desk or computer, when driving, or when sleeping. A stiff neck can also be caused by a psychological condition, such as severe STRESS.

WHIPLASH

This is when the neck is jerked forward and backward very rapidly, which sometimes happens during a car accident. The vertebrae often put pressure on the spinal nerves, which results in severe pain.

IT'S A FACT

The highest musical note (the B above high C) sustained by the human voice was sung by Madeleine Marie Robin (1918–60) in Donizetti's opera Lucia di Lammermoor.

◆

The human voice can be detected as far as 17km (10½ miles) across still water at night.

◆

Voodoo cult members in Haiti still believe that the human soul resides in the nape of the neck.

◆

The stretched necks of the Paduang women can be as long as 39cm (15¾in) and are the longest in the world.

WOMAN VS. ANIMAL

A woman's neck can only move about 90° from the front to each side and through about 180° from side to side. An owl's neck, in contrast, can move 180° from front to back, and all the way around through 360° if it starts from a backward-facing position.

THE PROMINENT NECK

Pleasure zone
The eroticism of the neck is emphasized in Japan by the kimono's stiff collar. This stands away from the back of the neck, allowing a view down the length of the neck to part of the spine while the wearer kneels.

The neck is a significant body area in a number of cultures, such as the Japanese (left). In Europe between the 16th century and the middle of the 17th century, in some countries and at elevated levels of society, women's necks were emphasized by elaborate neck ruffs. The ruff originated in the frilly edging of standing collars and, by 1570, had become a separate item from a woman's dress and was composed of stiffened pleats of linen or lace attached to a neckband (right). In some cases, these extraordinary items of dress became so large that women were unable to eat while wearing them.

In the West, the velvet neck choker has been popular at various times during the 20th century; it is usually seen as particularly erotic.

Sensory deprivation
A woman was cut off from the rest of her body by the neck ruff.

BREASTS

Breast size

Women's breasts are measured in terms of chest circumference (in) and fullness (cup sizes AA–DD). The average Canadian woman is a size 34C (see far right). All women have breasts that are not quite mirror images of each other, however slight the difference between them. The areolae can also vary in size, as well as in position and color. With time and during and following pregnancy, a woman's breasts will naturally droop and flatten if unsupported by a bra. Contemporary Western women wear bras to maintain a rounded breast shape.

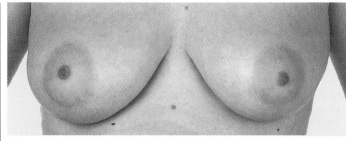

36C Larger-than-average circumference, average cup size.

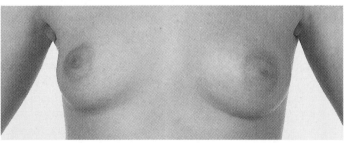

32B Narrow circumference, smaller-than-average cup size.

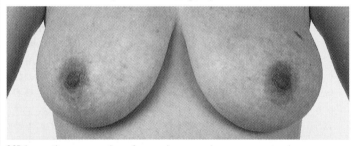

36D Larger-than-average circumference, large cup size.

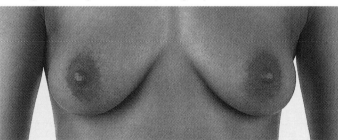

32A Average circumference, small cup size.

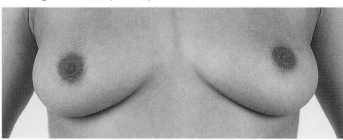

34C Average circumference and cup size.

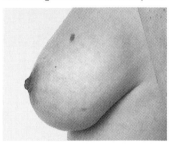

34C Average circumference and cup size.

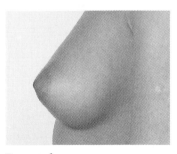

WOMAN VS. MAN

A woman's breasts are not only used for breastfeeding babies but are also powerful sexual signals. Prominent rounded breasts are exclusive to the human female. From woman to woman, breasts vary more in their size, shape, and appearance than most other parts of the anatomy. The male breast is an immature version of the female breast.

Breast shape

Larger breasts, like the one shown above center, are heavy and usually lie close to the chest wall; they sag very easily without support. Smaller breasts, like the one shown above, are lighter, and are usually rounder. They normally stand high and well away from the chest wall.

NIPPLES

Set in the areola at the tip of each breast, the nipples are darker than the surrounding skin and contain muscles that allow them to stand erect. They darken and enlarge during sexual arousal and pregnancy and contain tiny passages through which milk can pass. Extra (supernumerary) nipples (POLYMASTIA) develop very rarely, along a line that extends down to the groin. They do not usually have an internal structure of glands or fatty tissue.

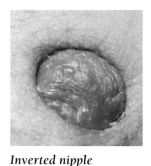

Inverted nipple
An inverted nipple is one that lies flat, and it may dimple inward. A normal nipple that suddenly becomes inverted may indicate the presence of breast cancer.

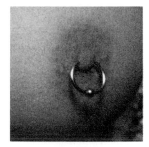

Pierced nipple
Piercing results in the nipple being kept in a state of constant stimulation.

BREAST STRUCTURE

Breasts have an envelope of fat and an internal structure of glands supported in fibrous and fatty tissue. Branching milk-collecting ducts emanate from the milk-secreting glands, and lead to the NIPPLES (left). Each breast is supported on the pectoral muscles and ribcage on one side of the thorax (chest) by the suspensory LIGAMENTS (fine bands of inelastic tissue).

Lactation
The blackberry-shaped alveoli (milk-secreting glands) do not mature until stimulated by the surge of the hormones estrogen and progesterone during pregnancy. Then milk reservoirs develop behind the nipples.

Pectoral muscles
Fatty tissue
Suspensory ligaments

Pigmented skin
Sensitive nipple

Alveoli (milk-secreting glands)

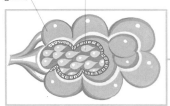

Alveolus (milk-secreting gland)   Milk

BRA STYLES

Breasts require support if the suspensory LIGAMENTS are not to be stretched. Medium-size breasts can each weigh more than 225g (8oz) each, while large breasts can weigh well over 500g (1lb) each. In addition to supporting the breasts, bras and corsets emphasize and shape them. Bras vary from simple triangles of cloth to veritable feats of engineering, and bra designs change to reflect fashions. The most lasting and popular designs include padded bras, which increase the size of breasts, and low-cut bras with underwiring that lift up the breasts and emphasize the cleavage.

The "racer back" doesn't restrict the shoulders

Push-up bra
Using padding, this bra can increase, or create, cleavage.

Sports bra
While the breasts are held firmly, the sports bra permits easy movement.

Conical bra
This costume is provocative and very aggressive.

EXTREMES OF BREAST DEVELOPMENT

Normal breast development begins at PUBERTY and is complete when a woman reaches the age of 18–20.

MUSCLES INSTEAD OF BREASTS

Female bodybuilders who take steroids lose rounded female breasts and develop enlarged pectoral muscles instead.

ANORECTIC BREASTS

Women who suffer from ANOREXIA NERVOSA have little BODY FAT and relatively asexual figures. Their breasts revert to their prepubertal size.

POLYMASTIA (SUPER-NUMERARY "BREASTS")

This condition, recorded in women throughout history, was often taken as a symbol of fertility. The "extra breasts" usually consist of just under-developed nipples. Anne Boleyn, one of the wives of Henry VIII, was reputed to have polymastia.

Fertility goddess
This figurine from Ephesus shows a fertility goddess; her "breasts" are represented by bulls' testicles.

COSMETIC BREAST SURGERY

Surgical procedures are carried out on the breasts to correct asymmetry, to ease dissatisfaction with size and shape, to support sagging breasts, or to aid in the quest for a youthful but voluptuous figure. Surgery may also be needed because breasts fail to develop or because other breast surgery, such as MASTECTOMY, makes BREAST RECONSTRUCTION an option. As a potent symbol of femininity, the loss of a breast has significant psychological repercussions – including depression and loss of confidence.

BREAST REDUCTION

Skin, fat, and excess breast tissue are removed in this delicate operation.

In addition to the cut made in the skin for the removal of tissue, an incision is made around the AREOLA, as well as a keyhole incision for the relocation of the nipple. The remaining tissue and fat are secured within the skin, and the nipple is relocated, where the keyhole incision was made, higher up.

BREAST AUGMENTATION

Skin and muscle are expanded and stretched gradually over a period of weeks to accommodate an implant. The incision for insertion of the implant can be made either in the armpit, around the areola, or underneath the breast, depending on the size and firmness of the breast.

The implant is inserted beneath the pectoral muscle, or behind the breast tissue, so that it lies against the pectoral muscle.

Breast implants (right)
These are small bags, usually filled with saline solution. The implant shown contains silicone gel. These implants have been used rarely in Canada since 1992, when concerns arose about their long-term safety.

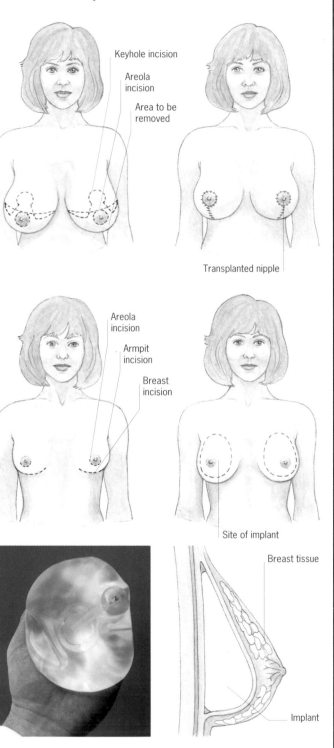

Keyhole incision
Areola incision
Area to be removed
Transplanted nipple
Areola incision
Armpit incision
Breast incision
Site of implant
Breast tissue
Implant

FIBROCYSTIC DISEASE

About 75% of all breast lumps are nonmalignant. This group includes cysts (fluid-filled tissue sacs), fibroadenomas (tumors), and connective tissue hyperplasia (enlarged glands). Such forms of fibrocystic disease (benign breast tumors) affect about 20% of women between the ages of 20 and 50 years.

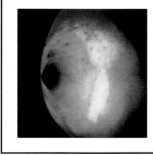

BREAST CANCER

The number of cases of breast cancer is rising in many countries, and it is the leading cause of death in Western women aged 35–50 years.

In Canada, breast cancer kills more than 5,000 women a year. As of 1993, one in nine Canadian women can expect to develop breast cancer.

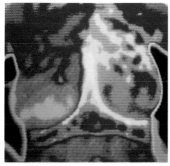

Cancer in the breast
From this thermal image, the breast cancer in the left breast shows clearly as a white (cooler) area.

BREAST CANCER RISK FACTORS

Apart from family medical history, lifestyle factors are major determinants of risk.

HIGH FAT INTAKE

According to some studies, varying rates of breast cancer closely match the amount of fat in a nation's diet. In Japan, breast cancer is one of the fastest-growing disorders, and the incident rate, which rose by 58% in the decade 1975–85, is strongly linked to a change to a fatty diet. The best diet to guard against breast cancer is one in which the fat intake is less than 20% of the total energy intake.

Breast cancer rates worldwide

Legend:
- Percentage of fat intake
- Breast cancer rate (per 100,000 women aged 45–69)

Country	Percentage of fat intake	Breast cancer rate
Japan	23	42
Romania	23	96
Israel	32	166
Britain	38	173
France	39	166
Switzerland	41	207
USA	42	232

HORMONES AND BODY SHAPE

Overweight women who are ENDOMORPHIC (apple-shaped), and therefore have more fat deposits around their abdomens and internal organs, have a greater risk of suffering breast cancer than women who are overweight and are MESOMORPHIC (pear-shaped), who deposit fat on their hips and thighs, or ENDOMORPHIC (beanpole-shaped).

HORMONE REPLACEMENT THERAPY (HRT), which involves taking tablets containing estrogen, changes hormone levels and is thought to raise the risk of cancer in a small proportion of women. The early onset of MENSTRUATION; childlessness or late child-bearing; and late MENOPAUSE are also believed to increase the risk.

FAMILY CONNECTIONS

A woman whose mother, grandmother, sister, or maternal aunt suffered breast cancer prior to menopause has three times the usual risk of developing breast cancer herself. If the cancer occurred in both breasts, the risk can rise to 10 times the norm.

ENVIRONMENTAL FACTORS

Cigarette smoking, industrial pollution, car emissions, and chemicals, such as fertilizers in or on food, are all thought to play a part in the occurrence of breast cancer.

Factors	High risk	Medium risk	Low risk
Family history of cancer	Close female relatives.	Distant female relatives.	No family incidence.
Own gynecological history	Early onset of menstruation. No children. Late start in sexual activity. Late menopause.	First child after 35 years. Benign breast disease.	Late onset of menstruation. Child before 20 years. Early sexual experience. Early menopause.
Diet	Obesity. Diet high in animal and dairy fat (over 35% of total daily intake).	Moderate animal and dairy fat intake (20–30% of total daily intake).	Low fat intake (under 20% of total daily intake).
Ethnic groups	Western CAUCASOID, NEGROID, and MONGOLOID.	Southern European. Latin American.	African Negroid. Eastern Mongoloid.
Body build	ENDOMORPHIC.	MESOMORPHIC.	ECTOMORPHIC.
Age	Over 40 years.	25–39 years.	Under 25 years.
Environment	Large cities.	Towns.	Rural areas.

BREAST SELF-EXAMINATION

With early treatment, BREAST CANCER can be beaten, so it is very important that women examine their breasts monthly to detect changes or lumps. Self-examination is particularly vital for women under 50 years, for whom regular MAMMOGRAPHY (below) has been shown to be ineffective. The best time to check is after menstruation. Many women have naturally lumpy breasts, and special guidance from a nurse may be necessary to detect changes.

VISUAL INSPECTION

Stand in front of a mirror with your arms relaxed, and look for any changes in breast size, shape, or condition. Be aware of any breast discomfort that occurs other than premenstrually. Raise your arms and look again.

MANUAL EXAMINATION

Lying horizontal with one arm raised, feel the breast on the side of the raised arm. To lubricate the skin so that the hand slides smoothly over the breast, use a soapy hand or a sprinkling of talcum powder. Repeat for other breast.

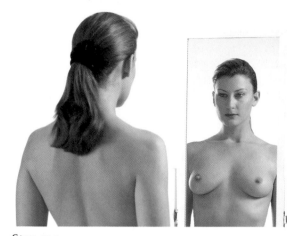

Step one
Look for any puckering or dimpling of the skin, or changes in the nipple – especially a discharge.

Step two
Raise both arms and look again.

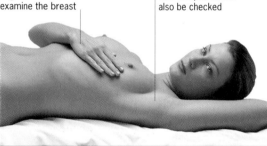

Use the flat palm and fingers to circle and examine the breast

Your armpits should also be checked

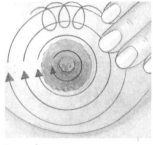

Step three
Lie down and feel around the breast and the nipple.

MAMMOGRAPHY

Using X-rays, mammograms can detect breast tumors as small as 0.5cm (0.2in), usually before they metastasize (begin to disperse cancer cells throughout the rest of the body). Early mammogram detection increases the five-year survival rate to 82%, compared with 60% for women whose lumps were not detected by mammograms. Regular mammograms only benefit women over 50 years of age. Recently, there has been some concern that a comparatively high level of radiation exposure during mammography may play a part in triggering the development of breast cancer.

Mammogram
Each breast is placed on a small examination plate and gently compressed. This flattens the breast so that as much tissue as possible can be X-rayed. Up to three different X-rays are taken.

CANCEROUS BREAST LUMPS

Only a small proportion of lumps are cancerous; most are benign cysts or fibrous lumps. The frequency with which cancer is detected in given parts of the breast is shown in percentages below; it can also occur in LYMPH NODES in the armpits.

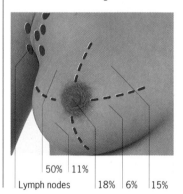

50%   11%
Lymph nodes   18%   6%   15%

MASTECTOMY

Breast biopsy, and partial or complete removal of the breast, are used to diagnose and treat BREAST CANCER. The type of surgery selected to treat the cancer depends on the size of the tumor and other factors. The amount of tissue removed depends on how much, if at all, the axillary LYMPH NODES have been affected.

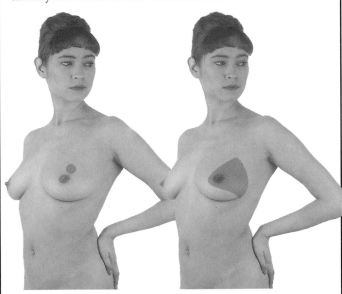

Breast biopsy
Only the "lump" or suspicious lesion is removed.

Lumpectomy
The tumor and some of the surrounding and underlying breast tissue are removed.

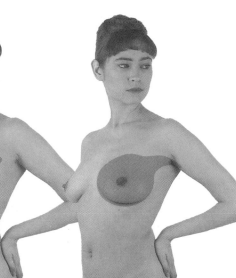

Total (or simple) mastectomy
This is when the whole of the breast is removed, but the pectoral muscle and axillary lymph nodes are left intact.

Modified radical mastectomy
The breast, axillary lymph nodes, and sometimes the pectoralis minor (the smaller pectoral muscle) are removed.

AFTER BREAST SURGERY

CHEMOTHERAPY

Several drugs are designed to target rapidly dividing cancer cells anywhere in the body. The use of these drugs can increase the average 10-year survival rate. Side effects, including hair loss and nausea, are unpleasant but usually only temporary. Other noncancerous cells that are rapidly dividing, such as those in bone marrow, are susceptible to damage from chemotherapy; they may require additional forms of treatment.

HORMONAL DRUGS

Tamoxifen, a hormonal anticancer drug, is used to block the effect of ESTROGEN, which is implicated in tumor growth. However, recent research suggests that tamoxifen may increase the risk of uterine cancer. It is also unclear how long tamoxifen use should continue after surgery and how beneficial it is when given as a preventative measure; research is ongoing. Women taking tamoxifen should not take the birth control pill.

RADIATION THERAPY

Ionizing radiation (given by X-rays) destroys or slows the development of cancerous cells. It is usually given after surgery, to kill any remaining cancerous cells, but may be used in place of surgery to relieve symptoms by reducing the size of breast tumors. A certain percentage of women may suffer pain and disability (especially in the upper chest area, and in the shoulders and arms) for many years (sometimes for life) following radiation therapy.

BREAST RECONSTRUCTION

This can be done at the same time as MASTECTOMY (left) or at a later date. Most breast reconstructions involve a flap of skin, fat, and muscle that is folded into a breast shape. An IMPLANT may be inserted. New nipples can be created by tissue grafting and tattooing.

BREAST PROSTHESES

Specially constructed bras and a variety of forms that can be fitted into regular bras are available for postoperative patients. Prostheses are designed to simulate the feel and appearance of a natural breast.

ARMS AND HANDS

The adaptable limb

When women began to walk erect, their front limbs were able to develop wholly manipulative, specialized human hands. Women were the main foragers and tool users, and their flexible and sensitive fingers produced the first craft items – pots and bowls. A particularly feminine gesture is the characteristic crooked elbow with a loose wrist. This may have its roots in the way women naturally carry an infant in the crook of one arm while performing tasks with the free hand. Some studies have shown that a baby will quieten quickest if held against the mother's left breast because of the sound of her heartbeat. This habit is said to have led to predominant right-handedness worldwide. In Caucasoid and Negroid women, the armpit is richly endowed with apocrine glands. Mongoloid women, in contrast, have few, if any, apocrine glands in the armpit.

WOMAN VS. MAN

Women have proportionally shorter and slenderer arms than men. A woman's arms are held closer to her body because her shoulders are narrower than a man's. Women tend to have flexible hands and fingers, which are frequently able to work with greater precision than those of men.

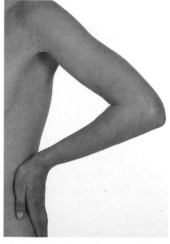
Medium-build ectomorph. Caucasoid.

Large-build mesomorph. Caucasoid.

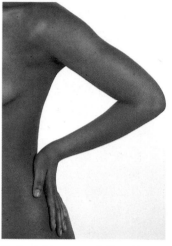
Medium-build mesomorph. Negroid.

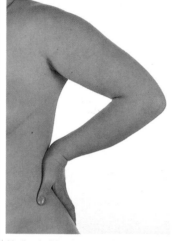
Medium-build endomorph. Caucasoid.

Small-build mesomorph. Caucasoid.

Large-build ectomorph. Negroid.

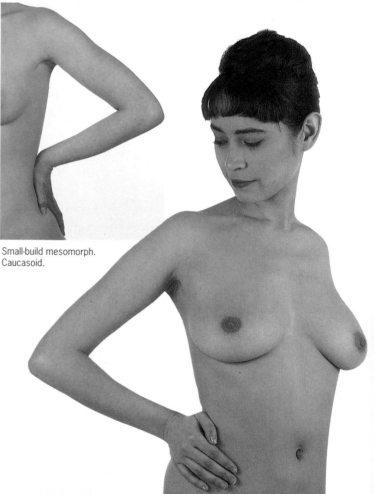
Medium-build mesomorph. Caucasoid–Mongoloid.

ANATOMY OF THE ARMS AND HANDS

Women use their arms in three main ways – for throwing, for lifting, and as a "crane" for the hands. There are three main bones in the arm: the large humerus and slimmer ulna and radius. It is the relationship between the ulna and radius that allows the hand to be swiveled. The arm is attached to the body by a ball-and-socket joint in the scapula. The deltoid muscle enables women to lift weights and raise her arms upward and away from her body. The biceps bend the arms, while the triceps straighten the forearms. Other upper arm muscles rotate the arms inward. The muscles in the lower arms rotate the forearms and are responsible for the strength and flexibility of the hands and fingers; the smaller muscles within the hands enable the fingers and thumbs to operate with great precision.

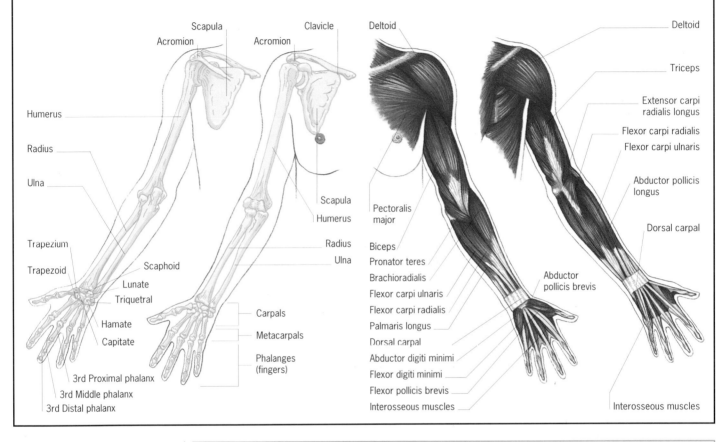

THE ARMPIT

Technically known as the axilla, the small hairy area of the armpit is richly endowed with APOCRINE GLANDS (specialized scent glands). Their secretions are somewhat oilier than ordinary sweat. While they are being exuded, apocrine secretions are strong and compelling sexual scent signals. When the apocrine secretions are trapped by clothing, however, the scent becomes a stale, sour, and wholly unattractive smell that is commonly termed body odor.

NAILS

The nails are a modified form of the EPIDERMIS (the upper layer of skin tissue), hardened with a protein called KERATIN. They protect the tops of the fingers and toes and are lifeless. Although the nails lack nerve endings, they are embedded in sensitive tissue (there are about 17,000 touch receptors in the hand; most are located in the fingertips). These allow nails to pick up the slightest tremor when they touch an object. The visible part of the nail is only 0.5mm thick and is usually pale pink owing to the rich supply of capillaries that lie beneath it in the nail bed. The nail grows out of the nail matrix underneath the skin. A white crescent called the lunula (half-moon) is often visible at the base, although it is sometimes covered by the eponychium (cuticle). The average fingernail takes about six months to grow from the root to the tip; toenails take twice this long.

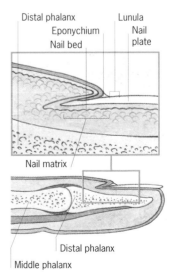

ARM AND HAND SIGNALS

A number of signals that women make with their arms and hands appear to be universal. These include hugging, raising the arms above the head in triumph or celebration, holding up the arms in surrender, waving, and shaking hands.

A woman's palms are pale, which makes signals involving the hands conspicuous (although this is less noticeable in pale-skinned women). The flat raised palm, for example, is always recognized as saying "keep away" or "keep back," while saluting implies a respectful greeting, from the stylized gesture of the soldier to the simple wave of the hand by an acquaintance. The extreme form of hand communication is the codified sign language for the deaf. Finger signals vary according to the finger making the gesture and

Crooking the little finger
Sexual independence may have characterized the model for the Virgin Mary in this painting.

Thumb signs
Pointing upward with the thumb is generally seen as a positive message; while "thumbs down" is perceived as negative.

the manner in which it is done. The forefinger is generally used to point at things or toward places – when giving directions, for example, or for signaling for attention, such as when summoning a waiter.

In depictions of female figures in early religious paintings, crooking the little finger is thought to indicate a high degree of sexual independence in the artist's model. The gesture was taken up by the members of the women's movement at the end of the 19th century, who crooked their "independent" little fingers while drinking from a teacup.

WOMAN VS. ANIMAL

Unlike other primates, a woman's palms (and soles) always remain pale due to lack of MELANIN. The theory of the AQUATIC PERIOD suggests this evolved as a signaling aid when body communication in the water would have been restricted. The universal "greeting" and "surrender" signals are also said to date from this time.

◆

As in other primates, a woman's arms are jointed so that they bend backward, facilitating the manipulation of objects. Dogs, cats, and horses have legs that are jointed so that the carpal bones, which form a woman's wrist, form their knees.

ANATOMY OF THE HAND

There are a total of 19 bones in the hand, interconnecting with muscles and tendons. The sensitivity of the hands is greater than just about any other area of the body; each fingertip contains literally thousands of nerve endings.

Extensor digiti minimi muscle

Distal phalanx bone

Extensor indicus tendon

Dorsal interosseous muscle

Synovial sheath

Carpal ligament

1st lumbrical muscle

Extensor pollicis longus muscle

Engineering miracle
The hand is such a complex unit that no robot can mimic it exactly.

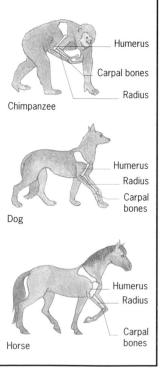

Chimpanzee

Humerus

Carpal bones

Radius

Dog

Humerus

Radius

Carpal bones

Horse

Humerus

Radius

Carpal bones

DECORATION

Women of all cultures have recognized the potential of the arms and hands for decoration and display. This has included permanent marks, such as scarring and tattoos, which are often used to define a woman's status, and temporary marks, such as the delicate hennaed tracery that is painted on the hands (as well as on the FEET) of many Arab and Indian women, especially brides-to-be.

Like necklaces and brooches, bracelets were originally worn to protect the wearer from the "evil eye." However, they soon became used to display wealth, denote status, and emphasize the slenderness of the female arm. The original protective purpose has survived to the present day (via the Victorians) in the form of the charm bracelet (below). The wristwatch has become the most "permanent" bracelet of all; one is worn every day of the year by practically every woman in the industralized world.

Rings tend to be both decorative and symbolic. The most enduring of all is the wedding ring, which in the West is usually worn on the fourth finger of the left hand. This dates from Roman times, when the ring finger was believed to have a nerve (or vein or artery) running straight to the heart. Another ring "symbol" is the engagement ring, signifying betrothal. Unlike the wedding ring, it is an almost completely feminine symbol, as is the eternity ring, which is often given to a woman on a wedding anniversary or after the birth of a child.

Indian dancers use red dye on the tips of the fingers to emphasize their delicate and intricate hand movements; finger extensions tipped with paper flowers are worn by Thai dancers for the same reason.

Charm bracelets (above)
These were popular in Victorian times, although this example is late 20th century. Each charm has a special significance.

Snake bracelet (left)
This was popular in ancient societies as a symbol of good health or rejuvenation.

HAND AND NAIL PROBLEMS

Problem	Causes and symptoms
Calluses	Thickened patches of skin formed by friction.
Chapped hands	Caused by the extremes of heating and chilling.
Whitlows	Small abscesses that form at the side of the nail.
LIVER SPOTS	Brown spots that are the result of sun damage.
Sweaty palms	Usually occur as a response to mental STRESS.
White flecks	Usually the result of injuries to the root of the nail.
Bursitis	Small sacs of fluid form where ligaments and tendons are overused and become inflamed.
RSI	Repetitive strain injury (RSI) is caused by constantly repeating the same actions over long periods. It involves muscle damage, inflammation, and trapped nerves.
Split nails	Usually result from rough treatment or from long immersion in water.
Hangnails	Painful splits in the skin folds around the nail. Usually caused by excessive dryness.
Black nails	Normally caused by an injury.
Whitish nails	Can indicate ANEMIA, poor circulation, or liver conditions.

LEFT-HANDEDNESS

The left hand has a long history of being the bad, clumsy, or sinister hand. This reputation probably arose because left-handedness affects only about 12% of the world population (this doesn't appear to alter with race) and was therefore usually the "unused" hand. In India and the Middle East, the left hand came to be seen as "unclean," and is still only used for dealing with feces, while the "clean" right hand is used for everything else. Left-handedness is severely discouraged in these cultures, although it has ceased to be discouraged in the West.

DECORATIVE FINGERNAILS

Long and decorated fingernails historically have been adornments and status symbols (the owner does not carry out any manual work). In some cultures, such as Mandarin China, the fingernails were often allowed to grow very long, becoming curved and hornlike in the process. In many Western societies today, women use colored polish on their nails, and some have realistic fingernail extensions applied over their natural nails.

Thai dancers wear finger extensions.

GENITALS

WOMAN VS. ANIMAL

The vaginas of practically all land mammals tend to be retro (positioned to the rear), and tucked just under the tail if there is one. (Their normal coital position is rear-entry.)

A woman's genitalia, however, are ventral (forward-facing).

She shares this characteristic with the majority of sea mammals, such as dolphins and whales, and it may be a legacy from the theoretical AQUATIC PERIOD.

It is thought that elephants had a semi-aquatic period in their evolution; this explains why elephant cows have ventral vaginas.

Retro vagina

Cow

Ventral vagina

Elephant

Ventral vagina

Dolphin

WOMAN'S PUBIC HAIR

This begins to appear between the ages of nine and 13 on a girl's LABIA MAJORA, gradually spreading upward over her MONS PUBIS and out onto the very tops of the thighs. Pubic hair is coarser in texture than other body hair and is often darker than the hair on the head. (It is not actually true that you can tell a "real" blond or redhead by the color of her pubic hair.)

Some women have scanty pubic hair or a very defined triangular area while others, particularly Northern CAUCASOID women have profuse pubic hair. Some women shave their pubic hair, while others trim it into different shapes and patterns, like the heart shape that Mary Quant made famous in the 1960s.

Pubic hair eventually goes gray and becomes thinner as a woman ages.

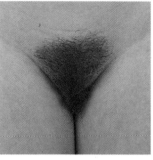

Mongoloid
This woman has a neat triangle of black-brown pubic hair. The short hair grows rather sparsely.

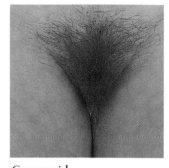

Caucasoid
This woman has light brown hair that is fine, long, and luxuriant; it is inclined to be bushy.

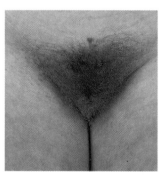

North-European Caucasoid
This woman has profuse, dark blond pubic hair. Her dense triangle tends to sprawl.

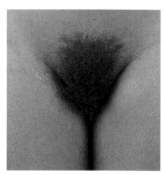

South-European Caucasoid
This woman has short, coarse, black pubic hair.

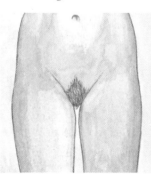

Pubescent
Scanty pubic hair first begins to grow on the outsides of a girl's labia majora.

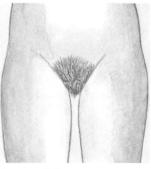

Young adult
By the age of 20, most women have a neatly defined area of pubic hair.

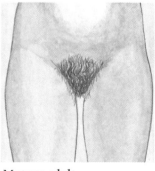

Mature adult
As the woman becomes fully mature, pubic hair grows out onto the very tops of her thighs.

VULVA

Also known as the pudendum, the vulva is the name for all of the external female genitalia: the MONS PUBIS, LABIA MAJORA, LABIA MINORA, urethral and vaginal openings, fourchette (fork), prepuce (clitoral hood), and the CLITORIS.

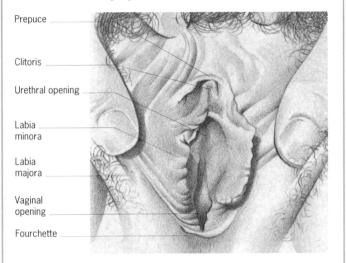

Prepuce

Clitoris

Urethral opening

Labia minora

Labia majora

Vaginal opening

Fourchette

VESTIBULE

The area that is enclosed by the LABIA MINORA ("small lips" – below left) is known as the vestibule. It contains the vaginal and the urethral openings, and the primary APOCRINE (scent) GLANDS – the ducts of which produce a mucous discharge during sexual arousal. The close proximity of the urethral and the vaginal openings to each other, and to the anus, is the reason why so many women suffer bacterial infections, such as CYSTITIS, and fungal infections, such as YEAST INFECTIONS.

MONS PUBIS

Also known as the mons veneris (mound of Venus), this is the soft fatty tissue that covers the pubic symphysis (union of the two pubic bones). After puberty, PUBIC HAIR, usually in a roughly triangular shape, covers the area. The mons pubis acts as a buffer during face-to-face sexual intercourse and gives pleasurable sensations if pressed or moved. If the hair on the mons pubis is lightly touched, an "electric shock" sensation is experienced.

LABIA (VAGINAL LIPS)

LABIA MAJORA

These two larger lips form the outermost parts of the VULVA (above). They lie together, extending forward from the PERINEUM, and fusing at the MONS PUBIS (above right). They usually conceal the other external genital organs completely and the outer surfaces are covered with pubic hair.

The labia majora are made up of fatty tissue, and their inner surfaces contain ECCRINE (sweat), APOCRINE (scent), and SEBACEOUS (oil) glands. Sebaceous glands provide vulval lubrication, while the apocrine glands release a mucous discharge that creates some lubrication and the characteristic musky smell during sexual arousal. The labia majora also contain many nerve endings.

LABIA MINORA

The inner lips of the vulva are very delicate folds of skin that lie between the labia majora, and extend from the FOURCHETTE (fork) behind the vaginal entrance to the CLITORIS, where they form the PREPÚCE (clitoral hood).

The labia minora have more nerve endings than the outer lips and also contain larger numbers of sebaceous glands that produce sebum (oil) to lubricate the VESTIBULE (above). The sebum also combines with secretions from sweat glands and the vagina to provide a waterproof protective covering against urine, menstrual blood, and bacteria. The labia minora are often asymmetrical; in some women, they can be quite long, even protruding out beyond the labia majora.

CHASTITY BELTS

The use of a chastity belt to ensure a wife's fidelity, while her husband was absent fighting in the Crusades, has long been a part of Western, particularly British, folklore. Chastity belts, however, are believed to have been invented in Italy in about 1400 – about 200 years after the last Crusade. Most of the chastity belts still surviving, like the one shown below, are thought to have been made during the 18th and 19th centuries as curiosities or jokes, although there is some evidence of chastity belts being in actual use, albeit occasionally, from the 15th century to the early part of the 20th century.

Actually wearing a chastity belt was a particularly unpleasant experience. Some chastity belts were equipped with a lock, while others were welded shut; all fitted tightly against the body. Although holes were provided for bodily evacuations, the wearer was prevented from wiping or washing herself thoroughly.

CLITORIS

An erectile organ that is homologous to the male penis, the clitoris gets its name from the Greek word for "key." The clitoris has exactly the same component parts as the penis (including the same number of nerve endings), which means that the small clitoridas (head or glans) is extremely sensitive to touch. The clitoral stem usually measures between 2cm (³⁄₄in) and 5cm (2in) in length, although it appears smaller because it is bent over on itself and only the clitoridas is visible.

From the clitoral stem, two slender ligaments, which are about 5cm (2in) long, run along either side of the vagina. The clitoridas is covered by the prepuce (clitoral hood), which draws back as the clitoris becomes erect and doubles in size during sexual arousal. Lack of clitoral erection may result in an inability to achieve orgasm.

VAGINA

A sheathlike elastic canal that usually measures about 9cm (3½in) along the posterior (back) wall and 7.5cm (3in) along the anterior (front) wall, although it is capable of great expansion. In its normal relaxed state, a woman's vagina has a width of about 1.5 – 2cm (½–³⁄₄ in), and the walls usually touch. Taller and heavier women tend to have longer vaginas.

The skin lining the vagina is similar to that on the palms of the hands but has a mucoid surface that secretes fluid. The walls of the vagina are corrugated, which enables it to expand greatly during childbirth.

The top third of the vagina contains the cervix. The vagina widens near the cervix, and its size increases during arousal, which means that most penis sizes can be accommodated without discomfort. The position of the vagina is either backward-angled or nearly upright and is determined by whether the uterus is angled forward or backward (as illustrated below).

During sexual intercourse, air occasionally becomes trapped in the area of the vagina that lies behind the cervix. When this happens, the trapped air may be expelled noisily during penile thrusting.

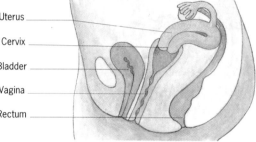

Uterus
Cervix
Bladder
Vagina
Rectum

Backward-angled vagina
Most women have an anteverted (forward-facing) uterus. The vagina is angled slightly backward.

Nearly upright vagina
When a woman has a retroverted (backward-facing) uterus, the angle of her vagina is more upright.

VAGINAL ODOR

A healthy vulva usually smells salty and slightly musky. Each woman, however, has a unique smell, which is more noticeable during sexual arousal, OVULATION, and MENSTRUATION.

The use of fragranced panty liners and vaginal deodorants, particularly among teenage girls, has increased in recent years. The chemicals used in the manufacturing of these products, however, can irritate the vagina and cause allergic reactions.

HYMEN

At birth, the vaginal entrance is often partly covered by a thin membrane called the hymen (Hymen was the Greek god of marriage). Theory suggests it evolved during the AQUATIC PERIOD as protection against sand entering the vagina. In most girls, the hymen erodes easily during activities such as running, jumping, climbing, lifting and carrying, bicycling, and horse-back-riding (the eroding hymen may be visible to a girl when she is bathing – it looks like a minute sea anemone). Consequently, by the time adulthood is reached, all that usually remains is a few tags of skin at most. In some women, however, the hymen is more thick and rigid and remains in place even after penile penetration. Approximately one woman in 2,000 has a hymen so tough that it must be removed surgically.

The existence of the hymen has long been seen as an evidence of virginity, although its significance has dwindled in the Western world. In the Middle and Far East, however, the intact hymen is still of great importance to unmarried women, and some surgeons are skilled in replacing and repairing hymens.

WOMAN VS. MAN

The basic blueprint of all living organisms is female. Consequently, the male genitals develop from the female genital structure. In the male fetus, the vulval tissue fuses and develops into a scrotum and penis. In the adult male, this fusion is still visible as a darker line running up the center of the scrotum and the underside of the penis.

The foreskin that covers the head of the penis is the equivalent of the PREPUCE (clitoral hood).

CYSTITIS

This is an infection in the bladder caused by bacteria that usually live in the intestine and around the anus, where they cause no problems at all. Cystitis is known as the "honeymoon disease." It is more common in women than in men because of the shorter distances between the anus and urethral opening, and because a woman's urethra is shorter. Once the bacteria enter the urethra, they multiply and irritate the urethral lining. The infection spreads to the bladder, where it causes irritation of the bladder lining. This leads to an increased desire to pass urine, as well as pain from the inflamed urethral lining upon passing urine. The pain is severe.

Cystitis requires prompt treatment, not only because it is very painful, but also because the infection can spread to the kidneys. A woman should always wash or wipe from front to back.

YEAST INFECTION

Characterized by a thick, curdy discharge from the vagina, dryness, soreness, severe itching, and a yeasty odor, yeast infection will affect 80% of all women at some point. It is caused by the yeast *Candida albicans*, which occurs naturally in the bowel. Problems occur when the yeast is able to grow uncontrolled by other organisms, such as often happens following a course of antibiotics.

CERVICAL CANCER

Cancer of the cervix most commonly occurs among young women. It has a long and well-defined pre-cancerous stage, which doctors are able to detect during a PAP SMEAR. Smoking increases the chances of developing the disease. Risk also increases with the number of sexual partners that a woman or her partner have had, and with first sex at an early age.

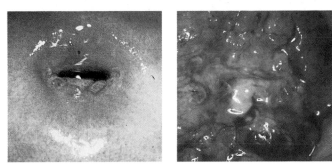

The vulnerable cervix
The picture on the left shows a healthy cervix, while that on the right shows one with precancerous cells. Cervical cancer occurs mainly in the 25–35 age group, and there appears to be a link with the presence of genital warts in the vagina or on a partner's penis.

FEMALE CIRCUMCISION

It has been estimated that 90 million women worldwide have suffered this form of genital mutilation, usually before they reach the age of seven. It occurs in Africa, Asia, and South America, and also in some ethnic communities in the Western world. Although referred to as circumcision, the process is usually far more radical than the male equivalent.

In addition, it is not performed for cleanliness, which is the main reason given for male circumcision, but for moral reasons: a woman is considered to be promiscuous if she is uncircumcised. There is even a belief that the clitoris will continue to grow like a boy's penis if it isn't removed. Female circumcision predates all modern religions.

Genital mutilation, usually performed under nonsterile conditions, carries the risk of pelvic and urinary infections, tetanus, septicemia, CYSTS and abscesses in and around the VULVA, problems during urination, MENSTRUATION, and childbirth, pain during sexual intercourse, DEPRESSION, frigidity, and severe psychological problems.

Paradoxically, the operation was performed in Victorian Britain as a "cure" for many so-called feminine weaknesses, including hysteria, depression, insanity, hallucinations, masturbation, nymphomania and, especially, EPILEPSY. In North America, female circumcision is a topic of growing concern.

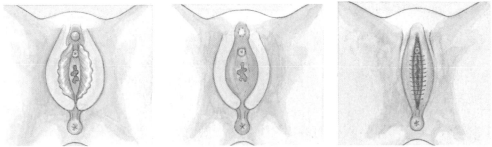

Circumcision
Known as sunna *(meaning "tradition") in Arabic Muslim countries, this involves removing the prepuce (the hood that protects the clitoris).*

Clitoridectomy
Also known as excision, this is when the clitoris and all or part of the labia minora are removed. Sometimes adjoining parts of the labia majora are also removed.

Infibulation
This procedure involves the vulva being totally removed and most of the opening being stitched up tightly. It is also known as Pharaonic circumcision.

LEGS & FEET

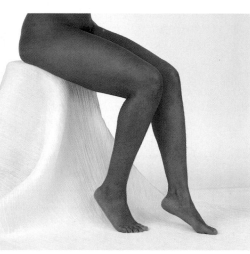
Medium-build mesomorph. Negroid.

Medium-build mesomorph. Caucasoid–Mongoloid.

The lower limbs

The legs account for approximately half of the total height of the adult human female. Leg length varies between body types: endomorphs have legs that are slightly shorter than their torsos, mesomorphs have legs that are equal in length to their torsos, and ectomorphs have legs that are slightly longer than their torsos. In addition to length, legs vary in size and shape, as do the feet, which support the weight of the body when it is erect.

Medium-build mesomorph.
Caucasoid–Negroid.

Medium-build endomorph. Caucasoid.

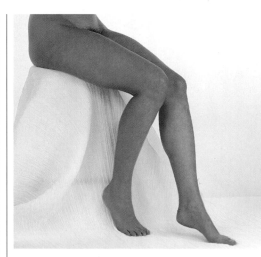
Medium-build ectomorph. Caucasoid.

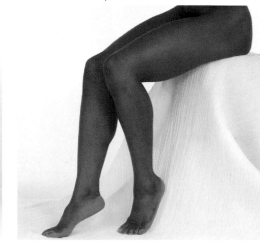
Large-build ectomorph. Negroid.

ANATOMY OF THE LEGS

The muscles and bones in the legs and feet maintain the body's balance and posture. The venous blood flow from the feet has to travel against gravity, so it is more sluggish than elsewhere. This can contribute to problems such as VARICOSE VEINS and CELLULITE.

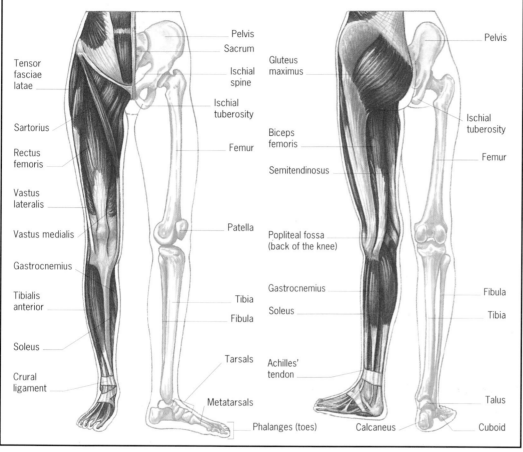

Tensor fasciae latae
Sartorius
Rectus femoris
Vastus lateralis
Vastus medialis
Gastrocnemius
Tibialis anterior
Soleus
Crural ligament

Pelvis
Sacrum
Ischial spine
Ischial tuberosity
Femur
Patella
Tibia
Fibula
Tarsals
Metatarsals
Phalanges (toes)

Gluteus maximus
Biceps femoris
Semitendinosus
Popliteal fossa (back of the knee)
Gastrocnemius
Soleus
Achilles' tendon

Pelvis
Ischial tuberosity
Femur
Fibula
Tibia
Talus
Calcaneus
Cuboid

THE BUTTOCKS

At the very tops of the legs are the buttocks. These are far more developed in women than in females of any other species, and may have developed during the hypothetical AQUATIC PERIOD, when a layer of subcutaneous fat was laid down and the buttock muscles became more highly developed as a result of adopting an erect posture. Women have larger and more rounded buttocks than men. Some peoples, such as the San (Bushmen), have particularly highly developed buttocks. Buttock veneration may have been more widespread in earlier times; many ancient carved stone icons (such as the one illustrated) show female figures with extremely protuberant buttocks.

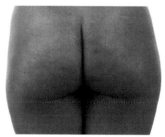

Fleshy protuberances
A woman's rounded buttocks (above) are immediately recognizable as feminine, whatever form they take (below).

UPS AND DOWNS

The point where a woman's legs meet is her primary sexual region, which makes her legs powerfully erotic. It also explains the preoccupation with skirt lengths throughout history; the shorter the skirt, the easier it is to imagine the point at which the legs meet. This interest was taken to its extreme in the Western world during the 19th century, when even a glimpse of ankle was thought deeply shocking, and references to legs were considered impolite. Legs were concealed by language as well as by skirts and became known as limbs, underpinners, and understandings, while furniture legs were covered with flounces of material. In the 20th century, Western skirt lengths (below) not only continue to have an erotic significance, but also are governed by economic conditions.

1921 1925 1933 1941 1948 1953 1960 1967 1971

LEG SIGNALS

Bared or partially clothed legs signal sexual confidence, while keeping legs covered downplays their significance. The leg positions chosen also convey a variety of nonverbal signals.

OPEN LEGS

Whether the woman is standing, sitting, or lying down, legs that are apart indicate a woman who is assertive, sexy, dominant, and relaxed. Because there is no attempt to hide or protect the genitals, open legs indicate that the woman is in control and is not worried about being thought vulnerable.

CLOSED LEGS

Positions in which the legs are drawn together signal politeness, formality, neutrality, inhibition, or subordination. They also indicate a readiness to take action, should it be required for courtesy's sake.

CROSSED LEGS

The informal posture of crossed legs signals that the sitter is unwilling to rise quickly. It is also protective because the leg is across the body. The crossed-leg position in which one leg is entwined around the other is almost exclusively female, owing to the shape of the female pelvis. This position has a particularly protective and defensive feel to it.

Leg language
When two people are sitting next to each other, the way in which they unconsciously cross their legs clearly demonstrates the feelings between them and the extent of communication. Legs that are crossed away from the other person signal lack of interest, while legs that are crossed top leg to top leg, as above, indicate intimacy and interest.

LEG CHAINS AND RINGS

Women in some societies are "shackled" by ornamental rings on their legs. Women of the Paduang tribe of Burma wear brass rings on their legs, and young women of the Waririke tribe of Nigeria have copper rings attached to their legs for a month while they are prepared for marriage (below). In the West, some women wear an ankle chain as an erotic accessory.

LEG LENGTH AND SEXUALITY

Long legs are seen as sexual and feminine because when they begin to lengthen in adolescence, sexuality is also developing. Legs in illustrations are often impossibly long compared to the torso, to emphasize this signal. The sexuality of the legs is highlighted by seams or patterns on hosiery, by skirts that almost reveal the crotch or give glimpses of the leg through a split, and by stockings or high boots that emphasize the thigh.

A glimpse of garter
During the first half of the 20th century, French can-can dancers made their living by revealing their legs, while other women kept their legs under wraps.

LEG AND FOOT PROBLEMS

Leg injuries Injury to the legs is potentially crippling, and even relatively minor problems can result in restricted movement. Knee injuries are among the most common and occur when the knee, which is an extremely flexible hinge joint, is subjected to a sudden degree of twisting, such as might occur during a skiing accident. This often results in damage to the cartilage or ligaments. If the ligaments are ruptured, the long-term stability of the knee is usually affected.

Ekbom syndrome About one person in 20, most of whom are women, suffer from Ekbom syndrome (restless legs), particularly at night. Ekbom syndrome is thought to have a hormonal cause, although some doctors dismiss it as psychosomatic. Sufferers often report that other (usually female) family members are also affected, and that the symptoms usually start in PUBERTY, then cease, to reappear during pregnancy and MENOPAUSE.

Foot complaints Two women out of five suffer from foot problems, which include the fungal infection ATHLETE'S FOOT, in-growing toenails, and BUNIONS. Women tend to have more problems with their feet than men because their footwear is often more restricting and poorly fitting.

THE SCENTED FOOT

The glabrous (hairless) skin on the soles of the feet is extremely well endowed with sweat glands. This means that a woman's foot leaves an individual scent mark that can be picked up easily by tracking dogs, even when the foot is covered by heavy footwear and the scent trail is over two weeks old.

Women's ape ancestors used scent to distinguish who had been where, and how long before, as they climbed barefoot along branches in the primeval forest. It is no longer useful for a woman to be able to track others in this way, and her once helpful scented feet have become nothing but a social nuisance to be doused in deodorant.

The Australian Aborigines are exceptional among humans in retaining the ability to follow a scented barefoot trail some time after the person has been past.

FOOT ANATOMY

The human foot is composed of 26 bones, 114 ligaments, and 20 muscles. The feet support the whole weight of the upright body, act as a springboard, and make constant, unconscious, tiny adjustments in order to maintain balance. Together with the hands, the feet contain half the bones in the body. One left-over foot feature may date from the theoretical AQUATIC PERIOD – approximately 6% of all girls are born with "webbed feet," which means they have webs of skin between some or all of their toes.

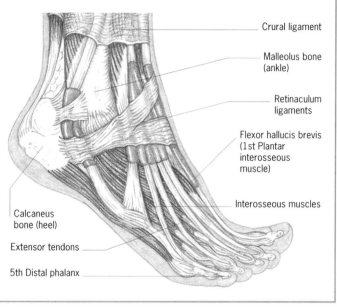

Crural ligament

Malleolus bone (ankle)

Retinaculum ligaments

Flexor hallucis brevis (1st Plantar interosseous muscle)

Interosseous muscles

Calcaneus bone (heel)

Extensor tendons

5th Distal phalanx

SHOES

In the Western world, most female feet spend about two-thirds of their lives encased in leather. This has a big impact on the foot, especially since bones do not finally harden until about the age of 20. By then, women have often spent a number of years squeezing their feet into shoes that are too narrow, too short, too high, or all three, in pursuit of super-feminine feet.

Shoes often have sexual connotations: it was appropriate for the old woman who had "so many children she didn't know what to do," to live in a shoe (a genital symbol), while old shoes and boots are tied onto the back of newlyweds' car.

FOOT FETISHES AND CUSTOMS

Because men are usually heavier and larger than women, small feet are seen as being essentially feminine, while large female feet are denigrated.

In China, the custom of foot binding was the social norm in high-ranking families for many centuries. Foot binding involved bending a young girl's foot under and tightly bandaging it so that her four small toes lay against her heel, leaving only her big toe free. The most prized feet of all were the "Golden Lotuses," which were 7.5cm (3in) long. Once bandaged, these feet could never be straightened and prevented their owners from walking normally. Women who were foot bound were considered very sexually desirable for a number of reasons – they had tiny (ultrafeminine) feet; they were physically unable to work (enhancing their social standing) or to wander; and their crippled feet provided an additional sexual orifice.

The fairy tale "Cinderella" originated in China. The Chinese Cinderella was only distinguished from her equally beautiful sisters by her tiny bound feet, which were the much-admired Golden Lotuses and could therefore fit into the Prince's slipper.

In India, women's feet (and hands) are often decorated with intricate tracery in henna, especially on special occasions.

The bound foot
A foot crushed by successive years of tight binding is a poignant symbol of total captivity and the submission of women.

Conspicuous extremities
Henna is used to paint a delicate pattern on this Indian bride's bare feet. After a few hours the henna is washed off; the golden-colored design will remain for several weeks.

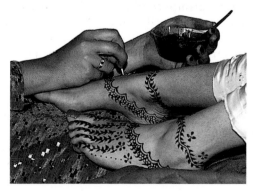

ENDOCRINE SYSTEM

ENDOCRINE ANATOMY

A system of glands (known collectively as the endocrine system) controls the workings of a woman's body through chemicals called hormones, which are released by the glands into the bloodstream. Hormones are responsible for numerous body processes, such as growth, METABOLISM, temperature control, sexual and reproductive activity, MENSTRUATION, LABOR CONTRACTIONS, MILK PRODUCTION and BREASTFEEDING, and the response to STRESS. The effect of hormones can be rapid or delayed, short term or long-lasting.

Hormones also provide the mechanism by which a woman "experiences" her emotions. As the central core of the brain (loosely known as the LIMBIC SYSTEM) is triggered by stimuli, it sends signals to the CEREBRAL CORTEX and other areas of the brain. The emotion is then "registered" by the master glands (the HYPOTHALAMUS and the PITUITARY GLAND) and the appropriate hormone is released (HORMONE PRODUCTION, below). Each emotion is experienced by the body as a separate hormonal response, which triggers a physical reaction. Fear, for example, triggers a release of CATECHOLAMINES, which are released by the ADRENAL GLANDS. Catecholamines trigger the FIGHT-OR-FLIGHT RESPONSE in the body.

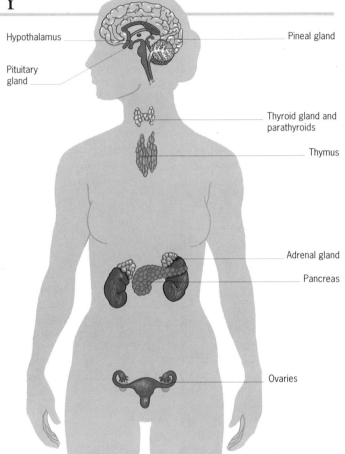

Hypothalamus — Pineal gland

Pituitary gland — Thyroid gland and parathyroids

— Thymus

— Adrenal gland

— Pancreas

— Ovaries

Hormone-producing glands
The glands that produce hormones are found throughout the body. Each produces different hormones, regulating different systems of the body.

HORMONAL PRODUCTION

The HYPOTHALAMUS and the PITUITARY GLAND are known as the master glands of the ENDOCRINE SYSTEM (above) because they regulate and monitor the endocrine system through an intricate feedback system. Most of the messages that travel between the brain and the body go via the hypothalamus, which consequently "knows" about all the sensations that are experienced, such as the pain that is felt when a toe is hurt or the pleasure felt on hearing music, or things that are not consciously realized, such as levels of the different hormones and nutrients. The hypothalamus balances the responses of the glands within the endocrine system through the pituitary gland, which is situated just below it. In response to the electrical or hormonal messages from the hypothalamus, the pituitary releases hormones of its own (known as trophic hormones) into the bloodstream, which carries them to the target cells – including other endocrine glands.

The hypothalamus also produces two hormones (OXYTOCIN and antidiuretic hormone, or ADH) that are stored in the posterior lobe of the pituitary gland for later release into the bloodstream. These ready-made hormones pass down to the pituitary via nerve fibers.

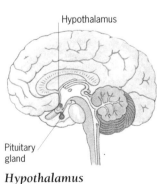

Hypothalamus

Pituitary gland

Hypothalamus
The controlling hormones from the hypothalamus are released into a special tract that passes directly to the pituitary gland.

HORMONE REGULATION

The production of each hormone is kept balanced by the feedback mechanism between an individual gland (the THYROID in the example below), the HYPOTHALAMUS, and the PITUITARY gland (master glands). If a gland overproduces or underproduces a hormone, the master glands register this from the amount of hormone in the bloodstream. The master glands then respond by regulating the hormonal production.

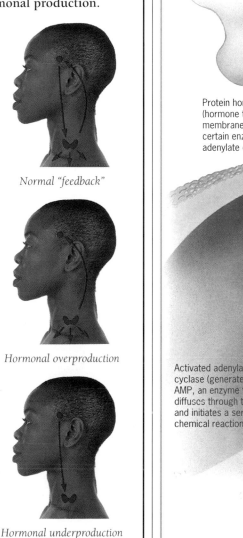

Normal "feedback"

Hormonal overproduction

Hormonal underproduction

HOW HORMONES WORK

HORMONE REGULATION (left) is controlled by the endocrine glands and the "master glands" (the HYPOTHALAMUS and the PITUITARY GLAND). The system works with great precision, despite the fact that the hormones are transported in the bloodstream and are disseminated throughout a woman's entire body. This is because each hormone can transmit only a certain chemical message (like a key), which can fit only into the correct receptor (like a lock) in particular target cells. Some hormones, such as the steroid hormones, work very precisely. Oxytocin, for example, acts on the uterus during labor and on the MILK DUCTS in the breast in response to the LET-DOWN REFLEX during breastfeeding. Other hormones, such as the protein hormones, are able to fit receptors in many target cells and therefore these trigger a much more general effect on the body. Hormones not only excite or inhibit the pace at which target cells perform their usual functions, but they can usually activate or deactivate particular GENES within the cell nucleus that are responsible for certain functions.

Hormones can have either a short-term effect, such as in the fluctuating amounts of INSULIN released by the pancreas in response to blood glucose levels for example, or they can have a long-term effect, such as in the extended activity of ANDROGENS on the sexual development of a woman's body throughout PUBERTY.

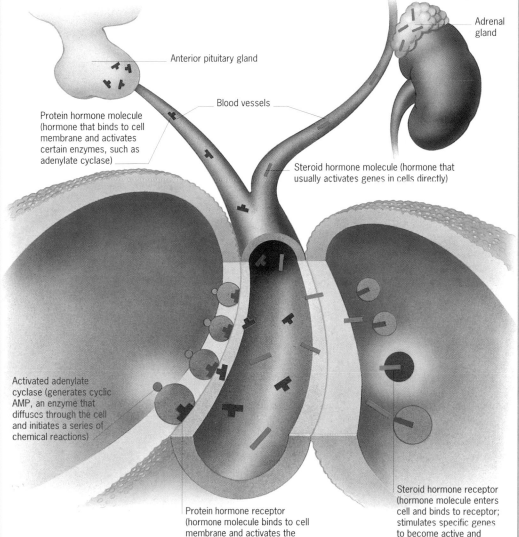

Anterior pituitary gland

Adrenal gland

Blood vessels

Protein hormone molecule (hormone that binds to cell membrane and activates certain enzymes, such as adenylate cyclase)

Steroid hormone molecule (hormone that usually activates genes in cells directly)

Activated adenylate cyclase (generates cyclic AMP, an enzyme that diffuses through the cell and initiates a series of chemical reactions)

Protein hormone receptor (hormone molecule binds to cell membrane and activates the enzyme adenylate cyclase)

Steroid hormone receptor (hormone molecule enters cell and binds to receptor; stimulates specific genes to become active and initiate chemical reactions)

THE PITUITARY GLAND

This pea-sized gland consists of two main parts – the anterior lobe and the posterior lobe. The pituitary gland is known as a master gland and produces six hormones: growth hormone; PROLACTIN, involved in the production and release of BREAST MILK; two hormones affecting METABOLISM – THYROID-stimulating hormone (TSH) and adrenocorticotrophic hormone (ACTH); two hormones that stimulate the ovaries to produce ova (eggs) and sex hormones – FOLLICLE-STIMULATING HORMONE (FSH) and LUTEINIZING HORMONE (LH). The pituitary also stores the two ready-made hormones from the hypothalamus – OXYTOCIN and antidiuretic hormone (ADH). Oxytocin is particularly important in initiating muscle contractions in the uterus during labor. ADH regulates the body's water balance.

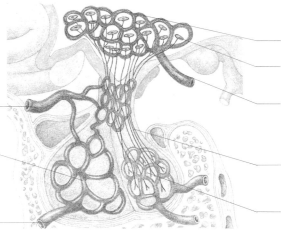

Superior hypophyseal artery (conveys hormones from the body cells and the other endocrine glands to the hypothalamus and the pituitary gland)

Anterior lobe of the pituitary gland

Hypophyseal vein (through which hormones from the pituitary and the hypothalamus reach and stimulate the body cells)

Hypothalamus

Hypothalamic neurosecretory cell

Hypothalamic artery (conveys hormones from the hypothalamus to the rest of the body)

Nerve fibers (carry neurosecretions from the hypothalamus)

Posterior lobe of the pituitary gland

Hormonal control
Hormones present in the blood reach the pituitary gland and the hypothalamus from the rest of the body cells through the superior hypophyseal artery and from the hypothalamus through neurosecretions. These hormones influence the pituitary gland to produce more or less of its controlling hormones, such as growth hormone or oxytocin. These reach the rest of the endocrine glands and the body cells through the hypophyseal vein.

GROWTH DISORDERS

These can occur if the PITUITARY GLAND either underproduces growth hormone, which results in a woman being of excessively short stature ("dwarf"), or overproduces growth hormone, which results in excessive growth, particularly of the woman's jaw and limbs. Dwarfism can also be caused by the inherited disorder achondroplasia, when the ends of the long bones fail to grow. This results in disproportionally short limbs.

Giantess
Rosita, born in 1865 in Vienna, was said to be 2m 34cm (7ft 8in) tall.

PITUITARY DISORDERS

Illness	Description
Cretinism	This is caused by low THYROID hormone levels in babies and infants. Symptoms include mental retardation, skin disorders, coarse facial features, and low METABOLISM, resulting in stunted growth.
Cushing's disease	This results from excessive secretion of adrenocorticotrophic hormone (ACTH). Symptoms include a "moon face," obesity, acne, wasted limbs, HIRSUTISM, easily bruised skin, and EDEMA (fluid retention). Sufferers often develop OSTEOPOROSIS and 20% develop DIABETES MELLITUS. Cushing's disease may also be caused by tumors of the ADRENAL GLAND, which results in excess secretion of steroids.
Failure of sexual maturity	This results from a deficit in FOLLICLE-STIMULATING HORMONE (FSH) and LUTEINIZING HORMONE (LH).
Diabetes insipidus	A deficit of antidiuretic hormone (ADH) may cause this type of diabetes. In contrast to DIABETES MELLITUS, the sufferer's urine does not contain excessive amounts of sugar.

JET LAG

When flying into, or across, another time zone, a woman usually suffers from interrupted sleep patterns, fatigue, and irritability. This is because each person has an individual body clock, controlled by the PINEAL GLAND (right), which regulates all the bodily functions, such as sleeping, waking, and eating, on a circadian (24-hour) cycle. When time zones alter quickly, the internal circadian body rhythms do not synchronize with local time, which results in the experience of jet lag. Jet lag tends to be more severe after an eastward flight than it is after a westward flight, because going east shortens the traveler's day.

THE PINEAL GLAND

This is a tiny pinecone-shaped gland, situated within the brain, which responds to daylight through nerve fibers from the eyes and brain. As daylight fades, the pineal gland produces a hormone called MELATONIN, which peaks at night and switches off again as day dawns.

Melatonin levels are highest in the winter when the days are short or, in some countries, nonexistent, and lowest during the summer months, when the opposite is true. Consequently, the pineal gland is thought to play a significant role in SEASONAL AFFECTIVE DISORDER (right). Melatonin is also thought to influence the circadian (24-hour) body rhythms, such as temperature control, sleep, and appetite, as well as the emotional BIORHYTHM (below).

Rhythm regulator
The pineal gland plays a significant part in regulating the internal rhythms of many species, including women – from the daily patterns of hunger, to the yearly cycles connected to the seasons and number of daylight hours.

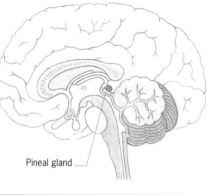

Pineal gland

SEASONAL AFFECTIVE DISORDER (SAD)

Otherwise known as winter depression, SAD occurs when the PINEAL GLAND (left) over-produces MELATONIN as a response to low light levels during the winter months. Excessive amounts of melatonin will suppress certain functions of the body, which will then result in depression characterized by acute anxiety, a lack of energy and enthusiasm, and the inability to look on the positive side of life. Sufferers report cravings for carbohydrates (such as chocolate); carbohydrates are thought to increase the level of SEROTONIN, a neurotransmitter that engenders contentment. SAD usually begins around the age of 20 and becomes less common after the age of 40. Women are four times more likely to suffer from SAD than men, although why this should be so is still unclear. It becomes more common the farther a country lies from the equator, and there appears to be a genetic link. Most sufferers find that their symptoms are relieved by spending time each day sitting in front of a special "daylight light." These lights give off a blue-white light that is very similar to daylight (and to the "grow" lights that are used to sprout seedlings). This appears to "fool" the pineal gland and consequently stops it from overproducing melatonin. Doctors recommend that sufferers try to spend the majority of the daylight hours outside during the winter months. Some sufferers seek relief by moving to a country that is nearer the equator and has a constant amount of daylight throughout the year.

A WOMAN'S BIORHYTHMS

A woman's hormones manage functions within her body on a regularly occurring basis, and so act as an "internal clock." One example is the menstrual cycle of between 25 and 32 days, while a more frequent cycle relates to sleep. The three biorhythmic cycles are depicted as waves of 23 days (physical, which is thought to be controlled by the MOTOR NERVOUS SYSTEM), 28 days (emotional, which has been linked to the PINEAL GLAND) and 33 days (intellectual, which it has been suggested is influenced by secretions of the THYROID GLAND). Only occasionally do all three cycles coincide. The most critical time is when the waves cross the central line: research shows that more accidents happen on these days than on other days.

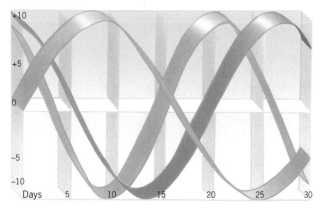
Days 5 10 15 20 25 30

■ Physical
■ Emotional
■ Intellectual

One month's biorhythms
This chart represents the biorhythms for October 1993 for a woman born on October 3, 1963. "Good" biorhythms (when two cycles are high and one is low) occurred only once.

THYROID GLAND

The butterfly-shaped thyroid is situated at the front of the neck under the larynx (voice box) and anterior to the trachea (windpipe). The thyroid gland's most crucial role is to produce the two hormones (thyroxine and triiodothyronine) that are

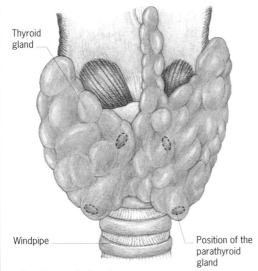

Thyroid gland

Windpipe

Position of the parathyroid gland

The thyroid gland
This important gland sits at the front of a woman's neck anterior to her trachea (windpipe).

vital for regulating the body's METABOLISM (below left), as well as a third hormone (thyrocalcitonin), which lowers CALCIUM levels (right) in the body by suppressing the uptake of calcium from the bone and increasing calcium excretion in the urine. There are two types of secretory cells in the thyroid: follicular and parafollicular. Follicular cells are in the majority, and secrete thyroxine and triiodothyronine, while parafollicular cells secrete thyrocalcitonin. Thyrocalcitonin is formed by the cells in the space between the follicles.

PARATHYROID GLANDS
These four darker glands lie at the back of the thyroid and produce parathyroid hormone. This monitors the level of calcium in the blood by balancing the effect of thyrocalcitonin. Parathyroid hormone is the most important hormone controlling calcium levels in the body. It does this by inhibiting the excretion of calcium from the kidneys, stimulating the uptake of calcium from the intestines, and causing calcium to be released from the bone.

CALCIUM

The average female adult body contains approximately 1kg (2lb) of calcium, 99% of which is in the bones and teeth. The other 1% is in the bloodstream, where it is necessary for the proper functioning of the nerves and muscles, as well as for blood clotting and for glandular secretions.

When the level of calcium in the diet is severely inadequate, the body takes it from the bones. This has serious implications on a long-term basis, particularly for women. This is because the action of ESTROGEN, which facilitates the uptake of calcium throughout the fertile years, is lost during MENOPAUSE as a woman's estrogen levels plummet.

METABOLISM

The collective term for the chemical processes that take place in the body, metabolism is categorized either as catabolism, when a complex substance is broken down into simpler ones, or anabolism, when a complex substance is built up from simpler ones. A catabolic process usually releases energy, while an anabolic process usually uses energy. The basal metabolic rate (BMR) is the level of energy required to keep the body functioning normally when it is at rest and is controlled by the THYROID hormones.

THYROID DISORDERS
THYROID
Both under- and overactivity of the THYROID GLAND (above) cause severe disruption to the body's METABOLISM (left) and functions. The disorders can be caused by a defect within the thyroid gland itself or by malfunction of the PITUITARY GLAND in releasing the hormones that stimulate the thyroid. Underactivity can occur when there is insufficient iodine in the diet. Iodine is needed for the production of functional thyroid hormone, and lack of it can result in cretinism in children (myxedema in adults) and GOITER. Overactivity of the thyroid gland can result in Graves' disease and other forms of hyperthyroidism.

PARATHYROID
Overproduction of the PARATHYROID HORMONE (above) is very rare. It usually occurs as a result of a tumor and leads to bone softening, high levels of CALCIUM (above) in the blood, causing muscular weakness and depression of the nervous system, and the formation of kidney stones. Deficiency in parathyroid hormone causes muscular twitches, convulsions, loss of nervous sensations, and, eventually, respiratory paralysis and death.

THYMUS GLAND

Lying behind the sternum (breastbone) and in front of the trachea (windpipe) and heart is the two-lobed thymus gland; each lobe is made up of LYMPHATIC tissue. The thymus plays a significant part in establishing the immune system from the 12th week of gestation until PUBERTY, after which it shrinks gradually.

Lung   Thymus gland

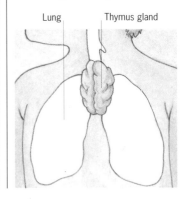

THE PANCREAS

This organ is found in the membrane between the intestine and the stomach and is often described as "two organs in one." This is because it secretes enzyme-rich pancreatic juices from the ACINAR CELLS and hormones from cells known as the islets of Langerhans.

The hormones GLUCAGON and INSULIN (below) that are secreted by the pancreas regulate the amount of glucose that is present in the blood and its uptake by the body cells (glucose provides energy).

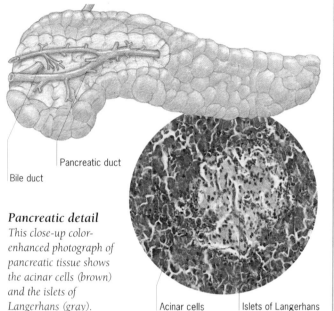

Pancreatic detail
This close-up color-enhanced photograph of pancreatic tissue shows the acinar cells (brown) and the islets of Langerhans (gray).

Bile duct

Pancreatic duct

Acinar cells

Islets of Langerhans

DIABETES MELLITUS

Deficiency in insulin secretion by the pancreas results in excessive levels of GLUCOSE in the blood (below); and subsequently in the urine. This odoriferous urine gives the disease its name (*mellitus* is Greek for sweet). This can be caused by either INSULIN undersecretion or a deficiency in its action due to insensitivity of the tissue receptors.

NON-INSULIN-DEPENDENT DIABETES MELLITUS
This usually occurs after the age of 40 and is the most common type of diabetes; it accounts for over 90% of all diabetes cases. Some insulin is produced by the pancreas but either it is inadequate or an abnormality of the insulin receptors on the tissues develops. Most sufferers are obese and obesity causes the insulin receptors to become less sensitive to the hormone. There is a strong genetic tendency to inherit this type of diabetes. It can be largely controlled by careful diet and exercise.

INSULIN-DEPENDENT DIABETES MELLITUS
Apparent in most sufferers before the age of 15 years, this type of diabetes occurs because the beta islet cells of the pancreas (which produce insulin) have been destroyed as a result of an autoimmune reaction, triggered by a viral infection. The disease is controlled by the administration of insulin by injections on a daily basis.

Sufferers are likely to develop vascular and neurological problems that have to be treated throughout their life. With age, women with diabetes can develop kidney problems, impaired vision, ATHEROSCLEROSIS, and a tendency to HEART ATTACKS and STROKES.

GLUCAGON AND INSULIN

The hormones glucagon and insulin are regulated by the islets of Langerhans (above) in the pancreas, which are made up of alpha and beta cells; the former secrete glucagon and the latter produce insulin. When glucagon is released from the pancreas it stimulates glycogen in the liver to break down and form glucose. This is then released into the bloodstream, raising the blood glucose level. When insulin is released, it causes muscle cells, fat, and other connective tissue cells to take in glucose, thus lowering the blood glucose level. Insufficient glucose uptake leads to hyperglycemia, increased urine output, and ultimately to unconsciousness, coma, and death. Excess insulin in the blood results in hypoglycemia (low blood glucose levels) causing anxiety, tremors, and muscular weakness.

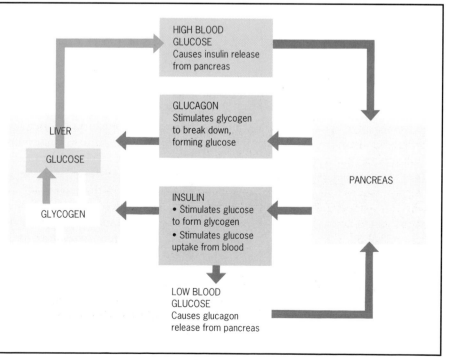

HIGH BLOOD GLUCOSE
Causes insulin release from pancreas

GLUCAGON
Stimulates glycogen to break down, forming glucose

INSULIN
• Stimulates glucose to form glycogen
• Stimulates glucose uptake from blood

LOW BLOOD GLUCOSE
Causes glucagon release from pancreas

LIVER

GLUCOSE

GLYCOGEN

PANCREAS

THE ADRENAL GLANDS

Situated on top of the kidneys, each of the two adrenal glands has an outer portion of glandular tissue, called the adrenal cortex, and an inner core of nervous tissue, called the adrenal medulla. These parts are so different that each adrenal "gland" is like two separate glands, one inside the other.

The adrenal cortex responds to the PITUITARY GLAND and produces many steroid hormones; mineralocorticoids control the balance of minerals and water in the blood, glucocorticoids control functions that enable the body to adapt to STRESS over a period of time. The adrenal glands also trigger the release of extra nutrients (such as glucose) in the blood, balance BLOOD PRESSURE, and stimulate tissue repair. In addition, relatively small quantities of sex hormones (ANDROGENS) are produced by the adrenal cortex and are responsible for sex drive and the growth of pubic hair.

The adrenal medulla responds to the NERVOUS SYSTEM and secretes only two hormones – the CATECHOLAMINES, epinephrine (formerly adrenaline) and norepinephrine. These are responsible for the FIGHT-OR-FLIGHT RESPONSES (below) to "emergency emotions," such as fear and anger.

Medulla hormones
- *Epinephrine*
- *Norepinephrine*
  (fight-or-flight response)

Cortex hormones
- Mineralocorticoids:
  aldosterone,
  deoxycorticosterone
- Glucocorticoids:
  cortisol, corticosterone
- Androgens:
  dehydroepiandrosterone,
  androstenedione

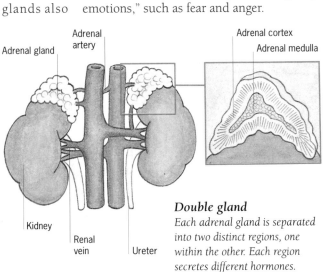

Adrenal gland | Adrenal artery | Adrenal cortex | Adrenal medulla | Kidney | Renal vein | Ureter

Double gland
Each adrenal gland is separated into two distinct regions, one within the other. Each region secretes different hormones.

WOMAN VS. ANIMAL

In common with all other mammals, one of a woman's reactions to fear is to scream. This is such a universal alarm call that it is instantly recognizable, from the high-pitched squeal of the rabbit to the the deeper shrieks of the elephant or horse. Women and children usually have higher-pitched screams than men owing to their different LARYNXES.

FIGHT-OR-FLIGHT RESPONSE

The hormones produced by the inner core of the ADRENAL GLANDS (above) control the body's immediate reaction to danger, triggering the "fight-or-flight" reaction. This reaction occurs when, in response to signals from the nervous system, the adrenal glands pour CATECHOLAMINES (epinephrine and norepinephrine) into the bloodstream. The release of epinephrine results in the coronary arteries dilating, which makes the heart beat faster, and the release of norepinephrine directs blood to muscles and constricts certain blood vessels, which causes blood pressure to rise. The body is thus primed for action, whether it is to fight or to flee. When this response evolved, it was ideally suited to contemporary dangers, which could be physically attacked or run away from. Today, however, the fight-or-flight response tends to occur most often in contexts in which it would be inappropriate either to fight or to run away, making it a major component of STRESS.

THE OVARIES

The ovaries produce two female sex hormones, estrogen and progesterone. Their production is controlled by the HYPOTHALAMUS and the PITUITARY GLAND with FOLLICLE-STIMULATING HORMONE (FSH) and LUTEINIZING HORMONE (LH), which target the ovaries.

Estrogen controls the maturation of the female REPRODUCTIVE ORGANS and the appearance of female sexual characteristics at PUBERTY. Acting in tandem with progesterone, it also controls the MENSTRUAL CYCLE and BREAST DEVELOPMENT. Most of the ovarian hormones are produced inside the ovary by minute saclike structures called FOLLICLES. The cells of each follicle surround an ovum (egg), a number of which are triggered to grow (and produce the bulk of estrogen that is present in a woman's body) by FSH during the first half of the menstrual cycle. One follicle (or sometimes more – some women release two or more ova (eggs) a month, which can result in TWINS or triplets) outstrips the other follicles (which are then reabsorbed by the ovary) and ruptures to release the mature ovum. The burst follicle changes into the *corpus luteum* and then produces less estrogen but more progesterone.

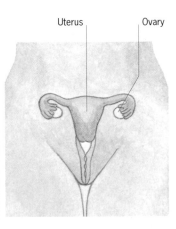

Uterus | Ovary

MENSTRUATION

For about half of her life, a woman will experience monthly menses, or periods (right). From MENARCHE (below), the onset of menstruation, to MENOPAUSE, the cessation of menstruation, the average woman will have about 400 periods. A girl will begin to menstruate when she has acquired at least 17% body fat (after the age of 11 years in Western societies). Peak fertility occurs in the late teens/early 20s, although most Western women have their first child in their mid-20s.

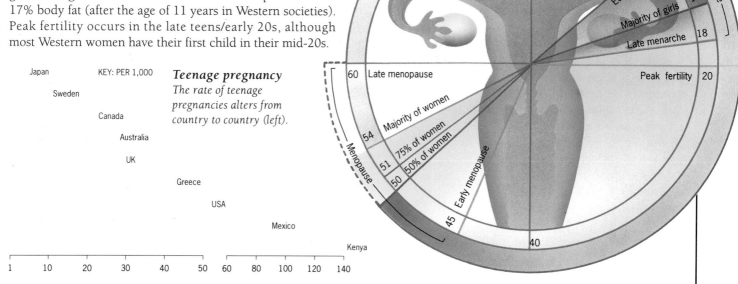

Teenage pregnancy
The rate of teenage pregnancies alters from country to country (left).

KEY: PER 1,000

Japan
Sweden
Canada
Australia
UK
Greece
USA
Mexico
Kenya

1 10 20 30 40 50 60 80 100 120 140

THE MENARCHE

This physical proof of female maturity is frequently marked by a special ceremony or ritual. The Atayal women of Formosa, for example, tattoo permanent, veil-like markings of three stripes on each cheek. In some of the tribes in Sierra Leone, girls' faces and arms are painted white and their bodies are decorated (below).

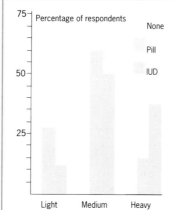

Blood loss
The average woman loses 60–75ml (2–2½fl oz) of blood at each menses.

Percentage of respondents

None
Pill
IUD

75
50
25

Light   Medium   Heavy

Duration
Some 48% of women bleed for 3–4 days; 35% bleed for 5–6 days. The majority of the outstanding 13% bleed for 7 days or more. Contraception can affect the duration of flow as well as amount of blood loss.

MENSTRUAL BLOOD

Women are able to perceive differences in the color, amount, consistency, and odor of their menstrual blood over the course of their menses, or period (below), as well as over the course of their fertile lifetimes. Young, childless women usually report their menstrual blood as bright, thin, profuse, and fresh. Older mothers tend to report dark, clotted blood with a strong odor. Menstrual blood contains red blood cells, cells shed from the ENDOMETRIUM (uterine lining), cervical mucus, and vaginal cells.

Progressive color changes of menstrual blood in an average period.

Duration of period in days

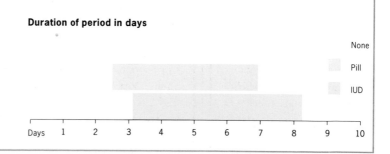

None
Pill
IUD

Days 1 2 3 4 5 6 7 8 9 10

MENSTRUAL PROTECTION

In Canada, millions of disposable sanitary napkins and tampons are used every year by menstruating women. Around the world, women in other cultures prefer to use homemade pads of cloth, cotton batting, or toilet paper, or factory-made, disposable sanitary napkins. Many working-class and rural women worldwide still wash and re-use homemade cloth pads for menstrual protection; 6% of women use no protection at all.

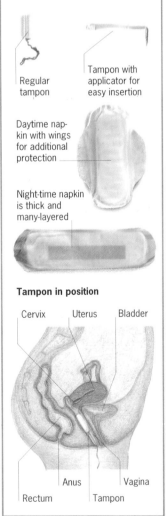

Regular tampon

Tampon with applicator for easy insertion

Daytime napkin with wings for additional protection

Night-time napkin is thick and many-layered

Tampon in position

Cervix   Uterus   Bladder

Anus   Vagina

Rectum   Tampon

THE MENSTRUAL CYCLE

Overall regulation of a woman's menstrual cycle is controlled by the HYPOTHALAMUS and PITUITARY GLAND in the brain. Feedback from the ovaries and uterus is essential for maintenance of the cycle. A breakdown in communication results in menstrual dysfunction.

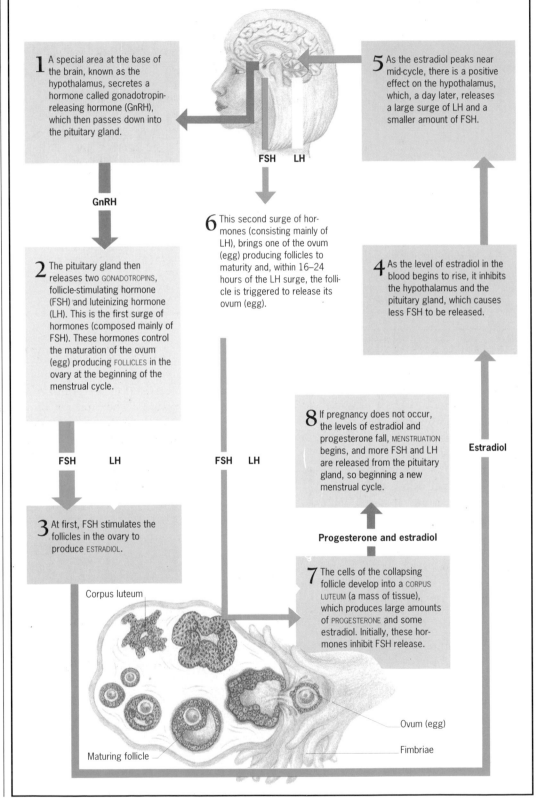

1 A special area at the base of the brain, known as the hypothalamus, secretes a hormone called gonadotropin-releasing hormone (GnRH), which then passes down into the pituitary gland.

GnRH

2 The pituitary gland then releases two GONADOTROPINS, follicle-stimulating hormone (FSH) and luteinizing hormone (LH). This is the first surge of hormones (composed mainly of FSH). These hormones control the maturation of the ovum (egg) producing FOLLICLES in the ovary at the beginning of the menstrual cycle.

FSH   LH

3 At first, FSH stimulates the follicles in the ovary to produce ESTRADIOL.

FSH   LH

6 This second surge of hormones (consisting mainly of LH), brings one of the ovum (egg) producing follicles to maturity and, within 16–24 hours of the LH surge, the follicle is triggered to release its ovum (egg).

FSH   LH

5 As the estradiol peaks near mid-cycle, there is a positive effect on the hypothalamus, which, a day later, releases a large surge of LH and a smaller amount of FSH.

4 As the level of estradiol in the blood begins to rise, it inhibits the hypothalamus and the pituitary gland, which causes less FSH to be released.

Estradiol

8 If pregnancy does not occur, the levels of estradiol and progesterone fall, MENSTRUATION begins, and more FSH and LH are released from the pituitary gland, so beginning a new menstrual cycle.

Progesterone and estradiol

7 The cells of the collapsing follicle develop into a CORPUS LUTEUM (a mass of tissue), which produces large amounts of PROGESTERONE and some estradiol. Initially, these hormones inhibit FSH release.

Corpus luteum

Maturing follicle

Ovum (egg)

Fimbriae

ENDOMETRIAL CHANGES

ESTROGEN causes the endometrium (uterine lining) to thicken and BLOOD VESSELS to spiral up the lining. PROGESTERONE causes uterine cells to secrete enzymes and hormones to support a fertilized ovum (egg). If an ovum doesn't implant, the levels of estrogen and progesterone dip; this, and changes to the enzymes and hormones secreted by the lining, cause spasms in the blood vessels. This vascular constriction results in the disintegration of the uterine lining and the tissue sloughs off. PROSTAGLANDINS cause contractions of the uterine muscles, which expel the lining as MENSTRUAL BLOOD.

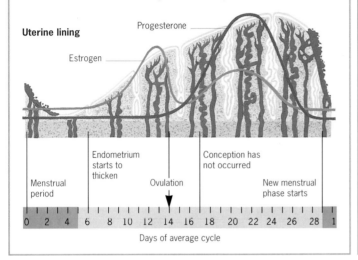

Uterine lining

Progesterone

Estrogen

Endometrium starts to thicken

Conception has not occurred

Menstrual period

Ovulation

New menstrual phase starts

Days of average cycle

TOXIC SHOCK

This is a rare condition, usually linked with the use of tampons left in place for extended periods encouraging excessive growth of normally occurring bacteria (Staphylococcus aureus); the same is true of cervical caps and diaphragms. The bacteria could also have been introduced into the vagina on the fingers. The bacteria produces a toxin that can cause shock, kidney failure, coma, and death. Tampons should always be removed after 4–6 hours, and a sanitary napkin should be worn during the night.

ABNORMAL PERIODS

Irregular, prolonged, and heavy menses (periods) are most common in adolescence and in the teens and the years prior to MENOPAUSE. These are often due to a hormonal imbalance. Menstruation is also influenced by diet, body weight, and activity levels; however, any deviation from the perceived norm is not necessarily abnormal for the individual woman. Irregular menses tend to be related to the level of ESTROGEN in the body. When the level of estrogen is low, blood spotting is light but sustained; when it is high, no bleeding may then be followed by quite profuse blood loss.

Prolonged and heavy menses are often the result of low PROGESTERONE levels, which means the progesterone takes longer to peak and trigger the shedding of the lining, so the lining is thicker than normal.

Dilation and curettage (D&C)

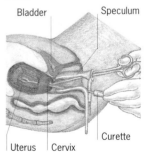

Bladder

Speculum

Uterus

Cervix

Curette

Most often used to diagnose the cause of and treat abnormal menstrual bleeding. A curette is inserted into the uterus and used to scrape away the lining.

MENSTRUATION: BELIEFS AND BEHAVIOR

Beliefs and behavior	Egypt	India: Hindu High Caste	India: Hindu Low Caste	Indonesia: Javanese	Indonesia: Sundanese	Jamaica	Korea	Mexico	Pakistan: Sind	Pakistan: Punjab	Philippines	UK
Menstruation is necessary for femininity	96	95	96	58	85	61	79	57	33	84	95	42
Menstruation is "dirty"	88	69	48	82	93	33	34	53	58	40	41	7
Menstruation is like a "sickness"	67	20	7	19	14	37	22	26	5	3	61	7
Intercourse should be avoided during menstruation	98	97	94	94	98	91	91	90	88	86	90	54
Washing hair should be avoided during menstruation	16	18	2	58	61	21	11	14	36	16	68	5
Cooking should be avoided during menstruation	1	79	75	1	2	27	2	3	3	3	6	0
Bathing should be avoided during menstruation	42	8	3	7	2	18	72	20	47	44	72	10
Visits to friends should be avoided during menstruation	55	49	56	2	2	39	7	16	12	7	24	0
Physical discomfort before or during menstruation	58	58	55	65	70	61	53	51	68	50	62	57
Mood changes before or during menstruation	42	44	40	34	23	42	52	38	58	39	48	71

Figures represent percentage of the respondents to a UNESCO survey.

PREMENSTRUAL SYNDROME

PMS is the term for a group of emotional, mental, and physical symptoms that affect many women during the days leading up to a menstrual period. The exact cause is unknown but is thought to be related to hormonal changes.

Symptoms

- *Fluid retention*
- *Mood changes*
- *DEPRESSION*
- *Weight gain*
- *Carbohydrate cravings*
- *Poor skin condition*
- *Back pain*
- *Low tolerance to alcohol*
- *Urinary tract infections*
- *Breathlessness*
- *Visual disturbances*
- *Numbness in fingers*
- *Headaches*
- *Clumsiness*
- *Nasal congestion*
- *Susceptibility to CONJUNCTIVITIS*

AMENORRHEA

When menses (periods) have never started, or are interrupted, the condition is known as amenorrhea. The most common causes are pregnancy and breastfeeding, but amenorrhea can also be a side effect of being severely under-weight or of excessive exercising. It may also result from STRESS, certain chronic diseases, or the long-term use of some medications.

ENDOMETRIOSIS

This is a condition in which fragments of endometrium (the uterine lining) are found in other parts of the abdominal cavity, or on organs within it. These displaced patches of the endometrium may respond to the MENSTRUAL CYCLE as if they were inside the uterus and so bleed each month. Because this blood cannot escape, slowly growing CYSTS form. These can cause intense pain along with severe and abnormal internal bleeding. Thirty to forty percent of sufferers are INFERTILE, although surgery and drug treatments may work for some.

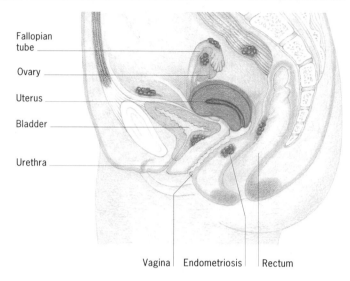

Fallopian tube
Ovary
Uterus
Bladder
Urethra

Vagina | Endometriosis | Rectum

Sites of endometriosis
Endometriosis can occur in many places within the pelvic and abdominal area, causing abnormal internal bleeding and scarring. This can result in internal organs becoming joined together with scar tissue.

DYSMENORRHEA (PAINFUL PERIODS)

Fifty percent of menstruating women suffer low abdominal pain, cramps, backache, and pains in the thighs, sometimes accompanied by nausea, vomiting, and diarrhea. Some form of period pain is experienced by 80% of girls under the age of 19. The pains often occur just before a menses starts and can last for two days. Menstrual pain is caused by high concentrations of prostaglandins; these stimulate excessive spasmodic contractions of the uterus, inter-mittently cutting off the blood flow and so depleting oxygen supply to the muscle. This also happens during LABOR CONTRACTIONS. The exercises shown below will increase the flow of blood to the pelvis and so help to relieve dysmenorrhea.

Hip circles
These will promote relaxation of the muscles in the pelvic area. Stand upright with feet apart and move the hips in a full circle, twice in one direction, and then twice in the other. Repeat 10 times.

Knee lift with arm pulls
This exercise helps improve circulation and loosens up the muscles. Stand upright with the arms straight above the head. Lift one knee up to the chest, while bending the arms down and outward. Lower the foot to the floor and extend the arms up again. Repeat with the other knee. Repeat 10 times.

OVARIAN PROBLEMS

Because the ovaries lie deep within the abdominal cavity, problems or disorders concerning them may be overlooked unless they manifest in a very obvious way.

OOPHORITIS

An ovary that becomes swollen and inflamed (known as oophoritis) isn't usually detected unless a pelvic examination is performed. Oophoritis is normally caused by the mumps virus or pelvic inflammatory disease.

OVARIAN CYSTS

These usually develop when an OVARIAN FOLLICLE fails to rupture and release an ovum (egg). The majority of such follicles fill with fluid, although some develop into benign tumors. They may cause a disturbance in the MENSTRUAL CYCLE, abdominal swelling, pain during intercourse, or unfamiliar pain or discomfort at any point in the menstrual cycle. Most ovarian cysts are spontaneously reabsorbed, although a few may have to be treated surgically. An ovary should never be removed just because of a cyst.

OVARIAN CANCER

Although cancer of the ovaries is relatively rare, it is the fourth most common cause of death in women, mainly because it is so difficult to detect. In most cases, there are no obvious symptoms until the cancer is widespread, although mild stomach upsets, gas, and abdominal pain may have been experienced. Sometimes there is a buildup of fluid in the pelvic region and the ovaries may be swollen. Ovarian cancer is more common after the age of 50. Risk factors appear to include:

- *Having borne no children*
- *Being postmenopausal*
- *Having had CANCER of the breast, intestine, or rectum*
- *Family history of ovarian cancer*
- *Being overweight*
- *Working in the electrical, textile, or rubber industries*
- *Living in an urban area*
- *High-fat diet*

HYSTERECTOMY AND OOPHORECTOMY

HYSTERECTOMY

This is the surgical removal of the uterus, and is performed for the following reasons:

- *Cancer of the uterus, cervix, vagina, fallopian tubes, ovaries*
- *Severe UTERINE PROLAPSE*
- *Severe pelvic inflammatory disease or other pelvic disease*
- *Uncontrollable bleeding*
- *Rupture of the uterus during childbirth (extremely rare)*
- *Severe ENDOMETRIOSIS*
- *Extensive FIBROIDS*

A hysterectomy can be performed either vaginally or abdominally. Get a second opinion before you agree to one, and be sure you understand the reasons why you need it.

OOPHORECTOMY

Usually performed because of ECTOPIC PREGNANCY, endometriosis, OVARIAN CANCER or CYSTS, (above) and pelvic inflammatory disease, oophorectomy is the removal of one or both ovaries. A few surgeons still remove healthy ovaries when performing a hysterectomy, arguing that it removes the risk of future ovarian cancer. The evidence suggests that the chance of developing ovarian cancer following a hysterectomy is one in a thousand, compared with one in a hundred in women over 45 who still have an intact uterus. If both ovaries are wholly removed, premature MENOPAUSE occurs.

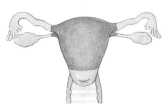

Partial hysterectomy
The uterus is removed through the abdomen, while the fallopian tubes and the ovaries are attached to the top of the cervix. Partial hysterectomy is only rarely performed today.

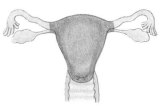

Total hysterectomy
Both the uterus and the cervix are removed through the vagina or the abdomen. The fallopian tubes and ovaries are attached to the top of the vagina. This is the usual type performed.

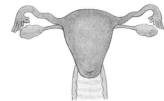

Total hysterectomy with oophorectomy
One or both ovaries, the fallopian tubes, the uterus, and the cervix are removed through the abdomen. It is fairly common.

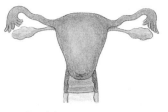

Radical hysterectomy
This involves total organ removal and the removal of the lymph nodes. It is performed through the abdomen and is relatively uncommon.

BLOOD & HEART

CIRCULATORY SYSTEM

This, the transport system of the body, consists of three parts. Blood is the fluid in which oxygen, food, water, and other essentials are carried to the tissue cells and in which waste is removed; the heart is the driving force that propels blood through the body; the BLOOD VESSELS (arteries, veins, and capillaries) are the routes through which the blood travels. The blood in the arteries is under high pressure, while that returning to the heart in the veins is under low pressure.

Consequently, the walls of the arteries are much thicker, stronger, and more elastic than those of the veins. The arteries can therefore expand under the pulse of high pressure as the heart beats, so smoothing out the blood flow.

Circulation of the blood
From the heart, the blood travels to various points of the body through the arteries. It returns to the heart through the veins.

Jugular vein
Subclavian artery
Superior vena cava
Inferior vena cava
Femoral vein
Femoral artery

Carotid artery
Heart
Pulmonary (lung) circulation
Aorta
Brachial artery
Iliac vein
Iliac artery

BLOOD

A healthy woman has about 4 liters (4.22 quarts) of blood circulating around her body; this forms about 5% of her total body weight. Blood is a thick red fluid: arterial blood contains oxygen and is bright red; venous blood is deoxygenated and is dark purplish red. Plasma is the carrying fluid for the blood cells. In addition to water, it contains many other substances, such as proteins, hormones, antibodies, minerals, uric acid, glucose, and cholesterol.

Plasma
Red blood cells
White blood cells

Blood composition
Plasma (which is composed of 90% water) makes up 55% of blood. The remainder consists of 43% red blood cells and 2% white blood cells.

BLOOD FORMATION

All the red and some white BLOOD CELLS are formed from stem cells within the bone marrow.

Monocyte
Lymphocyte
Red blood cell
Stem cell

Platelets   Neutrophil   Basophil   Eosinophil

BLOOD CELLS

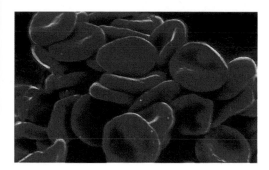

RED BLOOD CELLS (LEFT)

These doughnut-shaped blood cells have a large surface area and a flexible shape. The red blood cells transport oxygen from the lungs to the rest of the body, and there are approximately five million of them in every cubic millimeter of blood. Red blood cells are formed in the bone marrow and define a woman's BLOOD GROUP (below right) and her RHESUS FACTOR (right).

WHITE BLOOD CELLS (RIGHT)

These are twice as big as red blood cells but are much less numerous (8,000 in each cubic millimeter of blood). There are five main types of white blood cells, each with a slightly different role, although they all engulf bacteria. NEUTROPHILS, BASOPHILS, and EOSINOPHILS, known collectively as GRANULOCYTES, survive for only a few hours or days. Their job is to react quickly to an invasion of the body by attacking and destroying invading organisms. Granulocytes release substances that attract other defense cells to the sites of wounds. MONOCYTES are longer-lived. Their function is to clear away dead cells and digest invading

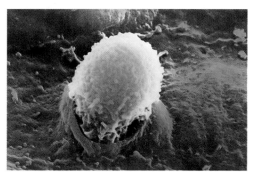

organisms. LYMPHOCYTES (above) play a central role in the immune system. T-lymphocytes reject foreign bodies and stimulate B-lymphocytes to produce antibodies. The antibodies then attack invading organisms.

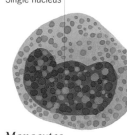

Nucleus is oddly shaped and segmented

Granulocytes

Neutrophils, eosinophils, and basophils make up 75% of white blood cells. Granulocytes are formed from the stem cells in the bone marrow.

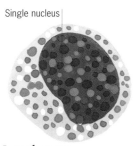

Single nucleus

Monocytes

These are the largest white blood cells and make up 5% of the total. They are formed from stem cells in the lymph nodes, spleen, and thymus, and some in the bone marrow.

Single nucleus

Lymphocytes

Formed mainly in the lymph nodes, spleen, and thymus, these make up 20% of the total. Lymphocytes are the cells that are attacked by HIV.

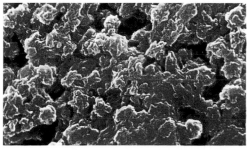

PLATELETS (LEFT)

The smallest cells in the body, platelets (left) are formed in the bone marrow and are involved in BLOOD CLOTTING. They stick to the COLLAGEN of the damaged lining of the blood vessel. There are about five hundred billion platelets in 1 liter (1 quart) of blood. This figure fluctuates with exercise.

RHESUS FACTOR

An important minor blood group, its presence means that the woman has Rhesus-positive blood. If the factor is absent, as in 15% of the population, the woman has Rhesus-negative blood. This generally only presents a problem during a second pregnancy if the blood of both her first and second babies is Rhesus-positive; during her first pregnancy, she may have formed antibodies that affect subsequent babies.

BLOOD GROUPS

Chemical structures in the cell membranes, which are known as antigens, vary between the blood groups. Blood group A can donate to groups A and AB and receive blood from groups A and O; O can donate to all other groups but can receive only from O; B can donate to B and AB and receive from B and O; AB can donate only to AB, but can receive from all other groups.

Group A (45%)
Group O (45%)
Group B (8%)
Group AB (2%)

A O B AB

BLOOD CLOTTING

When a vessel is damaged, blood immediately starts to escape. There is a spasm of the smooth muscle and the blood vessel wall constricts. Platelets in the immediate area congregate at the site and stick to the COLLAGEN of the damaged lining (right).

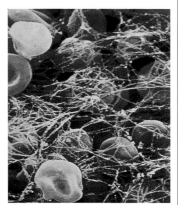

Blood-clotting agent
Platelets plug the hole by disintegrating and releasing blood-clotting factors, which are converted into an elastic protein called fibrin. This meshes across the wound.

Blood clotting begins
The platelets gather at the site of a breach in the blood vessel.

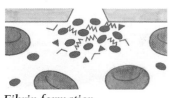

Fibrin formation
Blood-clotting factors are released by the platelets; strands of fibrin form.

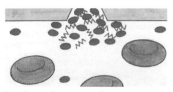

Sealing the wound
Fibrin and disintegrating platelets mesh together and seal the wound.

WOMAN'S BLOOD VESSELS

The two major types of blood vessel are the arteries and the veins. The arteries carry blood away from the heart; it is returned by the veins. The walls of both contain five layers: two protective layers; a middle layer of SMOOTH MUSCLE and elastic tissue; a thin layer of elastic tissue; and a single layer of cells called the endothelium.

ARTERIES

These have the thickest and most elastic walls, which enables them to expand with each surge of BLOOD PRESSURE following a heartbeat (felt as the pulse). Arteries become progressively smaller until they divide into arterioles.

VEINS

Blood flow in the veins is directed toward the heart by muscle contractions. Valves ensure that the blood moves in one direction.

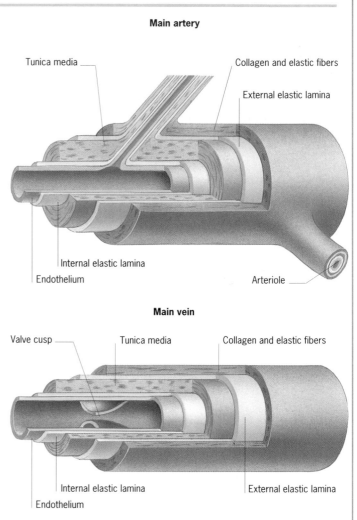

Main artery

Tunica media — Collagen and elastic fibers — External elastic lamina — Internal elastic lamina — Endothelium — Arteriole

Main vein

Valve cusp — Tunica media — Collagen and elastic fibers — Internal elastic lamina — External elastic lamina — Endothelium

AORTA

The body's largest BLOOD VESSEL is an artery – the aorta. Its diameter is 3cm (1¼in) where it exits from the heart, as shown below.

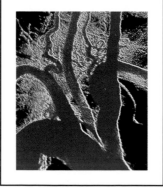

VENOUS BLOOD FLOW

Arterial pressure is high, but venous pressure is low, so the blood moves slowly in the veins. The veins can collapse or expand to accommodate variations in blood flow. Blood in the veins is propelled around the body by contractions of the surrounding muscles and pulsations of adjacent arteries. Semilunar valves found in the larger veins prevent blood from leaking backward. Veins divide into smaller blood vessels, known as venules.

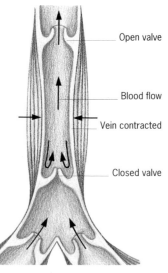

Open valve

Blood flow

Vein contracted

Closed valve

VARICOSE VEINS

When VALVES *in the veins become damaged, they allow blood to flow back. The veins then balloon (below). Women are at greater risk of developing varicose veins than men are.*

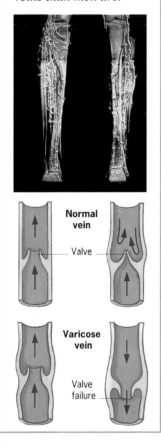

Normal vein

Valve

Varicose vein

Valve failure

BLOOD SUPPLY TO THE TISSUES

Tiny blood vessels supply the body's tissues. Blood enters the capillary bed from ARTERIOLES and is drained through the VENULES.

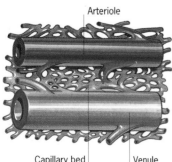

Arteriole

Capillary bed | Venule

BLOOD CIRCULATION

The heart and BLOOD VESSELS enable blood to flow continuously around the body and thus supply its tissues with oxygen and nutrients, as it removes waste products. All parts of the body, except the lungs, receive blood from the systemic circulation. The lungs have their own pulmonary circulation, in which carbon dioxide and oxygen are exchanged through the alveolar surface in the lungs. The heart is supplied with newly oxygenated blood by the coronary arteries, which are the first to leave the AORTA.

SYSTEMIC CIRCULATION

A 60-mile (96-km) network of blood vessels carries blood around the body. Blood is pumped out by the left VENTRICLE of the heart, through the aorta and its branches, the arteries and ARTERIOLES, to all parts of the body. As the blood travels through the body, it gradually gives up its oxygen and is finally pumped to the lungs to be reoxygenated.

The coronary arteries leave the aorta first and, a bit farther on, the brachial and carotid arteries branch off the aorta, going to the head and arms.

The aorta then runs in front of the spine and behind the ESOPHAGUS to the abdomen, with small and large branches going to the spine, abdominal cavity, diaphragm, SPLEEN, and the intercostal muscles.

Within the pelvis, the aorta divides into two large branches, the iliac arteries, which supply blood to the legs. Blood returns to the superior and inferior VENA CAVA and then finally to the right atrium of the heart.

In the lungs, oxygen is transferred from the LUNG ALVEOLI to the red blood cells and the reoxygenated blood then returns to the left atrium of the heart.

Heart

Right pulmonary circulation

Right lung

Renal circulation

Left pulmonary circulation

Left lung

Splanchnic (spleen) circulation

■ Arteries – oxygenated blood

■ Veins – deoxygenated blood

Blood flow
Oxygenated blood flows away from the heart through the arteries. Deoxygenated blood returns to the heart via the veins.

BLOOD PRESSURE

Blood needs to flow under pressure to maintain the CIRCULATION. The heart pumps in pulses, however, so a woman's blood pressure is rapidly and constantly changing. Blood pressure is highest during the contraction of the heart's VENTRICLES (systolic pressure) and is lowest between beats (diastolic pressure). Each ventricle in the heart ejects about 70ml (2½fl oz) of blood at each heartbeat. This means that just over half the heart's output of blood has to be stored as the heart contracts and then passes on as the heart rests. The conducting arteries are always under full pressure.

ATHEROSCLEROSIS

Clumps of atheroma, a fibro-fatty material consisting mainly of cholesterol, blood lipids, and fibrous tissue, build up within the arteries from childhood onward. This buildup is called an atherosclerotic plaque; with time, it may contain calcium deposits that cause the arteries to harden. Atherosclerotic plaques obstruct the lumen (cavity) of the artery and cause the flow of blood to become sluggish.

Atherosclerotic plaque

Blood flow

THE HEART

The average female heart weighs about 350g (¾lb) and is the size of a clenched fist. It is a hollow, muscular organ, which beats on average 100,000 times a day, and sits left of center in the chest. The heart is actually two pumps, each with two chambers; the right-hand chambers receive deoxygenated blood from the body and pump it to the lungs; the left-hand chambers receive oxygenated blood and pump it out to the body.

HEART CHAMBERS

The heart has four chambers: the atria are the two upper, thin-walled chambers, and the ventricles the two lower, thick-walled chambers. The heart's two sides are separated by the septum (a strong muscular wall).

MYOCARDIUM

A unique arrangement of branching fibers, the myocardium (heart muscle) gives a woman's heart the strength to pump approximately 7,200 liters (6,340 quarts) of blood around the body each day.

PERICARDIUM

Surrounding the heart, the pericardium is a tough, double-layered membranous bag. In the space between its two layers is a lubricating fluid that permits free movement of the heart muscle.

ENDOCARDIUM

A smooth membrane, the endocardium lines the inside of the heart and its valves.

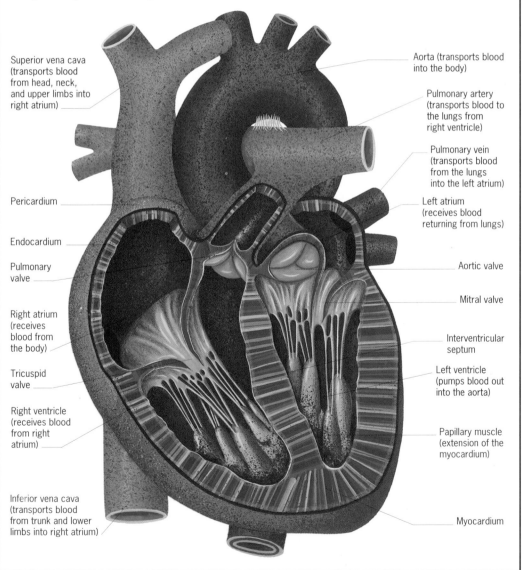

Superior vena cava (transports blood from head, neck, and upper limbs into right atrium)

Pericardium

Endocardium

Pulmonary valve

Right atrium (receives blood from the body)

Tricuspid valve

Right ventricle (receives blood from right atrium)

Inferior vena cava (transports blood from trunk and lower limbs into right atrium)

Aorta (transports blood into the body)

Pulmonary artery (transports blood to the lungs from right ventricle)

Pulmonary vein (transports blood from the lungs into the left atrium)

Left atrium (receives blood returning from lungs)

Aortic valve

Mitral valve

Interventricular septum

Left ventricle (pumps blood out into the aorta)

Papillary muscle (extension of the myocardium)

Myocardium

SMOOTH OPERATOR

The muscular walls and specialized valves of the heart combine to produce a pulsed, streamlined blood flow. The membranous valves at the entrance and exit of the ventricular chambers are extremely tough.

Throughout the course of a woman's lifetime, these membranous valves will open and shut some 80 million times.

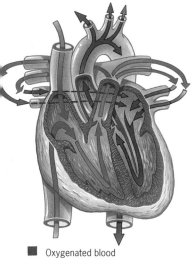

■ Oxygenated blood
■ Deoxygenated blood

The dual pump
Blood vessels connected to the heart carry blood to and from all parts of the body. Deoxygenated blood is pumped to the lungs through the heart and then returned to the heart to be pumped around the body.

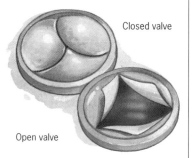

Closed valve

Open valve

Heart valves
Flaps in the heart valves open and lie against the heart walls so that the blood can flow through the chambers of the heart.

SPARE HEART PARTS

Several natural replacements and mechanical parts and equipment have been developed to treat heart problems. The hearts of human donors can be transplanted to replace the diseased hearts of patients with a similar tissue type. Alternatively, artificial hearts can reproduce the heart's function, although they have not performed successfully in the long term. Malfunctioning heart valves can be replaced with plastic and metal ones, or with biological valves, taken from a pig or from a human cadaver. Specialized pumping mechanisms can be installed in the body to assist a failing heart, and battery-operated pacemakers or automatic defibrillators (which deliver electric shocks to the heart) can be implanted to treat abnormal heart rhythms.

Mechanical valve
This caged-ball valve is durable but encourages blood clots. Anti coagulant drugs are needed.

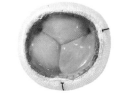

Biological valve
This valve works well, but is less durable than a mechanical one. There is no problem with clotting.

Electronic pacemaker
This is battery-powered and sends timed electrical impulses to the heart through a wire.

Artificial heart
Blood clotting has often been a fatal problem with these mechanical devices.

HUMAN HEART TRANSPLANT

In 1967, a 25-year-old South African woman's heart was transplanted by Dr. Christiaan Barnard into a man who subsequently lived for 18 days. Hearts that are to be transplanted are kept on ice (right) so they will keep "fresh" for as long as possible.

THE HEARTBEAT

Each beat of the heart has three phases. Initially, the heart chambers expand and fill with blood (known as diastole). The ATRIA then contract and squeeze more blood through the large VALVES so that the VENTRICLES fill up (atrial systole). Finally, the ventricle walls contract and pump blood outward (ventricular systole) to complete the heartbeat.

At rest, the average woman's heart beats between 70–85 times per minute. This rate increases by 40% during the FIRST TRIMESTER of pregnancy to 105–119 per minute.

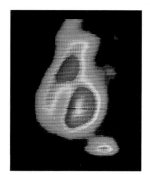

Diastole pressure
The right and left atriums of the heart fill up with blood from the lungs and the body.

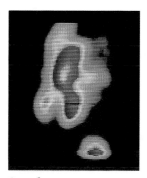

Systole pressure
The right and left ventricles of the heart contract, expelling the blood into the arteries.

THE HEART – A SYMBOL OF LOVE

Beating, fluttering, and palpitating hearts are closely associated with the concept of love. Heart-shaped tokens or beads worn around the neck, and settings or stones shaped into hearts, have historically been an expression of love. In most Western cultures, the wedding ring is traditionally worn on the fourth finger of the left hand because it was commonly believed that a blood vessel (vein) led from there directly to the heart. Heart-shaped golden lockets were frequently worn by women in Victorian times – a picture of the beloved was usually placed inside.

HEART ATTACK

Medically known as myocardial infarction, a heart attack is when an area of heart muscle is deprived of its blood supply, resulting in dead tissue. Almost all research into heart disease is based on men, because women tend to be at a much lower risk of a heart attack until after MENOPAUSE. After menopause, however, the risk to women is on a par with the risk to men in the same age group. Myocardial infarction is often the result of a buildup of ATHEROSCLEROTIC PLAQUES on the walls of the blood vessel, thus promoting the formation of a blood clot. Once the blood clot has formed, the blood vessel becomes blocked and prevents the flow of blood. The blood-starved tissue then goes into spasm, resulting in a heart attack.

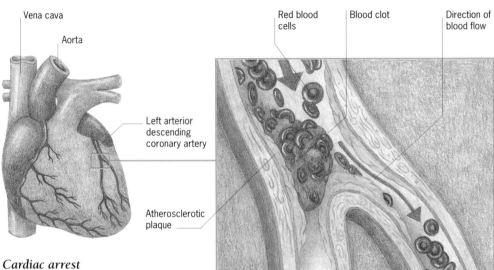

Vena cava

Aorta

Left arterior descending coronary artery

Atherosclerotic plaque

Red blood cells

Blood clot

Direction of blood flow

Cardiac arrest
A blockage in one of the blood vessels in the heart can deprive part of the heart of blood. The muscle fibers quickly go into spasm.

ETHNIC TYPE AND HEART DISEASE

Western Asian women are 46% more likely to contract HEART DISEASE than white women. The causes are not clear, but there is an association with STRESS and eating habits, and with the fact that Asian women are twice as likely to develop DIABETES MELLITUS as white women. Heart disease is also a contributing factor to STROKES, which kill 50% more black women than white women.

RISKS ASSOCIATED WITH HEART ATTACKS

Risk factor	Effect
High cholesterol	Low-density cholesterol lipoproteins (LDLs) damage arteries. Regular exercise can reduce LDL cholesterol levels by as much as 6%. This also increases the level of beneficial high-density cholesterol lipoproteins (HDLs), which help "remove" harmful fat deposits from the arteries.
Smoking	Nicotine can cause irregular heart rhythms. It also raises BLOOD PRESSURE.
Hypertension (high blood pressure)	This strains the heart and leads to hardening of the arteries.
Family history of heart disease	Heart attacks have a tendency to run in families, and a woman with a close relative who has suffered a heart attack is at increased risk.
Diabetes	DIABETES can damage the small blood vessels, which can prevent the CORONARY arteries from supplying the heart with blood.
Stress	This increases the level of the hormone norepinephrine in the blood, high levels of which can damage heart muscle.
Excessive alcohol	This can damage the heart muscle.

RESPIRATORY SYSTEM

ANATOMY OF THE LUNGS

Lying above the diaphragm are the lungs. They are not quite identical; the right lung has three lobes, while the left lung has two lobes and is indented where it molds itself around the heart. A layer of pleura covers the surface of the lungs and the inside of the chest cavity so the lungs can inflate and deflate smoothly. Air enters the lungs through the NOSE, PHARYNX, and TRACHEA. The trachea branches into two bronchi, which then rapidly divide into a branching mass of smaller air tubes called bronchioles, and then into the alveoli, which is where gas exchange takes place.

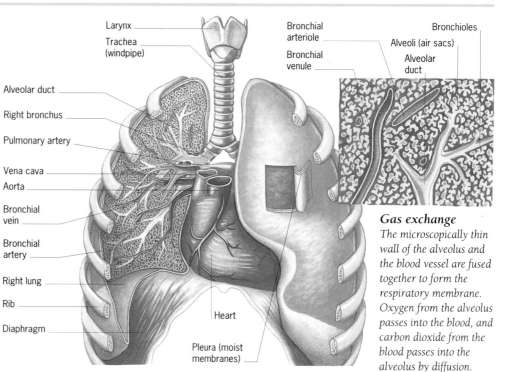

Larynx
Trachea (windpipe)
Alveolar duct
Right bronchus
Pulmonary artery
Vena cava
Aorta
Bronchial vein
Bronchial artery
Right lung
Rib
Diaphragm
Heart
Pleura (moist membranes)

Bronchial arteriole
Bronchial venule
Bronchioles
Alveoli (air sacs)
Alveolar duct

Gas exchange
The microscopically thin wall of the alveolus and the blood vessel are fused together to form the respiratory membrane. Oxygen from the alveolus passes into the blood, and carbon dioxide from the blood passes into the alveolus by diffusion.

BREATHING

The average woman breathes in and out nine times per minute (the average man's rate is 12 times per minute). This can rise to 60–80 times per minute with vigorous physical activity. When a woman breathes in, the external INTERCOSTAL MUSCLES of her ribcage and diaphragm contract, her lungs expand, and her diaphragm drops. The pressure inside the lungs drops to a lower level than the external air pressure, and air, of which 20% is oxygen, is inhaled. The volume of the lungs is increased by raising the ribcage and contracting the muscles of the diaphragm. This process is reversed when a woman breathes out; the external intercostal muscles of her ribcage and diaphragm relax, her ribcage is lowered, and her diaphragm then returns to its gently arched resting

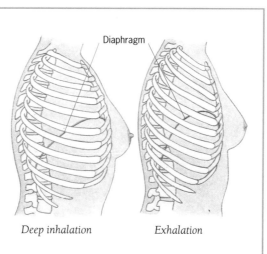

Diaphragm

Deep inhalation   *Exhalation*

shape. The lung volume decreases and the internal pressure rises above that of the external air pressure so that the lungs' gases (of which 13.7% are oxygen and 5.2% are carbon dioxide) are expelled.

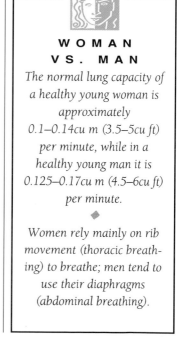

WOMAN VS. MAN

The normal lung capacity of a healthy young woman is approximately 0.1–0.14cu m (3.5–5cu ft) per minute, while in a healthy young man it is 0.125–0.17cu m (4.5–6cu ft) per minute.

◆

Women rely mainly on rib movement (thoracic breathing) to breathe; men tend to use their diaphragms (abdominal breathing).

HIGH ALTITUDE

When a woman lives at a very high altitude, such as in the South American Andean mountains or the mountainous region of Nepal, her body acclimatizes to the lower levels of oxygen available — 0.5kg (1lb) per sq cm (sq in) as opposed to twice that quantity at sea level. This is achieved by her developing larger lungs and by her body's enhanced ability to use the available oxygen in the most efficient manner.

Peruvian altiplano woman.

WOMAN VS. ANIMAL

A woman can hold her breath for about two minutes. In contrast, the sperm whale can hold its breath for nearly two hours. A woman's heartbeat, like the whale's, slows down when she dives (known as bradycardia). This may be a legacy of the AQUATIC PERIOD.

◆

Fish do not have lungs like mammals; they breathe using gills – sophisticated filter systems that remove oxygen from the water as it flows through. Oxygen is collected by thin capillaries in the gills and then relayed to the rest of the body.

ASTHMA AND HAY FEVER

Breathlessness, wheezing, and, in the case of hay fever, streaming eyes and a running nose are the body's reaction to allergens, such as atmospheric pollutants and pollen.

HAY FEVER

Otherwise known as allergic rhinitis, hay fever is the production of excessive mucus in reaction to the inhalation of allergens, such as tree, grass, and weed pollen, dust, and house-dust mite droppings. Pollen-activated hay fever is cyclical, while other types tend to be ongoing. Hay fever affects 5–10% of the population, and tends to run in families. It is more common among Northern CAUCASOIDS than among other racial types.

ASTHMA

Usually occurring when the allergen "trigger" is inhaled, asthma is the result of the sensitive bronchial muscles going into intense spasm. The air passages can close down to a pinhead diameter, which results in the sufferer's feeling of strangulation. Recovery can take from minutes to days. During severe asthma attacks, the sufferer may need to be hospitalized and may require the help of a mechanical respirator to recover fully. Asthma can be controlled by avoiding triggers (see the list of common causes given below), or by inhaling drugs that strengthen and dilate the BRONCHIAL TUBES.

Common causes of asthma attacks

- *Allergies to substances, such as the droppings of dust mites, mold spores, pollen, cigarette smoke, animal dander (shed skin), drugs, chemicals, and food.*

- *Viral infections, such as flu, and STRESS.*

- *Air temperature (cold), and air quality (dry, polluted).*

- *Hormones; some women find their asthma is affected by periods or pregnancy.*

CORSETS AND TOBACCO

During the 19th century, it became fashionable in the Western world to emphasize the narrowness of the female waist by the use of tightly laced corsets. "Wasp-waisted" women often achieved a 37.5–45cm (15-18in) waist (the smallest waist ever recorded was 32.5cm (13in), but at the cost of severely restricting the lungs, which often resulted in fainting. As soon as her stays were loosened, the sufferer recovered.

When cigarettes became available at the start of the 20th century, smoking was seen as racy and daring by the "Bright Young Things" of the 1920s. Women increasingly began to smoke during the 1930s and 40s in response to the independent, glamorous, and sexy image of smoking, as portrayed by cinema actresses such as Greta Garbo and Bette Davis. At the end of the 20th century, most new smokers in the West are likely to be female, despite the fatal damage to their lungs and the high risk of lung cancer.

Bette Davis demonstrates the habit she glamorized in her earlier films.

Stays constricted the lungs and caused a woman to faint easily.

RESPIRATORY BEHAVIOR

Yawning is a reflex action that forces oxygen into a woman's lungs. It results when the oxygen supply in the tissues is depleted.

Sneezing occurs when irritating particles, such as dust and pollen, settle on the sensitive mucous membranes in the nasal cavity. This triggers the airways to close and the respiratory muscles to expel air forcefully.

Coughing is the body's response to substances such as dust, which irritate the respiratory tract.

Hiccuping results when the nerves that control the DIAPHRAGM become irritated (because of eating too fast, for example) and contract involuntarily. As air is inhaled, the GLOTTIS (the space between the vocal cords) clicks shut.

Hyperventilating usually occurs when anxiety causes a woman to breathe in a rapid and shallow rhythm. This removes too much carbon dioxide from the body.

COLDS AND INFLUENZA

Common colds are caused by a virus. A typical cold lasts seven days and may be caused by one of over 200 different viruses.

Influenza has four major strains, all of which have a tendency to mutate. Symptoms are similar to those of a cold, but include others, such as aching muscles.

CHOKING

If a foreign body becomes lodged in the airways, preventing a woman from breathing, prompt action will be needed to prevent her from choking to death. (A choking victim's skin will start to turn bluish and she will clutch at her throat.) As a first step, strike the victim's back several times between the shoulder blades; a young child should be held across the lap, with her head below her torso. If the victim is an older child or an adult and the obstruction remains, the Heimlich maneuver (below) should be used.

Heimlich maneuver
The force of the fists should be applied to the abdomen, not the ribcage. This should be done only in emergencies. It carries a slight risk of damage to the victim's liver or spleen.

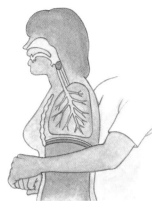

Clasp the victim
Clench your hands and place them under the victim's sternum.

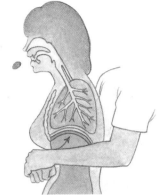

Compress the torso
Quickly thrust your clenched hands upward and inward.

LUNG DISEASE

LUNG CANCER

The most prevalent malignancy in women, lung cancer incidence peaks in women at 70, compared with 65 in men. Cigarette smoking is the major cause of lung cancer; the younger the age at which a woman starts to smoke, and the greater the number of cigarettes she smokes per day, the higher her chances of developing cancer. Smoking damages the CILIA in the cell lining so that the only way of clearing mucus from the throat and lungs is by coughing – hence the smoker's cough. Lung cancer occurs because the respiratory system's mechanism for clearing debris and bacteria is damaged and the immune system impaired. The lungs continue to grow new air sacs well into young adulthood, but teenagers who smoke stop air sac formation, and their lungs never mature to full capacity. Lung cancer has a low cure rate; 7% of sufferers survive after five years.

TUBERCULOSIS

This infectious disease results when mycobacteria in airborne droplets (from sneezing or coughing), are inhaled and cause inflammation in the lungs. The infection can then spread in the LYMPHATIC SYSTEM and be fatal; this development occurs in only 5% of cases.

IT'S A FACT

Together the two lungs weigh about 750g (1½ lb); only slightly heavier than a normal box of sugar.

◆

If all the ALVEOLI from both lungs were opened up and laid flat, they would cover a tennis court.

◆

When a woman is a newborn, her lungs are rose pink in color; by the time she is an adult, they are slate gray because of dust and pollution.

◆

A sneeze can reach a speed of 160km (100 miles) an hour and can travel up to 4m (13ft).

Lymphatic System

THE BODY'S IMMUNITY

Most infections enter the body through the DIGESTIVE SYSTEM, RESPIRATORY SYSTEM, urogenital tract, or skin. The immune system consists of white blood cells made by the SPLEEN, LYMPH NODES, and sometimes in bone marrow, and antibodies (proteins made by the white blood cells). These work together to identify and attack any invading foreign bodies. There are five types of white blood cells defending the body, and they all act in different ways. NEUTROPHILS engulf bacteria; EOSINOPHILS combat allergic reactions and detoxify foreign particles; BASOPHILS release anticoagulants; and MACROPHAGES in the tissues (derived from blood monocytes) swallow large foreign particles whole. LYMPHOCYTES produce antibodies when stimulated by antigens. The antibodies work with the white blood cells to eliminate infection and also help in the removal of cancerous or diseased cells.

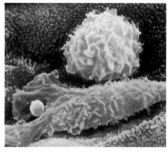

Macrophages in the lung
The macrophage in its normal spherical shape is at the top; the one beneath it has elongated itself to engulf a small, round particle (green).

WOMAN'S LYMPHATIC SYSTEM

An essential part of the body's defenses, the lymphatic system manufactures most white blood cells (see THE BODY'S IMMUNITY, left) and antibodies, cleanses body fluids, and drains excess fluid and TOXINS from body tissues. It also digests fats and transports nutrients. The lymphatic system consists of lymph (a clear, watery fluid that bathes all tissues of the body and is derived from BLOOD PLASMA), Peyer's patches (lymphoid tissue in the intestines), lymphatic capillaries, lymph vessels, LYMPH NODES (glands), the SPLEEN, TONSILS, ADENOIDS, and THYMUS GLAND.

Lymph is primarily moved around the lymphatic vessels by the pressure of breathing and muscular movements, rather than by being pumped in the way that the arterial blood is by the heart. This means that the efficiency of the lymphatic system is related to a woman's activity level and general fitness; a sluggish or overloaded lymphatic system may be one of the causes of CELLULITE.

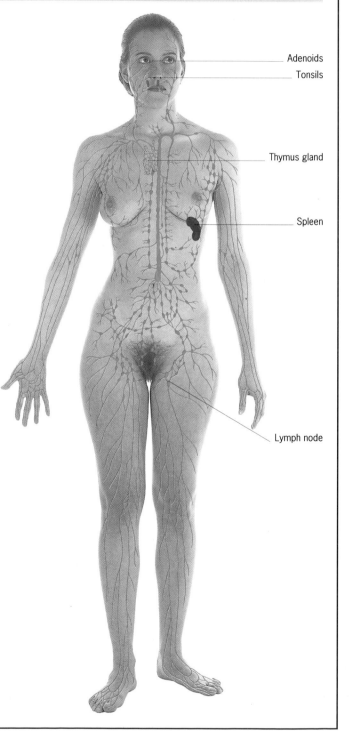

Adenoids

Tonsils

Thymus gland

Spleen

Lymph node

Lymphatic circulation
The circulation of the lymphatic system extends throughout a woman's body. Lymph nodes tend to be grouped together in clumps, particularly along the spine, around the groin, and in the abdomen, neck, and armpits.

SPLEEN

One of the main filters of the blood, the spongy spleen is about the size of the heart and is capable of holding 1 liter (1 quart) of blood. In addition to filtering the blood, the spleen removes old blood cells and also stores blood for times when the body's requirements increase, such as during exercise. The way that blood enters the spleen is unique; tiny ARTERIOLES empty the blood directly into the tissue of the spleen without passing via a network of capillaries, as is usual in any other organ. This means that the LYMPHATIC SYSTEM is able to come into direct contact with any abnormal substances present in the blood, so that antibodies can be formed immediately. It also means that old cells can be destroyed by the reticular (red pulp) and phagocytic cells of the spleen.

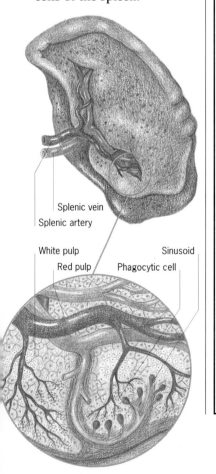

Splenic vein
Splenic artery

White pulp
Red pulp
Sinusoid
Phagocytic cell

HOW THE SYSTEM WORKS

The lymphatic system is composed of lymphatic capillaries, lymph nodes, the SPLEEN (left), THYMUS, TONSILS, ADENOIDS, and Peyer's patches (lymphoid tissue in the intestines). Lymphatic capillaries are tiny, open-ended, one-way vessels that collect fluid (which is known as lymph once it is in the lymphatic system) from the blood capillaries and transport it to and from the lymph nodes. Spread at various points along the lymphatic vessels, lymph nodes filter the lymph and destroy any microorganisms or TOXINS in it. They produce extra WHITE BLOOD CELLS to fight infection (causing swollen glands). The tonsils and adenoids are thought to work together in responding to foreign bodies present in anything swallowed (tonsils) or inhaled (adenoids). They produce white blood cells in response to infection, and are most active during childhood. Lymphatic vessels connect lymph nodes with other lymphatic tissue, such as the spleen, and are responsible for returning the filtered and cleansed lymph back into the blood system.

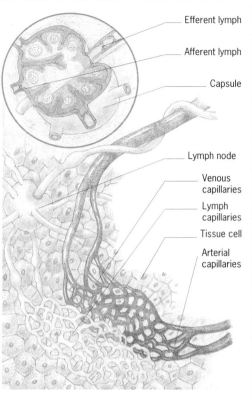

Efferent lymph
Afferent lymph
Capsule
Lymph node
Venous capillaries
Lymph capillaries
Tissue cell
Arterial capillaries

LYMPHATIC DISORDERS

LUPUS ERYTHEMATOSUS

A disorder in which the body's immune system attacks tissues, the skin, and the organs, such as the kidneys. It is nine times more common among women than men, and most often affects women of childbearing age. Lupus erythematosus is more common among NEGROIDS and MONGOLOIDS than CAUCASOIDS and, in high-risk groups, its incidence may be as high as one woman in 250. The symptoms tend to recur cyclically and include a red, circular or blotchy (almost butterfly-shaped) skin rash on the face, neck, and the scalp; nausea; fatigue; fever; loss of appetite and weight; ANEMIA; and joint pain. In severe cases, there may be kidney failure, inflammation of the lungs or of the membranes surrounding the heart, and arthritis. There is thought to be a genetic influence.

MONONUCLEOSIS

Also known as the kissing disease (it is spread by direct contact), mononucleosis is caused by a virus and usually develops during adolescence and early adulthood, when the immune system is at its most active. Symptoms are enlarged LYMPH NODES (swollen glands), severe sore throat (caused by inflamed tonsils), a fever, and an enlarged SPLEEN. Mild liver damage may also occur.

HIV

Infection with HIV (human immunodeficiency virus) results in a deficiency of the immune system and leads to AIDS. The virus attacks the immune system and is spread by sexual intercourse, sharing hypodermic needles, transfusions of infected blood, and in breast milk; practicing SAFE SEX is essential. AIDS has been fatal in all known cases.

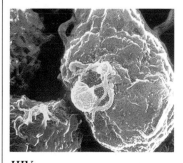

HIV
The HIV (yellow) buds from the plasma membrane (blue) of an infected lymphocyte.

INDIGESTION AND HEARTBURN

Indigestion is usually caused by eating food that is too rich or fatty, by eating too much or too fast, or by tension and anxiety. It is relatively common. Symptoms include GAS, colic (abdominal cramps), bloating, and nausea. Some women are especially prone to severe indigestion when under STRESS.

Heartburn is a painful burning sensation that occurs when acidic stomach juices regurgitate into the ESOPHAGUS (food pipe) through the CARDIAC SPHINCTER. This happens when the stomach is overloaded or compressed, or as a result of a hiatus hernia (rupture of a part of the stomach through the diaphragm). Many women suffer heartburn when they are pregnant because the growing fetus compresses the stomach upward.

WOMAN'S DIGESTIVE SYSTEM

Food is broken up in the mouth by the action of the teeth and further reduced by enzymes produced by the SALIVARY GLANDS. It forms into a ball (bolus) when it reaches a suitable consistency and temperature. The bolus is then swallowed and pushed down the esophagus by its contracting muscles. Food takes 4–8 seconds to pass from the mouth to the stomach; liquids take 1–2 seconds. Food is further digested in the stomach until it is semiliquid (known as CHYME), and then it passes through the small intestine, where digestive juices from the liver, gall bladder, and pancreas break it down into absorbable nutrients. What is left continues through the large intestine, where most of the water content is absorbed and it gradually becomes solid waste. This waste matter collects in the rectum and is finally expelled through the anal sphincters.

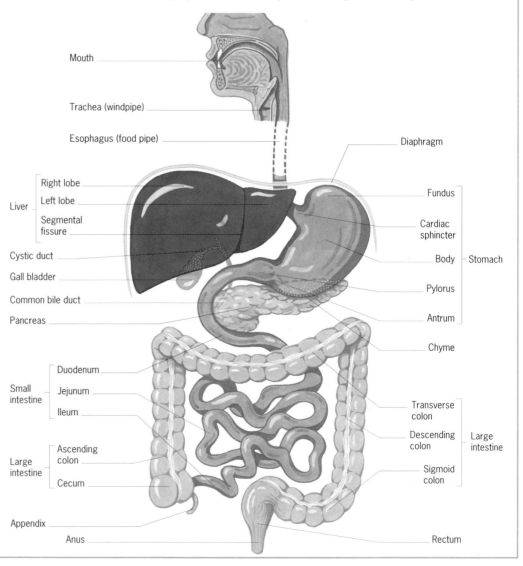

Mouth

Trachea (windpipe)

Esophagus (food pipe)

Diaphragm

Right lobe
Left lobe
Segmental fissure
Liver
Cystic duct
Gall bladder
Common bile duct
Pancreas

Fundus
Cardiac sphincter
Body — Stomach
Pylorus
Antrum

Chyme

Duodenum
Jejunum
Ileum
Small intestine

Ascending colon
Cecum
Large intestine

Appendix
Anus

Transverse colon
Descending colon — Large intestine
Sigmoid colon

Rectum

STOMACH

A muscular bag lying behind the lower ribs, the crescent-shaped stomach is about 25cm (10in) long when it is empty, but distends and changes shape depending on how much food it contains. The stomach wall is made up of three layers of muscle lined with alkaline mucus, which prevents the acid secreted by the stomach from damaging the stomach lining. Ulcers occur when the mucosal lining of the stomach wall becomes damaged. The stomach normally takes 3–6 hours to digest a meal; warm, thoroughly chewed food will be digested faster than chilled or chunky food. Fluids pass through the stomach quickest of all. Once food is in the stomach, it is broken down into a semi-liquid pulp called chyme. The stomach does this by kneading, tossing, and churning the food with the acidic gastric secretions.

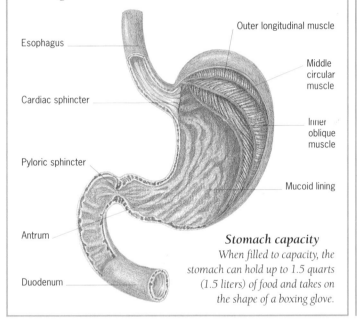

Stomach capacity

When filled to capacity, the stomach can hold up to 1.5 quarts (1.5 liters) of food and takes on the shape of a boxing glove.

LIVER

The largest internal organ in the body, the liver, weighs about 1.5kg (3lb) and has two lobes. The left lobe overlies the top of the stomach; the right lobe is larger and is sub-divided into three sections. The liver performs over 500 different functions, including stabilizing the blood glucose level, manufacturing bile and cholesterol, detoxifying the body, building enzymes, and processing waste products. Vitamins A, B, D, E, and K are all stored in the liver after being broken down by BILE (below left) in the DUODENUM. The liver is unique in being the only organ that is supplied with blood from two sources; the hepatic artery supplies oxygen-rich blood from the heart, while the portal vein supplies nutrient-rich blood direct from the STOMACH (left) and the intestines. Nutrients are processed, and then stored to be released as the body needs them. Most unusable substances are rendered harmless by detoxification.

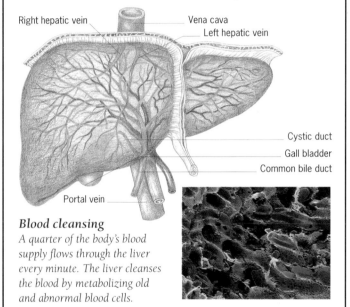

Blood cleansing

A quarter of the body's blood supply flows through the liver every minute. The liver cleanses the blood by metabolizing old and abnormal blood cells.

GALL BLADDER

Bile (which was traditionally known as gall) is produced by the liver and stored in the gall bladder before being released into the duodenum. Bile contains salts that have a detergent effect upon fats in CHYME (semidigested food), breaking them into minute droplets so that the enzymes in the pancreatic juices can digest them. Bile also renders cholesterol soluble and enhances the absorption of fatty acids and fat-soluble vitamins (such as Vitamin A).

PANCREAS

Besides having endocrine cells (which secrete hormones), the pancreas has a central duct surrounded by acinar (exocrine) cells, which secrete 1.5 liters (1.5 quarts) of digestive juice a day into the DUODENUM. The pancreatic juice contains enzymes, which digest proteins, fats, and carbohydrates, and is alkaline in order to neutralize the acidic CHYME (above).

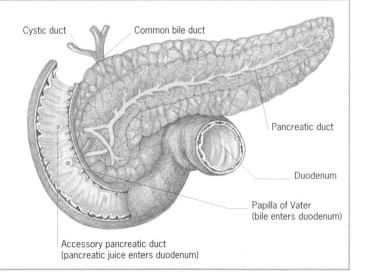

WOMAN VS. ANIMAL

A woman is an omnivore and has a medium-sized digestive tract that can cope with both animal and plant matter. In contrast, carnivores, such as cats, have very short digestive tracts because pure protein can be broken down relatively easily .

◆

A woman has only one stomach, while herbivorous ruminants, such as cows, have four. These enable cows to break down the cellulose in grass efficiently.

◆

Many birds deliberately swallow grit, which assists the breakdown of food in their crops before it enters their stomachs.

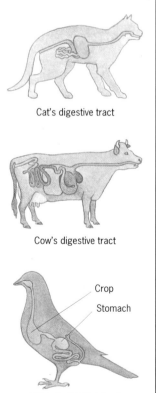

Cat's digestive tract

Cow's digestive tract

Crop

Stomach

Pigeon's digestive tract

THE SMALL INTESTINE

As CHYME enters the duodenum (first part of the small intestine), the liver, pancreas, and gall bladder release their enzymes. In addition, the small intestine produces mucus that helps protect the duodenum from acid damage. The inner surface of the small intestine is covered by villi (fingerlike projections), which are in turn covered with microvilli (hairlike projections). The muscles surrounding the intestine contract every 3–4 seconds, churning and mixing the chyme. The chyme takes 4–6 hours to pass through the small intestine, and during this time most of the nutrients are absorbed. Carbohydrates are absorbed quickly, while fats and protein take much longer.

Inside the intestine
Like aquatic plant life, the villi and microvilli sway continuously in the intestines. They increase enormously the amount of surface area in the intestines that is available for the absorption of nutrients from the chyme.

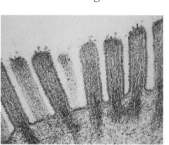

HEMORRHOIDS (PILES)

Distended veins in the lining of the anus, hemorrhoids can be internal (at the beginning of the anus), or external (at the anal entrance or protruding outside the anus, when they are known as prolapsed). They are very common during pregnancy, with increased blood flow and congestion in the pelvic area. They can also be caused by straining while passing stools or by a diet containing too much refined food, which fails to provide adequate amounts of fiber and, therefore, normal stools.

Symptoms include discomfort or pain, and sometimes blood on passing stools.

THE APPENDIX

Near the junction of the small and large intestines lies the pouchlike appendix, which is 7.5cm (3in) long. The appendix seems to have evolved as an "infection controller," in a way similar to the TONSILS (it contains a large amount of LYMPHATIC tissue) and, like them, it becomes significant only when it is inflamed – a condition known as appendicitis. Symptoms of appendicitis include sudden abdominal tenderness or pain, nausea, vomiting, and HALITOSIS (bad breath).

A ruptured appendix will lead to serious, widespread abdominal infection. Surgery to remove an inflamed appendix is immediate, but straightforward.

THE LARGE INTESTINE

The large intestine (bowel) reabsorbs water and passes waste out of the body as feces. Mucus secreted by the bowel binds together the waste material and ensures its smooth passage. Living in the colon are beneficial bacteria that digest nutrients and manufacture certain vitamins. The rectum is basically a storage pouch for fecal matter, and is a muscular tube 13cm (5in) long that expands to hold feces and contracts to expel them. The feces are further lubricated with mucus produced by glands in the rectal lining. The anus consists of two sphincters. The internal sphincter is controlled by the nervous system. The external sphincter is under conscious control and can be kept closed until it is convenient to pass feces.

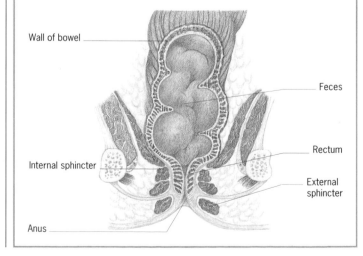

Wall of bowel

Internal sphincter

Anus

Feces

Rectum

External sphincter

GAS

Burping (belching) is usually caused by air being swallowed while eating or drinking, either because of a nervous habit, talking with the mouth full, or eating or drinking too quickly. Burping can help to relieve INDIGESTION.

Flatulence is gas expelled through the rectum. A considerable amount of gas is produced every day in the normal digestive system, although most of it is absorbed by the intestines.

URINARY SYSTEM ANATOMY

The urinary system is composed of the two KIDNEYS (below left), which secrete urine; the ureters, the tubes that convey urine from the kidneys into the urinary bladder, where it is stored temporarily; and the urethra, through which urine is discharged from the bladder.

It is the function of the kidneys to select and remove unwanted products from the blood and expel them. Millions of nephrons together form the kidney. Each nephron (below left) is composed of a knot of thin-walled blood vessels, called glomeruli, and a renal tubule. Each of the glomeruli filters substances from the blood plasma into the renal tubule, where selective reabsorption of some of the substances takes place until the fluid has the composition of urine and is fed back to the collecting renal tubule. This then carries the urine through a network of increasingly large ducts into the ureter.

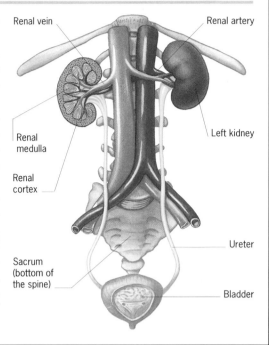

Renal vein · Renal artery · Left kidney · Renal medulla · Renal cortex · Sacrum (bottom of the spine) · Ureter · Bladder

KIDNEYS

Each adult kidney weighs about 170g (6oz), and is made up of an outer cortex and inner medulla containing millions of nephrons. The kidneys filter the entire blood volume about 40 times per day, converting the waste matter to about 1 liter (1 quart) of urine. In so doing they excrete the waste products of metabolism, regulate the body's concentration of water and salt, and maintain the acid balance of the plasma.

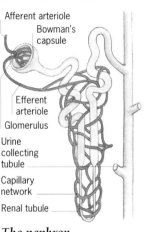

Afferent arteriole · Bowman's capsule · Efferent arteriole · Glomerulus · Urine collecting tubule · Capillary network · Renal tubule

The nephron
Each kidney contains millions of nephrons, which filter waste matter from the blood.

BLADDER

This is a muscular bag that expands to collect urine, which is delivered to the bladder via the ureters. At the bottom of each ureter there is a SPHINCTER that allows passage of urine into the bladder. When the bladder is full, nerves send a message to the brain transmitting the urge to urinate. The sphincter from the bladder can be opened under conscious control, allowing urine to pass into the URETHRA and out of the body. When empty, the bladder is a funnel-shaped sac 7.5cm (3in) long. When full, it may expand to 12.5cm (5in) long or more, and becomes almost round in shape.

TOILETS

The disposal of bodily waste has been a concern of human beings since the earliest civilizations. Simple latrines, complete with sewers to carry away waste matter, have been found in the ruins of the civilizations in the Indus Valley (2,000 years BC) and in ancient Babylon. Flushing toilets were usual in Minoan and Roman times; modern flushing toilets did not appear until 1889. In medieval Europe, the castle garderobe (toilet) was a simple affair, consisting of a hole in the wall or floor and a chute through which waste descended to a midden or a moat. In the 18th century, Madame de Pompadour had three sumptuously decorated commodes, complete with padded velvet seats. Her lover, Louis XV, would often grant audiences at his "throne."

Communal Roman toilets
The latrines in Roman times were often communal; going to the toilet was a social event.

Victorian toilet
As decorative as domestic toilets were, British sewers posed a threat to health until the 1870s.

GALLSTONES

Generally occurring in the GALL BLADDER, the most common type of gallstones are composed of cholesterol, although some contain BILE or calcium. Usually 1–10 gallstones form at one time, ranging in size from 1–25mm (0.05–1in); the surfaces can be either smooth or rough.

Gallstones are three times more common in women than in men, and high-risk groups include women who are overweight or who have had many children.

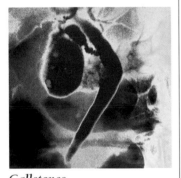

Gallstones
When the composition of bile is altered, tiny particles form and increase in the gall bladder. These develop into gallstones.

HALITOSIS (BAD BREATH)

Although there are a number of causes of halitosis, the most common are food-related. These include small particles of food becoming trapped in the teeth; drinking tea, coffee, or alcohol, and eating strong-flavored substances, such as spices, onions, and garlic. Smoking, sinusitis, and DIABETES can also cause bad breath.

Using mouthwash or spray will only mask halitosis, not cure it.

IRREGULAR BOWELS

Individual women pass feces at different rates. Irregularity can be the result of TOXINS (such as alcohol), disease, or hormones (such as during pregnancy or before MENSTRUATION).

Diarrhea results when CHYME travels through the digestive tract too fast for water to be reabsorbed. A prolonged period of diarrhea can lead to dehydration.

Constipation is when feces become very hard and difficult to pass as a result of food remaining in the colon for so long that an excessive amount of water is reabsorbed.

IRRITABLE BOWEL SYNDROME

Causing intermittent abdominal pain, a swollen abdomen, reduced appetite, and IRREGULAR BOWELS (left), irritable bowel syndrome is generally the result of a disturbance of the muscles around the LARGE INTESTINE. Irritable bowel syndrome is twice as common in women as in men. It usually starts in adulthood, and it tends to recur. It is thought that emotional STRESS and anxiety are the main causative factors and that it may be linked to an individual's inability to express particular emotions, such as anger.

NAUSEA AND VOMITING

The body's normal mechanism for rapidly getting rid of poisonous or dangerous substances, vomiting can also occur for other reasons, such as anxiety, foul smells, pain, motion sickness, pregnancy, infections, some drugs, or after eating or drinking too much. Vomiting is usually preceded by nausea, which stops the secretion of gastric juices and halts digestion. The normal contractions of the stomach cease and then the waves of contraction in the DUODENUM are reversed. Symptoms include salivating, sweating, becoming pale, and an increased heartbeat. During vomiting, the abdominal, diaphragmatic, and rib-cage muscles contract in the same way as when taking a deep breath. Pressure on the stomach is increased, pushing the contents up the ESOPHAGUS and out of the mouth.

DISEASES AND DISORDERS

Jaundice occurs when the liver is unable to remove a yellow pigment called bilirubin from the blood. This pigment builds up in the bloodstream and causes the skin, the whites of the eyes, and the tears to become yellowish. Jaundice can also result if GALL-STONES (above left) form and obstruct the COMMON BILE DUCT.

Hepatitis is an inflammation of the liver, accompanied by liver cell damage or death. It is usually caused by a viral infection; less often by some drugs, chemicals, or poisons. JAUNDICE is normally the first symptom.

Cirrhosis of the liver is a disease normally caused by chronic damage, which is usually the result of alcohol consumption. It is a serious condition that kills about one person in 70 in the West every year. Women are more susceptible to the disease than men.

Cystic fibrosis is an inherited disease that results when the PANCREAS fails to produce enzymes necessary to digest fats, as well as the overproduction of mucus by the glands in the lungs. Severe cystic fibrosis results in malnutrition and fatal lung infections.

Stomach cancer is generally thought to be linked to the consumption of salted, pickled, or smoked food. It is more common in the Far East than it is in the Western world.

Cancer of the intestines rarely affects the SMALL INTESTINE, but is very common in the LARGE INTESTINE. Contributory factors appear to be inherited susceptibility and a diet rich in meat and animal fats and poor in fiber.

Bladder cancer is linked to smoking and to exposure to compounds used in the rubber, printing, and textile industries. It is more common in industrialized countries and among urban dwellers. Although at present it affects three times more men than women, this is likely to change as a result of the increasing numbers of women smokers.

THE
*I*NNER
WOMAN

INNER WOMAN

INSIDE A WOMAN'S MIND

The character of a woman, how she reacts to external stimuli and interacts with the world around her, is determined by her mind. Inherited elements ("nature"), such as intelligence, and elements that she has been taught ("nurture"), such as learned patterns of behavior, all contribute to the individual woman's personality.

EMOTIONS

Triggered by internal or external stimuli, emotions are signals that pass from the central areas of the brain (known loosely as the LIMBIC SYSTEM) to the CEREBRUM and back again. The appropriate hormone is then released by the ENDOCRINE SYSTEM and the emotion can be "experienced." Emotions are essential to life – they enable women to react to STRESS, to achieve goals when interacting with others, and to act when there is no time to "think." Basic emotions are short-term but can become long-term in response to some circumstances (happiness can turn into love, for example), especially where the specific trigger for the emotion is known. Some emotions are generally viewed as "good" (such as love), while others are usually viewed as "bad" (such as anger). All emotions, however, are neutral, and contain the potential for both good and bad, depending on how the individual woman responds.

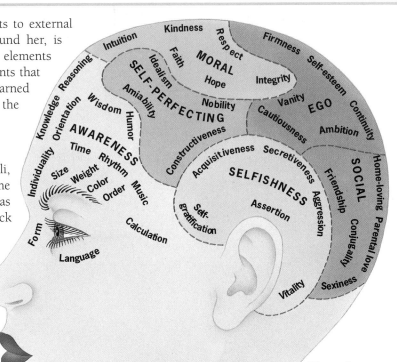

Phrenology
This study, which has no scientific basis, assigns emotions and abilities are to specific areas of the brain.

SENSES

A woman is mainly sight-dependent, but her other senses are extremely important. Touch is the most fundamental sense, and arguably the most essential – without the ability to feel a woman would be unable to stand upright or walk, and when deprived of the power of touch, babies do not develop properly and may even die. Smell tends to be the most evocative sense, mainly because it connects straight to the limbic system without being processed by other areas of the brain, as is the case with sight and sound. Some women have a condition known as synesthesia. This is when the limbic system interprets sensory stimuli differently than normal.

A musical note or key, for example, may be seen as a specific color; a taste may be experienced as a shape. Individual numbers or letters are often seen as particular colors.

Women are generally recognized as having more acute senses than men. Some studies have suggested that the least touch-sensitive woman is more sensitive to touch than the most touch-sensitive man. Stereo manufacturers use women to check the sound quality of their products.

INTUITION

The ability of many women to perceive the subconscious signals in any human contact can appear uncanny to many men. Research suggests that intuition is probably the combination of a woman's greater sensual sensitivity and the greater integration of functions of the two sides of the brain.

PSYCHOLOGICAL HISTORY

Woman is the primary sex and the blueprint of the human race itself. All life is basically female; "triggers" are required for mammalian fetuses to become male, and there are some people who are physically female but genetically male. In most parts of the world, however, women have been discriminated against as the inferior and inadequate sex for centuries. Strongly identified with nature through her procreative abilities, a woman's (and nature's) power was perceived as threatening to a man. Male-based religions developed as a form of control. They promulgated a male supreme creator and man created in his image. Woman was therefore subordinate. Over the centuries, and around the world, a woman's status in comparison with a man's was eroded until she became, in common parlance, the "second sex."

This cumulative history has had a profound effect on modern female psychology. Despite the many changes that occurred in Western countries during the 20th century, unwritten codes of female behavior often still operate subconsciously. Although these codes are impossible to satisfy, many women attempt to alter themselves to fit them, thus setting themselves up for inevitable failure.

Adam and Eve

In the Bible, man's response to the unalterable (and unpalatable) fact that he was produced from a woman's body was to proclaim that the first man was created by God in his image. The first woman (Eve) was created from the man's (Adam's) body and ultimately led man (the species) into sin and damnation.

THE FEMALE CODE OF GOODNESS

All women inherit ideas and codes of behavior about what it is to be a woman. These are absorbed from the outset of a girl's life and become a "natural" part of how a woman behaves. American family therapists Claudia Bepko and Jo-Ann Krestan have identified what they term the female code of goodness (below).

The code of goodness	Maxim	Result
Be attractive.	A woman is as good as she looks.	External approval is more important than her internal satisfaction.
Be a lady.	A good woman stays in control.	Suppresses anger, underplays her achievements, doesn't compete.
Be unselfish and of service.	A good woman lives to give.	Works for the good of everyone else and feels guilty for saying no.
Make relationships work.	A good woman loves first, most, and unconditionally.	Takes on sole responsibility for all her relationships.
Be competent without complaint.	A good woman does it all and never looks overwhelmed.	Juggles everything and everybody and sets impossibly high standards.

Mary Wollstonecraft.

WOMAN VS. ANIMAL

A woman's feelings and emotions issue from the core of her brain. This is the oldest part of the brain, and its basic structure is shared by women with all other animal species.

Emotion is believed to be the prerequisite for thought and action; recent research suggests that consciousness (the ability to perceive oneself as separate from the rest of the world) is the result of emotion ("I feel, therefore I am"), rather than intelligence ("I think, therefore I am"), as has long been held.

If emotion is seen as the force that propels an organism to react to an unexpected, possibly life-threatening, situation, small creatures, such as birds and mice, as well as women and the large mammals, can be held to have emotions and therefore to be conscious.

This has been found to be the case in a recent work published in the US by Marion Stamp Dawkins on domestic chickens.

She formulated the idea of "asking" the fowl how much something mattered to them by making them work to achieve it. Dawkins found that what mattered most to chickens (what they would work hardest to obtain) was a nest box or a scratchable floor, over and above food or companionship.

FEMALE INTELLIGENCE

Like personality, intelligence is the result of a woman's genetic inheritance, combined with the way in which she is socialized and educated. Research has defined seven areas of intellectual competence (right), which are considered to be relatively independent of one another. Intelligence is not set at the same level throughout a woman's life; it develops with the effort to learn and understand (such as occurs during childhood) and with mental stimulation (when exposed to unfamiliar information and ideas), and decreases with lack of stimulation and activity (such as during old age). Growing older does not preclude exposure to new ideas, nor does it necessarily mean a loss of intellectual ability. In addition to these variations, there are differences in each woman's inherent ability, with some women being quicker and more perceptive than others. Studies indicate that the average woman tends to be quicker on the uptake than the average man.

Intellectual competence

- *Linguistic: sensitivity to the meaning and order of words.*
- *Logical-mathematical: ability to handle chains of reasoning and recognize patterns of order.*
- *Musical: sensitivity to pitch, melody, rhythm, and tone.*
- *Bodily-kinesthetic: awareness of the body; ability to use the body skillfully and to handle objects adroitly.*
- *Spatial: ability to perceive the world accurately and re-create or transform aspects of that world.*
- *Interpersonal: ability to understand people and relationships.*
- *Intrapersonal: access to one's emotional life as a means to understanding oneself and others.*

HUMOR AND COMEDY

Mae West encapsulated bawdy female humor.

Comedy is a product of its culture and looks at familiar situations, people, behavior, and attitudes from an unexpected angle. Jokes and comedy are also used to express forbidden or frightening ideas (hence racist or sexist jokes).

Women are less likely than men to tell jokes to large groups. They also tend to feel more comfortable joking and "taking the floor" in small (preferably all-female) groups, where status is more equal. Women who do tell jokes to large, mixed groups often come from families, upbringings, and ethnic backgrounds in which oral expression is highly valued and encouraged.

COMMUNICATION

Language is thought by many anthropologists to have been created and refined by women. There are many myths to this effect in different cultures.

The style in which modern women and men communicate varies. Studies indicate that women are more likely to feel relaxed in a small group, where they can feel intimate and connected to the other people present. Their conversation usually centers on "troubles talk" (sharing their own personal problems, and those of people they know), and concentrates on the detailed and the domestic. Linguistic psychologists, such as Professor Deborah Tanner, call this type of conversation "private" talk and note that it makes women much more able than men to connect intimately with other people and to use small talk to maintain a conversation. Men, on the other hand, tend to prefer larger groups and will use "public" speaking even with friends – monologue performances rather than a conversational to-and-fro – and use language as a powerful tool to establish status.

Both styles have their positive and negative points. "Private" talk establishes rapport and makes the participant feel that she is not alone or singular. If a time comes when there is nothing to talk about that reinforces shared values, however, the information exchanged may be used in a damaging way.

"Public" talk establishes respect and creates independence. It can, however, be used to dominate others and prevents the speaker from becoming intimate with others.

Maria Montessori devised the Montessori method of education through communication and play.

Gossiping is private speaking and could be correctly described as information gathering and social linking. People gossip because they are fascinated by what other human beings think and do and want to learn what is acceptable behavior in their society. In general, public life in the West is becoming increasingly "private." There is an insatiable interest in the private lives of the rich and famous, reflected in the rise of "gossipy" magazines. The modern tendency to spend less time communicating as a community has led to the immense popularity of soap operas as substitutes for real communities.

Over the garden fence

Gossiping allows women to gather information on others not present and enables social relationships to become stronger and more intimately connected. In addition, by talking about, and agreeing upon, the behavior of those not present, the people who are gossiping reinforce their shared values and view of the world. A difference should be drawn, however, between good gossiping (talking about) and bad gossiping (talking against).

FEMALE CREATIVITY

Women are intrinsically creative and have always managed to find ways of expressing themselves, despite being barred from the stereotypically "male" artistic fields for much of Western history. Women are likely to have made the first pots or tools out of necessity, and their creativity in later times was often solely restricted to those areas connected with the home. While some women did manage to excel in nondomestic areas, their work has been credited to men in most instances (Fanny Mendelssohn published some of her musical compositions under her brother's name; author Marian Evans used the pseudonym George Eliot). The birth of language and the written word is ascribed to a

2000 BC pinch pot.

woman in many myths worldwide. Medusa, for example, gave the alphabet to Hercules, while Queen Isis gave it to the Egyptians, and the priestess-goddess Kali invented the Sanskrit alphabet. The world's first known novel, *The Tale of Genji*, was written in Japan by the Lady Murasaki in 1004.

Scientific ability and discovery rely to a great extent on creativity. The earliest healers were women, because of their involvement with children and their position as the plant gatherers. Later, despite centuries of male persecution and discrimination, some women still managed to succeed, such as the 16th-century Swiss surgeon Marie Colinet, who pioneered CESAREAN surgery, and the early-20th-century French physicist, Marie Curie, who won the Nobel Prize twice.

The creative quilt

Undeniably useful and practical, quilts were also important female works of art, as well as historical and social records. In certain groups in 18th-century America, a bride was expected to make 12 quilts for her bottom drawer; the 13th would be her marriage quilt. Certain quilt designs, such as the Whigs' Defeat, were made by disenfranchised American women to express their political affiliations. The Drunkard's Path design was often made by members of the 19th-century temperance movement. The above is a 19th-century American "Feathered Star and Garden Maze" quilt.

Aphra Behn (far left)

As well known in her day as her contemporary William Shakespeare, Aphra Behn wrote the first known novel in English in 1680. She also composed poetry, wrote one play a year for nearly 20 years, and translated French literature into English. A one-time spy and experienced world traveler, Behn was the first woman known to have made her living as a professional writer.

Barbara Hepworth (left)

This distinguished British sculptor once described her celebrated carving as a "biological necessity." She was a key member of Unit One in the 1930s, a group that brought together the most outstanding abstract artists of the period.

PERSONALITY

The definition of personality is that it is the sum of the emotions, thoughts, and experiences of the individual. Although each woman is born with a unique set of characteristics, her personality is then molded and influenced by her environment. So personality is not as firmly fixed as many believe; a woman has the potential to modify and alter her personality traits in response to stimuli.

What exactly constitutes personality has intrigued human beings throughout history; different methods have been used to try to predict different personality types. Some examples are PHRENOLOGY, astrology (right and below), graphology (handwriting analysis), and analysis of body build (ENDOMORPHIC women are thought to be relaxed and sociable, MESOMORPHIC women energetic and assertive, ECTOMORPHIC women introverted and artistic).

Chinese fire horse
An inauspicious year for Chinese female babies to be born was the year of the fire horse, which occurs every 60 years (the last was 1966). The personality of the fire horse is seen as argumentative, hot-headed, and dominant. Male fire horses were regarded as very lucky, but up until the 20th century, most newborn female fire horses were killed.

Western astrology
The first known reference to astrology dates from Babylonian times, in 1700 BC. Then, astrology was used to predict the fate of a nation or of its ruler. Today, astrology is usually used to define a woman's personality and to highlight her strengths and weaknesses. It may also be used to determine auspicious and inauspicious times in her life, suitable mates, courses of action, and a future career. Positions of the planets at the time of a woman's birth aid astrological interpretation.

SPIRITUALITY

Worldwide, women throughout history have been more connected to nature and the mystical and spiritual forces of life than men have been. This is probably a consequence of their intimate link with the rhythms of life and death through MENSTRUATION, pregnancy, childbirth, and child care. Women generally tend to be more religious than men, and to have greater commitment to causes, particularly ones that have the potential to improve, or threaten, the world they live in or to affect the lives of those they love.

Greenham Common
During the 1980s and 90s, as part of a campaign to force the UK government to remove US nuclear warheads and return the Common to the people, many women camped out for years in terrible conditions. Media reaction was extremely hostile.

PHOBIAS

When a particular object or situation is regarded with intense fear and panic, it is known as a phobia. There are hundreds of different phobias, affecting both men and women. Women are more likely than men to suffer from arachnophobia (fear of spiders), ophidiophobia (of snakes), and agoraphobia (of open spaces). Specific phobias, such as a fear of a particular species (spiders, snakes) or situations (enclosed spaces, heights), are the most common. These phobias tend to run in families and appear to be learned rather than inherited. Some anthropologists, however, think that some phobias are so widespread that they may be part of a racial memory. Ophidiophobia, for example, is said to have originated during the AQUATIC PERIOD, since most sufferers say they hate snakes because they are "slimy." Land snakes, however, are dry-skinned, unlike water snakes and electric eels, which are slimy and much more dangerous than most land snakes. More complex situational phobias, such as agoraphobia, are thought to arise from intense anxiety experienced during childhood, although the phobia may not become apparent until adulthood.

WOMAN VS. MAN

Although men are more likely to be murdered than are women (a ratio of 3:2), women are more likely to be murdered by their partners than men (43% of female murder victims compared with 9% of males). They are also less likely to be murdered by people outside the family (11% of female murder victims compared with 27% of males). Women make up the vast majority of rape victims, and many more rapes than those cited below go unreported. In Canada, rape is classified as one of several types of sexual assault. In 1992, there were 125 sexual assaults per 100,000 people.

Australia 13.8

Austria 5.3

Chile 10.6

Denmark 7.7

England & Wales 2.7

France 5.2

Germany 9.7

Greece 0.9

Hungary 6.1

Japan 1.6

Spain 3.6

Sweden 11.9

Switzerland 5.8

Venezuela 17.4

USA 35.7

Rapes per 100,000 people per year.

SOCIALIZATION OF WOMAN

Expectations about how women behave can be seen in terms of sex (being female by nature) and gender (being a woman as a result of nurture). Roles are shaped by assumptions and expectations as to how girls and women should behave. These assumptions have a long history, although they are socially, rather than genetically, determined and have frequently become stereotyped. Being submissive, dependent, gentle, cooperative, subjective, affectionate, and suggestible in behavior, for example, is viewed as essentially feminine, whereas being aggressive, independent, objective, competitive, and autonomous is seen as being characteristically masculine.

This oppositional view crops up in many cultures, although anthropological research has shown that it is not universal. Margaret Mead's studies of three tribes in New Guinea showed much diversity in female/male roles. For example, in the Arapesh tribe, both men and women were taught to help each other, care about one another's feelings, and avoid aggression. In contrast, in the Mundugamor tribe, both women and men were ruthless, aggressive, and appeared to be devoid of parental feelings toward their children. Women were dominant in the Tchambuli tribe, where they fished and traded, and often initiated sex, while the men were more passive and emotional, spending their time playing music, dancing, and painting.

The most persistent female stereotypes (woman as virgin, mother, or whore) have been around for centuries and are thought to have their roots in the male rejection of the universal goddesses of early human history. Female sexual freedom and voracity were major tenets of goddess religions and were seen by the newly developing paternalistic religions as requiring control to ensure lineage and thus protect property.

By the time of Jesus, for example, it was considered sinful if a woman had sex outside of marriage or if she enjoyed sex within marriage. Sexual intercourse was purely for procreation, the means by which she would become a mother, and not for enjoyment. This was further emphasized by the dogma of the virgin birth of Jesus, which promulgated that although Mary was the mother of Jesus, she conceived without having had sexual intercourse.

Sleeping beauty
Many fairy tales emphasize the theme of the good maiden (young, virginal, beautiful) awaiting her prince (strong, virile, brave, handsome).

Witches
Women condemned throughout history as witches (Joan of Arc was burned as a witch) were usually accused of being in spiritual and intellectual darkness, although persecution appears to have been prompted by the threat to man's superiority posed by their real or imagined knowledge of healing.

FASCINATING WOMEN

Cleopatra (above)
Renowned for her beauty and as a symbol of love, she was also a shrewd politician and leader.

Amy Johnson (right)
In 1930, she was the first woman to fly solo around the world and from east to west across the Atlantic.

The media and advertising image of women is often very stereotypical; women are portrayed mainly as sex symbols, housewives, or mothers. Although it is claimed that the media reflects reality, it would be more true to say that the way women are portrayed emphasizes the CODE OF GOODNESS. *This is particularly noticeable in many newspapers, where women may be discussed in terms of their marital status, appearance, and age; successful women are trivialized, while those who take positive (un-feminine) action are condemned. In addition to being derogatory, this does not even start to acknowledge the many fascinating women who have influenced the course of history.*

Emmeline Pankhurst
The foremost British voice in the women's Suffrage movement, she was a charismatic leader who risked her life for the cause.

Josephine Baker
In the 1930s, this black American dancer's cabaret acts helped change racist attitudes in France.

Marie Stopes
She worked tirelessly for women to have control of their bodies and fertility.

Anne Frank (left)
The poignant diaries of Anne Frank have become a world famous record of her short, but very courageous, life.

Dian Fossey (right)
Her work with endangered mountain gorillas captured world attention. It is thought that her murder in 1985 was the work of poachers.

WOMAN AS LOVER AND WIFE

In the Western world, the myth of romantic and all-fulfilling love is very strong; every year thousands of single people join dating agencies in order to find their perfect partners. In many societies, the unconscious view is that a single (particularly female) person cannot be fulfilled and is somehow not "normal." The barometer of relationships (marriage), however, appears to be in crisis, with one marriage in two currently ending in DIVORCE (below). The expectations of love and marriage have been increasing in the West throughout the 20th century, until the husband and wife are expected to be everything to each other – lover, best friend, confidante, and support person. This appears to be in conflict with the desire or expectation that the first romantic and intense "falling-in-love" stage will last. Partners in successful marriages have qualities in common: the ability to express feelings and to listen to what the other person is saying, the ability to preserve a balance between intimacy and personal space, a strong commitment to the relationship, and the ability to adapt to changing circumstances and to each other.

In the modern Western world, it is generally accepted that a "normal" family is nuclear. This myth of the husband as sole breadwinner, with a wife who stays at home and two children, is one that is frequently portrayed by the media. The evidence suggests otherwise, however, with only a minority of all families in the West actually being nuclear. Most women work outside the home; a recent study found that 18% of British families are headed by a single parent (usually female). In others, more than two generations live under the same roof, the children are not the biological offspring of one or of either of the parents, the couple are of the same sex, or the household consists of unrelated friends living together.

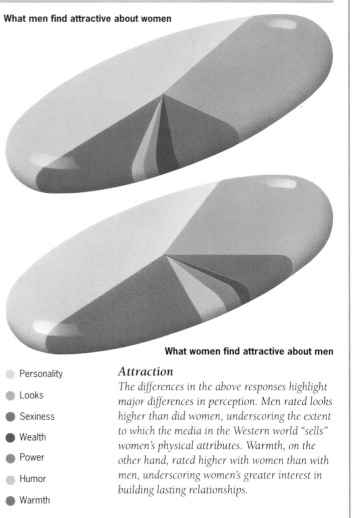

What men find attractive about women

What women find attractive about men

- Personality
- Looks
- Sexiness
- Wealth
- Power
- Humor
- Warmth

Attraction
The differences in the above responses highlight major differences in perception. Men rated looks higher than did women, underscoring the extent to which the media in the Western world "sells" women's physical attributes. Warmth, on the other hand, rated higher with women than with men, underscoring women's greater interest in building lasting relationships.

ADULTERY

A recent survey found that during their first marriage, 66% of women and 68% of men reported having at least one affair. The study listed a number of reasons for having an affair, and the participants were asked to choose five reasons and put them in order of importance. The reasons that they gave for having an affair were generally similar; the results are listed below.

Women

1 *I felt compelled by my emotions to have an affair.*

2 *My spouse and I had grown apart.*

3 *I had sexual needs that were not being met at the time.*

4 *Life felt very empty.*

5 *Life was for living.*

Men

1 *With care, the affair would not harm my marriage.*

2 *I was curious to know what sex would be like with someone else.*

3 *Life was for living.*

4 *I had sexual needs that were not being met at the time.*

5 *I felt compelled by my emotions to have an affair.*

DIVORCE

As women's expectations of marriage have risen in the Western world, the number of divorces has risen and the number of marriages has fallen. In Canada, there were 172,251 marriages in 1991. In the same year, there were about 77,000 divorces. Almost one in two Canadian marriages ends in divorce.

In Canada, up to 61% of all divorce proceedings were initiated by the woman. A lack of communication and intimacy is the most common reason cited by women for divorce.

The underlying reasons for divorce appear to be the result of a conflict between socially prescribed roles and expectations, and the personal expectations of women and men.

The increasing incidence of divorce in the Western world has resulted in the increasing numbers of one-parent families and stepfamilies.

WOMAN AS MOTHER

Mothering is central to the history and development of human beings. The bond between mother and infant was the first long-term pair-bond, and it was the relationship from which all others sprang. The germ of social organization is the woman, her children, and her children's children. Food gathering and sharing food with the child resulted in tribal cooperation and socialization, as it still does in many primate groups. Men were primarily the protectors of the tribe. Research also suggests that women, specifically in their roles as mother, played the primary role in the emergence of Goddess religion. Mother Goddess worship, which is thought to have spanned about 25,000 years, was built on the miracles of birth and creation. These were seen as being wholly female processes because primitive human beings had no idea that intercourse resulted in pregnancy. The Mother Goddess was all-powerful, sexually voracious, and awe-inspiring. She was the font of all life, the creator of the world itself. She was the "good mother" who gave life, and the "bad mother" who would punish her children. Myths such as these still impinge upon modern life. One of the most persistent is that of the "good mother," who stays at home to look after her children or stepchildren while her partner goes out to work. Working mothers are seen as "bad," as are SINGLE MOTHERS (below right).

Mother Goddess
Her generous proportions reflect her link with fertility.

The virgin mother
The myth of Mary, the mother of Christ, provides an impossible role model for Roman Catholic women. Not only was she herself conceived without sin, unlike the rest of the human race, she also became pregnant with Jesus without engaging in sexual intercourse. The image above is an unusually intimate portrayal of Mary and baby Jesus.

STEPMOTHERS

Between the myth of the evil stepmother, who figures prominently in countless fairytales, such as Snow White, and the myth of the utterly self-sacrificing stepmother, such as Maria in *The Sound of Music*, lies the real flesh-and-blood stepmother. The problems of stepmothering are myriad, and include the "ghost" (whether alive or dead) of the real mother; the fact that the only role models are mythic and therefore impossible to emulate; and the stepchildren themselves – often badly hurt and bitter, with the defensiveness that is the result of incomplete mourning. In addition, expectations on all sides often run high, and in most countries, the law is vague about where a stepparent's responsibilities start or end (the relationship may be held to be for life or to finish if the marriage ends). Despite this, some stepmothers do eventually have a successful relationship with their stepchildren, although tensions can run high for many years.

Wicked stepmother
One enduring myth of the stepmother is that of a wicked, vain, and cruel woman, featuring in fairy tales such as Snow White.

SINGLE MOTHERS

Family breakdown has often been blamed on single mothers. While boys reared by single mothers do appear to have a higher chance of being delinquent, this is far more likely to be a consequence of the poverty in which some of these families live than a result of inadequate mothering, unless the mother is teenaged. Most women become single parents as the result of divorce. If the father is irresponsible or absent, and there is no social pressure on him to perform as a "father," his son is unlikely to develop a sense of responsibility.

WOMAN VS. MAN

Women usually work more hours than men as they take responsibility for domestic tasks in addition to doing a "real job." This dual responsibility continues because women embody the enduring myth of "home" – the birthplace and permanent safe haven. Home appears to function effortlessly and running it is not seen as real work, hence the label "only a housewife."

◆

It has been predicted that about 90% of the jobs that will be created by the end of the first decade of the 21st century will be filled by women.

◆

Since wage records have been kept, women have been paid about 30% less than men for doing the same job. This continues to the present day in most countries (below).

Australia 78.2

Burma 88.8

El Salvador 85.9

France 78.1

Germany 73.0

Japan 43.1

Kenya 75.8

Korea 45.1

Canada 71.8

Sweden 90.3

UK 68.8

USA 57.2

Women's wages as a percentage of men's.

WOMAN AS WORKER

The idea of a working woman is not a modern one, although the value of women's work has been consistently underestimated by both men and women. Throughout history, women, in addition to bearing and rearing children, a huge and essential task in itself, have gathered food (in hunter/gatherer societies typically 80–90% of the tribes' food is provided by the women). They have also tilled fields, reared and harvested crops, and husbanded animals, washed, cooked, and cleaned, nursed the sick and dying, lain out the dead, spun yarn, woven cloth, and tanned

US astronaut Sally Ride.

leather for clothes that they made themselves. In Roman times women worked as doctors, midwives, and librarians, while in ancient Greece there were female musicians and teacher/philosophers (Pythagoras was taught by one, Aristoclea, and married to another, Theano; Socrates was taught by two – Diotima and the "first lady of Athens," Aspatia). In ancient Egypt, the pyramid builders were female as well as male, as were the canal navvies in Burma, whereas Inuit, Kurdish, and Chinese women have frequently been reported as carrying up to 150kg (300lb) at a time. In medieval Europe, widows often took on their husbands' professions (such as glover, perfumer, gold-, silver-, and blacksmith, tailor, wagonmaker, and cooper) despite being barred from the all-powerful male guilds. In Africa, markets were historically controlled by a women's council. During the Industrial Revolution, women worked alongside men in British mines from the age of five years onward.

In the modern Western world, women frequently work at mundane, yet essential, jobs, such as child care, cleaning, and secretarial work. They have also entered the professional workforce in increasing numbers during the second half of the 20th century. Many still choose "caring" jobs, such as nursing, which have traditionally been seen as suitable for a woman; many others, however, have jobs that have traditionally been seen as male, such as in high finance or as jockeys.

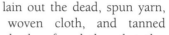

Chinese coolie
In rural areas of China, the transportation of agricultural crops, and other heavy goods, often falls quite literally on the shoulders of the women. Women are also involved in other manual labor and construction work.

Female soldiers
Soldiering has been a particularly male preserve at all points throughout history. Women have often been involved, however, from the British warrior queen Boudicca, to the soldiers in the Gulf War.

WOMAN AS LEADER

Women have always had a major role to play in the domestic sphere – for centuries the housewife was responsible for managing all aspects of the family's domestic life. For the most part, however, a woman's influence was never allowed to become apparent in the public sphere – she always remained "the power behind the throne" so to speak. There were, of course, exceptions, and these have tended to be extremely influential and remarkable women. British queens such as Elizabeth I and Victoria were lauded by their subjects and have remained firmly fixed in the popular imagination ever since. In the latter part of the 20th century, Sri Lanka, India, and the UK all had their first female prime ministers, Sirimavo Bandaranaike, Indira Ghandi, and Margaret Thatcher. Thatcher stayed in office for three terms – the only British prime minister in parliamentary history to have done so.

Other women are leaders in the inspirational sense. Some have spoken out for equality, such as Emmeline Pankhurst, or for peace, such as Mairead Corrigan and Betty Williams of Northern Ireland (they were jointly awarded the Nobel Peace Prize

in 1976). Yet more women have broken new ground in science, such as Marie Curie, Dorothy Hodgkin, and Evelyn Fox Keller (Nobel Science prize winners); in female health and reproduction, such as Elizabeth Garrett Anderson and childbirth educator and anthropologist Sheila Kitzinger; and in the arts, such as the celebrated artist Georgia O'Keeffe, photographers Lee Miller and Annie Liebovitz, fashion designer Coco Chanel, and choreographer Martha Graham.

Queen Victoria (right)
Ascending to the British throne while still in her teens, Victoria soon made her presence known by immersing herself in the daily running of the state.

Helena Rubenstein
The remarkable, energetic, and visionary Helena Rubenstein founded her world-famous cosmetic company in Australia; she later opened salons in over 100 major cities and pioneered modern marketing methods.

Marie Curie
In 1900, Marie Curie achieved her driving ambition to isolate pure, elemental radium.

WOMAN VS. ANIMAL
As with women, the ways in which animals cooperate are diverse and may depend on group dynamics, as well as self-interest.

◆

A hive of bees is composed of many workers, a few drones, and a single queen. The whole community is female, apart from the drones, who change sex in order to fertilize the eggs. All the bees in a hive work as a single entity.

◆

Lionesses do the bulk of the hunting for the pride. The male will occasionally join a stalk, but even then it is usually the females who make the kill.

◆

Although the stallion appears to be the sole leader of a herd of horses, he in fact works with the lead (usually eldest) mare. She usually will be the one who decides to move the herd – to better grazing, for example – and she will lead the way. The stallion keeps the herd moving from the rear. Even without the protection of a stallion, the lead mare will keep the herd together as an integrated unit.

AQUATIC THEORY

A radical theory of evolution was put forward by Sir Alister Hardy in an article in The New Scientist *in 1960. It barely made a ripple in the collective consciousness until the 1970s when Elaine Morgan, a British writer with an interest in evolution, developed the aquatic theory in her books* The Aquatic Ape *and* The Descent of Woman. *She argues two main points. The first is that woman's simian ancestors evolved throughout a 12-million-year period spent on the seashore and in the sea during the severely drought-ridden Pliocene age, which started 20 million years ago. Her second is that the female of the species and her babies played a major part in this transition.*

The very first ancestors were insignificant, fruit-eating African apes that were driven out of dwindling jungle; a fortunate few ended up near a beach. These foraged along the shore, occasionally going into the water to cool down and to escape from water-shy, carnivorous predators. Apes can stand up if necessary (which it would have been for females with babies); this trait eventually evolved into a permanent bipedal stance. The aquatic theory makes sense of many so-called "unique" human features, such as tears, hairless skin, a subcutaneous fat layer, bipedal locomotion, manipulative use of tools, the ventral VAGINA, *the* HYMEN, *and* SPEECH. *Many are unique only in relation to other land animals; many sea creatures, such as seabirds, dolphins, seals, and sea crocodiles shed tears, for example.*

WOMAN AS THINKER

Foremost among early female intellectuals was Christine de Pisan, an Italian 15th-century scholar of philosophy, poetry, history, and biology. De Pisan was lionized by royalty and was enormously successful. The first Italian woman to qualify as a doctor was Maria Montessori in the 20th century; she also had a great influence on modern education. Other women thinkers have also profoundly altered the way in which people view the world. American anthropologist Margaret Mead had a particular interest in social interaction and studied diverse cultures worldwide. In the 1970s, Elaine Morgan expanded the radical AQUATIC THEORY of evolution (left). British Labour politician Barbara Castle saw the inherent problems in the Trade Union Movement and tried to modernize the legal framework. If she had succeeded, British Coal would probably have survived the Thatcher years. Writers such as Simone de Beauvoir, Marilyn French, Toni Morrison, and Margaret Atwood have had tremendous influence.

Christine de Pisan
She argued tirelessly that women should be educated.

20th-century intellectual
In her groundbreaking book The Second Sex, *Simone de Beauvoir argued for women's emancipation.*

WOMEN'S STATUS WORLDWIDE

Throughout the world, the status of women differs according to local traditions and customs, religious beliefs, and economics. In many countries, such as Canada, women expect equality with their male peers. Although this doesn't necessarily occur, and inequality tends to take subtle and insidious forms, at least the forum is usually open for discussion and negotiation between men and women. In other countries, such as Afghanistan, and many countries in the Middle East and in Africa, the public lives of women are very constrained. The situation can vary even within one nation. In the US, for example, abortion laws vary widely from state to state. In China, official pressure is exerted on a woman who already has a child to have a subsequent fetus aborted (abortions can occur up to term in China) and to have herself sterilized. This is reinforced by the educational privileges that are accorded to one-child families. The policy is more successful in urban China, where space restrictions reduce desire for larger families, than in rural China, where women feel less pressured by policy and space.

IT'S A FACT

The year in which female suffrage occurred illuminates a country's attitude toward women.

New Zealand – 1893
Austria & Australia – 1901
Finland – 1906
Norway – 1913
Russia – 1917
UK & Canada – 1918
Germany – 1919
USA – 1920
Japan – 1945
France – 1946
China – 1947
Greece – 1952
Switzerland – 1971
Iraq – 1979

THE
SEXUAL
WOMAN

Sexual pleasure

A woman's ability to experience sexual pleasure increases until she reaches her thirties, after which it remains at a constant level for the next 30–40 years.

IT'S A FACT

The frequency of sexual activity of the average woman varies according to her age. The statistics below, which show the frequency of sexual intercourse in a wide cross-section of women, were taken from the Janus survey, published in the United States in 1993.

Age in years	Daily	Twice weekly	Weekly	Monthly	Rarely
18–26	13	33	22	15	17
27–38	8	41	27	12	12
39–50	10	29	29	11	21
51–64	4	28	33	8	27
65+	1	40	33	4	22

Figures represent a percentage of respondents.

The sexual woman is passionate . . .   and tender.

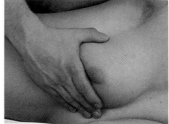

Her buttocks and inner thighs . . .   her feet, and . . .   her breasts are pleasure zones,

. . . as are her lips.   Sensuality is integral to a woman's sexuality.

A woman's sexuality can be a purely singular pleasure.

EROTIC REPRESENTATIONS

Throughout the history of human civilization, representations of the sexual act have been made. Some have been simple, such as the Stone-Age cave drawings of copulating couples (one of these shows the man's erect penis inside some sort of sheath; the earliest known illustration of a condom). Other cultures have produced erotic paintings, such as those in Japanese "pillow books" and the Indian *Kama Sutra*. Ancient African and American cultures produced erotic statuettes in metal, pottery, bone, or wood, some of which were used for practical purposes.

Sexual imagery
Erotic representations are widespread throughout all cultures. Indian and Persian artists specialized in lavishly colored paintings, like the one shown on the left. The Ashantis of Ghana produced stylized statuettes; the one shown above is made of brass and was used to weigh gold.

CLITORAL SYSTEM

A woman's genitals are made up of a large amount of sexually responsive tissue, of which the clitoris is only the visible tip. This system is believed to be as big, sensitive, and responsive as a man's. When fully aroused, a hidden network of bulbous spaces, nerves, veins, and arteries becomes swollen with blood, and the clitoris becomes erect. Lack of understanding about the origins of a woman's orgasm, which is the result of clitoral stimulation but a vaginal experience, is due to the clitoris being the surface manifestation of a much larger internal system.

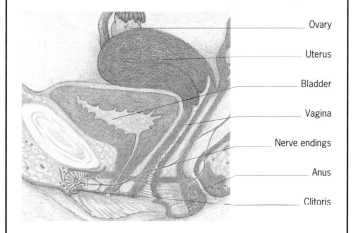

- Ovary
- Uterus
- Bladder
- Vagina
- Nerve endings
- Anus
- Clitoris

THE G-SPOT

Named after Dr. Ernst Grafenburg, a German obstetrician and gynecologist, the G-spot is an area that some women report produces intense excitement and orgasm when stimulated. Despite the fact that pathologists have failed to locate the G-spot in autopsies, some people believe that the G-spot is a rudimentary prostate gland situated around the urethra.

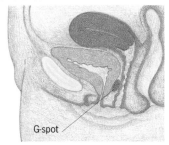

G-spot

Rudimentary prostate
The front wall of the vagina, the supposed site of the G-spot, responds to deep vaginal stimulation.

A WOMAN'S EROGENOUS ZONES

Every single part of a woman's body will respond to touches, caresses, and kisses, but certain areas produce more intense sensations when stimulated and trigger sexual arousal. These are called erogenous zones. Most women relish having their body parts rubbed or stroked with the fingertips or lips.

Good	Better	Best
• Hairline	• Mouth and lips	• Breasts
• Forehead	• Earlobes	• Nipples
• Temples	• Throat and neck	• Vulva
• Eyebrows	• Armpits	• Clitoris
• Eyelids	• Abdomen	• Buttocks
• Cheeks	• Navel	• Topmost inner thighs
• Arms	• Back	
• Hands	• Toes	

WOMAN AND FOREPLAY

Although the vagina will usually lubricate naturally within a few moments of a woman being sexually stimulated, to become fully aroused and ready for intercourse some women need a lot of stimulation. Foreplay may also be enjoyed as an end in itself. Actions such as massage, kissing, petting, MASTURBATION, and ORAL SEX can increase sexual tension and stimulate sexual desire; erotic material may have the same effects. Most women enjoy using sexually explicit material to increase their arousal, but many prefer to read an erotic text rather than looking at pictures or videos.

Most men also enjoy foreplay, or find it necessary for erection. A woman can use her entire body, in addition to her hands, to stimulate and caress her partner.

Massage oils

Wooden massager roller

Petting
Touching, stroking, nibbling, caressing, and kissing a woman's body will encourage the buildup of sexual tension, which prepares her body for sexual intercourse. Brushing her hair, blowing gently in her ear, and massaging her body parts can make her tingle all over. Being clothed or semiclothed can add to the excitement.

Your partner can bestow kisses all over your body

Kissing
Appreciated by every part of the body, kisses can be tender, explorative, hard, passionate, or sensuous, and involve both closed and open lips. A gradual progression of kisses down the body is highly arousing.

Massage
A variety of pressures and strokes across a woman's entire body will help to increase her sexual desire, particularly if applied to her erogenous zones. Scented massage oils (above) can be used to relax or arouse, and their fragrance will perfume the air and add to the atmosphere. Wooden massager rollers (above), feathers, and fabrics such as silk and velvet can be applied to the body to vary the sensations.

MASTURBATION

The majority of Western women learn about their sexuality through MASTURBATION between the ages of 12 and 16. The surge of hormones at adolescence encourages girls to experiment in this way. The entire genital area is extremely sensitive to touch, and orgasm can be attained by rubbing the MONS PUBIS, VULVA, and CLITORIS. Other techniques include rubbing against objects or clenching the perineal muscles. No two women masturbate in exactly the same way.

Self-stimulation
Using circular and vibratory movements and various degrees of pressure, a woman will rub and press on her mons pubis and clitoris and stimulate the inside of her vagina to achieve orgasm. Seventy percent of women experience orgasm as a result of masturbation, but only 30% do so from penetration during sexual intercourse.

Vibrators
These are among the most popular of all sex aids and come in a variety of sizes and designs. A vibrator is a useful means of ensuring that a woman achieves orgasm.

Tube-shaped vibrator

WOMAN AND ORAL SEX

Cunnilingus involves licking and sucking a woman's clitoris and vulva. Women often require direct clitoral stimulation to reach orgasm, and the tongue, which is softer and more flexible than the fingers, can be used to stroke the clitoris – where sensation is greatest – as well as to penetrate the vagina. Some women enjoy performing fellatio on their partners; with her tongue and mouth, a woman can enclose and suck her partner's penis and can bring him to orgasm. During oral sex, partners must take great care not to hurt the delicate genital tissue.

Cunnilingus
The man should stroke upward with his tongue from below the clitoris.

One modern sexual myth is that all women need a lot of foreplay to become fully aroused, while men need no foreplay and are "always ready." The truth is actually less clear-cut. Some women undoubtedly do need prolonged foreplay if they are to achieve orgasm; many others become fully aroused easily and quickly. A few men are "always ready," while others need foreplay; some think it superfluous to penetration. Still other men, however, frequently require a lot of foreplay to achieve orgasm.

BODY CHANGES DUE TO SEXUAL STIMULATION

The production of vaginal lubrication is a woman's first response to sexual stimulation. This can occur after 10–30 seconds of excitement, although it can take longer depending on the individual woman and the situation. If the stimulation continues, changes will occur to her entire body as well as to her genitals. The blood supply to the pelvic area will increase and will bring about the greatest changes to the genitals.

Changes to the genitals
- *The inner two-thirds of the vagina lengthens and distends.*
- *Lubrication increases.*
- *The color of the vagina darkens to a purplish hue.*
- *The cervix and uterus are pulled backward and upward into the pelvis.*
- *The LABIA MINORA and MAJORA become separated, elevated, and turned out.*
- *The clitoris enlarges and becomes erect.*

Changes in the whole body

Pupils dilate

Lips darken in color

Sweating increases

Nipples become erect

Skin becomes flushed

Breathing quickens

Heart beats more rapidly

Breasts enlarge

ANAL SEX

A recent US survey revealed that 43% of female respondents had engaged in anal intercourse, 19% of them occasionally and 2% often. Forty percent of those who had experienced anal sex said that they enjoyed it, while the majority said they didn't or that they had no particular feelings about it. Although anal sex is used as a method of CONTRACEPTION, these respondents used it for sexual enhancement.

Penetration is not normally very deep, and a woman can help by assuming a man-on-top, rear-entry position and relaxing her anal SPHINCTER as much as she is able to. The penis should always be well lubricated.

Anal sex is a causative factor in spreading AIDS; other infections can also be spread by this activity.

SEXUAL FANTASIES

The majority of women (over 70%) fantasize to enhance sexual arousal. Often, a woman's fantasies concern a partner other than her own, and may feature sexual activities not previously engaged in. Many women "set a scene," while other women will use a single word or image to increase their sexual arousal.

WOMAN VS. MAN

The average woman appears to fantasize about sex differently from the average man. Most men focus exclusively on the sexual act when fantasizing, while most women tend to place sex in a wider context – such as on a tropical beach or in a luxurious boudoir, for example. Women are also more likely to fantasize about being "forced" to have sex than men are.

EXERCISES FOR SEXUAL ENHANCEMENT

Taoist philosophy embraces activities that are claimed to enable women to balance the female hormones, encourage sexual energy, and help them look more beautiful. These daily exercises involve stroking the breasts and contracting the vaginal muscles.

Vaginal pressure (right)
Place the heel of the foot against the vagina (a small ball can also be placed between the foot and the vagina). Pressure from the heel or ball stimulates and releases your sexual feelings.

Sit cross-legged on the floor or the bed

If using a ball, place it between the heel of your foot and your vagina

Breast massage (left)
Stroke your breasts slowly, a minimum of 36 times to a maximum of 360, morning and evening. Caress your right breast counterclockwise and your left breast clockwise.

Massage your breasts in opposite directions

Stroke your breast with one hand

Drawing up energy (right)
While massaging a breast with one hand, use the other to press against your vagina, contracting your vaginal muscles and anus at the same time. Hold for as long as possible, then relax. Repeat 20 times.

Press against your vagina with your other hand

LESBIANISM

It is not known exactly how many women are homosexual, but in one famous study, Kinsey estimated that 12–13% of American women had experienced orgasm through sexual behavior with another woman. Probably no more than 2–5% of women worldwide are exclusively homosexual, however.

The sexual techniques women use with each other include kissing, petting, ORAL SEX, and manual stimulation of the clitoris. (Few lesbians appear to use phallic objects inserted into the vagina for stimulation during sex.)

Lesbians claim that lovemaking between two women is far more satisfying than between the opposite sexes. This may be because lesbian lovemaking focuses on ensuring that both women experience orgasm. Most lesbians have had at least one heterosexual encounter, mainly as a result of social expectations and pressure.

TRIBADISM
A sexual practice commonly engaged in by lesbians, in which one woman lies on top of the other and moves her MONS PUBIS against that of her partner to stimulate the genital area.

BISEXUALITY

Most women are capable of being attracted to, and loving, members of both sexes, but it is estimated that only about 10% of all women engage in sexual behavior with both women and men. While same-sex experimentation is not uncommon, true bisexuality is unusual.

FEMALE SEXUAL RESPONSE

As a woman experiences sexual pleasure, she responds by passing through a recognized number of stages, each of which takes a certain amount of time. A woman's sexual tension tends to build slowly, but the more stimulating and varied the foreplay, the more rapidly a woman will become aroused and reach the plateau phase. If her clitoris is stimulated directly and constantly, she will rapidly approach orgasm. Most women prefer a slower pace, however, as well as the use of visual and aural stimulation, FANTASIES, caressing of the whole body, and clitoral stimulation. After orgasm, sexual tension subsides and a woman's breasts and genitals (right) will gradually return to normal.

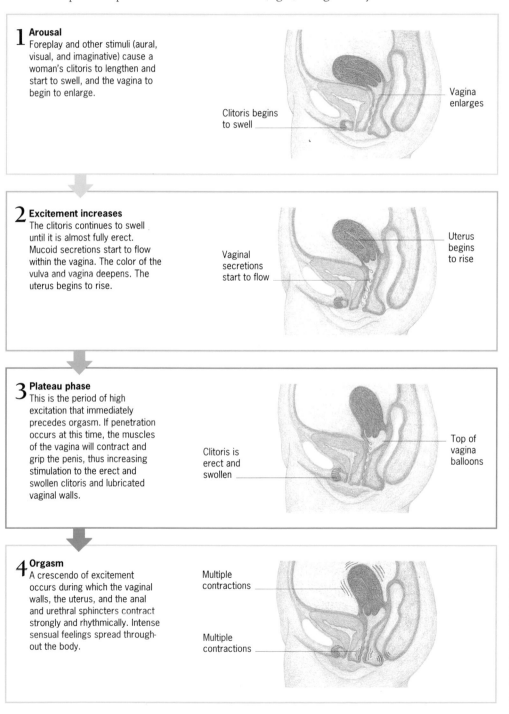

1 Arousal
Foreplay and other stimuli (aural, visual, and imaginative) cause a woman's clitoris to lengthen and start to swell, and the vagina to begin to enlarge.

Clitoris begins to swell

Vagina enlarges

2 Excitement increases
The clitoris continues to swell until it is almost fully erect. Mucoid secretions start to flow within the vagina. The color of the vulva and vagina deepens. The uterus begins to rise.

Vaginal secretions start to flow

Uterus begins to rise

3 Plateau phase
This is the period of high excitation that immediately precedes orgasm. If penetration occurs at this time, the muscles of the vagina will contract and grip the penis, thus increasing stimulation to the erect and swollen clitoris and lubricated vaginal walls.

Clitoris is erect and swollen

Top of vagina balloons

4 Orgasm
A crescendo of excitement occurs during which the vaginal walls, the uterus, and the anal and urethral sphincters contract strongly and rhythmically. Intense sensual feelings spread throughout the body.

Multiple contractions

Multiple contractions

REACTIONS

BREASTS
As well as being a powerful sexual attractant, the breasts are among a woman's most sensitive EROGENOUS ZONES, and respond to direct stimulation by becoming as much as 25% larger. The nipples and surrounding areolae darken, and the former become erect. In 75% of women (compared to 25% of men), a flush extends over the front of the body, particularly over the chest area, during sexual arousal.

CLITORIS
When a woman is sexually aroused, her genital system becomes swollen with blood, resulting in the erection of her clitoris. Priapism (permanent erection) does occur, but is a rare condition, as is a lack of clitoral erection. Lack of erection may prevent orgasm. The clitoris, like a man's penis, becomes erect about every 90 minutes while a woman is asleep.

Nipple erection
This is universal among women during sexual arousal, and can increase the nipple's length by as much as 1cm (1/2 in) and diameter by 0.5cm (1/4 in).

SEXUAL POSITIONS

Variety is the spice of love and, as in all things human, inventiveness has produced a large number of positions for sexual intercourse. Most couples experience different needs and situations that require different positions.

Woman on top
A woman controls the pace of intercourse and the depth of penetration in this position (above). It is also easy for her partner to fondle her breasts, inner thighs, buttocks, and genital region. Positions in which a woman faces away from her partner (left) encourage sexual fantasies.

Man on top
The "missionary position" can be varied in a number of ways to increase a woman's pleasure. By locking her legs across those of her partner (left), she can increase the amount of pressure against her mons pubis. If she raises her legs (right), this will directly stimulate her clitoris.

Sitting positions
Generally, these allow a woman to be the more dominant partner; her movements set the tempo and pace of lovemaking, while the man's movements are very restricted. A chair can be used as a support for rear penetration (left), so that the hands of the woman's partner are free to fondle her thighs, breasts, and clitoris. The woman can also sit in her partner's lap (right).

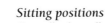

Standing positions

If both partners stand, penetration during lovemaking may be difficult to achieve if the two are not approximately the same height. The woman can aid penetration by rising up on her toes and turning one leg slightly sideways, while the man bends slightly at the knees. The couple can face each other or the man can penetrate from behind (left). If a woman is smaller and lighter than her partner, she can be lifted up onto his hips. She can then support herself on his shoulders and wrap her legs around his hips (right).

Side-by-side positions

These are among the most comfortable and relaxed lovemaking positions. In the "spoons" position (above), the man lies against the woman's back and penetrates her from behind. With the woman's legs bent over those of the man (right), a couple can make love face-to-face.

Rear-entry positions

In the "doggie" position (left), the man is able to caress the woman's breasts, clitoris, and buttocks. Direct stimulation of the woman's mons pubis can be achieved by pressing her against the floor (below).

WOMAN VS. ANIMAL

A woman can enjoy sex even when she is menstruating. Pleasure rather than procreation is the usual impetus.

◆

A female porcupine is in heat for four hours a year.

◆

A female chimpanzee is sexually active for about 10 days each month. When she is most fertile she will mate with the dominant male. Until then she mates with every other male in the troop.

◆

When scorpions mate, the male holds the female's pincers to prevent her from attacking him. They then perform an elaborate "courtship dance," which can last several hours, before copulating.

◆

Dolphins usually mate belly to belly as they swim together just below the surface of the sea.

◆

Indian pythons copulate for up to 180 days at a time.

◆

Courting otters play chase, and swim and dive together, racing and corkscrewing through the water. Otters mate underwater, either belly to belly or with their bodies twisted around each other.

◆

Female black widow spiders often poison their mates during copulation.

A WOMAN'S ORGASM

Although this varies with each experience, as well as from woman to woman, usually during orgasm the outer third of the vagina produces 3–5 contractions 0.8 seconds apart. The first come quite close together, the later contractions are spaced out slightly. The number, duration, intensity, and intervals between the contractions can and do differ. A woman may experience 10–15 contractions, of which the first may last 2–4 seconds and be quite profound, while the others last less than a second.

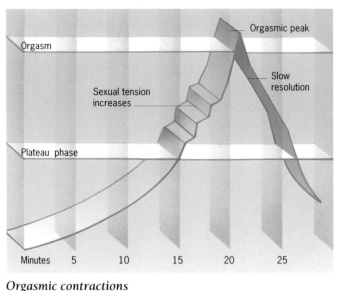

Orgasmic contractions
After the plateau level, contractions rise in stages to a peak of sensation.

MULTIPLE ORGASMS

Some women are capable of experiencing more than one orgasm, as long as their partners are able to control their ejaculations. The potential for having multiple orgasms may be increased if women keep their PELVIC FLOOR MUSCLES in good shape, engage in sex on a regular basis, and communicate their needs to their partners.

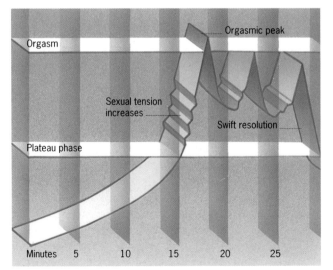

Multiple orgasmic contractions
Once the plateau stage has been reached, sexual tension quickly increases. The woman then experiences a flurry of minor contractions, followed by the first intense contraction. This pattern is swiftly repeated for a second, and then a third time.

VAGINAL ACHE

This is the "anticipatory hollowness" that is experienced by some women just prior to the moment of orgasm. This feeling has a physiological basis in the ballooning out of the upper end of the vagina at this time.

FEMALE EJACULATION

During orgasm, some women experience a spurting of clear fluid, which recent studies have discovered contains enzymes, such as acid phosphatase, found in male seminal fluid. It is thought that female ejaculate is produced by Skene's glands, which are near the urethral opening. Skene's glands have also been linked by some research to the G-SPOT.

RESOLUTION

- *Five to ten seconds after orgasm: clitoris returns to its normal position; normal coloration of the LABIA MINORIA returns.*

- *Ten to 15 minutes after orgasm: vulval folds reappear and normal coloration returns.*

- *Up to 30 minutes after orgasm: the CLITORIDAS (head) returns to its usual size. If there is no orgasm, it can take several hours to subside.*

LEVELS OF TAOIST ORGASM

Taoist sexology defines a woman's orgasm as having a possible nine stages. A woman needs sustained stimulation, however, to progress further than level four (below), which is what most women experience as orgasm.

- *Level 1: the woman sighs, breathes heavily, and salivates.*

- *Level 2: while kissing her partner, she extends her tongue into his mouth.*

- *Level 3: she grasps him tighter.*

- *Level 4: she experiences a series of orgasmic contractions, and her vaginal secretions flow copiously.*

- *Level 5: her joints loosen, and she starts to bite him.*

- *Level 6: she wraps her arms and legs right around him.*

- *Level 7: her blood is "boiling," and she frantically tries to touch him all over his body.*

- *Level 8: the woman's muscles totally relax. She bites and grabs at his nipples.*

- *Level 9: she collapses in a "little death," surrenders to her partner, and is completely "opened up."*

UNRESPONSIVENESS

Many women engage in sexual intercourse without enjoying it. Rarely due to physical reasons, unresponsiveness may be the result of a partner's selfishness or lack of technique, or it may be because the woman had a disturbing sexual encounter when she was young, was brought up to think of sex as dirty, or just does not know how to respond to sexual sensations in her body. Therapists use various methods to treat inhibited sexuality, the most effective of which is "sensate focus." This aims to reacquaint partners with their sexuality.

SENSATE FOCUS
The exercises below are designed to reawaken a woman's sexual feelings and to enable both partners to give and receive pleasurable touch freely.

Stage one (right)
Using different touches, a woman learns to focus on her sensuality by concentrating on what gives her pleasure.

Stage two
Now aware of erotic sensations, both partners practice giving and receiving pleasure, without genital contact.

Stage three (below)
Touches become more intimate and attention is paid to the genitals. This sensual massage will inevitably lead to pleasurable intercourse.

LACK OF ORGASM
About 12% of women never experience orgasm, while up to 70% do not achieve orgasm solely from penetration; women usually require direct stimulation of the clitoris to be able to achieve orgasm. MASTURBATION is the best way to learn how to achieve orgasm; a continued inability to climax may be because of a lack of clitoral erection.

VAGINISMUS
Psychologically induced muscle spasms, which can cause the vaginal entrance to close so tightly that it is very painful and intercourse becomes impossible, affect 2–3% of adult women, although as many as 9% have suffered from vaginismus at some time in their lives.

With proper counseling, this condition is almost always completely curable. In addition to guidance on sexual practice and anatomy, treatment sometimes involves the use of vaginal dilators.

PAINFUL SEX

Psychological factors, including resentment, anger, fear, or shame, are the commonest causes of painful sex, which is technically known as dyspareunia. Several medical conditions, however, including vaginal infections, pelvic inflammatory disease, ENDOMETRIOSIS, a PROLAPSED UTERUS, URINARY TRACT infections, HEMORRHOIDS, irritation of the VULVA, and hormonal deficiencies can make intercourse painful. Consequently, it is first necessary to rule these out or treat them if present. Sex therapy, including SENSATE FOCUS (left), may be able to help with psychological causes.

VULVITIS
Symptoms of vulvitis (essentially DERMATITIS of the vulva), include allergic or irritant reactions resulting in inflammation and severe itching or burning. Ulcers may also occur.

VESTIBULITIS
This condition causes particular vaginal glands to become extremely tender and painful when pressure is applied. It is especially severe during, or immediately following, sexual intercourse. The most commonly affected glands are those at the vestibule (bottom of the entrance) to the vagina in the perineal area (between the anus and vulva) and either side of the urethral opening. Symptoms also include redness or inflammation of the area. Many women suffer pain from their teenage years. There appears to be a long-term cyclical pattern to the symptoms.

No single consistent cause has been identified as yet, but triggers appear to include vulval warts, skin diseases, exposure to chemical irritants (in bath products, for example), and trauma to the genital area, such as during rape or childbirth. Foods containing yeast or sugar also appear to aggravate vestibulitis.

SAFER SEX

This comprises forms of sexual activity thought least likely to expose a woman to HIV infection and AIDS, as well as to CHLAMYDIA, YEAST INFECTION, nonspecific urethritis, and other SEXUALLY TRANSMITTED DISEASES (right). Sensual MASSAGE, mutual MASTURBATION, and the use of unshared VIBRATORS hold minimal risks. Using a latex condom or female condom is recommended during sexual intercourse or ORAL SEX; any practice when body fluids (wet sex) are exchanged should be avoided.

Sources of HIV infection

Highest risk	Some degree of risk
Vaginal sexual intercourse without a latex condom.	Vaginal sexual intercourse with a latex condom.
Anal intercourse with or without a latex condom.	Love bites or scratching that breaks the skin.
Fellatio, especially to climax.	Anal licking or kissing.
Any sexual activity that draws blood, whether accidentally or deliberately.	Sexual activities involving urination.
Sharing penetrative sex aids, such as vibrators.	Mouth-to-mouth kissing, especially if either partner has bleeding gums or cold sores.
Inserting fingers or hands into the anus.	Fellatio using a condom.

CHLAMYDIA

The commonest sexually transmitted disease, chlamydia is frequently symptomless. If undetected or left untreated, it can cause generalized pelvic infection that may result in infertility due to a blockage of the FALLOPIAN TUBES by scarring.

The test for chlamydia can be done easily during a pelvic examination. Symptoms of chlamydia are rare, but abdominal discomfort, particularly during sexual intercourse, fever, and an unusual or offensive yellow cervical or vaginal discharge should be investigated. It may damage the mucoid lining of the mouth, eyes, urinary tract, rectum and vagina. Chlamydia can be treated using antibiotics.

SEXUALLY TRANS-MITTED DISEASES

Genital herpes is an infectious, recurring disease caused by the herpes simplex II virus, characterized by large, painful, fluid-filled blisters. Herpes is more common in women than in men. It is highly contagious and incurable, although medication can help to control outbreaks.

Gonorrhea has an incubation period of two to 10 days. Symptoms include pain on urination and vaginal discharge, although 60% of women are symptomless. Gonorrhea is curable, although if left untreated it can be fatal.

Syphilis is caused by bacteria that can enter the body through broken skin, or during kissing or sexual intercourse. The most obvious symptom is a skin rash. Early syphilis is usually treatable.

AIDS

The HUMAN IMMUNODEFICIENCY VIRUS (HIV) causes AIDS, which leaves the body prey to opportunistic diseases, such as pneumonia and cancer, and is ultimately fatal. HIV can be spread by unprotected sex because the virus is present in the semen of infected men and in the vaginal secretions of infected women, so a condom should always be used (below) and SAFER SEX guidelines (above) should be followed. Shared hypodermic needles and infected blood transfusions can also spread the virus, and women can pass the virus to their babies during pregnancy and birth, and in their breast milk, although screening in early pregnancy is available. HIV can be passed on before the carrier has any symptoms or tests positive for HIV. Skin infections, swollen LYMPH GLANDS, weight loss, diarrhea, and oral thrush (known as AIDS-related complex) develop first. Once AIDS develops, life expectancy is about two years.

Risk-free activities
- *Dry kissing or cheek-to-cheek kissing.*
- *Self-masturbation.*
- *Masturbating a partner's genitals or being masturbated by your partner.*
- *Sitting on a toilet seat.*
- *Swimming in a pool.*
- *Using another person's bed linen or towels, or wearing another person's clothes.*
- *Sneezing or being sneezed on.*
- *Shaking hands, embracing, or cuddling.*
- *Sharing a glass or dishes.*

Squeeze out air
Press the tip of a condom so that there is no air inside (which could cause the condom to split).

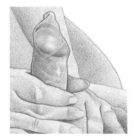

Put on a condom
Roll the condom carefully down the length of the erect penis, from the tip down to the base.

THE HEALTHY WOMAN

DIET & NUTRITION

WOMAN VS. ANIMAL

A mammal can be a carnivore (eats meat only), herbivore (eats vegetation only), or omnivore (eats meat or vegetation). Wholly carnivorous species are relatively uncommon. Women are omnivores.

Carnivore
Cats, as a species, are at the top of the carnivore league.

Omnivore
Badgers eat practically anything, from mice to berries.

Herbivore
Grazers, like the wallaby, eat mainly grasses and leaves.

MACRONUTRIENTS

These are substances that are needed by the body in large amounts to maintain health and growth.

CARBOHYDRATES

The body's main sources of energy (energy is measured in calories) are carbohydrates, which are either sugars or starches. Sugars are simple carbohydrates and include sucrose (cane or beet sugar), glucose (fruit and honey), fructose (fruit and vegetables), and galactose (milk). Starches are complex carbohydrates and include grains, potatoes, and beans. When unrefined, they also contain VITAMINS, MINERALS, and FIBER. Complex carbohydrates provide a steady supply of energy, while sugars supply instant energy. Sugars taken in anything but very small quantities will actually lower energy and will tend to increase the amount of fat stored.

FATS

Like carbohydrates, fats are also used for energy, but tend to be stored in the body first; they are very concentrated and hence very high in calories. Fats consist mainly of fatty acids, which are essential for cells to function correctly. There are three types of fatty acids: saturated (animal and dairy fats), monounsaturated (olive oil), and polyunsaturated (vegetable fats). Although all fats have an equal calorie value, they are thought of as "good" or "bad" according to

their contribution to HEART DISEASE. In this respect, polyunsaturated fats are "good," saturated are "bad," and monounsaturated are "good" if taken in moderate amounts and not heated. Excessive intake of any fat is thought to contribute to CANCER.

PROTEINS

These consist of strings of amino acids that form the main structural elements of cells and tissues. Hence, amino acids are known as the building blocks of the body. There are 23 different amino acids, of which eight (known as the essential amino acids) can't be manufactured by the body. Protein that contains good amounts of these eight amino acids is known as a complete protein (meat, cheese, soy beans); protein that does not is known as incomplete (nuts, beans, rice). When they are eaten in combination, incomplete proteins can provide the body with its complete amino acid requirement.

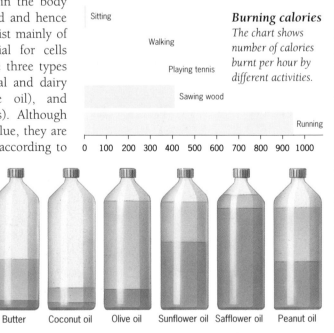

Sitting
Walking
Playing tennis
Sawing wood
Running

0   100   200   300   400   500   600   700   800   900   1000

Burning calories
The chart shows number of calories burnt per hour by different activities.

Fat proportions
Oils and hard fats, such as butter and lard, contain the three types of fats (saturated, polyunsaturated, and monounsaturated) in different proportions.

☐ Saturated
▨ Monounsaturated
■ Polyunsaturated

Butter   Coconut oil   Olive oil   Sunflower oil   Safflower oil   Peanut oil

MICRONUTRIENTS

Although essential for health, these substances are needed by the body in fairly small amounts.

MINERALS

These are chemicals that are needed by the body. Major minerals, such as calcium, sodium, potassium, and magnesium, are needed in larger amounts than are those known as essential trace elements, such as iron, copper, selenium, and zinc.

VITAMINS

These complex structures are either water- or fat-soluble. The B-complex vitamins and vitamin C are water-soluble; any excess is excreted in the urine. Vitamins A, D, E, and K are fat-soluble, and are stored in the liver or fatty tissue; excess can be toxic. Some vitamins, such as vitamin D, can be manufactured in the body.

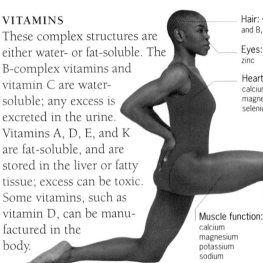

Hair: vitamins A and B, zinc

Eyes: vitamin A, zinc

Heart function: calcium, copper, magnesium, potassium selenium, sodium

Muscle function: calcium magnesium potassium sodium

FIBER IN THE DIET

Unrefined vegetable food, such as the husks of grains, the skins and flesh of fruits and vegetables, and tough vegetable matter, is known as fiber, and it plays an important role in a healthy diet.

Fiber helps to maintain a healthy BOWEL because of its remarkable ability to bind water during digestion. This promotes bowel activity by ensuring that feces are soft but well formed; they are easy to pass, but are large enough to stimulate the necessary contractions of the bowel.

Research suggests that soluble fiber, such as that found in apples and oats, is helpful because it lowers the amount of cholesterol in the blood.

Food	Dietary fiber per 25g (1oz)
Unprocessed bran	12.3
Dried apricots	7
Prunes	4
Almonds	4
Raisins	2
Whole-grain bread	2
Dried beans	2
Spinach or peas	2
Whole-grain pasta, potatoes, brown rice	2
Broccoli or leeks	1
Boiled lentils	1
Apples, bananas, or strawberries	0.5
Oranges or pears	0.4

Measurements above are in grams.

A BALANCED DIET

The food pyramid (below) was developed by American nutritionists at the beginning of the 1990s. It represents the proportions in which it is now considered that the main food groups should be eaten each day to achieve a perfectly nutritionally balanced diet.

(Sweets, fats, and oils are not actually considered to be a food group and should be used sparingly.) All the food that a woman eats should be as fresh as possible and preferably organically raised. (For details of the sizes of the various servings in each food group, see chart on page 172.)

Sweets, fats, and oils (use sparingly)

Dairy products (2–4 servings)   Meat, seafood, eggs, legumes, nuts (2–3 servings)

Vegetables and fruit (5–10 servings)

Carbohydrates (5–12 servings)

WATER

About 60% of the body consists of water. Drinking fluids provides most of the body's water; the rest comes directly from food, as well as from the METABOLISM of food. The body loses water via sweat, urine, breath, and feces. Output of water increases in hot weather.

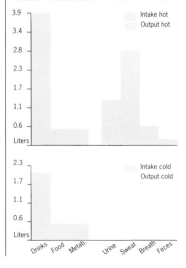

Intake hot
Output hot

| 3.9 |
| 3.4 |
| 2.8 |
| 2.3 |
| 1.7 |
| 1.1 |
| 0.6 |
| Liters |

Intake cold
Output cold

| 2.3 |
| 1.7 |
| 1.1 |
| 0.6 |
| Liters |

Drinks Food Metab. Urine Sweat Breath Feces

FOOD PRODUCTION AND TECHNOLOGY

The production of food in the Western world developed into an industry during the 20th century, with the application of science playing a bigger and more involved part. This has led to the availability of fresh food throughout the year and a reduction in food-related diseases.

In addition, the use of chemicals (herbicides, pesticides, and fungicides) on vegetable and fruit crops and of hormones in animal feed, enabled the demands of an increasing population to be met. Now, however, the Western world overproduces, and very little of its food is sold in its pure, unadulterated state. Even that known as an intact food (a food that is recognizable as a plant or animal) has usually been subjected to chemicals or hormones during its life, with

the exception of organically produced food. Effects on health from the use of chemicals and hormones have led to an upsurge in public outcry against food that has been tampered with (or artificially manufactured, as in the cases of many flavorings and colorings), and a corresponding rise in the popularity and production of organic foods. Intensive farming of animals and poultry has caused many women to change to diets that exclude meat altogether, or exclude meat or animal products that have been "factory farmed."

Food manufacturers are now required to label additives such as coloring and preservatives. The 1980s saw a rise in public awareness of food product labeling and contents. Some food additives have now been banned.

Bread production

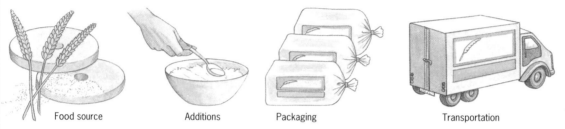

Food source   Additions   Packaging   Transportation

Food processing
Even the most basic foods available in the West have usually been highly processed before reaching the consumer.

SNACK FOOD

Food such as chocolate, cookies, candies, potato chips, and soft drinks is low in nutritional value and usually contains high levels of fat, salt, and sugar, as well as additives such as colors and flavor enhancers. Some of this type of food contains MACRO- or MICRO-NUTRIENTS, but large amounts of poor-quality

snack ("junk") food increase the likelihood of short-term health problems such as weight gain, poor skin, and DENTAL CARIES, as well as of long-term health problems, such as CANCER and HEART DISEASE. Snack foods like fruit and vegetables, however, are low in fat and sugar, and high in nutrients.

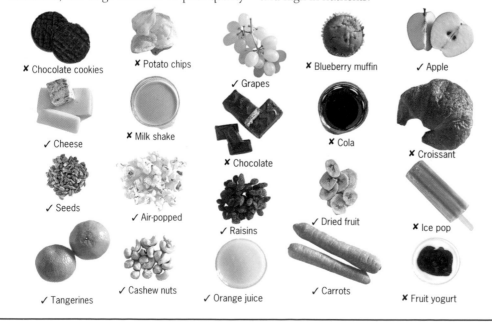

✘ Chocolate cookies   ✘ Potato chips   ✓ Grapes   ✘ Blueberry muffin   ✓ Apple

✓ Cheese   ✘ Milk shake   ✘ Chocolate   ✘ Cola   ✘ Croissant

✓ Seeds   ✓ Air-popped   ✓ Raisins   ✓ Dried fruit   ✘ Ice pop

✓ Tangerines   ✓ Cashew nuts   ✓ Orange juice   ✓ Carrots   ✘ Fruit yogurt

ALCOHOL

Regular ALCOHOL consumption among women rose sharply between 1930 and 1971. In addition, surveys indicate that one woman in 11 drinks over 14 units a week (the maximum usually recommended). Women are affected by alcohol more than men because the average woman's body weight includes a higher proportion of fat and a lower amount of water than that of an average man. Alcohol thus becomes more concentrated more quickly in a woman's body and, because fat absorbs alcohol inefficiently, more is left circulating in the body for longer. A woman's liver is also less able than a man's to process alcohol, so women are more susceptible to cirrhosis of the liver. This has been traditionally a male disease, but about 40% of cases now occur in females.

FOOD NEEDS

There are five levels on which women need food. Each need arises once a more fundamental need has been met, and levels of needs can and do change.

The need for security often expresses itself when a woman becomes anxious, depressed, or lacking in self-confidence. "Security foods" are often chosen for their sweetness (which evokes the taste of breast milk), and their strong links with memories of a woman's childhood home.

Mothers who continually try to "fill up" their loved ones are using food to fulfill their need to give and receive affection.

1 Survival
Regular, preferably daily, sustenance is essential for human physical survival.

2 Security
Once food supplies are regular enough to ensure survival, a woman becomes concerned with the security of the supply. Hoarding may result. Certain foods usually represent security through association with home.

3 Affection
Food may be prepared or given as a sign of affection. Eating the food or making complimentary comments reciprocate this affection, while rejection of the food equals rejection of the person.

4 Status
Food preparation is used to affirm status by demonstrating proficiency. It also establishes and maintains self-esteem.

5 Individualism
Food becomes an expression of the individual through the creation of new dishes and menus, the discovery of a personal style, and experimentation.

DIET AND CULTURE

Eating is more than just the taking in of nourishment; it is an experience that is both social and cultural. What people consider to be "food" (substances they will eat) varies from culture to culture. The way substances are categorized is largely a subconscious process and is highly resistant to change.

This is because food fulfills emotional needs and defines which social and cultural groups a woman belongs to. Studies of immigrants show that clothes and language are readily adapted to fit in with the adopted culture, but food habits tend to be retained for much longer. Within every social group, there are (usually) unwritten rules specifying what is acceptable as food and what is not. "Food," therefore, is drawn from a wide selection of potential foodstuffs (substances that will provide the body with nourishment, but which may not be considered food); no culture classifies all available foodstuffs as food. Hence dog meat is acceptable in China, but not in Europe, while millet, a staple cereal in much of Africa, is dismissed as "bird food" in other countries. Examples of potential foodstuffs include:

- *Cereals – wheat, rye, oats, corn, rice, millet.*
- *Fruit – apples, limes, quinces, breadfruit.*
- *Vegetables – turnips, beets, eggplants, artichokes, okra, chilies, celery root, pumpkin.*
- *Dairy produce – from cows, goats, sheep, camels, llamas, donkeys, horses.*
- *Meat protein – from cows, pigs, shellfish, sharks, dogs, horses, snails, grubs, insects.*

THE SIGNIFICANCE OF FOOD

In many Indian, South American, and African societies, food is seen as being either "hot" or "cold" and, to keep the body in harmony, a balance must be maintained between the two extremes. A similar dichotomy is evident in the Chinese principles of YIN/YANG; food is regarded as either yin (cold) or yang (hot). In the West, food tends to be categorized as either "fattening" or "nonfattening."

RITUALIZED FOOD

In every culture, certain foods have acquired a ritual significance, such as food that is served on special occasions (pumpkin pie at Thanksgiving, for example). Some cultural rituals were originally associated with food, but have become separated over time, as is true of many wedding traditions. Confetti originated in the rice or wheat that was thrown at a couple (above) to ensure fertility. A similar Roman custom was to throw nuts at newlyweds; this has survived in the form of the sugar-coated almonds that are sometimes given as favors at wedding receptions.

RELIGION AND FOOD

Millions of people have their eating habits dictated by their religion. In India, for example, a large percentage of the population is vegetarian in respect for the Hindu tenet that all life is sacred. Other religions also place restrictions on the consumption of meat, such as pork (Jews, Muslims), beef (Sikhs), and shellfish (Jews). Most religions also have rules governing when certain foods can or can't be eaten (many Roman Catholics traditionally eat no meat on Friday, for example), and many have special foods or dishes that are eaten at certain times (Jews have a symbolic Passover dish, below, Anglicans often eat Simnel cake at Easter).

OBESITY

A woman is obese when she has excessive body fat in relation to the rest of her body. Obesity is measured using the BODY MASS INDEX (see p.13), calipers to gauge skin folds, and a waist/hip girth ratio. With these measurements, the 1988 Campbell's Survey on Well-being in Canada found that 39% of Canadians 15 years and older are obese. Obesity occurs almost exclusively in industrialized nations. Obese people are discriminated against throughout their lives. This often has a psychological effect on women who are even slightly overweight, and results in many of them having a negative self-image.

Possible consequences of obesity include CANCER, ARTHRITIS, VARICOSE VEINS, HYPERTENSION, DIABETES, and CORONARY HEART DISEASE.

BULIMIA NERVOSA

When suffering from this disorder, a woman will binge rapidly on a lot of food, and then make herself sick or take laxatives to avoid digesting it. Bulimia nervosa is commonly associated with feelings of powerlessness and of anxiety similar to those experienced by anorexic women. In addition to other health problems, tooth decay can be caused by stomach acid washing over the teeth during repeated episodes of vomiting.

WOMAN AND DIETING

In the Western world, a slim body shape is seen as the ideal, both for health and for physical attractiveness. Slimness has become associated, via the mass media, with wealth, popularity, and success, and many people follow strict and often nutritionally unbalanced diets in response.

Supermodel
Embodying the current Western obsession with thinness, many models are extremely ectomorphic and so are naturally very thin. Others, however, are not; they fast constantly and so eat very unhealthfully. It is ironic, therefore, that they are emulated by so many Western women.

"Being on a diet" is a state of normality for many Western women; 90% of Canadian women have been on a diet at some point, but only 5% have achieved lasting success. The passion for dieting ignores the fact that women are different shapes and sizes and have different metabolic rates.

Dieting is unhealthy because it does not change a woman's basic eating habits, nor does it take into account that exercise is also necessary for weight loss. Instead, dieting depends on deprivation. Most of the weight lost in a fast-acting diet is water, then stored energy, and then muscle. Fat is lost last because the body interprets a diet as a time of famine, and reacts by becoming more efficient at functioning on less food, leading to increased weight gain when the diet is abandoned.

The total amount of money spent on diet aids in the Western world is enough to feed all the world's hungry populations.

ANOREXIA NERVOSA

A woman who is suffering from this psychological disorder purposely starves herself, sometimes to the point of death. Although the cause varies, the classic sufferer of anorexia nervosa tends to be a female with low self-esteem who feels she is not in control of her life. The disorder may be triggered by a desire to lose weight and comply with the Western cultural norm of excessive slimness. Anorexia nervosa usually starts during the teenage years and early twenties, and is characterized by an obsession with food and food rituals (such as eating

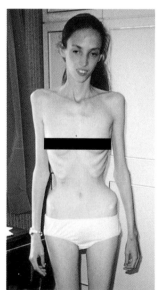

Fatal thinness
A sufferer sees herself as fat.

exactly the same food every night). Hospitalization rarely results in a cure because one food regime is simply substituted for another. As in the case of OBESITY (above left), recovery from this disorder depends on the sufferer being able to see herself as a worthy individual.

MALNUTRITION

This is most often seen in women from countries that are suffering from drought, famine, or war. The symptoms of malnutrition include craving for food, thirst, weakness, feeling cold, AMENORRHEA, abnormally low body temperature, slow pulse, low BLOOD PRESSURE, diarrhea, apathy, DEPRESSION, and an increased susceptibility to illness. In some countries, such as Africa and South America, malnutrition may result following infectious diarrhea. This is because these cultures regard diarrhea as a "HOT" illness and so "hot" foods (which are usually nutritious, such as milk) are not given to the patient. Malnutrition may also occur if women deliberately restrict their food intake, for example, while on strict weight-loss diets or when suffering from ANOREXIA NERVOSA (left).

MINERAL-LINKED DISORDERS

Iron-deficiency anemia is the most common form of anemia and occurs when the hemoglobin (the oxygen-carrying pigment) in the RED BLOOD CELLS is reduced. The result is that adequate oxygen cannot be transported from the lungs to the body tissues. Symptoms include tiredness, lethargy, headaches, dizziness, and palpitations. Women are more prone to suffer from anemia than men.

Osteoporosis is the thinning of the bones caused by the loss of connective tissues and calcium. OSTEOPOROSIS frequently follows a woman's MENOPAUSE.

Osteomalacia is the demineralization of the bones and occurs if an adult's diet contains insufficient VITAMIN D (known as rickets in children). It is exacerbated if the sufferer has had inadequate exposure to sunlight. (Dark skins require longer exposure than pale skins.) Demineralization results in the bones softening and weakening.

Goiter is an enlargement of the THYROID GLAND and appears as a swelling at the base of the front of the neck. Goiters are usually caused by iodine deficiency.

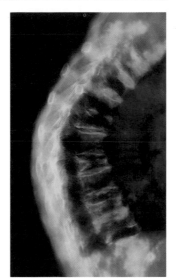

Dowager's hump
After menopause, many women suffer from osteoporosis, which can cause the spine to become deformed.

Goiter-prevalent areas
Enlarged thyroids generally occur where the soil lacks iodine (indicated by dark green areas on the map, right, and including the Alps, Himalayas, Andes, and Derbyshire in the UK). About 400 million people are affected worldwide – women more than men. Iodine deficiency in women can result in cretinism in their infants.

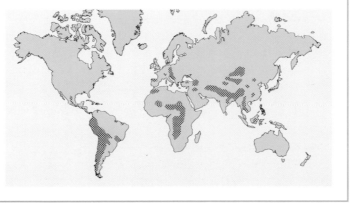

CANCER AND DIET
Some studies estimate that dietary factors, such as fat intake, lack of dietary FIBER, and benzopyrene, may be responsible for 35% of all of the cancers that occur in developed countries.

FAT
The clearest statistical evidence so far is of the link between fat intake and some cancers. Colon and BREAST CANCERS, for example, are far more prevalent in those countries where there is a high intake of fat, as in much of the industrialized Western world. In addition, the children of immigrants from countries with a low-fat intake, such as Thailand or Japan, show greatly increased incidence rates of breast and colon cancers in those countries with a high-fat intake.

BENZOPYRENE
This is a chemical substance that occurs in the charred surfaces of barbecued or burned food and in cigarette smoke. Benzopyrene has been shown to cause cancer in animals, although no conclusive studies have been made yet in human beings.

FOOD POISONING
This is an illness caused by food or water contaminated by bacteria, viruses, molds, chemicals, or TOXINS. Some foods are polluted by the environment in which they were produced (seafood, by raw sewage discharged into the sea). Listeriosis can contaminate soft cheeses or pâté as a result of infection from unwashed hands or inadequate storage. A few foods are naturally toxic (some mushrooms; kidney beans, unless properly prepared).

FOOD ALLERGIES
A food allergy is the common term for sensitivity to or intolerance of a substance that has been eaten or drunk; the immune system responds abnormally to some food, such as milk, eggs, wheat, strawberries, or shellfish. Food sensitivity or intolerance can occur for a number of different reasons, including ENZYME deficiencies that prevent proper digestion of some foods; reactions to chemicals, such as additives or spices; or psychological reasons, such as religious beliefs or traumas connected to certain foods. Symptoms of a food allergy include ASTHMA, ECZEMA, IRRITABLE BOWEL SYNDROME, fatigue, nausea, inflammation (particularly of the skin and joints), HAY FEVER, and migraine. Food allergies are increasing worldwide, and it is thought that this increase is linked to the growing levels of pollution, chemicals in the food chain, and intensive farming. Women appear to suffer from allergies more frequently than men do, and allergy-prone women tend to have babies with allergies. It can be difficult to diagnose a food allergy. Elimination diets, where certain foods are omitted from the diet temporarily, are one of the best, if the most time-consuming, methods of diagnosis.

PHYSICAL WELL-BEING

WHAT IS PHYSICAL FITNESS?

The measure of a woman's ability to do a particular physical task is known as fitness. All-round, or general, fitness means that a woman's body is able to perform many different and demanding tasks equally well. This is possible because she has a healthy heart and lungs, endurance, strength, flexibility, balance, coordination, and suppleness. These are the elements that are necessary for general fitness, and they can be achieved by combining different types of exercise.

ARE YOU FIT?

When you exercise, your pulse should not exceed that caused by a bout of mild exertion, such as running in place for 30 seconds. If you are fit, your pulse rate will stay at about the level indicated below for 20 minutes of continuous exercise.

Age in years	Pulse rate
15-19	146
20-24	142
25-29	138
30-34	134
35-39	130
40-44	126
45-49	122
50-54	117
55-59	113
60-64	109

Beats per minute.

A HEALTHY LIFESTYLE?

A woman's body has certain basic requirements that need to be fulfilled to enable her to follow a healthy lifestyle. These requirements date from early human evolution and are often incompatible with the demands of industrialized societies.

For example, the body is designed to spend the majority of the time either erect or lying down. Sitting for any lengthy period of time sets up stresses within the body that lead to the tension and stiffness that modern life often generates. The body is also designed to be physically active, whereas many working women in the Western world are generally inactive for long periods.

Even a woman who is very active and fit and who eats a good, well-balanced diet, is vulnerable to environmental TOXINS (exhaust

Modern-day stress
In the industrialized nations, working women often spend long hours in sedentary occupations.

fumes, cigarette smoke, industrial waste), that affect her body's IMMUNE SYSTEM and its ability to cope with STRESS and disease.

THE BENEFITS OF EXERCISE

Most women are motivated to exercise by the resulting improvements in their body shape and posture, as well as the changes in health and lifestyle. The benefits of exercise have been conclusively proven: it decreases STRESS, helps to maintain an ideal weight, increases energy levels, prevents insomnia, and may help a woman to live longer. Not all exercise provides the same benefits. Aerobic fitness, strength, and flexibility can all be promoted by different activities; a very few activities, most particularly swimming, are beneficial for all three. Regular exercise is also essential for good health, and has been shown to protect against CANCER, HEART DISEASE, OSTEOPOROSIS, and poor circulation, and to help prevent anxiety, DEPRESSION, and insomnia, and may also relieve menstrual problems in some cases. Excessive exercise, however, has been found to increase vulnerability to disease by suppressing the IMMUNE SYSTEM.

Activity	Aerobic fitness	Strength	Flexibility
Swimming	✓✓✓	✓✓✓	✓✓✓
Cross-country skiing	✓✓✓	✓✓✓	✓✓
Jogging/running	✓✓✓	✓✓✓	✓
Cycling	✓✓✓	✓✓✓	✓✓
Dancing	✓✓	✓✓✓	✓✓
Volleyball	✓✓	✓✓✓	✓✓
Brisk walking	✓✓	✓	✓
Tennis	✓✓	✓✓✓	✓✓
Climbing stairs	✓✓	✓✓	✓
Digging garden	✓✓	✓✓✓	✓✓
Housework	✓	✓	✓✓
Golf	✓	✓	✓✓
Roller skating	✓✓	✓✓	✓✓
Downhill skiing	✓✓	✓✓✓	✓✓

A WOMAN'S EXERCISE WEAR

Unless a woman plays for a team that has a special uniform, the choice of exercise clothing is very much an individual one. Cotton clothing is ideal as it allows the evaporation of SWEAT, which regulates body temperature, while spandex offers a close fit and good support. Wearing a sports bra is important when doing any exercise that involves vigorous movements. Many sports also require a degree of protective clothing. Helmets, goggles, gloves, and mouth, elbow, or knee guards are used in a variety of activities. When horseback riding, for example, a hard hat is a requirement, and many riders also choose to wear protective goggles. Sunglasses are vital where glare is a problem, as when skiing.

Correct clothing
Comfortable and appropriate clothes and shoes are essential, whatever the form of exercise.

SPORTS SHOES

Choosing the correct shoe to support the feet while pursuing a particular activity is of the utmost importance; poorly fitting or badly designed shoes can result in injury, from blisters to a twisted ankle or jarred knee. The types of movements performed in the activity will dictate the type of shoe chosen.

Mountain biking
Bikers wear a helmet, gloves, tight shorts, and special shoes.

TYPES OF EXERCISE

Different aspects of fitness are maintained by specific types of exercise. AEROBIC EXERCISE (below), such as swimming, dancing, jogging and brisk walking, burns fat and conditions the heart, lungs, and circulation; training improves STRENGTH and muscular endurance; STRETCHING increases flexibility; and balance and coordination exercise MOTOR FITNESS. For total fitness, it is necessary to perform activities from each of these areas. Some activities, such as sprinting, lifting heavy weights, and squash, are anaerobic. This means that they are high-intensity activities that are performed over a short space of time and concentrate on increasing muscle tone.

AEROBIC EXERCISE

This is the usual name given to exercise in which the body's need for oxygen is met continuously; the rate at which the muscles use up the available oxygen is matched by the rate at which oxygen reaches the muscles. This type of exercise increases fitness and should be done nonstop for at least 20 minutes three times a week. Aerobic exercise is not confined to fitness classes (below); many other physical activities, such as tennis, cycling, digging in the garden, and ballroom dancing (right) are aerobic.

Relaxed shoulders

Bottom tucked in

"Soft" knees

Aerobics
A correct start position (above), will ensure that the rest of the exercises will be done safely.

Ballroom dancing
This is aerobic if done vigorously.

MOTOR FITNESS

This is concerned with balance, speed of reactions, and coordination. Women tend to be better than men at performing activities requiring a high degree of motor fitness. Gymnastics, for example, is one of the highest disciplines of motor fitness, and is a very female-dominated sport.

Motor fitness activities

- *Horseback riding*
- *Surfing*
- *Windsurfing*
- *Skiing and waterskiing*
- *Competition diving*
- *Acrobatics*
- *Figure skating*
- *Ballet dancing*
- *Rock climbing*
- *T'ai chi*

Balance and coordination
Rock climbing (above) and t'ai chi (left) are seemingly very different activities, but each requires high levels of balance and coordination.

STRENGTH

Increasing the strength of the body's muscles can be done either by dynamic exercise, which involves changing the length of the individual muscles, or by isometric exercise, which involves the muscle contracting without shortening.

DYNAMIC EXERCISE

This involves repeated movements of a particular muscle group against a force, such as when training with weights. It is not necessary to move heavy weights to tone the muscles. Indeed, if toning rather than muscle building is the aim, then instructors advise that a moderate circuit of a range of equipment (such as that found in a good gym) be made no more than three times a week.

ISOMETRICS

Muscles contract without shortening during isometric exercise, whereas other strength exercises alter the length of muscles. One example of an isometric exercise is pushing your palms together to exercise your arm muscles. Isometric exercise is thought to give rapid results in shaping muscles. If done improperly, however, such exercises can be dangerous, so it is important to attend a class rather than do them at home.

MUSCLE TONING

Women are able to tone up their muscles as well as improve muscular strength and endurance through weight training. Overdeveloped and bulging muscles will not result unless the weight-training program has been tailored specifically for body-building purposes.

Rowing machine (below)
Regular use of a rowing machine tones most of the major muscles in the body, particularly those in the arms, back, legs, and buttocks.

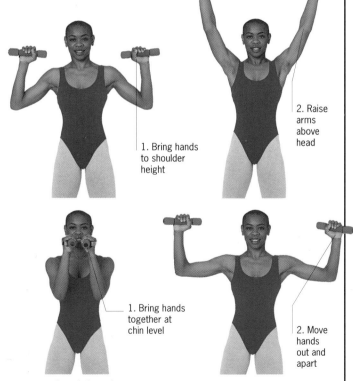

1. Bring hands to shoulder height

2. Raise arms above head

1. Bring hands together at chin level

2. Move hands out and apart

Free weights (above)
Exercising using hand weights is a good way of toning the arm, shoulder, and pectoral muscles. Toning the pectoral muscles can improve a woman's cleavage.

STRETCHING

All mammals stretch their muscles after they have been in one position for a long time, such as after sleeping. Stretching elongates the muscles and thus prevents injury, relieves muscle soreness, relaxes the body, and relieves tension. The exercise shown below is known as the good-morning stretch. It should be one continuous movement.

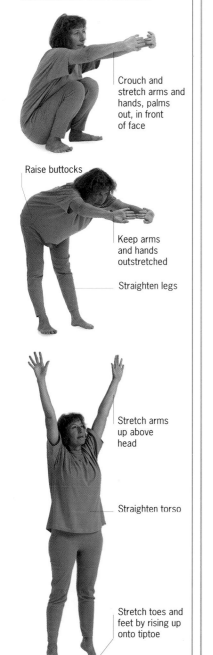

Crouch and stretch arms and hands, palms out, in front of face

Raise buttocks

Keep arms and hands outstretched

Straighten legs

Stretch arms up above head

Straighten torso

Stretch toes and feet by rising up onto tiptoe

RELAXATION TECHNIQUES

There are a number of ways in which a woman can help herself to relax. Most methods of relaxation are easily learned and practiced at home, although some require a teacher to begin with.

YOGA

There are different types of yoga, some of which emphasize exercise and others meditation. All types teach relaxation and breath control. Yoga postures exercise every part of the body and result in increased suppleness, endurance, and strength. Harmonization of breathing with yoga postures helps a woman to achieve a state of relaxation, and yoga is very useful at relieving STRESS.

TENSE-AND-RELAX TECHNIQUE

Once the body's major muscle groups are loosened, the mind will also ease, resulting in a state of deep relaxation. Knowing if a muscle is very tensed is easy, but it is less easy to be sure when it is relaxed. In the tense-and-relax technique (below), the main muscles are deliberately tensed (as a breath is inhaled), and then consciously relaxed (as the breath is exhaled) consecutively from the feet up to the face.

Shoulder relaxation
Tense your shoulder muscles (above left), hold for a few seconds, and then let them relax (above right).

Tense and relax
Find a comfortable position, with your back flat against the floor (below). Close your eyes and take deep breaths. Starting with your feet, tense each group of muscles in turn, then let them relax.

MEDITATION

The aim of meditation is to free the mind from the usual everyday "chatter." This promotes mental relaxation, which is then followed by physical relaxation. A relaxed mind is achieved either by giving the brain a phrase, word, or mantra (sound) to concentrate upon, or an object, such as a candle flame, on which to focus very intently.

The head is held in alignment with the spine

The hands are relaxed

Lotus position
Energy flows through a straight spine, and a body in balance in this yoga position allows the mind to relax.

DEEP BREATHING

The depth and speed of breathing alter depending on a woman's emotional state. If she is emotionally upset, her breath comes in short, shallow pants from the top of the lungs. When she is relaxed, on the other hand, her breath is slower and deeper, and utilizes more of the capacity of the lungs. This physiological fact can be consciously used in breathing exercises to lower stress levels.

WOMAN AND STRESS

Life-enhancing stress
Moving from one state in life to another provokes a degree of short-term pleasurable stress.

Although many people still think of stress as a wholly negative state, it can, in fact, be either positive or negative. Stress is energy that is associated with change; this can range from something as minor as getting out of bed in the morning to a major life event, such as bereavement or giving birth. As such, it can be seen that life without stress of any kind would be a non-event. Too much (particularly continuous) stress, however, can cause serious health problems, although the occurrence and severity of these vary from woman to woman because everybody has a different stress threshold. Excessive stress also leads to an increase in the use of, and dependency upon, addictive substances such as caffeine, nicotine, and alcohol, and can lead to "comfort" behavior, such as overeating.

Response to stress	Why it occurs	Effects if stress is long-term
EPINEPHRINE and NOREPINEPHRINE released into bloodstream.	Physical and mental faculties focused.	High BLOOD PRESSURE, frustration, worry, impatience, anxiety, insomnia.
Liver releases energy stored as GLYCOGEN.	Energy provided.	Inability to relax, hyperactivity, irritability, fatigue, buildup of cholesterol in blood.
Raised breathing and pulse rate.	Oxygen supply in bloodstream increased and diffused.	Breathlessness and raised blood pressure.
Muscular tension.	Readiness for action.	Dizziness, faintness, heart palpitations, headaches, hypertension, muscles continually tensed or aching.
Digestive process inhibited.	Energy diverted to muscles.	"Butterflies" in stomach, nausea, indigestion, constipation, ulcers.
Perspiration increases.	Body cools as it prepares for action.	Clammy hands, sweating, nervous rashes, ECZEMA.
Need to empty bladder, evacuate bowels.	Body weight reduced in preparation for FIGHT OR FLIGHT.	Very frequent urination, defecation.
Emotional tension.	Preparation for effort.	Crying, nervous laughter, aggression, angry outbursts, depression.

STRESS-RATING SCALE

In the late 1960s, doctors in Seattle, Washington, published (below) the degrees of stress, on a scale from 1 to 100, that their research showed as being commonly associated with life events. A stress score incorporates events of the previous year. Over 150 is considered high.

Cause of stress	Score
Death of spouse	100
Divorce	73
Marital separation	65
Prison term	63
Death in family	63
Personal injury or illness	53
Marriage	50
Losing a job	47
Marital reconciliation	45
Retirement	45
Illness of family member	44
Pregnancy	40
Sexual problems	39
New baby	39
Business readjustment	39
Change in financial circumstances	38
Death of a close friend	37
Change in work	36
Increased arguments with spouse	35
Large mortgage or loan	31
New responsibilities at work	29
Children leaving home	29
Trouble with in-laws	29
Outstanding personal achievement	28
Spouse begins or stops work	26
School or college ends or begins	26
Living conditions change	25
Personal habits change	24
Trouble with boss	23
Change in working conditions	20
Change in residence	20
Change in school or college	20
Change in social activities	18
Change in sleeping habits	16
Change in eating habits	15
Vacation	13
Christmas	12
Minor violations of law	11

TOXINS IN A WOMAN'S BODY

These are poisonous substances that can cause illness and which the body can harbor for years. The most common toxins are introduced into the body by alcohol, nicotine, environmental pollution, saturated fat, food additives, and chemicals. These poisons cause the body to work harder to rid itself of them. This can take a while – for example, the average female liver takes 1½ hours (below) to process one unit of alcohol (right). Women's bodies contain 10% less water than men's, so toxins like alcohol become more concentrated in a woman's blood.

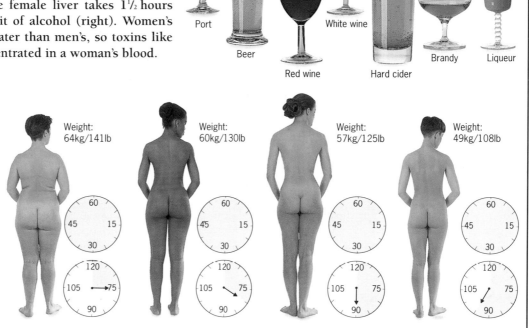

A single measure
Despite the discrepancies in volume, these drinks all contain one unit of alcohol.

Port

Beer

Red wine

White wine

Hard cider

Brandy

Liqueur

Processing alcohol
One "unit" of alcohol is equal to 8,000 milligrams of absolute alcohol, and the liver processes alcohol at the rate of 100mg per 1kg (2.2lb) of body weight per hour; therefore, a woman who weighs 60kg (130lb) will process one unit in 1½ hours. A woman who is very over- or underweight will process alcohol at a slower rate. The women shown right, who are all at their ideal weights, take varying amounts of time to process one unit of alcohol (as illustrated by the clocks).

Weight: 64kg/141lb

Weight: 60kg/130lb

Weight: 57kg/125lb

Weight: 49kg/108lb

WOMAN AND CELLULITE

Unsightly bumps and bulges occurring predominantly on the thighs and buttocks are a uniquely feminine condition, and one that continues to be dismissed by many doctors as ordinary fat. Other doctors, however, believe that cellulite is a form of water retention. When the circulation is sluggish, often because of a sedentary lifestyle and lack of exercise, circulating TOXINS (above) in the bloodstream become lodged in fat cells in areas away from a woman's reproductive organs (because of the action of ESTROGEN). The capillaries then become dilated and PLASMA seeps out until the LYMPHATIC SYSTEM becomes overworked, is unable to drain the cell fluid away, and the whole area gradually becomes stagnant. This gives the skin over the affected area an orange-peel appearance and, as the cells harden over time, deeper dips and dimples. In addition, the area often feels cold, due to sluggish circulation. Some women are more vulnerable to developing cellulite than others, and high levels of estrogen, such as occur during pregnancy, also increase its incidence.

Cellulite can be encouraged to disperse by limiting the amount of toxins entering the body, by stimulating the lymphatic system by brushing the skin and by deep AROMATHERAPY massage, and by increasing physical activity levels.

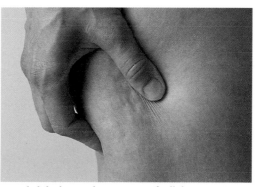

Dimpled thighs are characteristic of cellulite.

WOMAN VS. MAN

The bodies of women and men deal with TOXINS (above) in different ways. If toxins that the liver can't deal with are introduced into a woman's body, they are deposited in fat cells far away from the body's vital organs owing to the action of ESTROGEN. This protective function is thought to be one reason why CELLULITE (left) occurs only in women. When estrogen levels drop after MENOPAUSE, excess toxins tend to clog the arteries and cause higher rates of heart attack.

ACUPUNCTURE

Originating in China over 2,000 years ago, acupuncture is based on the concept of the flow of life energy, or chi (pronounced "key"), through 14 meridians (channels or pathways) that run through the body. On each meridian are numerous points at which this energy can be tapped to influence the organs that are linked on a specific meridian. In acupuncture, very slender, sterilized needles are used to tap the energy (which may result from stimulation of the LYMPHATIC or NERVOUS SYSTEMS),

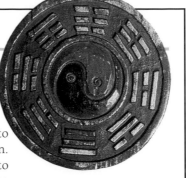

The ancient symbol of yin/yang.

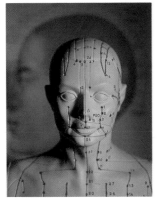

Meridians
The acupuncture points on each meridian are numbered.

while acupressure, or SHIATSU, applies pressure to precise points. The aim of acupuncture, shiatsu, and REFLEXOLOGY (below) is to bring yin and yang (the two opposite flows) of chi into balance within the body. Yin is characterized as being feminine, dark, cold, solid, and passive, while yang is perceived as masculine, light, hot, hollow, and active. Both are equally important, and a balance between the two forces is considered essential if good health is to be maintained. The yin meridians are on the inside or front surfaces on the body, while the yang meridians are on the outside or back. Chi flows up the yin meridians and down the yang meridians.

Acupuncture may be used in treating high BLOOD PRESSURE, digestive disorders, fatigue, poor circulation, ARTHRITIS, and sciatica. It can also be used to help a woman fight addictions, to ease menstrual cramps, and to stimulate childbirth.

WOMAN VS. ANIMAL

Acupuncture is not only effective in treating women; in China it has been used successfully for centuries to treat animals. Some vets in the Western world also use acupuncture.

COLOR THERAPY

The psychological effects of color are well documented. Color therapists also believe that individual color wavelengths affect the cells and organs of the body and can influence mood and perceptions (below). Good health can be maintained or regained by exposure to one or more pure colors.

Red
Increases vitality; can be exhausting.

Orange
Encourages enthusiasm; antidepressant.

Yellow
Promotes detachment and insecurity.

Green
Creates indecision and harmony.

Turquoise
Promotes objectivity; refreshes.

Blue
Encourages relaxation; recharges energy.

Violet
Promotes sensuality and peacefulness.

Magenta
Increases composure and individuality.

REFLEXOLOGY

This therapy involves stimulating reflex points on the feet that correspond to the meridians in ACUPUNCTURE. Most reflex points (zones in reflexology) are on the soles, with a few on the top of the feet and around the ankles. Each foot is slightly different; the illustration is of the left foot.

Reflexologists believe that sensitivity in one part of the foot indicates a disorder or weakness in the corresponding body area.

Problems with the feet, such as corns and BUNIONS, can cause problems in the corresponding parts of the body. Many women with bunions, for example, often suffer from neck problems.

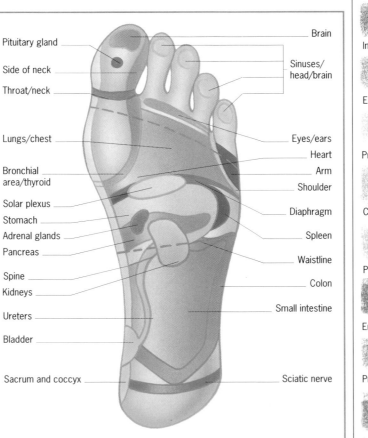

Pituitary gland
Side of neck
Throat/neck
Lungs/chest
Bronchial area/thyroid
Solar plexus
Stomach
Adrenal glands
Pancreas
Spine
Kidneys
Ureters
Bladder
Sacrum and coccyx

Brain
Sinuses/head/brain
Eyes/ears
Heart
Arm
Shoulder
Diaphragm
Spleen
Waistline
Colon
Small intestine
Sciatic nerve

MASSAGE

Touch is essential for health: a woman can become depressed and irritable if she is not touched. In addition, touch lowers BLOOD PRESSURE. Massage arose out of innate human desire to touch and groom others, just as other mammals do. Massage not only relaxes and soothes, it also stimulates the CIRCULATORY and LYMPHATIC systems – both of which are important in preventing EDEMA and CELLULITE from developing. Some cultures, such as in northern European countries and the US, have strong social taboos against touching because sensuality is closely linked with sexuality. In others, such as India, children are massaged from birth and taught from an early age how to give massages in return.

Keep elbows out while pulling the flesh up

Warmth is important for relaxation

Kneading
Muscles are stretched and relaxed by kneading. The blood circulation and the lymphatic system are also stimulated by kneading.

Pressure is exerted by thumbs on either side of the spine

Pressure
The pressure of the hands gently stretches the spine.

Stroking
This reduces muscle tension and improves the circulation.

SHIATSU

Also known as acupressure, this type of Eastern therapy follows ACUPUNCTURE in theory. In shiatsu, pressure is applied with fingers, thumbs, or palms to points on the MERIDIANS. It is used to release muscular tension or to improve the health of the internal organs, each of which is linked to a meridian.

Pressure is firmly applied

Applying pressure
Direct pressure is held for three to five seconds on certain key areas and may be repeated.

AROMATHERAPY

Smells are interpreted by the inner core of the brain, the area that is concerned with emotions. Scents therefore tend to have powerful effects on mood and health. Concentrated essences, such as are used by aromatherapists, are a complex mixture of chemicals. Different essences have specific properties.

Warning
Aromatherapy oils should never be taken internally. Except for bergamot, rose, and neroli, the oils in this chart should be avoided by pregnant women, although lavender and chamomile need be avoided only for the first three months of the pregnancy.

Oil	Properties
Bergamot	Antiseptic, astringent, antidepressant. Used for acne and greasy skin or hair. Sensitizes the skin, so do not use just before sunbathing.
Chamomile	Calming, soothes the nerves. Suitable for sensitive skins. Used in hair products to lighten blonde hair.
Clary sage	Astringent, stimulating. Stimulates UTERINE CONTRACTIONS. Used as a fixative in perfume.
Eucalyptus	Antiseptic and stimulating. Used for treating coughs and colds, and aching muscles.
Geranium	Astringent, diuretic, antidepressant. Tones the skin, helps blend fragrances, and repels insects.
Jasmine	Antidepressant, aphrodisiac. Stimulates uterine contractions. Good for treating depression.
Lavender	Antiseptic, analgesic, calming. Treats headaches, insomnia, depression, aches, wounds, insect bites.
Marjoram	Analgesic, sedative, warming, comforting. Treats aches and pains, DYSMENORRHEA (menstrual pains), insomnia, and headaches. Increases local blood circulation, so useful after exercise.
Neroli (orange blossom)	Sedative, calming, aphrodisiac. Helps relieve anxiety and insomnia. Neroli is especially suitable for dry skin.
Rose	Antiseptic, sedative, antidepressant. Extremely expensive, but only a little is needed to add its distinctive fragrance.
Rosemary	Stimulating, helps memory and clear thinking. Treats RHEUMATIC PAIN, and aches and pains. Used in shampoo and hair conditioner to enrich dark hair color.

SAUNAS AND STEAM BATHS

Developed by the Finns, saunas use intense dry heat of not less than 38°C (100°F) in order to stimulate perspiration. Users sit naked in a cabinet or in a small room that is heated by a stove in the center. The sauna is then followed by a swim or shower in cold water. Those who want a more vigorous sauna may also be struck with birch twigs, which causes a stinging sensation. The profuse perspiration caused by a sauna can cause water weight loss, relieve aches and respiratory problems, and cleanse the skin.

STEAM ROOMS

These use moist (steam) heat rather than dry heat. Steam heat induces far more profuse perspiration than dry heat does and so promotes a quicker loss of water-retained TOXINS. A steam session is then followed by a shower or cold swim, and is frequently combined with a sauna.

Sauna cabinet
Heat (either dry or moist) is fed into a body-encasing cabinet.

HYDROTHERAPY

Water has been renowned for its therapeutic qualities since Greek and Roman times. In hydrotherapy (*hydro* is Latin for water), water is used for relaxation, toning the skin, relieving muscular aches and pains, and even reshaping the figure. The first modern hydrotherapy center was set up during the early 19th century. Hot and cold water are frequently applied alternately to stimulate BLOOD CIRCULATION. Heat increases blood flow to the skin as the blood vessels dilate; cold causes the vessels to constrict, sending blood back to the heart. One recent study found that regular cold baths stimulate the IMMUNE SYSTEM and boost ESTROGEN levels.

THALLASOTHERAPY

There is a close affinity between the minerals present in seawater and those in the human body. Thallasotherapy can involve being sprayed with, or lying in, seawater, or being wrapped in seaweed.

Turkish baths inspired many 19th-century artists.

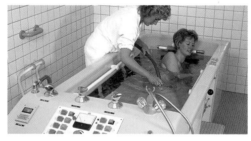

Hydrotherapy is used to tone the skin.

TURKISH BATH

Hamams (Turkish baths) remain an essential part of daily life in such cities as Istanbul, although they are no longer popular in the rest of Europe. Turkish baths are built as two separate units (one for women, one for men), and are recommended to free the body of TOXINS, clean the skin, and relieve high fever, ARTHRITIS, and DEPRESSION.

BEAUTY TREATMENTS

Facials are used to cleanse and exfoliate the skin and come in many forms. Warmth opens up the pores, and various products are used to remove dirt and dead skin cells. Massage is usually given to stimulate the CIRCULATION.

Wrapping is becoming more popular as a way of toning and smoothing the body. Blankets, bandages, or plastic film are used to help treatment creams or minerals penetrate the skin, reshape the body, and achieve loss of inches.

THERAPEUTIC BATH ADDITIVES

Volcanic mud contains many therapeutic minerals. During a mud-filled bath, these minerals coat the skin and stimulate perspiration, which then releases water-retained TOXINS from the body. Other therapeutic substances that can be used in a bath are Epsom salts, which help stimulate CIRCULATION; mustard, which warms the skin and soothes ARTHRITIS; sea salt; and seaweed (above).

Therapeutic bath additives are not recommended for anyone suffering from DERMATITIS.

OSTEOPATHY

First developed at the end of the 19th century, osteopathy is concerned with the maintenance of the structural and mechanical efficiency of the body's framework. Central to osteopathy is a belief that the body is an interrelated whole and that slight displacement of the spine causes a blockage of the blood vessels.

Osteopaths believe that diverse disorders can be treated using manipulation, massage, and exercise. Consequently, they think osteopathy is useful in relieving structural problems, such as joint pain, as well as problems such as PMS (premenstrual syndrome) and DYSMENORRHEA (menstrual pains). Further scientific studies are needed in this practice for it to receive medical acceptance. Osteopaths are rare in Canada for this reason.

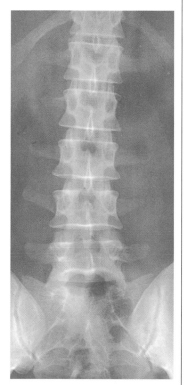

Healthy spine
Osteopaths believe that even slight displacement of the vertebrae affects the rest of the body.

HOMEOPATHY

Based on the belief that like cures like, homeopathy treats diseases and disorders with substances that, in a healthy individual, would provoke the same kinds of symptoms as the patient is manifesting. Symptoms are thought to be a sign of the body's attempt to heal itself; homeopathy seeks to stimulate this healing process.

Homeopathic remedies may be taken from mineral, plant, or animal sources and are always extremely diluted. This is believed to increase their effectiveness and is known as potentization. It is also thought to make the remedies harmless.

An increasing number of women in the Western world are looking into alternatives to conventional medicine, such as homeopathy, for relief from various complaints. These include PMS (premenstrual syndrome), DYSMENORRHEA (menstrual pains), YEAST INFECTIONS, ECZEMA, ASTHMA, and colds. However, further scientific studies would be needed in this area for it to gain medical approval. Homeopathic remedies can be prescribed by private practitioners as well as by doctors who are qualified homeopaths. They are also available in some pharmacies.

Surukuku snake
Lachesis, from surukuku venom, relieves menopausal hot flashes.

Pulsatilla
Menstrual problems can often be treated with pulsatilla.

CHIROPRACTIC

A slight displacement of a woman's spine is thought by chiropractors to be detrimental to a variety of her bodily functions. They believe this to be the result of nerve transmission being hindered, which causes the nerves to become inflamed. Chiropractors believe that manipulation of joints and muscles can realign the spine and allow the nerves to function freely, and therefore enables the body to recuperate. They perform physical examinations, use X-rays, and carry out joint and nerve tests to diagnose the problem. Chiropractic can help to relieve headaches, back problems, ARTHRITIS, and neuralgia (chronic pain). It is a popular form of treatment in Canada.

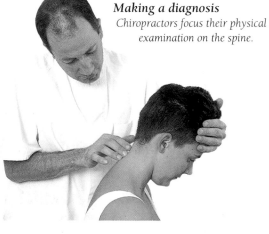

Making a diagnosis
Chiropractors focus their physical examination on the spine.

Spinal examination
The entire spine, from the neck (left) to the small of the back (right), is minutely examined for any deviations or lesions (inflamed areas).

CERVICAL SMEAR (PAP) TEST

Regular cervical smear tests are important for a woman's health because they are the best method of detecting precancerous and early cancerous cells on the cervix. These types of cells cause no noticeable symptoms and otherwise would be able to develop undetected. Also known as a Pap test (after Dr. George Papanicolaou, the Greek-American physician who developed the test), a cervical smear test is performed during an internal examination, and cells normally shed by the cervix are collected. The cells are then smeared on a glass slide and sent to a laboratory to be tested for abnormalities.

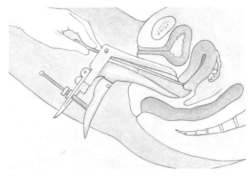

Receiving a Pap test
An instrument called a speculum is inserted into the vagina and opened to hold the vaginal walls apart and reveal the cervix. A spatula and small brush are then used to scrape some cells from the cervix.

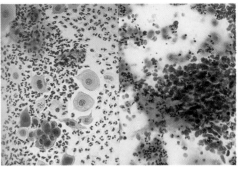

Cervical cells
Abnormal or atypical cervical cells (above right) usually have larger nuclei that stain much darker than normal cervical cells (above left) when exposed to particular laboratory dyes.

WOMAN VS. MAN

Compared to women, men have fewer routine medical checks of specific areas of their bodies. Men do, however, have blood tests for problems such as high levels of cholesterol.

Breast cancer in women is often detected following self-examination; men are now encouraged to check their testicles on a regular basis because testicular cancer is treatable if detected early enough. If a man finds one or more distinct pea-sized or larger lumps on his testicles, he should ask his doctor for a checkup.

GUIDELINES FOR MEDICAL CHECKUPS

Name of test and purpose	When recommended	When to begin	Frequency of follow-up
Blood pressure To check on the state of the heart and arteries.	If you have a family history of high BLOOD PRESSURE, heart or kidney disease, STROKE, or DIABETES; if you are overweight; if you had TOXEMIA during pregnancy.	Once as a child, then from the age of 30 onward. Earlier, as determined by prescription drugs or medical problems.	Annually, or depending on reason for which blood pressure was taken originally.
Blood tests To check for specific disorders, particularly during pregnancy.	If you have a family history of HEART DISEASE, STROKE, or DIABETES; if ANEMIA is suspected; in pregnancy.	From the age of 30 onward, or earlier if you are pregnant or anemia is suspected.	According to your doctor's recommendation.
Complete physical examination To check on the general health of heart, lungs, brain, and major internal organs.	After a serious illness or surgery; if you are worried by a nonspecific symptom. If you have been subjected to severe levels of STRESS.	Rarely needed before the age of 30, unless there is a specified reason.	According to your doctor's recommendation.
Internal examination To examine the pelvic floor, PERINEUM, and pelvic organs.	On a regular basis as a preventative measure, and if you have menstrual problems or a persistent complaint of the pelvis, vagina, or perineum.	Before you start any new contraceptive; when first pregnant or if you have a pelvic inflammation.	According to your doctor's recommendation.
Cervical (Pap) test To detect premalignant changes in the cervix.	If you have intermenstrual bleeding; irregular periods, or a family history of risk factors.	As soon as you are sexually active.	One year after first test; then every three years unless abnormality is noted or risk factors are increased.
Vaginal smear To detect premalignant changes in the vaginal cells.	If your mother took the drug DES when pregnant with you; after hysterectomy for CERVICAL CANCER.	From the age of 20 onward if in risk group.	According to your doctor's recommendation.
Mammography To detect breast cancer.	If you fall into a high-risk group for BREAST CANCER.	From the age of 50 onward.	Every 2 years, or as recommended by your doctor.

THE
FERTILE
WOMAN

REPRODUCTION

UTERINE SUPPORT

A woman's uterine support system is the same as that of other female mammals. The uterosacral LIGAMENTS attach the uterus to a woman's lower spine and pelvis; this offers adequate support for a nonpregnant human uterus. This system developed in early mammalian evolution, when all mammals walked on four legs. It is a very efficient system, which allows the weight of a FETUS to be suspended from the pregnant animal's horizontal backbone in the most balanced way.

A woman, however, who now walks upright on what were once her hind legs, would be better served if her uterus was supported by ligaments that were strung from her shoulders. This ideal support system has not evolved because all species tend to adapt, rather than rearrange, their existing anatomy to meet changing environmental requirements and behavior.

Consequently, during pregnancy, the weight of the developing human fetus causes the woman's enlarging uterus to sag downward, pulling the uterosacral ligaments at the wrong angle from the bottom of her spine.

This results in backache, which is one of the most common symptoms of pregnancy, particularly in the THIRD TRIMESTER as the fetus becomes heavier. This also frequently results in the woman suffering from a PROLAPSED UTERUS in later life.

REPRODUCTIVE ORGANS

THE OVARIES

Located on either side of the uterus, each ovary is roughly ovoid in shape and about the size of a walnut. An entire lifetime's supply of ova (eggs) is present in a woman's ovaries at birth; these ova are released during ovulation at a rate of approximately one per lunar month between PUBERTY and MENOPAUSE. The ovaries are joined to the top of the uterus by narrow flexible tubes, known as the fallopian tubes.

THE FALLOPIAN TUBES

These vary in diameter along their length, and are about 0.4mm (0.016in) at their narrowest point. They are the pathways down which the mature ovum (egg) travels and meets the sperm. FIMBRIAE (frilly projections) cluster around the trumpet-shaped ovarian ends of the tubes. The ovaries and

fimbriae lie in the small pool of fluid that forms behind the uterus, at the lower end of a woman's abdominal cavity (illustrations of the reproductive organs normally show the ovaries and fallopian tubes laid out above the uterus, as below, for clarity). The ovum is usually shed into this pool and then enters the fimbriae of the nearby fallopian tube. Once an ovum has been "caught," it is held in the outer two-thirds of the fallopian tube for the first two or three days, after which contractions move the ovum along the fallopian tube toward the uterus.

THE UTERUS

This is a hollow organ with thick muscular walls, which is about the size and shape of a pear. It is situated at the top of the vagina and may be tilted either forward (70% of women) or backward (30% of women).

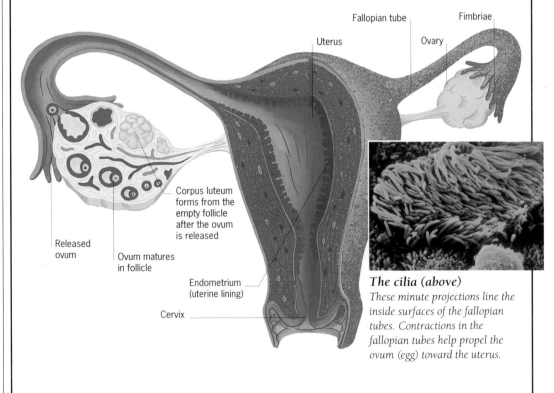

Fallopian tube

Fimbriae

Uterus

Ovary

Corpus luteum forms from the empty follicle after the ovum is released

Released ovum

Ovum matures in follicle

Endometrium (uterine lining)

Cervix

The cilia (above)
These minute projections line the inside surfaces of the fallopian tubes. Contractions in the fallopian tubes help propel the ovum (egg) toward the uterus.

THE OVARIAN CYCLE

The ovaries ripen ova (eggs) in cycles throughout a woman's fertile life. On about day five of the average 28-day menstrual cycle, about 20 ova begin to mature in the ovary within fluid-filled sacs known as FOLLICLES. By day 14, one follicle has out-grown the others and releases its ripe ovum. The other developing follicles shrivel, die, and are reabsorbed, while the ruptured follicle develops into the CORPUS LUTEUM.

Throughout the second half of the cycle, the corpus luteum produces PROGESTERONE, which causes the ENDOMETRIUM (uterine lin-ing) to thicken and soften in readiness to receive the fertilized ovum. If fertilization does not occur, the ovum dies and disinte-grates and the corpus luteum shrivels. The resulting drop in progesterone triggers the shedding of the endometrium during MENSTRUATION. Usually one ovum is released at a time, although some women tend to release several ova, resulting in multiple births, and occasionally no ovum is released. The ovaries ovulate in random order, but over many cycles, each ovary ovulates about an equal number of times.

The mature follicle ripens until it bursts.

GENES AND CHROMOSOMES

All the information required for each woman's unique physical and mental development is carried in her chromosomes. Every cell in the body, except the female ovum (egg) and the male sperm, contains 46 chro-mosomes, in 23 pairs. (An ovum or sperm contains only 23 single chromosomes). Each chromosome consists of two linked, spiraling chains of DNA (deoxyribo-nucleic acid), known as a "double helix." Thousands of pairs of genes, each one a minute unit of the DNA, are arranged along the helix like the rungs of a ladder.

HOW GENES WORK

All the cells in a woman's body contain exactly the same genetic information, but only a few genes are active in each cell – which ones are active is determined by the site and function of the individual cell. If a cell is in the iris of the eye, for example, the genes concerned with eye color are active; if in a blood cell, different genes of the chromosome are active. Genes are either recessive or dominant. A dominant gene will mask a recessive gene, so a genetic trait that is carried by a recessive gene, such as RHESUS-NEGATIVE blood, only manifests itself when a woman inherits two Rhesus-negative genes.

Double helix

Cell

Chromosome

Nucleus

Genes

Cell membrane

Cell division

*New cells are created in the body by
the chromosomes in an existing cell
splitting in half, down the rungs of the
"ladder," and then duplicating to form
the genetic material for two new cells.*

GENETIC AND CHROMOSOMAL DISORDERS

Everybody carries cells with faulty genetic material as a result of imperfect copying during CELL DIVISION (left). Most are harmless, but some cell changes, or mutations, can have a detrimental effect. CYSTIC FIBROSIS is a genetic disorder. Faulty genes can also increase susceptibility to certain diseases, such as CANCER. Chromosomal disorders occur when there is a prob-lem with the amount or the arrangement of the chromo-somal material. Problems usually occur in either the ovum or sperm, or when they combine during FERTIL-IZATION. Down's syndrome (when there is an extra chro-mosome, which results in distinctive characteristics, such as EPICANTHIC FOLDS, a large tongue, and a degree of mental handicap) is an example.

CONCEPTION

When the sperm meet the ovum (egg) in the FALLOPIAN TUBE, several start to penetrate the granulosa (nutrient) cell layers that surround the ovum, and the ovum's tough, elastic outer membrane. To enter the ovum, a sperm has to penetrate through the membrane, and then create a hole through which it can enter. The sperm is able to do this because it has an "acrosome cap." This is made up of enzymes and reacts with, and dissolves, the cells surrounding the ovum. Once the first sperm has successfully entered the ovum, a chemical reaction occurs in the ovum that makes it impenetrable to any other sperm. After the successful sperm has penetrated the ovum's outer membrane, it sheds its tail.

Some sperm do not have an acrosome cap, which means that although they seem completely normal, they are unable to penetrate the ovum. Andrologists (doctors who specialize in the male reproductive tract) can now provide them with a temporary, but workable, acrosome cap.

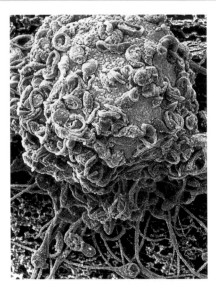

Fertilized ovum (left)
The surface of the ovum is smothered by lots of "loser" sperm.

Fallopian tube (below)
The inside of the tube is lined with ciliated cells (green), which beat rhythmically and thus move the ovum toward the uterus, and secretory cells (magenta), some of which produce substances that maintain a moist environment within the fallopian tube, while others nourish the rapidly dividing fertilized ovum.

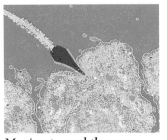

Moving toward the ovum
Before a sperm can actually penetrate the surface of the ovum, it must first pass through the granulosa cells that surround the ovum.

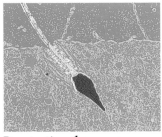

Penetrating the ovum
Enzymes in the sperm's acrosome cap react with cells in the ovum's membrane until they both begin to dissolve. This creates a hole in the membrane through which the sperm can pass.

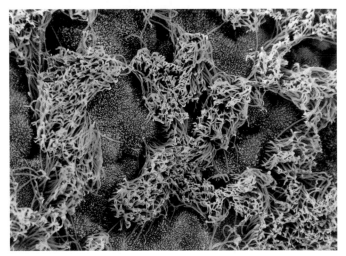

THE PROCESS OF FERTILIZATION

The sperm and the ovum are known as germ cells and each contains individual and unique genetic material (called CHROMOSOMES) in its nucleus. Once the sperm's nucleus (head) is inside the ovum, the two nuclei are drawn together until they fuse in the process of fertilization. Both germ cells carry only half the usual number of chromosomes (23) that are present in every other cell in the parent's body. The single cell that results when they combine (known as a zygote) therefore has 46 chromosomes. A few hours after the fusion, the fertilized ovum divides for the first time. It is now known as a morula, and its two cells each contain a full complement of genetic material. The cells in the morula divide every 12–15 hours, and they are partly nourished by a secretion from the lining of the FALLOPIAN TUBE. Later the morula, which is now composed of about 100 cells, becomes hollow and it is then known as a BLASTOCYST. While the germ cells' nuclei fuse, and the cells begin to divide, more and more sperm try in vain to penetrate the outer membrane, until over 100 may be present on the surface. The lashings of their tails make the fertilized ovum rotate slowly counterclockwise and, since this can continue for some days, these "loser" sperm may play an important role in moving the blastocyst down the fallopian tube toward the uterus.

TRAVELING TOWARD THE UTERUS

The blastocyst's journey down the fallopian tube begins about three days after fertilization. It is propelled by millions of rhythmically beating tiny CILIA that line the inside of the tube, the contractions of the fallopian tube itself, and possibly the lashings of the tails of the loser sperm. The fallopian tube is not the same diameter all the way down, and there is a SPHINCTER muscle between the widest and narrowest parts, through which the tiny blastocyst cannot pass. However, the CORPUS LUTEUM is by now producing increasing amounts of PROGESTERONE, which allows the muscle to relax and open.

WOMAN VS. MAN

A woman's entire supply of about seven million ova (eggs) has been created in her ovaries by the fifth month of her development before birth. This process begins in the very first weeks of her life when the cells that ultimately become the ova are formed within the yolk sac that sustains the embryo before the PLACENTA has developed. About 100 of these cells travel from the yolk sac, across the tissue that will become the umbilical cord, and into the minute areas of tissue that will become the ovaries. They then start to multiply into ova. About five million of these die before birth, and the process of degeneration continues until puberty, when between 200,000–500,000 ova remain. Roughly one ovum per month, or 500 in a lifetime, are actually released via ovulation. Sperm are produced continuously in a man's testicles throughout his life, but take seven weeks to mature before ejaculation. Quality and quantity start to diminish after the age of 40. Sperm are tadpole-shaped and about 0.05-0.06 mm long – much smaller than the ovum, which is about the same size as the period at the end of this sentence. Genetic material is located in the sperm's head, and the sperm "swims" by lashing its tail.

IMPLANTATION

By the third day after FERTILIZATION, the ovum has divided into more than 100 cells and is known as a blastocyst. Before it can enter the uterus, it has to travel through the narrowest part of the FALLOPIAN TUBE. An ECTOPIC PREGNANCY can occur at this point if the fallopian tube has been damaged or blocked, or if the blastocyst gets stuck in one of the folds of the tube's mucous membrane. Once the blastocyst enters the uterus, it ruptures and sheds the zona pellucida (its protective shell) before it implants in the thickened endometrium (uterine lining).

The blastocyst now consists of many hundreds of cells, and small sugar molecules form on its surface. These give it a firm "foothold" in the uterus as they become attached to similar molecules on the endometrium. An exchange of chemicals (HORMONES) then takes place to modify the woman's immune system and prevent it from expelling the "foreign" blastocyst (it is perceived as foreign because it consists of cells that contain genetic material from the father).

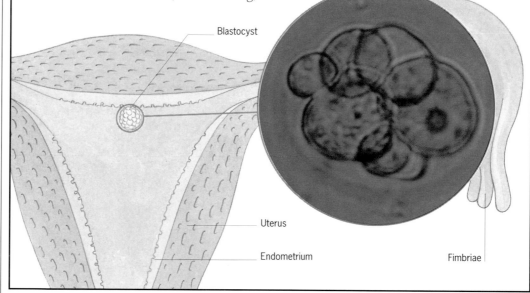

Blastocyst

Uterus

Endometrium

Fimbriae

ELECTIVE TERMINATION (ABORTION)

The termination of an unwanted pregnancy (called elective termination or therapeutic abortion) is not illegal – or legal – in Canada; there is no law against or for it. After discussion and counseling with the physician, abortion is performed by one of a variety of methods, depending on the age of the pregnancy. The earlier it is performed, the fewer risks and problems. An abortion is performed after 20 weeks only under exceptional circumstances.

VACUUM ASPIRATION
Akin to a D&C, this is the most common method used until about 12 weeks. After the cervix is dilated, a small plastic tube is inserted to suction out the uterine contents.

HORMONALLY INDUCED ABORTION
In more advanced pregnancies (12–20 weeks), a prostaglandin suppository or similar device is placed against the cervix. This makes the cervix dilate when the uterus contracts. A hormone causing contractions is injected into the uterus.

DILATION AND EVACUATION (D&E)
In later pregnancies (up to 24 weeks), the cervix is dilated with the help of a drug. Fetal tissues are removed in fragments with specialized evacuating forceps. In the most advanced pregnancies, another treatment, now seldom used, is to inject saline solution into the amniotic cavity, which kills the fetus. The uterus then contracts to expel it.

CONTRACEPTION

PROLONGING LACTATION

Breastfeeding tends to suppress OVULATION and is often used as a method of contraception in developing countries. It is only really effective, however, if the baby is allowed to suckle for as long and as often as it wants, receiving no supplements at all. In the Western world, prolonged lactation as a form of contraception has a high failure rate, due to differences in diet and lifestyle and in what is perceived as correct feeding procedure.

COITUS INTERRUPTUS

This is certainly the oldest, and probably still the most widely practiced, form of contraception.

Coitus interruptus involves withdrawing the penis from the vagina before ejaculation occurs, and it depends on extremely rigorous self-control on the part of the man. No sound data exists on the effectiveness of this method, but it is intrinsically unsound. A delay in withdrawal is likely to cause failure, and sperm are also often present in the preejaculatory fluid.

SAFE-PERIOD METHODS

These methods involve knowing precisely when OVULATION occurs, and avoiding intercourse during this period. Success relies on a predictable ovulatory cycle and, crucially, a woman being aware of her bodily changes. Such methods are often used in conjunction with another contraceptive, such as the diaphragm, during the fertile phase.

RHYTHM OR CALENDAR METHOD

Most women ovulate midway through their cycles, and sexual intercourse is therefore avoided during this fertile phase. It is advisable for a woman intending to use this method to keep a "menstrual calendar" (below) for some months beforehand. This enables her to calculate her fertile period, and to become familiar with changes in her mucus or temperature at this time. Women with irregular cycles generally find this method of contraception unworkable.

CHANGES IN THE CERVIX

In the two to three days preceding ovulation, cervical mucus becomes slippery and clear, and the woman feels "wet." During ovulation, the cervix sits higher in the vagina and feels softer to the touch (more like the lips than the nose). Not all women will be able to distinguish these changes.

CYCLICAL TEMPERATURE CHANGES

Using a thermometer that is in fractions of degrees Celsius, the woman takes her temperature each morning upon waking. Ovulation is indicated when there is a rise of 0.5°C, or more, maintained for three days.

Menstrual calendar

Length of cycle	21	22	23	24	25	26	27	28	29	30	31	32	33	34	35	36
First fertile day	3	4	5	6	7	8	9	10	11	12	13	14	15	16	17	18
Last fertile day	10	11	12	13	14	15	16	17	18	19	20	21	22	23	24	25

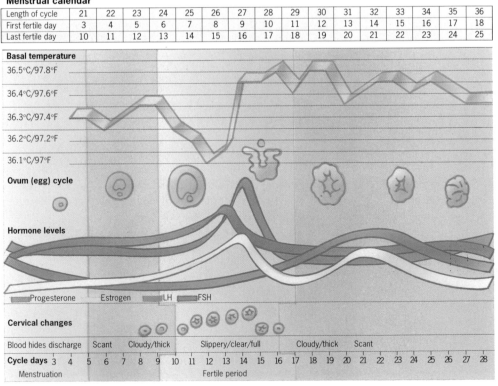

HORMONAL CONTRACEPTION

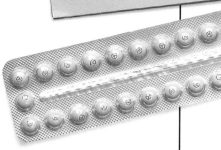

COMBINED PILL

This contains ESTROGEN and one of several progestins – synthetic hormones that have a similar effect to natural PROGESTERONE. One pill is taken every day for 21 days. A further course is begun after a break of seven days (some brands provide inactive tablets for these days). The synthetic hormones "switch off" the HYPOTHALAMUS so that the ovarian FOLLICLES cease to ripen and OVULATION does not occur. The pill hormones take over the control of the ENDOMETRIUM (uterine lining).

During pill-free days, a bleed is experienced because the endometrium has lost this hormonal support. Modern pills contain just sufficient hormone to prevent ovulation, but this is not always enough to maintain the endometrium, with the result that there may be some breakthrough bleeding. A change to a pill with a slightly higher amount of progestin usually prevents this side effect.

PROGESTIN-ONLY PILL (MINI-PILL)

A very small amount of a progestin is taken every day. This makes the mucus in the cervix thick and impenetrable to sperm. The process of ovulation is impeded and may cease altogether. The menses, or periods, tend to be irregular and occasionally stop completely.

HORMONAL INJECTIONS

These contain one of two long-lasting progestins and are given to a woman at two- or three-month intervals. The process of ovulation is impeded and ovulation usually ceases. The menses may be prolonged, although scanty, and irregular.

In about 30% of women, MENSTRUATION ceases completely after two or three hormonal injections; this is regarded as a convenience by many women. Menstruation, and fertility, will return within a few months once the injections are no longer given.

Oral contraceptives
The different varieties of the "pill" are packaged in convenient day-by-day packs.

THE PROS & CONS OF THE PILL

Combined pill	Progestin-only pill	Hormonal injections
Advantages	**Advantages**	**Advantages**
Regulates menstrual loss.	Minimal metabolic disturbances.	Highly effective and convenient.
Less mittelschmerz (which is literally German for "middle pain" – pain on ovulation).	Minor side effects of combined pill are not experienced.	Decreased risk of pelvic inflammatory disease.
Reduced menstrual flow.	The return of fertility is more rapid than in the case of the combined pill.	Decreased risk of ectopic pregnancy.
Can be used during lactation		Reduced menstrual flow.
		Can be used during lactation.
Disadvantages	**Disadvantages**	**Disadvantages**
Weight gain.	Menstrual pattern often erratic.	Irreversible for 2–3 months.
Fluid retention.	Increased risk of OVARIAN CYSTS and ECTOPIC PREGNANCY.	Weight gain.
Greater incidence of breakthrough bleeding, GALLSTONES, and nausea.		Increased incidence of acne.
Contact lens problems.		
Increased vaginal discharge.		
Increased incidence of migraine and headaches, venous thrombosis (deep vein blockage), raised BLOOD PRESSURE, jaundice, and urinary tract infection.		
Delayed return of fertility.		

LEVONOR-GESTREL IMPLANTS

Capsules of progestin are implanted under the skin on the arm, and last for five years. Contraceptive effects are similar to those of the MINI-PILL.

EMERGENCY CONTRACEPTION

Known as the morning-after pill, this combination of ethinyl estradiol and levonorgestrel is usually effective against pregnancy if taken within 72 hours after unprotected sexual intercourse.

The high dose of hormones required for this form of contraception has associated medical risks. It should therefore be taken in an emergency situation only.

DIAPHRAGM

Diaphragms are made of thin latex and fit obliquely across the vagina, covering part of the front wall and the cervix, thus blocking the passage of sperm. The diaphragm is used in conjunction with SPERMICIDE. It is left in place for at least six hours after sex. Correct insertion can be difficult at first, although it becomes easier with practice. The fit should be reassessed following childbirth or significant weight gain or loss.

Diaphragm

Cervical cap

Vault cap

Cervical caps
In addition to the diaphragm, the cervical cap (which fits the cervix closely) is sometimes used. Another type of cap, the vault cap, is available in Europe.

INSERTING THE DIAPHRAGM
This is best done with one leg propped up. Before insertion, apply a 10cm (4in) length of spermicide inside the dome and around the rim.

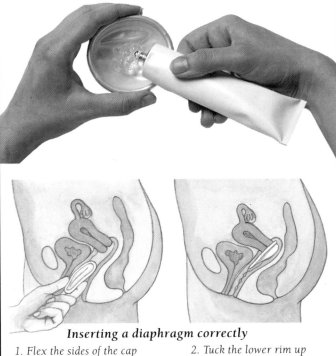

Inserting a diaphragm correctly
1. Flex the sides of the cap together, and push it gently, but firmly, into and up your vagina.

2. Tuck the lower rim up behind your pubic bone, and check that the dome covers your cervix completely.

CONDOMS

Most are made of very thin latex. Condoms for women have recently become available in the United States. Condoms for men are available in a variety of thicknesses, colors, and flavors. Condoms have undergone something of a revival since the advent of AIDS.

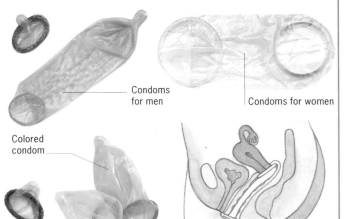

Condoms for men

Condoms for women

Colored condom

Condom for men
This fits snugly over the penis, preventing sperm from entering the cervix.

Condom for women
This lines the vagina and the open end protrudes out beyond the vulva.

SPERMICIDES

These are available in a number of different forms, such as foam, gel, or cream, and work as chemical barriers that are hostile to sperm. Spermicides are usually used in conjunction with the diaphragm or condoms, and are not normally designed to be used alone. Spermicides should always be applied, or reapplied, before sexual intercourse takes place. Perfume-free spermicides are available for women who find they have an allergic reaction to ordinary spermicides. This sensitivity often occurs in women who have used VAGINAL DEODORANTS.

SPONGE

Made of polyurethane foam impregnated with spermicide, the sponge is inserted high in the vagina against the cervix and has a loop for easy removal. The sponge works as a barrier method, but is not very effective, so its use is generally restricted to those with low fertility or for whom contraception is not crucial.

The sponge fits snugly against the cervix

INTRAUTERINE DEVICES

Copper-T IUD

Multiload IUD

Also known as the coil, these are 2.5–5cm (1–2in) long, flat, flexible devices made of white plastic that is partially sheathed with copper or wound around with copper wire. IUDs are inserted by a doctor through the cervix into the uterus, leaving threads that form the "tail" that hangs down into the vagina. The tail is used to check that the device has not been expelled. IUDs should be changed every three to five years by a doctor. IUDs work by irritating the ENDOMETRIUM (uterine lining), which then prevents implantation of a fertilized ovum. IUDs are best inserted during, or shortly after, MENSTRUATION, because the cervix is then slightly open. There is about a one in 500 risk of uterine perforation at the time of insertion. The majority of women experience some discomfort when the IUD is inserted. In past years there have been some complications associated with IUDs, including perforation of the uterus and pelvic inflammation. Problems are less common now, but about 10% of IUDs are removed in the first year because of pain or irregular bleeding, and infection can occur, particularly in those women who change partners frequently, or whose partners have other sexual partners.

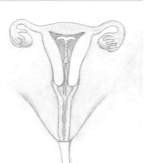

An IUD in position
The hollow tube containing the IUD is inserted by the doctor into the uterus. The IUD is carefully released into the uterine cavity and the plunger is removed, leaving the IUD in place. The threads are trimmed so that they extend 5cm (2in) from the cervix.

STERILIZATION

This is an increasingly popular method of contraception for couples who don't want children or who have completed their families. Full information and some counseling are necessary before a decision is made, because the operation must be viewed as irreversible. Female sterilization often involves "blocking" the fallopian tubes, usually with clips (below), although they may be cut and sewn up. Clip sterilization can be reversed by microsurgery in about 50% of cases.

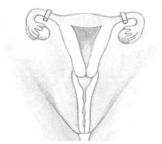

Filshie clips
These are hinged clips that compress the fallopian tube, which then usually divides, leaving two healed stumps.

CONTRACEPTION FAILURE RATES

Method	Careful Users	Typical Users	Disadvantages (perceived or actual)
Combined pill	0.5	1–7	Adverse side effects.
Progestin-only pill	1	1–4	Adverse side effects.
Hormonal injections	0–1	0–1	Can't be reversed; adverse side effects.
IUD	1	1–3	Risk of infection or ECTOPIC PREGNANCY.
Diaphragm plus spermicide	2	2–15	Messy; problematic to use.
Condom plus spermicide	2	2–15	Interrupts sexual intercourse.
Safe-period methods	2	2–25	Need to be disciplined and organized.
Contraceptive sponge	9	9–25	Messy; unreliable.
Sterilization	0–0.5	0–0.5	Requires surgery; must be considered irreversible.

Figures refer to percentage of couples, having regular intercourse, who conceive per year.

VASECTOMY

Male sterilization, or vasectomy, involves severing the *vas deferens* (the tube through which the immature sperm travel from the testicles). The immature sperm are absorbed by the body. Seminal fluid is made in the prostate gland and the seminal vesicles, so vasectomy does not interfere with a man's ejaculation. As with sterilization, the couple should have full information and counseling first.

INFERTILITY

WOMAN VS. MAN

Of all cases of infertility, 30% originate with the woman, 30% originate with the man, 30% are the result of combined factors; 10% remain unexplained. Female infertility has been studied for years by gynecologists, whereas the study of male fertility, known as andrology, is a newer discipline. Nonetheless, doctors are more likely to be able to ascertain the cause if there is a male problem, rather than a female one.

WHAT IS INFERTILITY?

As many as one in six couples consult a physician because of an inability to conceive. Doctors consider that investigation is necessary once a couple has failed to conceive a child after two years of regular sexual intercourse. Many of the people who are infertile according to such criteria, however, do eventually conceive a child. Therefore, fertility is not always a straightforward case of an "all or nothing" ability to conceive.

CAUSES OF INFERTILITY

Female infertility can be caused by many factors: chromosomal problems, such as DOWN'S SYNDROME, which can cause congenital (present at birth) infertility, inability to OVULATE, ENDOMETRIOSIS, blocked FALLOPIAN TUBES, OVARIAN CYSTS, or an abnormal uterus. In addition, a woman's cervical mucus may be hostile to her partner's sperm.

SUBFERTILITY

When a woman's fertility is marginal, such as when she ovulates infrequently, the conditon is known as subfertility. Usually this only becomes a problem if her partner's fertility is also marginal – if a man has a low to average sperm count, for instance – because subfertility in one partner can be balanced by strong fertility in the other.

SECONDARY INFERTILITY

The term secondary infertility applies if a woman who already has a child is unable to conceive another. The problem is usually caused by an infection of the fallopian tubes, which are particularly vulnerable to SEXUALLY TRANSMITTED DISEASES (STDs) and pelvic infections following childbirth or abortion. Many causes of primary infertility can also result in secondary infertility.

HORMONAL PROBLEMS

About 30% of female infertility is due to a failure to OVULATE. Ovulation is controlled by the same finely orchestrated release of hormones that controls the MENSTRUAL CYCLE. If the reason for a failure to ovulate can be pinpointed, it can be treated, usually by the use of synthetic hormones (fertility drugs).

A hormonal imbalance can result in the ovary failing to produce properly mature FOLLICLES in which the ova (eggs) can develop fully. A slightly different hormonal imbalance can mean that although the ovum (egg) matures, the ovary is not triggered to release it.

A malfunctioning hypothalamus may result from underactivity or from physical and emotional stress. The hypothalamus is the part of a woman's brain that is responsible for sending signals to the PITUITARY GLAND. The gland then sends hormonal messages to the ovaries, causing them to produce ova.

A malfunctioning pituitary gland, if it is under- or overactive or has been injured in some way, may not produce the precise amount of FOLLICLE-STIMULATING HORMONE (FSH) and LUTEINIZING HORMONE (LH) necessary for normal ovulation to occur.

CHECKING OVULATION

If a problem with a woman's ovulation is suspected, the physician will test for the level of PROGESTERONE in her blood on day 21 of a 28-day cycle, or seven days before an expected period if her cycles are usually shorter or longer than 28 days. This is because progesterone levels rise when ovulation occurs.

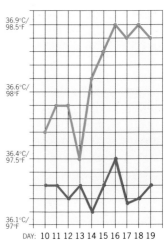

Ovulation temperatures
Temperature rise (blue line) indicates ovulation. Pink line shows failure to ovulate.

STRUCTURAL PROBLEMS

OVARIES

In addition to hormonal problems, the ovaries may be affected by CYSTS, surgery, radiation or chemotherapy, or by environmental factors, such as cigarette smoke inhalation. An otherwise healthy ovary may simply exhaust its store of ova (eggs) owing to the premature onset of MENOPAUSE.

FALLOPIAN TUBES

About 50% of infertile women have blocked fallopian tubes. Healthy fallopian tubes are essential for conception because they are the pathways that allow the ovum and sperm to meet and fuse, and then enable the resulting blastocyst to reach the uterus. The fallopian tubes usually become blocked because of previous abdominal disease or surgery, SEXUALLY TRANSMITTED DISEASE, or pelvic inflammation resulting from such infections. They are extremely delicate structures and it is difficult for them to be made fully functional again if damaged.

UTERUS

Uterine problems account for 10% of all cases of female infertility and may be due to FIBROIDS and congenital (present at birth) abnormalities, such as a SEPTATE UTERUS. Other, more rare, uterine problems include internal adhesions known as synechiae, which can cause the walls of the uterus to stick together, or polyps. The majority of these problems can be successfully treated.

CERVIX

Although the cervix itself does not suffer structural problems that can prevent conception, cervical mucus that is hostile to sperm may play a part, although it is extremely rare for the cervical mucus to be completely sperm-resistant.

FIBROIDS

These benign rounded masses can grow anywhere in the wall of the uterus and range in size from a pea to a small melon. Fibroids affect one in five women over the age of 30, and one in three women over 35. An operation known as a myomectomy can be tried, but it is not always effective in increasing fertility. Fibroids can cause infertility by:

- *Protruding into, and altering the shape of, the uterus.*
- *Compressing or blocking the FALLOPIAN TUBES.*
- *Distorting the relationship between the tubes and ovaries (if growing in the wall near where the tubes enter the uterus) and so reducing the chance of the ovum (egg) entering the tube.*

MALE INFERTILITY

This can be caused by hormonal problems (LH and FSH need to be in balance for sperm to be produced, for example), anatomical problems (with the penis or testes, or the man's ability to ejaculate), or immunological problems (when a man's immune system produces antibodies that attack and destroy his sperm). Studies suggest that male fertility has decreased over the course of the 20th century owing to environmental problems. These include TOXINS, and the use of indestructible chemicals that then enter the food chain.

INVESTIGATING INFERTILITY

When a couple decides to consult a doctor about infertility, the doctor will first assess their health and will ask them about their sex life. The woman will be asked about her menstrual history. Further investigation may include referral of the couple to a fertility specialist. The woman may be asked to keep an OVULATION TEMPERATURE CHART and may have a blood test to check that ovulation has occurred. Her partner will be asked to provide a semen sample. A postcoital test (when sperm and cervical mucus are taken from the woman's vagina six hours after intercourse) may be done to make sure that her cervical mucus is not hostile to her partner's sperm. The woman will be offered a LAPAROSCOPY if she is ovulating and her partner's sperm is normal, and she may be offered an ULTRASOUND SCAN if pelvic abnormalities are indicated. Once the cause of infertility is pinpointed, treatment will be offered.

Primary reason for infertility	Frequency	Causes	Results
Failure to ovulate.	30%	Underactive pituitary gland. Polycystic ovarian syndrome.	No ova (eggs). Ova not maturing. Mature ova not able to be released.
Damaged fallopian tubes.	50%	Abdominal or pelvic disease or surgery. ENDOMETRIOSIS.	Ova cannot reach uterus.
Uterine problems.	10%	FIBROIDS. SEPTATE UTERUS. Synechiae (adhesions in the uterine cavity).	Fertilized ovum (egg) unable to implant. Embryo unable to develop properly.

LAPAROSCOPY

A slender telescope that is equipped with fiberoptics, a laparoscope is about the width of a pen. It can be inserted through a tiny incision in the navel to view the abdominal and pelvic cavity directly. In addition to offering the surgeon a superb view of the organs, high-quality videos can be taken through the laparoscope for later reference.

Laparoscopy allows the normality of the reproductive organs to be assessed. Blue dye is injected through the cervix to check if the FALLOPIAN TUBES are open – the dye trickles from the ends of the tubes. Laparoscopy is often timed for the second half of the cycle to confirm ovulation has occurred and a corpus luteum has formed.

Viewing the ovary
This picture, taken through a laparoscope, shows a healthy ovary (top of the picture) with a mature follicle that will soon burst and release its ripe ovum (egg). The frilly shapes at the bottom are the fimbriae.

ENDOMETRIAL BIOPSY

In this procedure a tiny amount of the endometrium (the uterine lining) is removed and then microscopically examined for any changes. An endometrial biopsy is performed to assess whether a woman's hormones (ESTROGEN, PROGESTERONE, FOLLICLE-STIMULATING HORMONE [FSH], and LUTEINIZING HORMONE [LH]) are bringing about changes to her endometrium during the second half of her cycle. When the hormones are balanced correctly, there is an increase in the production of progesterone, which causes the endometrium to thicken. If progesterone is being under-produced, then the uterine lining will not develop sufficiently for a BLASTOCYST to implant. If there is no, or little, change, then fertility drugs may be prescribed.

HYSTEROSALPINGOGRAPHY

Hysterosalpingography (HSG) is an X-ray view of the interior of the uterus and FALLOPIAN TUBES, and is a useful diagnostic tool in infertility. Injected dye is monitored on an X-ray screen as it travels into and through the tubes. Dye is useful for checking the fallopian tubes as it will only enter, and travel through, open tubes, thus showing up any damage.

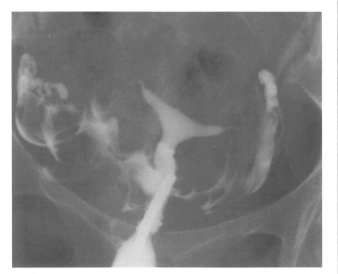

HSG X-ray
Dye billows out of the end of the fallopian tube (left of picture).

ULTRASOUND SCANNING

Using ultrasonography (ultrasound scanning) to check the development of the ovarian FOLLICLES, doctors can track the maturation of the follicles and the release of the ovum or ova at ovulation. The absence of these processes will also show up.

Ultrasonography is particularly useful during ARTIFICIAL INSEMINATION and IN VITRO FERTILIZATION treatment, when knowing the precise time of ovulation is crucial.

MICROSURGERY

Microsurgery, now used for many previously inaccessible areas of the body, involves the use of specialized instruments and optical magnification beyond what the surgeon's naked eye can see.

Microsurgery has been especially useful in treating damaged fallopian tubes, whose interior width is tiny (0.4mm) and whose tissue is delicate and easily damaged by traditional surgery.

Microsurgery has been used to reopen blocked tubes and to remove adhesions (bands of scar tissue), such as those resulting from ENDOMETRIOSIS, that have frozen the tubes into a position that does not allow them to function properly.

The degree of success of microsurgery depends on the amount and type of damage encountered.

HORMONAL TREATMENTS

When failure to ovulate is the reason for female infertility, fertility drugs are the usual treatment. The most common fertility drug prescribed to women is clomiphene, which is taken for only five days at the beginning of each menstrual cycle.

Clomiphene stimulates the release of FOLLICLE-STIMULATING HORMONE (FSH) by the PITUITARY GLAND. This acts on the ovaries and often initiates the ripening of a FOLLICLE and OVULATION. Clomiphene's advantages are that it is free from major side effects and has a multiple pregnancy rate of only 5–10% (usually twins and occasionally triplets; quadruplets and quintuplets are very rare even when a woman is taking a course of fertility hormones).

Clomiphene is an anti-ESTROGEN (the drug was first developed as a contraceptive), so it may actually impede conception if prescribed inappropriately. In addition, women who have been given clomiphene must be monitored regularly using ultrasound, because the ovaries may occasionally develop CYSTS.

If clomiphene fails to stimulate ovulation, a combination treatment with FSH and LH preparations can be used. But this is a complicated treatment that requires close monitoring of the ovaries with blood tests and daily ultrasound scans to avoid the risks of a high multiple pregnancy or ovarian cysts. Some women require even more complex medical management to ovulate.

DONORS

SPERM DONATION

Ideally, sperm donors should be healthy, fertile men who have children of their own. Some donors are the partners of pregnant women, although most donors are students recruited from universities. All sperm is screened for infectious diseases, such as AIDS, and all donors are asked about their genetic family background. Clinics also try to match the donor's physical characteristics to those of the couple but, because a different donor's sperm is usually used at every attempt, the closest match may not be the one that actually results in pregnancy.

EGG DONATION

More complicated than sperm donation, this involves the female donor using fertility drugs so that her ovaries will be stimulated to produce several ova (eggs). The donation process also involves a couple of trips to the fertility clinic and perhaps an overnight stay when the ova are collected. For this reason, many egg donors are women who are undergoing IN VITRO FERTILIZATION (IVF).

Medical data on each donor is archived and can be accessed by the child once she or he is 18.

ARTIFICIAL INSEMINATION

In this procedure, a partner's sperm (TIH) or a donor's sperm (TDI) is routinely introduced onto the surface of the cervix from a syringe. If the sperm are substandard, they are first processed and the more motile selected for introduction through the cervix into the uterus via a syringe. Insemination is done just before or during OVULATION.

TDI may be considered when a woman's partner has a very low sperm count, is sterile, or is known to be the carrier of a hereditary abnormality. Single women who want a baby may also consider TDI. They are assessed by criteria comparable to those applied to couples.

Normal sperm count
Over 30 million sperm per mm.

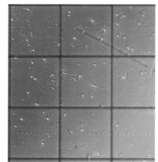

Low sperm count
Under 20 million sperm per mm.

ADOPTION

Owing to changes in society's attitude toward sex outside marriage and to single mothers, the number of babies available for adoption has dropped greatly in recent years. Most couples want to adopt newborn babies, particularly healthy ones.

This means that the screening of prospective adoptive parents is now extremely rigid, and that many children with special needs are not adopted. Many couples do not feel able to cope with special-needs children, however, especially if they have had no experience with parenting.

SURROGATE MOTHERS

Surrogacy involves a woman bearing a child for another woman. In full surrogacy, a surrogate conceives and carries the child of an infertile woman's partner. The surrogate conceives by artificial insemination with the father's sperm. Partial surrogacy involves the introduction of an embryo into a surrogate's uterus. Surrogacy raises many ethical dilemmas for the commissioning couple and the surrogate mother, such as what should be done if the child is born handicapped, or if the surrogate mother does not want to give up the baby after the birth. Historically, a mother's rights were determined by gestation and delivery. Even today, agreements made before a child's birth by surrogacy may not hold in court.

IN VITRO FERTILIZATION (IVF)

Children conceived in this way are commonly known as test-tube babies. IVF was pioneered by British doctors Patrick Steptoe and Robert Edwards in 1978, when the very first IVF baby, Louise Brown, was born. Since then, thousands of test-tube babies have been born. Although this may sound like lots of babies, IVF actually only has about a 20% success rate per cycle of treatment, although it can be as high as 30% under the best circumstances; the process is very physically demanding and stressful.

Once her partner's sperm have been tested for viability, the woman is given fertility drugs to stimulate her ovaries into producing a number of ova (eggs). She is then carefully monitored using ULTRASONOGRAPHY until the FOLLICLES are ripe, when the ova will be collected by her gynecologist. A laparoscope on a probe (long hollow needle) will be inserted through the upper vaginal or the abdominal wall to reach the ovaries, under constant monitoring with ultrasonography. The ova are gently suctioned out of the follicles into the probe, transferred to a culture medium in a glass dish, and then stored in an incubator, where they continue to grow. Once they have reached full maturity (within 2–24 hours), the sperm are introduced. FERTILIZATION usually occurs within 18 hours. The fertilized ova are then kept inside the incubator for an additional 48 hours, by which time each will have divided into about four cells. Embryos are then transferred into the woman's uterus.

A harvested ovum
The ovum is transferred into a Petri dish.

FETAL REDUCTION

During the early stages of a multiple pregnancy, some of the embryos may be destroyed, to reduce the physical risk of the pregnancy to the woman and increase the chances of survival for the remaining embryos. Reduction carries a risk that all of the embryos will be reabsorbed.

ETHICAL CONSIDERATIONS

If an infertile couple decides to go for fertility treatment, and by no means all do, there are a number of important factors to be taken into account:

Issues to consider

- *What if the FETUS was found to have abnormalities?*

- *How would you cope if you had a multiple pregnancy?*

- *Would you consider FETAL REDUCTION (above)?*

- *Would you be prepared to conceive with an unknown man's donated sperm or with a donated egg? Would this affect your feelings toward the resulting child?*

- *If the donor was known to you, what would happen if he or she wanted some involvement in your child's life?*

- *If you did have a child using assisted conception, would you keep it secret, or would you be totally open about it?*

- *If you kept it a secret from your child, how do you think she would cope if something so fundamental came out at a time of stress — or even after your death?*

- *What if your child wanted to find out details about her genetic heritage?*

- *If there were any extra ova, or embryos, would you want them destroyed, donated, or used for research?*

- *Would it be difficult for you to let your "miracle" child grow up and become independent?*

DILEMMAS AND EMOTIONS

Infertility treatment has changed so rapidly in recent years that there are many gray areas within the law. A child born to a married or unmarried woman after DONOR INSEMINATION is assumed to be the child of the woman and her partner.

The ability to have a child is inextricably linked to most women's fundamental sense of self – it is, after all, the way most women "achieve immortality." Whether subconsciously or consciously, many view having children as the ultimate purpose of life. In addition, fertility is often seen, mistakenly, as proof of of being a good lover, or virility in the case of the man. Consequently, many women feel ashamed, hopeless, and angry about infertility. Some report having had dreams of self-mutilation owing to the anger they feel toward themselves and their reproductive organs. If the woman is fertile, she may feel angry with her infertile partner, and he may also feel very guilty. If she is the infertile one, she may feel quite desperate, as well as feeling guilty.

Both partners in a couple may ride an emotional roller coaster during the woman's monthly cycle, as they wait for a successful fertilization attempt. Many women find that counseling helps them come to terms with their situation and enables them to mourn the child they never had; others actively pursue adoption or fertility treatment.

THE
PREGNANT
WOMAN

THE CHANGING BODY

Pregnancy

An average pregnancy is nine months and two weeks long; this can vary by up to two weeks. Despite pregnancy being a biological imperative, and a very real desire for many women, the fetus' relationship with the mother is parasitical. The mother's body chemistry has to be altered so that her immune system will allow the pregnancy to become established and, once it is, the fetus will take what it can from her body to meet its needs.

IT'S A FACT

Greatest number of children

Madame Fedor Vassilyev of Shuya, Russia, gave birth to 69 children during the period 1725–65. In 27 confinements over 40 years, she had 16 pairs of twins, seven sets of triplets, and four sets of quadruplets.

◆

Late starter

Senora Maria Aparecida Brito of Mandaguari, Brazil, had her eighth child at the age of 60 in September 1993. She had her first child at age 41.

◆

Surprise pregnancy

Karen Toole of Watford, UK, unexpectedly gave birth to a 3.7kg (8lb 4oz) boy in October 1992 following abdominal pains after a fall. She had been taking the pill for five years.

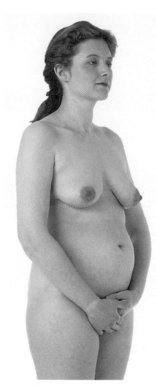

16 weeks

20 weeks

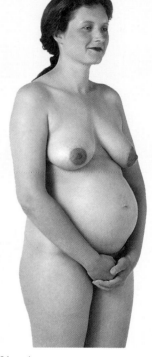

24 weeks

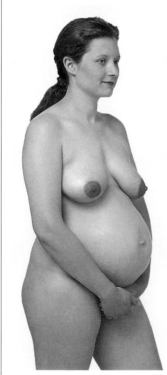

28 weeks

32 weeks

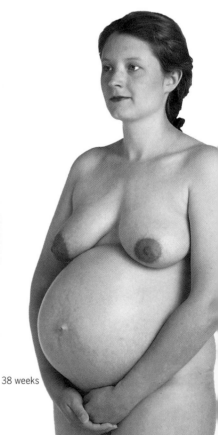

38 weeks

PHYSICAL SIGNS

AMENORRHEA
The cessation of periods is often the first sign of pregnancy. However, some women have been known to have light periods up to the sixth month, and occasionally all the way through pregnancy.

MICTURITION
An increased desire to pass urine is common, owing to the increased blood flow to the pelvic area, which results in congestion. Consequently, organs such as the bladder become extremely sensitive.

FATIGUE
This can be overwhelming, and is the result of the pregnant woman's body working hard to support and nourish the new life growing within her.

NAUSEA
Although this is most common early in the morning, it can occur at any time or be continual. It is caused by ESTROGEN levels and low blood glucose levels.

BREAST CHANGES
These are noticeable from the start of pregnancy. Changes include increased sensitivity to touch, lumpiness, enlarged veins just beneath the skin, and the deepening of the color of the nipple area (below).

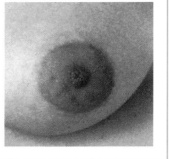

PREGNANCY TESTS

URINE TESTS
These check for the presence of hCG (human chorionic gonadotropin), the hormone that is manufactured initially by the EMBRYO and then later by the PLACENTA.

BLOOD TEST
hCG can be accurately detected in the blood eight days after CONCEPTION. Blood tests are performed by a laboratory.

Not pregnant

Pregnant

INTERNAL EXAMINATION
Usually, if performed by a doctor more than four weeks after conception, an internal examination is very accurate. The uterus begins to enlarge about this time and, because of the increase in blood flow to the pelvis, the color of the vagina and cervix deepens.

Home testing
Urine tests indicate the presence of hCG in the woman's urine. They can be used at home to confirm a suspected pregnancy, unlike blood tests and internal examinations, both of which have to be done by a doctor. Although urine tests do tend to vary in their accuracy, it is possible for hCG to be detected in the urine as soon as two weeks after conception. The best urine tests are over 90% accurate. The majority of the kits include two tests so that the result can be confirmed.

WORKING OUT THE ESTIMATED DATE OF DELIVERY (EDD)

Month	1	2	3	4	5	6	7	8	9	10	11	12	13	14	15	16	17	18	19	20	21	22	23	24	25	26	27	28	29	30	31
January Oct/Nov	8	9	10	11	12	13	14	15	16	17	18	19	20	21	22	23	24	25	26	27	28	29	30	31	*1*	*2*	*3*	*4*	*5*	*6*	*7*
February Nov/Dec	8	9	10	11	12	13	14	15	16	17	18	19	20	21	22	23	24	25	26	27	28	29	30	*1*	*2*	*3*	*4*	*5*			
March Dec/Jan	6	7	8	9	10	11	12	13	14	15	16	17	18	19	20	21	22	23	24	25	26	27	28	29	30	31	*1*	*2*	*3*	*4*	*5*
April Jan/Feb	6	7	8	9	10	11	12	13	14	15	16	17	18	19	20	21	22	23	24	25	26	27	28	29	30	31	*1*	*2*	*3*	*4*	
May Feb/March	5	6	7	8	9	10	11	12	13	14	15	16	17	18	19	20	21	22	23	24	25	26	27	28	*1*	*2*	*3*	*4*	*5*	*6*	*7*
June March/April	8	9	10	11	12	13	14	15	16	17	18	19	20	21	22	23	24	25	26	27	28	29	30	31	*1*	*2*	*3*	*4*	*5*	*6*	
July April/May	7	8	9	10	11	12	13	14	15	16	17	18	19	20	21	22	23	24	25	26	27	28	29	30	*1*	*2*	*3*	*4*	*5*	*6*	*7*
August May/June	8	9	10	11	12	13	14	15	16	17	18	19	20	21	22	23	24	25	26	27	28	29	30	31	*1*	*2*	*3*	*4*	*5*	*6*	*7*
September June/July	8	9	10	11	12	13	14	15	16	17	18	19	20	21	22	23	24	25	26	27	28	29	30	*1*	*2*	*3*	*4*	*5*	*6*	*7*	
October July/Aug	8	9	10	11	12	13	14	15	16	17	18	19	20	21	22	23	24	25	26	27	28	29	30	31	*1*	*2*	*3*	*4*	*5*	*6*	*7*
November Aug/Sep	8	9	10	11	12	13	14	15	16	17	18	19	20	21	22	23	24	25	26	27	28	29	30	31	*1*	*2*	*3*	*4*	*5*	*6*	
December Sep/Oct	7	8	9	10	11	12	13	14	15	16	17	18	19	20	21	22	23	24	25	26	27	28	29	30	*1*	*2*	*3*	*4*	*5*	*6*	*7*

How to use this chart
The date on which a baby is due assumes a regular 28-day menstrual cycle and is taken from the date of the start of a woman's last menstrual period (LMP)..To use the chart on the left: find the date of the LMP on the line where the months and days are marked in bold type. The date underneath is the baby's estimated date of delivery (EDD). If the EDD falls in the following month, this is indicated by a change in type style on the line giving the EDD. For example, the change from October to November (November 1 is the EDD for a LMP of January 25) is indicated by a change from plain to italic numbers. Less than 5% of babies arrive on the day that they are expected.

THE FIRST TRIMESTER

The trimesters are a convenient way of measuring pregnancy. They are of uneven lengths, and the third trimester varies according to how long the pregnancy lasts. The pregnant woman's body has to work very hard during the first trimester (1–12 weeks) to adjust to the developing EMBRYO and PLACENTA.

- *The metabolic rate increases by 10–25%, so that the body accelerates all of its functions.*
- *The HEART RATE and cardiac output rise, and the breathing rate increases as more oxygen is sent to the FETUS, and more carbon dioxide is exhaled.*
- *The muscle fibers of the uterus quickly thicken and grow, and the enlarging uterus will tend to press against the bladder, increasing the desire to urinate.*
- *The size and weight of the breasts increase rapidly.*
- *The breasts become very sensitive, often from the first few weeks of the pregnancy.*
- *New MILK DUCTS grow.*
- *The AREOLA around each nipple becomes darker; sebaceous glands increase in number and become more prominent.*
- *As the BLOOD supply to the breasts increases, the breast veins become more noticeable.*

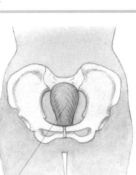

The uterus thickens but remains contained within the pelvis

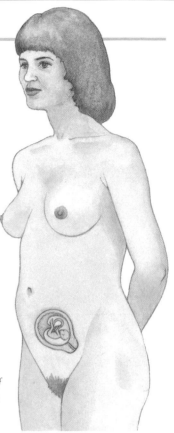

The early weeks
The muscle fibers of the woman's uterus thicken from the beginning of pregnancy, increasing the size of the uterus. The pregnancy is rarely prominent at this time, however.

THE SECOND TRIMESTER

This runs from the 13th to the 28th week. At the start of this trimester, the enlarging uterus protrudes above the pelvic brim, which results in the gradual loss of the waistline.

- *The musculature of the intestinal tract relaxes, causing gastric secretions to decline and food to remain longer in the stomach.*
- *There are fewer bowel movements because the intestinal muscle is more relaxed than usual.*
- *The breasts may tingle and feel sore.*
- *Skin pigmentation is likely to increase, especially in the areas that are already pigmented, such as freckles, moles, and nipples.*
- *The linea nigra (a dark line running down the center of the abdomen) may appear.*
- *The gums may become slightly spongy as a result of the increased action of pregnancy hormones.*
- *Esophageal reflux (regurgitation of the contents of the stomach into the esophagus) may cause HEARTBURN because of the relaxation of the SPHINCTER at the top of the stomach.*
- *The heart is working twice as hard as that of a nonpregnant woman and is circulating 6 liters (10 pts) of blood a minute.*
- *The uterus needs 50% more blood than usual.*
- *The kidneys need 25% more blood than usual.*

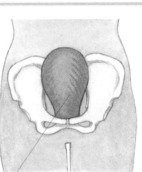

The uterus enlarges and rises above the pelvic brim

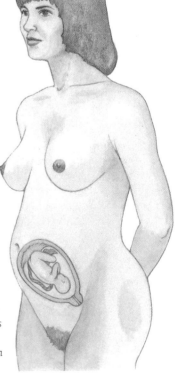

Midterm
As the fetus grows larger, the woman's uterus expands to accommodate it. This results in her uterus growing out and above the pelvic brim. The woman's waistline is then "lost" and her abdomen enlarges.

THE THIRD TRIMESTER

During this trimester (from the 29th week onward), the growing FETUS presses upon, and restricts, the diaphragm. Because of this, pregnant women breathe more rapidly and deeply, taking in more air with each breath. This increases the consumption of oxygen.

- *The ventilation rate rises by 40%, from the normal 7 liters (12 pts) of air per minute breathed by a non-pregnant woman to 10 liters (17pts) per minute, while oxygen consumption increases by only 20%. Increased sensitivity of the respiratory center to rising levels of carbon dioxide in the blood can sometimes result in breathlessness.*

- *As the fetus grows larger and the woman's abdomen increases in size, her lower ribs may spread outward.*

- *Ligaments, including those in the pelvis and hips, stretch (which can make walking uncomfortable).*

- *Swollen, puffy hands and feet may be bothersome and may indicate PREECLAMPSIA.*

- *Low back pain may occur, caused by the shift in the body's center of gravity and the slight loosening of the pelvic joints (owing to the stretching of the ligaments).*

- *The nipples may secrete COLOSTRUM (a thin, milky substance).*

- *Frequency of urination increases.*

- *The need for rest and sleep increases.*

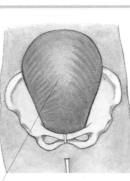

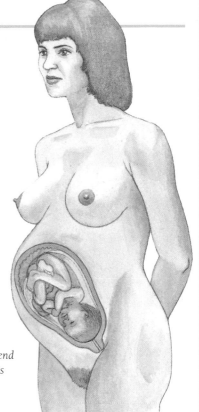

The uterus fills the abdominal cavity by the end of the third trimester, displacing the woman's digestive tract and compressing her stomach and bladder

The last months
The fetus is fully formed by the end of the third trimester. During this trimester the fetus will become engaged (settled deeply into the woman's pelvis).

PREGNANCY AND CULTURE

There are many different cultural beliefs surrounding conception and pregnancy. In medieval Europe, most unmarried women believed that babies were conceived through a woman's navel. Some groups of Aborigines believed that the spirit of a baby entered the mother when the baby "quickened" (made the first fetal movements felt by the mother). Since spirits were believed to reside in natural features, the place where the woman felt the baby quicken indicated the spirit that had entered her. The Anglo-Saxons also believed that the baby's spirit entered the mother's body when she felt the baby quicken; some Inuit people still hold this belief. Roman Catholics believe that the baby's spirit enters at conception.

Food beliefs concerning pregnancy are prevalent in most cultures. In Western societies, some foods are restricted from fear of bacterial infection. In Bolivia, it is believed that pregnancy is a hot state and therefore "COLD" foods are avoided. In Puerto Rico, however, while pregnancy is seen as being hot, "HOT" foods are avoided to prevent the baby from being born with a rash. In China, cold foods are not eaten during pregnancy because of a fear of MISCARRIAGE.

In many parts of the Caribbean, it is believed that if the mother eats eggs during pregnancy, the fetus will become too big and the baby will cry like a bird.

WOMAN VS. ANIMAL

A woman's pregnancy usually lasts nine months and two weeks; most women have a single baby. CONCEPTION can occur between the ages of 10 and 60, but most women conceive between the ages of 20 and 35.

◆

The average elephant's gestation lasts two years and six months, and produces just one calf; the cows breed when aged 16–80 years.

◆

A nine-week gestation is usual for cats. Litters average 3–5 kittens; 19 is the record. A queen usually starts to breed at 18 months.

ODD TASTES AND CRAVINGS

The taste in a pregnant woman's mouth often changes with the rising hormone levels, which are reflected in her saliva. This can lead to her disliking food and drink that she normally enjoys (coffee is an extremely common example) or having cravings for food that she doesn't usually eat. Occasionally, pregnant women have been known to eat nonfood substances, such as soil or coal (a practice known as pica).

Although pica generally has been thought to occur if the woman's body is deficient in trace minerals, pica is often a culturally determined activity. In such a context, the practice is not usually confined to the pregnant women.

WEIGHT GAIN IN PREGNANCY

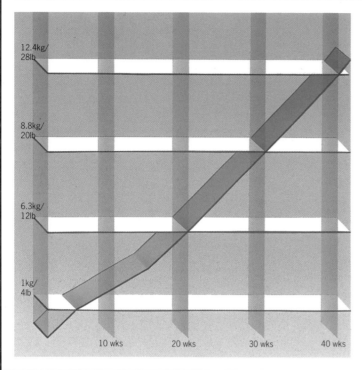

During pregnancy, the recommended weight gain for a woman of average weight experiencing an average pregnancy is approximately 8.8–14.2kg (20–32lb) for the entire gestation period. This allows 2.6–3.5kg (6–8lb) for the FETUS and 6.3–10.6kg (14–24lb) for the fetus' support system (below). Most women gain very little weight during the first month. During the last month of pregnancy some women may lose weight.

Breakdown of weight gained (right)
The weight gained during pregnancy is not purely because of the fetus. The average baby accounts for only about 25% of the total weight gained.

- ○ Maternal weight gain
- ● Fetus
- ● Amniotic & maternal fluid
- ● Larger uterus and breasts
- ● Placenta

VITAMINS AND MINERALS NEEDED BY MOTHER (AND BABY)

Substance	Source	Needed to
Vitamin A	Dairy products, eggs, fish, red or orange fruit and vegetables	Promote cell growth and development, eye development and health, healthy skin and mucous membranes, bone growth, reproductive health, fat metabolism, and resistance to infection.
Vitamin B_1	Whole grains, nuts, pork	Metabolize carbohydrates.
Vitamin B_2	Whole grains, eggs	Metabolize carbohydrates and protein; maintain tissue function and oxygenation.
Vitamin B_5	Whole grains, eggs	Metabolize carbohydrates and fats; maintain healthy cells, nervous system, skin, intestines.
Vitamin B_6	Whole grains, mushrooms	Metabolize protein, fats, and carbohydrates.
Vitamin B_{12}	Meat, fish, eggs, milk	Maintain normal cell formation – particularly of red blood cells – and healthy nervous system.
Folic acid	Peas, bananas, nuts	Synthesize essential nucleic acids for cell division; promote formation of red blood cells.
Vitamin C	Citrus fruits, tomatoes	Support material for bones, vascular system, muscles, cartilage, tissues; promote formation of hemoglobin and red blood cells.
Vitamin D	Oily fish, eggs, dairy products	Promote absorption of calcium and phosphorus in the gastrointestinal tract, and their retention and utilization in bones, blood, and other tissues.
Vitamin E	Wheat germ, eggs, fish, broccoli	Maintain cellular and intercellular structures and enzymes; antioxidant – believed to render dangerous free radicals harmless; deficiency can lead to infertility or miscarriage.
Calcium	Dairy products, fish with bones (sardines), nuts	Promote strong bones and teeth, normal muscle contraction, heart rhythm, blood clotting, transmission of nerve impulses, enzyme activity.
Iron	Meat, fish, egg yolks	Transfer and transport oxygen.
Zinc	Eggs, nuts, shellfish	Promote development and maintenance of the brain and nervous system.

The human body best absorbs the vitamins and minerals that it needs from food, not from vitamin supplements. Only minute amounts of vitamins and minerals are required.

DAILY DIETARY NEEDS IN PREGNANCY

Each of the suggested food sources that are listed below represents one serving of that nutrient. It is important for a pregnant woman to eat a variety of foods, as outlined in *Canada's Food Guide to Healthy Eating* (Health Canada 1992).

Using the Food Guide (Health Canada 1992) gives detailed information about healthy eating. Every woman, but particularly a pregnant woman, should try to ensure that she eats foods that have been organically grown or reared.

Vitamin A-rich foods	Calcium-rich foods	Protein-rich foods	Complex carbohydrates	Vitamin C-rich foods

Vitamin A-rich foods	Calcium-rich foods	Protein-rich foods	Complex carbohydrates	Vitamin C-rich foods
25g/1oz spinach, broccoli florets	50g/2oz hard cheese	75g/3oz hard cheese	75g/3oz cooked barley, brown rice, millet, bulgur	25g/1oz sweet peppers
13g/½oz carrots	325g/13oz cottage cheese	165ml/⅓ pint skim milk	25g/1oz whole-grain or soy flour	225g/9oz tomatoes
250g/10oz peas, beans	250ml/9fl oz yogurt	300ml/12fl oz yogurt	1 slice whole-grain or soy bread	200g/8oz blackberries or raspberries
25g/1oz sweet pepper	165ml/⅓ pint milk	3 large eggs	6 whole-grain breadsticks	100ml/4fl oz citrus juice
150g/6oz tomatoes	75g/3oz canned sardines, with bones	100g/4oz fresh or canned fish	75g/3oz kidney beans, soy beans, chickpeas	75g/3oz strawberries
50g/2oz melon	100g/4oz canned salmon or mackerel, with bones	100g/4oz shellfish	100g/4oz lentils, peas	1 large lemon or orange
6 plums	100g/4oz almonds	75g/3oz red or white meat	1 whole-grain pita or tortilla	½ large lime or tangerine
1 mango, orange, grapefruit		75g/3oz almonds, walnuts, peanuts, or pine nuts	6 whole-grain crackers	½ medium-sized grapefruit
2 apricots				
4 peaches, apples, pears				

FOOD HAZARDS

Certain foods can become contaminated and be a risk for pregnant women.

TOXOPLASMOSIS

This can cause MISCARRIAGE of a FETUS, and blindness and brain damage in a baby. Toxoplasmosis is usually contracted by eating raw or undercooked meat, particularly poultry, or by coming into contact with the feces of infected animals, such as foxes and cats. The majority of the Canadian population has already had toxoplasmosis and developed antibodies; this is more likely the older a woman is. Symptoms develop 2–3 days after infection, and include diarrhea and fever.

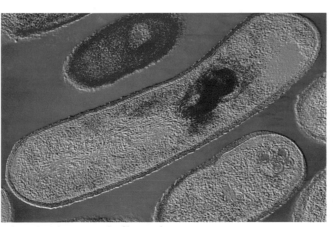

False-colored micrograph of listeria bacteria.

LISTERIOSIS

The listeria bacterium can cause miscarriage. It occurs in cooked, chilled foods; soft cheese; pâtés; and improperly cooked meat. It can also be spread by contact with infected animals, such as sheep. Symptoms are flulike.

WOMEN AT RISK

A woman who is pregnant has greatly increased nutritional needs if she:

- *Has had a recent MISCARRIAGE or STILLBIRTH, or her children were born less than 18 months apart.*

- *Smokes; drinks alcohol.*

- *Is ALLERGIC to key foods, such as milk or wheat.*

- *Suffers from a chronic medical condition.*

- *Is under the age of 18 or over the age of 40.*

- *Is carrying more than a single FETUS.*

- *Has been subjected to injury or a lot of STRESS.*

- *Was run down or underweight before CONCEPTION.*

POSTURE AND PREGNANCY

The growing fetus often forces a pregnant woman to over-arch her back to counteract the weight of her enlarging abdomen. This means that her spine is thrown out of alignment, and it frequently results in lower back pain, especially in the second half of pregnancy. Extra pressure is also put on the hip and knee joints.

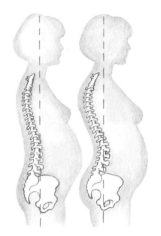

Good and bad posture
When a woman stands correctly (left), an imaginary line can run down through her body. Bad posture displaces this (right).

Correct lifting
Keep the back upright and lift by straightening the legs. Hold the item close to the body with both hands. This is important to remember when lifting a child, for example.

PHYSICAL ACTIVITIES

During pregnancy, a woman can continue to participate normally in the majority of physical activities with no ill effects. Many, in fact, will be beneficial. Some activities can pose a risk, however, and a pregnant woman should be aware of the potential problems. Backpacking, for example, puts a great deal of strain on the back and should be avoided, as should contact sports, such as judo. Sports involving a lot of balance, such as horseback riding and skiing, will probably be fine until the second half of pregnancy, when a woman's abdomen becomes big enough to upset that balance.

Exercising
Activities that involve the whole body harmoniously, such as swimming (left), yoga (above), and dancing, are very beneficial during pregnancy.

Relaxation
This is vital for well-being during pregnancy. Lying on your side with pillows under your head and knees (below) will help to alleviate pressure on the major blood vessels and the abdomen.

SEX DURING PREGNANCY

Unless there are medical problems, such as a history of MISCARRIAGE, PLACENTA PREVIA, or episodes of bleeding, sex can be enjoyed throughout pregnancy. Positions where the man's weight is off the abdomen are best (right).

The FETUS is well protected by the amniotic fluid and membranes, and the cervix is sealed with a mucous plug to prevent infection. After the water breaks, sex should cease.

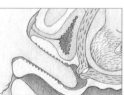

Protected fetus (left)
The cervix is sealed with a mucous plug throughout pregnancy, which provides complete protection for the fetus. This means that the penis cannot touch the fetus' head during sexual intercourse.

PRENATAL CARE

URINE TESTS

A regular check is kept on every pregnant woman's urine for the presence of certain agents that might indicate problems – a kidney infection can be detected in this way, for example. A doctor will also be concerned if urine contains protein, which may indicate PREECLAMPSIA; sugar, which suggests developing DIABETES MELLITUS; and ketones (chemicals that result when the body burns FATTY ACIDS for energy), a sign of advanced diabetes or that there has been excessive vomiting and starvation in pregnancy.

BLOOD TESTS

These will be done to ascertain both basic and RHESUS (Rh) blood groups. This is vital if a later transfusion or treatment for RHESUS INCOMPATIBILITY proves necessary. To rule out anemia, hemoglobin levels will be checked. Blood tests can also reveal the presence of a SEXUALLY TRANSMITTED DISEASE, whether there are antibodies to RUBELLA (German measles) present, and indicate the level of ALPHA-FETOPROTEIN. The latter is used to diagnose certain fetal disorders. Some genetic disorders, such as sickle-cell anemia, are detectable in blood.

EXTERNAL EXAMINATIONS

Checkups and tests make up a large part of prenatal care and help doctors and midwives identify potential problems at an early stage.

BLOOD PRESSURE
Taken at every visit, a higher BLOOD PRESSURE than normal may indicate PREECLAMPSIA.

The average reading in pregnancy is 120 over 70, although blood pressure varies with age, and there is a range at every age that is considered to be normal.

Sphygmomanometer
(blood pressure gauge)

HEIGHT
Tall, large-boned women tend to have larger babies than women who are very petite.

WEIGHT
This is monitored regularly to provide an indication of fetal growth. Sudden weight gain may reflect fluid retention and preeclampsia.

LEGS AND HANDS
Legs will be examined for VARICOSE VEINS, and ankles and hands will be checked for EDEMA (swelling and puffiness) that could signal preeclampsia.

BREASTS
Particular attention is paid to nipples to make sure that potential problems for breastfeeding are recognized early.

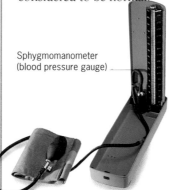

Twins (weeks)
In a multiple pregnancy, the woman usually experiences rapid weight gain from the start

28	36
24	32
20	28
16	24
14	20
11	16
	12

Single (weeks)
When the woman is carrying only a single baby, she is often fairly slow to start gaining weight.

ABDOMINAL PALPATION
Checks on fetal position are made by examining the mother's abdomen with the hands. From 12 weeks onward, the *fundus* (top) of the uterus protrudes into the abdomen and can be felt externally. The doctor will measure the distance between the *fundus* and the pelvic bone to check fetal growth, and will feel for the head and rump to determine the fetus' position.

INTERNAL EXAMINATION

This test is carried out to check on a pregnant women's pelvic size and the condition of her cervix. It may be done at the first antenatal check, or, occasionally, at about 36 weeks. The doctor or midwife will insert two gloved fingers of one hand into the vagina to check on the pelvic inlet and ischial spines. Finally, she will measure the woman's pelvic outlet.

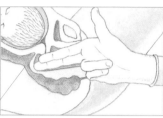

Sacral promontory

Measuring pelvic inlet
The doctor will check if she can feel the sacral promontory through the back of the vagina to judge the pelvic inlet (distance between the pelvic bone and the sacrum, or lower backbone).

Checking disproportion
The pelvis is usually assessed by internal examination (far right) to ensure that the baby's head will pass through easily during childbirth. The doctor or midwife will also press on the abdomen to feel the uterus (below).

Ischial spine

Measuring ischial spines
The doctor will feel right and left through the sides of the vagina for the two ischial spines. They may be barely noticeable or quite distinct, blunt or pointed.

Measuring pelvic outlet
Making a loose fist, the doctor may check that the distance between the ischial tuberosities is more than 10cm (4in).

Ischial tuberosity

ULTRASOUND SCANNING OF THE UTERUS

This diagnostic technique detects and analyzes reflected echoes, from high-frequency sound waves, to build up a picture of the FETUS in the uterus. The resulting sonograms provide valuable information on the development of the fetus. They also clarify an uncertain delivery date. Ultrasound is used with other diagnostic tests, such as AMNIOCENTESIS, to test for DOWN'S SYNDROME.

Ultrasound is painless and considered safe, although long-term studies have not yet been completed.

Having a scan
After gel or oil is smoothed on the woman's abdomen to give an airtight seal, the scanner is slowly moved across it.

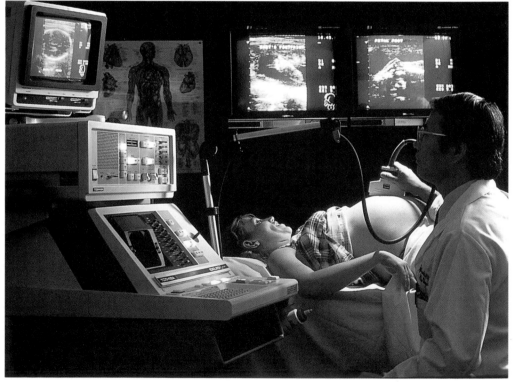

CHORIONIC VILLI SAMPLING (CVS)

The chorionic villi on the edge of the PLACENTA are genetically identical to the FETUS and so can be tested to detect certain disorders, including CYSTIC FIBROSIS and DOWN'S SYNDROME in the fetus. Performed between 10 and 12 weeks, this test will usually give a result within one to two days. This is an earlier result than that obtained by AMNIOCENTESIS (right). However, the risk of MISCARRIAGE is approximately 2% higher than that of amniocentesis. In a transcervical CVS (above), the uterus is approached vaginally, and a catheter is used to scrape cells from the chorionic villi; in a transabdominal CVS, the technique is similar to that used in amniocentesis.

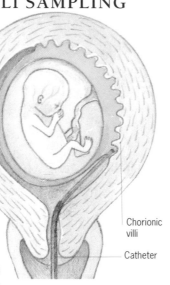

Chorionic villi

Catheter

Transcervical route

A catheter is inserted into the uterus via the vagina and the cervix. Cells are then taken from the surface of the placenta.

AMNIOCENTESIS

While in the uterus, a FETUS sheds skin and other cells into the amniotic fluid. These can be collected during amniocentesis to provide clues to the condition of the fetus. This examination is normally offered to mothers over the age of 35, or to those women whose other screening tests have given results outside the normal range. There is a one in 200 risk of MISCARRIAGE following amniocentesis.

Using ULTRASOUND as a guide to the fetus' position, the doctor will draw up a small amount of fluid for analysis through the anesthetized abdominal wall.

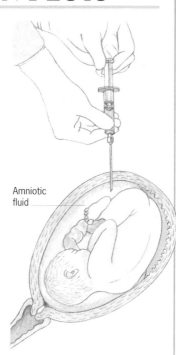

Amniotic fluid

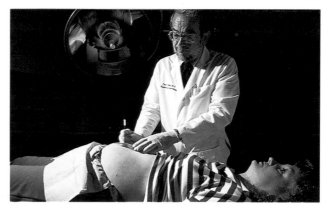

Taking a sample

The doctor passes a needle through the woman's skin into the uterus. A small amount of the amniotic fluid is withdrawn for analysis.

FETOSCOPY

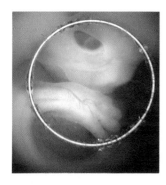

A flexible viewing tube with a powerful lens is passed into the uterus (either via the vagina or through an incision in the abdomen) to view the FETUS or amniotic fluid. Any abnormalities may then be pinpointed.

ALPHA-FETOPROTEIN TEST

Produced by the embryo's yolk sac, and later by the fetal liver, alpha-fetoprotein is found in a woman's blood in varying amounts throughout her pregnancy. A very low level may indicate DOWN'S SYNDROME in the FETUS, while a high level may point to neurological problems, such as spina bifida (unfused spinal vertebrae often resulting in paralysis). A maternal blood test will reveal the level of alpha-fetoprotein in the woman's blood, and ULTRASOUND and AMNIOCENTESIS (above right) will usually be offered if thought necessary.

TRIPLE TEST

This recently developed blood test is performed at 14–16 weeks to measure three substances. The levels of estriol (a form of ESTROGEN), HUMAN CHORIONIC GONADOTROPIN, and ALPHA-FETOPROTEIN (left) in the maternal blood can be correlated with the mother's age to assess the possibility of chromosomal abnormalities, such as DOWN'S SYNDROME, in the FETUS. Any suspicious findings are then further investigated, and AMNIOCENTESIS (above) and ULTRASOUND will be offered to the woman if any problems are indicated.

FETUS' KICK CHART

The number of kicks the FETUS makes in a six-hour period can indicate its well-being in the THIRD TRIMESTER. Charts should be marked to indicate the time by which five kicks are felt; if fewer than five movements within the specified period are felt, this should be noted in the bottom panel.

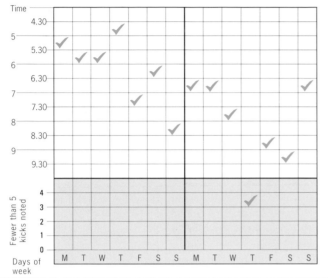

KEEPING IN TOUCH WITH BABY

Knowing what her baby is experiencing helps the mother (and father) to stay in touch with it before birth. The FETUS *can feel, hear, and see, and can also experience its mother's emotions through the release of certain chemicals. For instance, elation releases* ENDORPHINS, *and anger and fear* CATECHOLAMINES.

From the fourth month, the fetus will turn away from strong light from outside the uterus. From the sixth month, it will become agitated by loud music.

FETAL HEARTBEAT

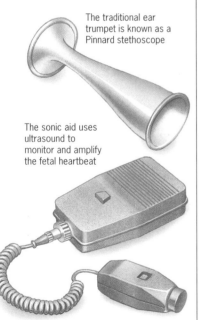

The traditional ear trumpet is known as a Pinnard stethoscope

The sonic aid uses ultrasound to monitor and amplify the fetal heartbeat

From the third month onward, the fetal heartbeat will be monitored at every prenatal visit. The fetal heartbeat is about twice as fast as an adult's heartbeat (140 beats per minute, compared with 72 beats per minute).

THE LIE OF THE FETUS

The lie refers to the position the FETUS adopts in the uterus. Doctors and midwives use abbreviations for the different longitudinal positions of the fetus. They note where the occiput (back of the fetus' head) is in relation to the mother's body – whether it is on her right or her left, and whether it is anterior (pointing forward) or posterior (backward). If the fetus' spine lies parallel to that of the mother's, it is known as longitudinal lie. The abbreviation ROA, for example, means that the occiput is on the right of the mother's uterus, facing forward.

In a few cases, the fetus' spine may lie across that of the mother's (transverse lie).

ROL

LOA

ROA

LOL

ROP

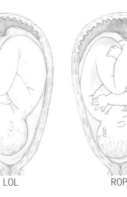
LOP

A TWIN PREGNANCY

Problems during pregnancy can be exacerbated if a woman is carrying more than one FETUS. Feelings of fatigue and nausea may be intensified, and the chances of developing raised BLOOD PRESSURE, ANEMIA, EDEMA, and PREECLAMPSIA are increased. A woman who is carrying more than one fetus will notice that the size of her abdomen is large compared with an average pregnancy. In addition, the shape of the abdomen tends to bulge out sideways to accommodate the extra fetus(es). A woman expecting twins is encouraged to restrict her physical activity in the THIRD TRIMESTER to minimize the risk of going into premature labor. Twins tend to have a shorter gestation period than single babies (35 weeks, as opposed to 40). Identical twins result from one ovum (egg) splitting and they usually, although not always, share a placenta; fraternal twins result from two fertilized ova (eggs).

Identical twins — Single placenta

Fraternal twins — Two placentae

CHANCES OF HAVING TWINS

There are a number of factors that increase a woman's chances of conceiving fraternal twins. The chances of identical twins stays constant.

There are twins on your mother's side of the family:

Yes	(5)
No	(0)

You are:

Negroid	(3)
Caucasoid	(2)
Mongoloid	(1)

Your age is:

Under 20 years	(0)
21–30	(2)
31–40	(3)
Over 40 years	(1)

You have the following number of children:

1 or none	(1)
2	(2)
3 or more	(3)

For your racial type, your height and build is:

Petite	(1)
Medium	(2)
Well-built	(3)

You conceive within:

2 months	(3)
6 months	(2)
12 months	(1)

SCORE

Result	Chance of having twins
0–5	0–20%
6–15	20–60%
16–20	60–100%

WHO HAS TWINS?

The incidence of identical twins is generally believed to be completely random, although there is slight evidence that in a few families they may be hereditary. Fraternal twins occur because a woman has an increased tendency to release more than one ovum (egg) during OVULATION.

This tendency can be inherited (fraternal twins often run in families, being inherited down the mother's side), or it can develop in an individual. The chance of having noninherited, fraternal twins increases until a woman is in her mid-thirties, and then drops again. It also seems to increase if she is tall, well-built, and conceives easily. The chances of having fraternal twins also appears to rise with each subsequent child that she has.

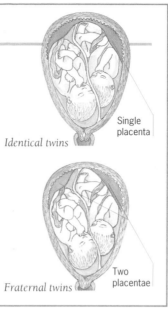

TWINS AND RACE

The occurrence of fraternal twins varies according to the mother's RACIAL TYPE, while that of identical twins stays constant. The lowest rate of fraternal twinning occurs among MONGOLOID women, and the highest among NEGROID women.

	Total	Fraternal	Identical
Negroid	46.2	42.3	3.9
Caucasoid	11.2	7.5	3.7
Mongoloid	6.4	3.1	3.3

Number of twins per 1000 births.

IT'S A FACT

Longest natural interval between twins

Diana and Monica Petrungaro were born 36 days apart. Mrs. Danny Petrungaro of Rome, Italy, gave birth to Diana on December 22, 1987, and to Monica on January 27, 1988.

◆

Longest interval between "test-tube" twins

Mrs. Mary Wright gave birth to twins 18 months apart, following the fertilization of her ova (eggs) by her husband's sperm in March 1984. The first twin was born in November 1985, and the second twin was born in April 1987 from an ovum that had been in frozen storage for 29 months.

◆

Most sets of twins

Madame Vassilyev (1707–70) of Shuya in Russia gave birth to 16 sets of twins.

◆

Fastest triplet birth

On March 21, 1977, Mrs. James E. Duck of Memphis, Tennessee, gave birth naturally to Bradley, Christopher, and Carmon in just two minutes.

◆

Oldest female twins

Identical twins Mildred Widman Philippi and Mary Widman Franzini were born on June 17, 1880. Mildred died first on May 4, 1985, 44 days short of their 105th birthday.

PROBLEMS

SMOKING AND ALCOHOL

Smoking This adversely affects the FETUS, but is largely avoidable. Women who continue to smoke while pregnant risk MISCARRIAGE, having a baby that has a low birthweight and congenital abnormalities, and a child who has learning difficulties or suffers impaired growth. Smoking before CONCEPTION can damage the GENES carried in the ovum (egg) and sperm. Passive smoking may carry a risk for a fetus as well as for a newborn baby, and may be a factor in causing crib death. If you must smoke after giving birth, do it outdoors or in another room from the baby.

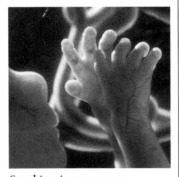

Smoking in pregnancy
When a pregnant woman inhales cigarette smoke, the oxygen level in the blood supply, and that reaching the fetus, drops dramatically. This quickly affects the amount of blood reaching the fetus' extremities.

Alcohol A poison that is potentially damaging to the ovum, sperm, and fetus. The risks include miscarriage, retarded mental and physical growth, and fetal alcohol syndrome, where there is damage to the brain and the nervous system.

DRUGS TO AVOID

Drug	Use	Fetal effect
Accutane	Treats acne	Can cause birth defects.
Anabolic steroids	Bodybuilding	Can have a masculinizing effect on a female fetus.
Amphetamines	Stimulants	May cause heart and blood disorders.
Narcotics (codeine, etc.)	Treats pain	Baby may suffer withdrawal symptoms.
Streptomycin	Treats tuberculosis	Can cause deafness.
Antihistamines	For allergies, travel sickness	Some may cause malformations.
Antinausea drugs	Combat nausea	Can cause malformations.
Acetylsalicylic acid	Treats pain and fever	Can cause problems with blood clotting.
Diuretics	Rid body of excess fluid	Can cause blood disorders.
Tetracycline	Treats acne	Can cause both first and second teeth to be colored yellow.
LSD, marijuana, etc.	Recreational or hallucinogenic	Risk of chromosomal damage before and after conception, and miscarriage.
Sulfonamides	Treat bacterial infections	Can cause jaundice in the baby at birth.

HEALTH HAZARDS IN PREGNANCY

HOME
Practices or situations that may affect the FETUS include:

- Using chemicals, such as oven cleaner, aerosols, gasoline, paint, varnish, some glues, and garden pesticides.
- Taking saunas or long, extremely hot baths.
- Eating raw or undercooked meat.
- Drinking caffeine-based drinks, alcohol, or nonorganic herbal teas.
- Cleaning out litter boxes, using a pooper scooper, and gardening without gloves.
- Receiving live vaccinations, such as for rubella (German measles).

WORK
A pregnant woman's occupation can mean that she or her FETUS may be placed at risk. Situations to avoid include:

- Taking physical risks (jockey, policewoman).
- Working with animals (vet, farmer).
- Exposure to chemicals, such as lead, mercury, toxic waste, dry cleaning fluids, solvents.
- Contact with anesthetic gases (nurse, doctor).
- Exposure to high levels of cigarette smoke (bar worker, waitress, nightclub worker).
- Exposure to infections (doctor, teacher).

ENVIRONMENT
Eating out, shopping, and even socializing can present potential hazards. These include:

- Inhaling exhaust fumes (especially in towns or cities on warm days).
- Contact with fertilizers or pesticides sprayed on crops or in gardens.
- Passive smoking and exposure to infections.
- Eating infected or contaminated food.

COMMON COMPLAINTS IN PREGNANCY

Problem	Why it happens	What you can do	Risk to fetus
Backache General discomfort across the back. It may go right down the legs.	High PROGESTERONE levels cause ligaments to soften and stretch, putting extra strain on the back and hips.	Exercise to strengthen the back; sleep on a firm mattress; correct your posture, and wear low heels.	None.
Carpal tunnel syndrome Sensation of pins and needles in the fingers, and sometimes in the hand and forearm.	The carpal tunnel (the ring of fibers around the wrist) becomes swollen owing to EDEMA (water retention), and pinches a nerve.	Take diuretics if prescribed by doctor; wear a splint on your wrist at night; hold your hand above head and wriggle fingers.	None.
Constipation Dry, hard stools that are difficult to pass.	Progesterone relaxes the intestinal muscles, so there are fewer contractions and more water is absorbed.	Drink lots of water; eat lots of fruit and vegetables (particularly dried fruit, such as figs and prunes).	None.
Cramps Painful, spasmodic contractions, usually in the thigh, calf, or foot.	Thought to be caused by low calcium levels or salt deficiency.	Have a firm massage. Maintain good nutrition.	None.
Diarrhea Soft, watery stools.	Usually caused by bacteria or a virus.	Drink more to replace lost fluid; a doctor can test stools for infection.	Can cause dehydration and low nutritional levels.
Heartburn Burning sensation behind sternum (breastbone). Stomach acid regurgitated into mouth.	Progesterone relaxes the SPHINCTER valve at the entrance of the stomach, allowing stomach acid to flow up into the esophagus.	Eat small meals to avoid overfilling your stomach; drink milk to neutralize stomach acid; avoid eating protein and carbohydrates at the same meal; sleep propped up. A doctor may prescribe antacids.	None.
Hypertension (high blood pressure) Test shows raised blood pressure. Often there are few, if any symptoms, although edema is a classic indication.	The cause is not fully understood.	Keep your weight gain to the recommended level; rest in bed; a doctor may suggest hospital admission if the problem is severe.	Reduces the blood flow to the uterus, so the oxygen and food supply to the fetus are restricted, leading to a low birth weight. A CESAREAN will be performed if the fetus is at risk.
Morning sickness Nausea that can actually occur at any time, usually when the woman hasn't eaten for a while.	Thought to be a result of the woman's body adjusting to supporting the FETUS and protecting it against TOXINS. Caused by pregnancy hormones and low blood glucose levels.	Eat little and often, particularly complex carbohydrate foods such as potatoes and rice; suck hard candies.	The severe form, hyperemesis gravidarum, can deplete the body of fluid and nutrients. Hospital admission may be required.
Hemorrhoids Dilated rectal veins that may bleed or protrude through the anus.	As the baby grows, it presses down on the woman's pelvic floor and impedes the blood flow. This causes the blood to pool in the veins, which dilate to accommodate it.	Increase your intake of fiber; don't lift or carry heavy loads (this increases pressure in the abdomen). Avoid constipation (see above).	None.
Yeast infection Characterized by a white, curdy discharge from the vagina, and dryness and itching around the vagina, VULVA, PERINEUM, and anus.	The yeast Candida albicans occurs naturally in the body. Infection sets in when it is able to multiply uncontrolled, following a course of antibiotics for instance. Alcohol, sugar, and yeast products exacerbate yeast infections because Candida albicans feeds on yeast and sugar.	Wear loose cotton under- and outerwear and avoid pantyhose; avoid alcohol and food containing sugar or yeast; eat live yogurt and lots of fresh fruit and vegetables every day; a doctor may prescribe an antifungal cream.	The baby can become infected as it passes through the birth canal. The infection most often manifests itself as white curds in the baby's mouth. This will not harm the baby.
Varicose veins Swollen veins, usually in the legs or anus (see hemorrhoids, above). They can also occur in the vulva.	See hemorrhoids (above).	Avoid standing for any length of time; put your feet up while resting; wear support hose or stockings; massage around the swollen veins.	None.

TUBAL PREGNANCY

Fallopian tube

Endometrium

Uterus

Cervix

Blastocyst inside the fallopian tube may also adhere to the outer surface of the internal organs

In this, the most common form of ectopic pregnancy, the fertilized ovum becomes "stuck" in the FALLOPIAN TUBE. If the embedded BLASTOCYST is left to develop, the tube will eventually burst, with life-threatening consequences. Pain caused by the growing blastocyst usually signals the condition and the blastocyst can then be removed surgically.

PLACENTA PREVIA

If the placenta implants low down in the uterus and blocks the cervix, this can have fatal complications for baby and mother. When labor starts, the placenta will separate too early, causing major hemorrhage. Episodes of bleeding should be checked by ULTRASOUND. A CESAREAN will usually be done.

Placenta

Cervix

The cervix is covered
When the placenta is centrally implanted, it covers the cervix.

INCOMPETENT CERVIX

If the normally tightly closed cervix begins to open long before term, it allows the amniotic sac and its contents to protrude into the vagina, resulting in MISCARRIAGE (right). To prevent this, a cervical suture is inserted at the 16th week of the following pregnancy.

Cervix

Thread

Sutured cervix
A thread is sewn through the cervix. This will be cut seven days before the due date.

RHESUS INCOMPATIBILITY

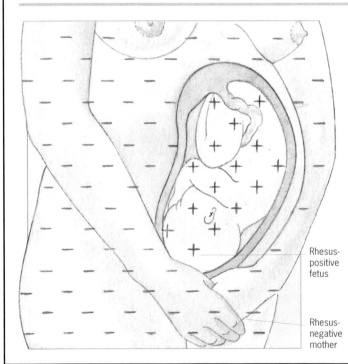

Rhesus-positive fetus

Rhesus-negative mother

If a woman has RHESUS-NEGATIVE BLOOD and her FETUS has Rhesus-positive blood (left), she may produce antibodies that could put subsequent Rh-positive babies at risk. When the blood of the firstborn Rh-positive baby enters the mother's bloodstream (most commonly during delivery – bottom left), it stimulates production in her blood of Rh-positive antibodies (green triangles). These will attack and destroy the red blood cells of her next Rh-positive baby (bottom right), resulting in fatal fetal anemia. This is usually prevented by the woman having an Rh-immune globulin injection to prevent Rh-positive antibodies from forming.

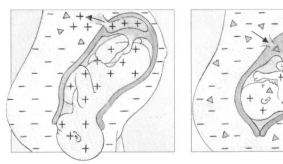

MISCARRIAGE

This is the loss of a FETUS of less than 28 weeks' gestation and is medically known as spontaneous abortion. About 30% of early pregnancies miscarry although, in at least 25% of these cases, the pregnancy has not been diagnosed. Older mothers and those carrying more than one fetus are at greatest risk. The most common cause of miscarriage is a chromosomally abnormal BLASTOCYST failing to implant in the uterus or to develop properly, although other causes include uterine abnormalities, hormonal imbalances, viral and bacterial infections, and INCOMPETENT CERVIX (left). If the sperm is slightly abnormal, it may still be able to penetrate the ovum, but the blastocyst may then miscarry. A miscarriage may also occur if the father's blood is incompatible with that of the mother. Doctors differentiate between threatened (the only kind that may not result in a miscarriage), inevitable, incomplete, complete, missed, habitual, and recurrent abortion.

- 1–6 wks gestation
- 6–40 wks gestation
- Live births

Pregnancy outcome
Any calculations regarding the percentage of conceptions that results in miscarriage are estimates owing to the difficulty in compiling firm data concerning early miscarriages (before six weeks). Most early miscarriages go unrecognized and are dismissed as late or heavy periods.

GESTATIONAL DIABETES

During pregnancy, a small number of women do not produce sufficient INSULIN to keep blood glucose levels normal. Women at risk include those who have a family history of DIABETES. Gestational diabetes is usually detected in the second half of pregnancy, when a blood test is done for diabetes, or increased glucose levels appear in the urine. It disappears once the baby has been born.

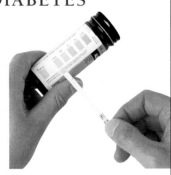

Urine testing
Chemically impregnated strips are dipped in urine, then read against a color chart that indicates glucose levels.

PREECLAMPSIA

Also known as toxemia, this syndrome may occur before eclampsia, a potentially life-threatening situation for the mother and FETUS. Preeclampsia is experienced by 15% of pregnant women and is more common in women over 35, those having their first babies, and those carrying more than one baby. It most often occurs after the 20th week of pregnancy. Symptoms include EDEMA (water retention) and HIGH BLOOD PRESSURE (which is why blood pressure is checked once a month throughout pregnancy). Proteinuria (when protein is present in the urine) may also occur, as may nausea, headaches, and dizziness. Preeclampsia is treated by bedrest and sedation; drugs may also be given to reduce blood pressure. Early delivery of the fetus may be performed if the mother or fetus is at risk.

Range of normal blood pressure		
Age	Upper systolic blood pressure	Lower diastolic blood pressure
15–25 years	100–150	60–95
25–35 years	100–160	65–95
35–45 years	110–170	68–100
45–55 years	110–180	70–105
55–65 years	115–180	70–110

UTERINE SEPTUM (WALL)

A woman's uterus, like the uteri of other mammals, develops from two separate embryonic tubes. Human female embryonic tubes fuse to form a single uterus in the same way as do those of horses and monkeys, but unlike those of cats and dogs. In a small percentage of women, however, the two embryonic tubes do not fuse completely, and such uteri then develop with restricted dimensions (right). If a pregnancy occurs in a woman who has this sort of uterus, the fetus is forced to adopt positions that tend to be inconsistent with a normal delivery. A CESAREAN SECTION will generally be necessary, particularly if the forced fetal position is a persistent transverse lie (sideways across the uterus).

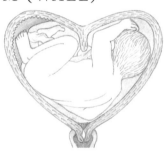

Bicornuate uterus
This uterus is horn-shaped. A normal delivery may be possible.

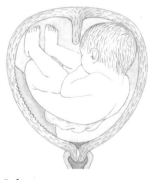

Subseptate uterus
An interior wall, or septum, protrudes into the uterus.

BIRTH PROCESS

Squatting opens the woman's pelvis.

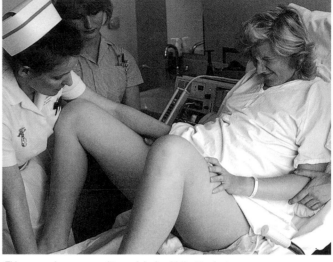

This woman is encouraged to push by her birth attendants.

66 Darkness, or almost, and ... silence. A profound peace settles in the room. You can feel the respect which naturally attends the arrival of a baby. One doesn't shout in a church. One spontaneously lowers one's voice. (We) enter into another rhythm; the profound rhythm of life, which is also the tempo of the child. 99

Frederick Leboyer

66 During childbirth ... a woman is completely caught up in the passionate act of creation, utterly committed to the feelings of the moment and to the vivid sensations with which her whole being is flooded. 99

Sheila Kitzinger

Water softens a woman's vaginal tissues and is also very relaxing.

The baby's head is crowning.

Giving birth

Women in the process of giving birth (above) become ultrasensitive to light and to sound. Consequently, a quiet, darkened, and preferably familiar place is the most desirable birthing place for most women. Giving birth is usually straightforward, if very hard work, and is a profoundly moving experience.

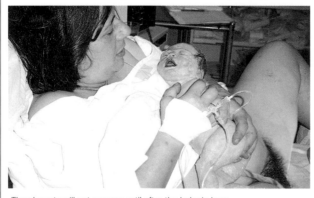

The placenta will not emerge until after the baby is born.

CONTRACTIONS

Early in the FIRST STAGE of labor, contractions are usually about 30–60 seconds long and occur at regular intervals – frequently of about 20 minutes. As labor progresses, they intensify and become more frequent until they last about 60–90 seconds, at intervals of 2–4 minutes.

Initial contractions pull up and efface (thin) the cervix; subsequent contractions dilate (widen) the cervix. Most women experience contractions as a wave of intense pain that peaks and then fades away. This is because the uterus, which is a huge muscle, becomes short of oxygen when the blood vessels are compressed during contractions.

Average times of stages of labor

1st stage

| Hours | 3 | 6 | 9 | 12 | 15 | 18 | 21 | 24 |

2nd stage

| Minutes | | 30 | 45 | 60 | 75 | 90 | 105 | 120 |

3rd stage

1st birth
2nd birth

| Minutes | | 30 | 45 | 60 | 75 | 90 | 105 | 120 |

FETAL ENGAGEMENT

Usually after 36 weeks of pregnancy in a primigravida woman (first pregnancy) and at the onset of labor in a multiparous woman (more than one pregnancy) the baby's head (or, occasionally, bottom, if it is a BREECH baby) will descend into the woman's pelvis until it is opposite her ISCHIAL SPINES. This is when the baby is said to be engaged.

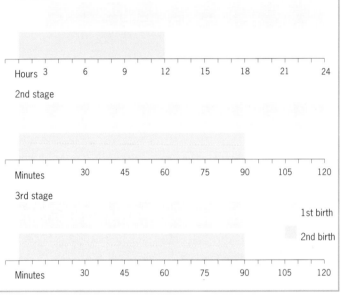

Pelvic inlet

Widest part of baby's head

PRELABOR

Certain phenomena signal that the birth process is beginning, although not all women experience them in the same way.

THE SHOW

There is a plug of mucus that seals the cervix, protecting the uterus from infection. This plug falls away (the show) as the cervix softens in prelabor. The plug may be stained due to tearing of the capillaries that attached it to the cervix.

CRAMPS

The physical and emotional changes that a woman may experience before and during MENSTRUATION may also be experienced before labor begins. Most women feel the need to empty their bowels and to pass urine frequently.

NESTING INSTINCT

Many women feel a surge of energy just before the start of labor, and experience an urge to clean things and "put the house in order."

WATER BREAKING

When the membranes rupture, they release the amniotic fluid as a trickle or a rush, depending on the size and site of the break. The waters usually break near the end of the FIRST STAGE, unless they are ruptured artificially. They can break just before labor or during the second stage.

INDUCTION

If necessary, labor can be induced (started artificially). Induction involves the use of OXYTOCIN, which is usually administered as an intravenous drip, and PROSTAGLANDIN suppositories inserted into the vagina. Labor may also be induced by rupturing the membranes of the amniotic sac (below). Induction may take place if a woman is suffering from HYPERTENSION, PREECLAMPSIA, HEART DISEASE, or DIABETES; if the FETUS appears to be distressed in any way; or if the pregnancy is prolonged two weeks or more after the EDD (estimated delivery date).

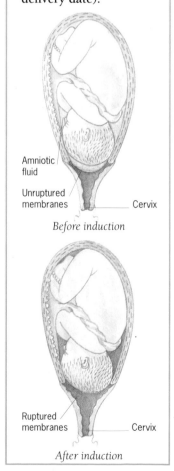

Amniotic fluid

Unruptured membranes — Cervix

Before induction

Ruptured membranes — Cervix

After induction

BIRTH AND CULTURE

In Canada, birth is viewed as a medical procedure, as it is by the Cuna Indians of Panama. In Sweden, birth is seen as a fulfilling personal achievement, while in Holland, and among the Indians of the Yucatan, it is regarded as a natural process. The Siriono of Bolivia see birth as such a straightforward event that it happens in front of everyone.

Most cultures have a tradition of older women assisting the laboring mother, and of men not being allowed near her, although this is not the case in many parts of the West. In some cultures, such as among the Tuareg of the Sahara, the mother is encouraged to be very active, while in many parts of Russia, the mother is kept practically immobile. A vertical position for the actual birth is favored by over 80% of all cultures.

EPIDURAL

The epidural block prevents the transmission of PAIN from the uterus by acting as a "nerve block" in the SPINAL CORD. An epidural removes sensation between a woman's waist and knees, although it also masks the body's signals to change position. A woman with an epidural in place is confined to bed and may require medical assistance to deliver the baby. When an epidural is administered (see below), a very fine, hollow needle is inserted into the epidural space in a woman's spinal column (right) and the catheter, or thin tube, is threaded through the needle, which is then removed. An anesthetic drug is injected through the catheter into the epidural space.

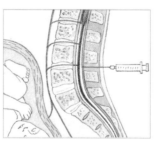

Epidural injection
Anesthetic is injected into the epidural space; it takes effect quickly and can be topped up.

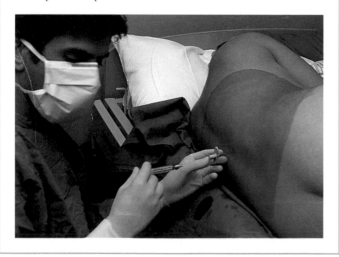

BREATHING

During labor, a woman's breathing patterns change in response to contractions.

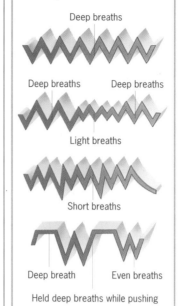

Deep breaths

Deep breaths   Deep breaths

Light breaths

Short breaths

Deep breath   Even breaths

Held deep breaths while pushing

NATURAL PAIN RELIEF

- *Walking and rocking your pelvis will probably feel most comfortable during the first stage of labor.*

- *Having your lower back massaged can help to relieve pain, especially if you are suffering from backache.*

- *Water pools are often used to soothe and relieve pain. Being in water can help to trigger the release of ENDORPHINS.*

- *Visualizing restful images, such as waves, during labor can effectively help to reduce pain and anxiety.*

TENS

Transcutaneous electrical nerve stimulation (TENS) works by passing a mild electrical current through the skin on a woman's back. The current blocks nerve impulses, so helping reduce pain.

OTHER DRUGS USED IN LABOR

Inhalation anesthetics are pain relievers that are administered by the woman herself by breathing through a face mask. They numb the pain center in the brain and produce a floating sensation. A mixture of gas and oxygen is widely used for pain relief.

Painkillers such as meperidine are usually given by injection in a woman's buttock. They dull the sensation of pain by acting on the nerve cells in the brain and spine.

Sedatives and tranquilizers work by dampening the activity of a woman's central NERVOUS SYSTEM and cause drowsiness. They are rarely used, but small doses may be given if a woman is very tense or anxious.

CHILDBIRTH POSITIONS

As childbirth became more medically controlled in the middle of the 20th century, women in labor were required to deliver while lying flat on their backs. Now women are encouraged to take up more comfortable positions.

FIRST STAGE LABOR

Resting with your shoulders dropped is helpful

Sitting (left)

Sit facing the back of a chair and rest while leaning on a pillow or cushion. Lean forward and keep your legs wide apart.

Rotate your hips, keeping your legs wide apart

Standing (right)

When you lean forward, the baby's weight will be taken off your spine and the contractions will be more efficient.

Rocking your pelvis backward and forward during contractions will help relieve backache

Kneeling (right)

This helps alleviate backache.

Resting (below)

Lying on your side, with pillows underneath your head and one thigh may help you to rest.

Relax your shoulders and concentrate on your breathing

TRANSITION

The pressure is off your lower back

Lean forward (below)

Kneeling with your head down and bottom raised can help to slow down the baby's descent if the cervix is not fully dilated.

Relaxing (right)

During transition, it may be comfortable to lean on a pile of cushions or pillows with your legs wide apart.

You can lean back against your birth assistant

DELIVERY

Supported squat (right)

When you are upright and supported under your arms, your pelvis will be completely open and you will be able to take full advantage of gravity. This is one of the most popular positions for a vaginal delivery.

Semi-upright positions (below)

A supported kneeling position can be very effective.

Your birth assistants can support your entire weight

DILATION OF THE CERVIX

The cervix is the neck of the uterus. In its normal state, the cervix is a thick-walled canal about 2.5cm (1in) long. During labor, the cervix dilates (opens up) to a diameter of 10cm (4in) and becomes one with the body of the uterus.

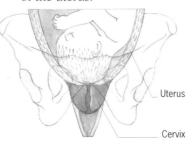

The normal cervix
Like the neck of a sack, the cervix hangs below the main body of the uterus, protruding into the top third of the vagina.

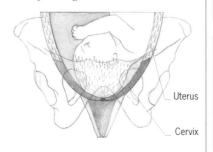

The cervix effaces
During the first stage of labor, the contractions slowly soften, pull up, and thin the cervix.

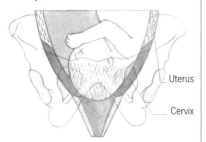

The cervix dilates
As the contractions intensify, they dilate (open up) the cervix. At this point, the vagina and the uterus have become a continuous cavity (known as the birth canal) along which the baby will be slowly pushed during the second stage of labor.

PARTOGRAM

This is a chart that doctors and midwives use to monitor a woman's cervix during labor. It shows the expected cervical dilation (left) for a primiparous (having her first pregnancy) woman and a multiparous (has had more than one pregnancy) woman.

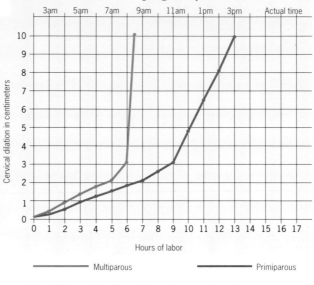

FETAL DESCENT

An internal examination will be made to check the descent of the FETUS through the pelvis. Imaginary lines, described as "stations," measure the level of the fetal head above and below a woman's two ISCHIAL SPINES, in intervals of 1cm ($^1/_2$in) from −5 to +5 (below). The fetus is considered to be ENGAGED when the top of its head is level with its mother's ischial spines, which are at station 0.

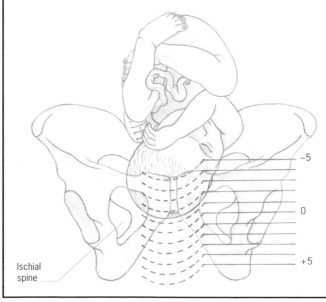

FETAL MONITORING

The heartbeat of the fetus is routinely monitored in all high-risk pregnancies, and in many low-risk ones, too. The process requires two electronic monitors – one is used to monitor the woman's CONTRACTIONS, the other to track the fetus' heartbeat.

Contractions are registered by an external monitor that is strapped to the woman's abdomen and are usually shown as visible waves on a video screen or as a printout.

The fetal heartbeat is recorded by an external or internal monitor. With the second, an electrode is screwed to the skin of the fetus' presenting part (usually the head). The heartbeat is shown as a printed, continuous wave pattern on a paper printout.

Monitoring
There are two types of monitor: the abdominal belt (above) and the internal monitor (below).

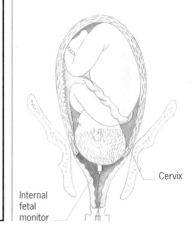

FETAL POSITION AT BIRTH

The majority of babies present head down (cephalic). The usual cephalic presentation is when the baby is facing the woman's spine (known as the anterior presentation). Sometimes, however, the baby faces the other way, so that the baby's spine lies next to the woman's spine (posterior presentation). If the baby is in this position, labor may be prolonged. Approximately 3% of babies in Canada present in the BREECH (bottom down) position at birth.

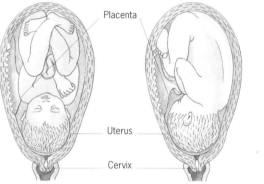

Placenta

Uterus

Cervix

Posterior presentation
The baby's back is against the mother's back, which can result in painful back labor.

Anterior presentation
The baby faces the mother's spine and can traverse the birth canal in the most effective way.

EPISIOTOMY AND TEARS

Before delivery, a cut in the PERINEUM may be made with surgical scissors. The perineum is the area between the anus and vagina, and it is where the pelvic muscles are at their thickest. Episiotomies are done to enlarge the vaginal opening (such as when forceps must be used) and prevent tearing. They are most common in forceps deliveries, during premature labor, and with first pregnancies. Use of episiotomies in other circumstances is controversial.

If the perineum tears during delivery, it tends to tear straight back toward the anus. This can lead to incontinence later. If circumstances permit, a controlled, gradual delivery of the baby's head will help the perineum stretch without tearing. Pre-natal classes can teach a woman how to slow down the second stage, and so give the perineum time to stretch.

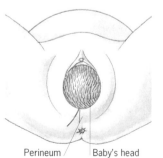

Perineum   Baby's head

Episiotomy
The most common cut angles away from the anus, although a straight cut may be used.

VAGINAL DELIVERY

Once the laboring woman's cervix has dilated fully and has formed part of the birth canal, the uterine activity switches from contractions that pull up and open the cervix to ones that push down on the baby until she is finally born (right).

Progress is monitored
A heartbeat monitor is used to check the baby's condition.

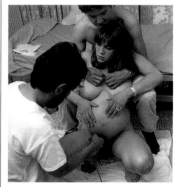

The head appears
The baby's head is the first part to emerge from the birth canal in the majority of vaginal births.

The body follows
With two tiny shrugs, the baby's shoulders and body are free.

THE EXPULSIVE STAGE

The expulsive stage of labor, when the baby is pushed out through the birth canal, is known as the second stage. From full DILATION OF THE CERVIX to the birth of the baby, the second stage usually takes about an hour, although it can be as short as 15 minutes and as long as two hours.

Uterine contractions at this stage last for about 60–90 seconds and occur every 2–4 minutes. Most women experience an involuntary urge to push, caused by the baby's head pressing down on the pelvic floor.

CROWNING

When the baby is about to be born, the anus and PERINEUM will bulge and the top of the baby's head will crown.

Crowning describes the point at which the baby's head appears at the vaginal opening and doesn't slip back between contractions.

As the head stretches the opening of the vagina, the woman will feel a stinging or burning sensation. The tissues then go numb because they are stretched very thin as the baby emerges.

CESAREAN SECTION

A cesarean section (surgical incision through the abdominal and uterine walls) is performed when a vaginal birth is dangerous or impossible. This operation can be done either under general anesthetic (when the woman is unconscious – right), or under EPIDURAL anesthetic (when she is conscious). The entire operation takes 45–60 minutes, and the baby is delivered within the first 10 minutes (see insets). Cesarean sections can be either elective (decision is made before labor) or emergency (problems arise during labor).

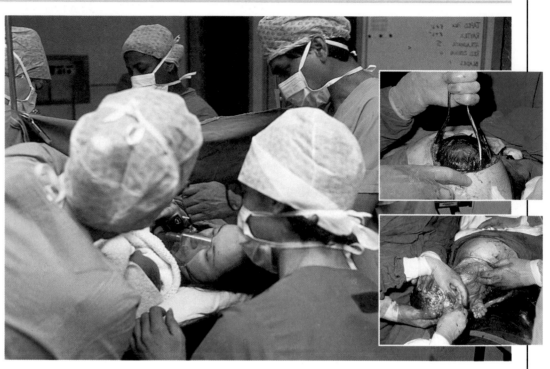

REPEAT CESAREAN

Until the 1960s, doctors used a vertical cut when performing a CESAREAN SECTION. The resulting scar was prone to rupture during subsequent labors, so repeat cesarean sections became the norm. Now the horizontal, lower-segment incision is always made, and the risk of the resulting scar rupturing is very low.

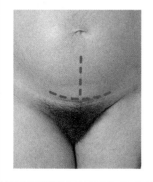

TWIN DELIVERY

Because TWINS tend to be somewhat premature (mainly owing to the limited space in the uterus) and the second twin experiences the powerful expulsive CONTRACTIONS twice over, twin deliveries are always managed in a hospital to minimize risk to the babies.

Twin babies are also treated as two separate births, so if the first twin is delivered vaginally, it doesn't necessarily follow that the second twin will be delivered in this way as well.

To "co-habit" the same uterus comfortably during gestation, the second twin may have assumed a position that is awkward for delivery.

SUDDEN BIRTH

Some women give birth so quickly that there is little, if any, time to call for assistance. These births are usually straightforward, the main risk being a vaginal tear because of the speed of the birth. Very rarely, the baby's head isn't ENGAGED properly, and the umbilical cord is washed past it into the vagina by the amniotic fluid when the waters break. This is very dangerous because, as the baby descends, her head can pinch the cord and cut off her oxygen supply. In this situation, the woman should maintain a head-down, bottom-up, kneeling position (below) in order to prevent the cord from being compressed. A head-down position is also used to ease the pressure of the baby's head against the cervix when the cervix is not fully dilated.

BREECH BIRTH

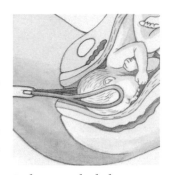

Placenta

Cervix

Baby in flexed breech position

Umbilical cord

Approximately 3% of all babies are born in the breech position, when the buttocks or feet are presented first. There are three main breech positions: frank (when the legs are flexed straight upward), flexed (when the thighs are up against the body and the knees are bent – left), and footling (when the buttocks are high in the uterus and the feet dangle above the cervix). Vaginal breech births are associated with increased risk to the baby. An increasing number are delivered by CESAREAN section.

VAGINAL BREECH BIRTH

An EPISIOTOMY is usually performed because the baby's buttocks can't stretch the birth canal sufficiently for her head to pass through easily. In addition, FORCEPS may have to be used if the baby attempts to breathe while her head is still inside the birth canal.

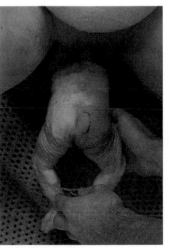

The buttocks emerge
In a breech birth, the baby's buttocks are the first part to appear.

The legs descend
The baby's legs uncurl and drop down, and her body follows.

The baby is almost born
Her head is delivered carefully. She will then take her first breath.

FORCEPS DELIVERY

Resembling sugar tongs in appearance, forceps come in various shapes and are used during the second stage of labor to assist the baby's descent if there is a delay. They may be used in a BREECH BIRTH and CESAREAN SECTION delivery. An EPISIOTOMY is often performed if the forceps are applied. Once forceps are applied, they provide traction and a rotational force. Babies delivered by forceps may seem to have misshapen heads, which is temporary and due to difficulty passing through the pelvis.

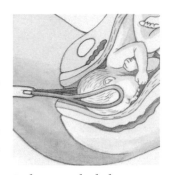

Delivering the baby
An episiotomy is performed and the forceps are then carefully fitted over the baby's head. Gentle traction is then applied.

VENTOUSE DELIVERY

Vacuum extraction, or a ventouse, is used in some parts of Canada as a more gentle alternative to FORCEPS. It consists of a metal or plastic plate or cup that is placed over the baby's scalp. An attached pump produces a vacuum to make the ventouse adhere. The ventouse causes less discomfort to the mother than do forceps. However, its usefulness in aiding delivery is limited when compared with forceps.

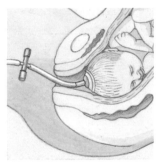

Delivering the baby
The ventouse is attached to the lowest point of the baby's head illustration above), and the baby is slowly drawn down by gentle traction, and out of the birth canal.

DELIVERY OF THE PLACENTA

After the baby is delivered, the uterus will contract again (sometimes with the help of a drug) in what is known as the third stage of labor. Contractions will then continue until the PLACENTA (right) shears off the uterine wall and is expelled.

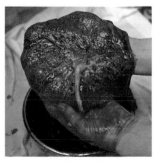

POSTPARTUM

LOCHIA

Postpartum (after delivery), there is a discharge from the uterus, known as lochia. For the first three or four days after delivery, lochia is bright red. It then turns pink or brown and finally yellowish white. Once the uterus has returned to its normal size, the flow of lochia will cease. Lochia loss may continue for as little as two weeks, or as long as six, although the average duration is three. A doctor should be consulted if the lochia becomes foul-smelling or if, after the flow has slackened, it increases or becomes bright red again.

UTERINE CHANGES

During pregnancy, the uterus enlarges greatly and expands upward into the woman's abdominal cavity. Immediately postpartum, it can be felt just below the navel and weighs approximately 1kg (2lb). It then shrinks back until, about six weeks after delivery, it has regained its normal size, weight, and position. In a nonpregnant woman, the uterus weighs about 50g (2oz) and measures 7.5–10cm (3–4in) long.

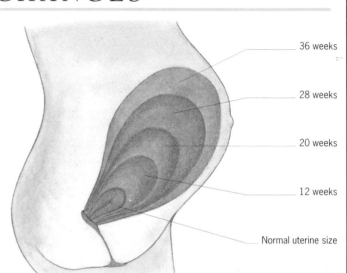

36 weeks

28 weeks

20 weeks

12 weeks

Normal uterine size

PELVIC FLOOR MUSCLES

Supporting the bowel, bladder, and uterus, these can become stretched during pregnancy owing to the weight of the FETUS.

Ischiocavernosus muscle
Bulbocavernosus muscle
Perineal muscle
Anus
Vaginal opening

Ischial tuberosity
Pubococcygeus muscle

POSTPARTUM EXERCISE

Muscles become stretched during pregnancy, and exercise is needed to get them back into shape. Special attention should be paid to firming the abdomen, shaping the waist, and toning the PELVIC FLOOR MUSCLES (below left). If the latter are not toned, urine may escape when a woman sneezes, laughs, or coughs.

Pelvic tuck-in (left)
Kneel on all fours with your knees apart. Tighten your buttock muscles, tuck in your pelvis, and arch your back. Hold and repeat.

Abdominal toner (below)
Lie on your back with your knees bent. Breathe in deeply. Breathe out and raise your head. Hold for two seconds, and then relax. Repeat 10 times.

Waist stretch (right)
With your feet apart, slowly bend to the left and run your left hand down your leg without straining. Raise your right arm over your head, hold your breath. Breathe out as you straighten up. Repeat on left side. Do 10 times on each side.

EXPRESSING BREAST MILK

A manual or electric pump is the quickest way of collecting milk wanted for feeding at a later time, or if the breasts become engorged. The breast also can be massaged by hand to remove milk.

Milk pump
Using a pump to express your milk is convenient and easy.

BREASTFEEDING

Each breast contains 15–20 groups of milk-secreting GLANDS; MILK DUCTS connect them to the nipple. The hormones ESTROGEN and PROGESTERONE stimulate the glands to produce first COLOSTRUM (below) and then BREAST MILK, (below right) but the continued production of milk depends on the sucking action of the breastfed baby.

Nerve endings in the AREOLAE send signals to the HYPOTHALAMUS and the PITUITARY GLAND to release PROLACTIN, the milk-stimulating hormone, and OXYTOCIN, a hormone that causes the muscle fibers around the milk glands to contract so milk enters the milk ducts.

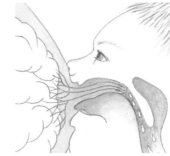

Sucking mechanism (above)
When a baby presses the tip of her tongue against the areola at the base of the nipple, she will stimulate the flow of milk.

"Let-down" reflex (right)
As the baby suckles, the nerves in the areolae send signals to the brain. This causes hormones to be released, thus stimulating the woman's milk to be "let down" into the ducts.

PRENATAL PREPARATION

Learning the proper positioning for the baby at the breast is the best way for a woman to ensure that breastfeeding will be a joyful experience. The mother should consult her doctor, lactation consultant, or community nurse for advice. The whole of the areola must be inside the baby's mouth, and the baby should be allowed to suck frequently for only a few minutes at a time, for the first few days, so the mother's nipples become accustomed to breastfeeding. There is no need for a woman to "toughen" her nipples with rough towels during pregnancy.

MILK VERSUS FORMULA

BREAST MILK (right) is the ideal food for human babies; cow's milk is for calves and soy "milk" is derived from a vegetable. Additions to formulas don't result in their compositions matching that of breast milk. If used, the composition of the formula chosen should match breast milk as closely as possible. Individual formulas will vary slightly from the analysis on the right.

Nutrient	Human milk	Cows' milk formula	Soy-based formula
Energy (kcal)	68	66	65
Fat (g)	3.8	3.7	3.6
Protein (g)	1.25	1.45	1.8
Carbohydrate (g)	7.2	7.22	6.9
Vitamin A (mg)	60	80	60
Vitamin D (mg)	0.02	1.0	1.0
Vitamin C (mg)	3.7	6.8	5.5
Iron (mg)	0.07	0.58	0.67

Per 100 milliliters

COLOSTRUM

This is produced by the breasts during late pregnancy and the first few days after birth. Colostrum is not as fatty and sweet as BREAST MILK (right), but is higher in minerals and protein. Colostrum contains maternal antibodies that protect a baby from infection.

BREAST MILK

The perfect food for a human baby, breast milk contains all the essential nutrients (fat, protein, carbohydrates, vitamins, and iron) that a baby needs. Moreover, like COLOSTRUM (left), breast milk contains maternal antibodies that protect the baby from common respiratory and intestinal infections. During a feeding, the first true milk that issues from the breast is known as foremilk; it is thirst-quenching and low in fat. The milk that follows is known as hindmilk; this is highly nourishing and rich in fat. Breast milk requires no special preparation, although the mother must make sure she is eating a balanced diet.

Breastfeeding will also help the mother lose some of the maternal fat stores she accumulated during pregnancy.

BABY BLUES

Approximately 80% of women experience the "baby blues" following delivery. They normally set in three to five days after the birth, and are characterized by tearfulness, sudden mood changes, irritability, anxiety, and indecision.

The principal cause of this mild postpartum depression appears to be the abrupt decline in levels of the pregnancy hormones. Baby blues often coincide with the start of a woman's milk production.

HORMONAL CHANGES

During pregnancy, the amount of PROGESTERONE in a woman's blood measures about 150 nanograms (thousand millionths of a gram) per milliliter. Immediately following the delivery of a baby, the level of progesterone drops to about 7ng/ml, while the level of estrogen in her blood falls from around 2,000ng/ml to 20ng/ml.

ng/ml

2000 —

　　　　Estrogen

　　　　Progesterone

1000 —

500 —

0 —

BREAST PROBLEMS

Women are designed to breastfeed their offspring, just as other mammals are. There are several problems that may occur while BREASTFEEDING, however.

MASTITIS
Characterized by swelling, tenderness, and reddening of the breast, this infection is usually accompanied by flulike symptoms. It can be successfully treated with antibiotics.

SORE NIPPLES
Slightly tender nipples are normal during the first few days of feeding. However, incorrect latching on and carelessness taking the baby off the breast can result in sore or cracked nipples. Immediate soreness can be relieved with special cream (right). But consult your doctor for a longterm remedy.

BLOCKED DUCTS
Engorgement, or milk that dries on the nipple and so blocks the opening, may result in blocked ducts. The breast feels tender and sore, and the skin may be red. Feeding the baby while massaging the breast just above the sore area will generally clear the blockage. If not, your doctor should be consulted as a breast abscess can develop.

ENGORGEMENT
This may prevent the baby from latching on and usually occurs if the breasts are overfull or not totally empty. The best solution is to express some milk from the breast.

MATERNAL MORTALITY

Abortion- or maternal-related deaths are a leading cause of female mortality worldwide; in India one woman dies from a septic abortion every 10 minutes. Maternal mortality can mostly be prevented by better prenatal care.

6　Canada

　　　　　　　　　　　　　　　Maternal mortality rate related to
　　　　　　　　　　　　　　　childbirth per 100,000 live births

　　14　UK

　　　　19　China (urban)

　　　　　　　　　　61　China (rural)

　　　　　　　　48　China (national)

　　　　　　　　　　　590　Sub-Saharan
　　　　　　　　　　　　　　Africa

POSTPARTUM CUSTOMS AND BELIEFS

There is a tradition in most cultures of a period of rest for a new mother. Cultures in which the mother gets back to work within a day of giving birth are exceptional. This period of rest was historically known as the "lying in" period or "confinement" in Europe and Canada, and would normally last about a lunar month, although, infrequently, it might last as long as 40 or 60 days.

During a period of "lying in," the mother is usually kept in seclusion and is often given special food and treatment. In traditional Judaic culture, the new mother is cared for entirely by women, the fire is kept burning, even on the Sabbath when all work normally ceases for orthodox Jews, and she is fed sweet and nourishing food. In many parts of Southeast Asia, a blazing fire is maintained to keep the mother very hot. This is believed to be effective in relieving postpartum soreness. In Mexico, new mothers have steam baths, and in India they receive special massages, especially on the abdomen and VULVA.

A small quantity of cooked placenta forms part of a new mother's food in some Southeast Asian cultures. In Burma, the traditional food for a new mother is a soup made of fish, fruit, and vegetables, while in many parts of India, new mothers are given a nourishing drink of sweet coconut milk mixed with dill seed. The Arapesh tribe of New Guinea reserve fresh coconut for breastfeeding mothers.

THE
OLDER
WOMAN

THE CLIMACTERIC

What is menopause?

The number of ova (eggs) in a woman's ovaries dwindles throughout her lifetime. From about the age of 40 onward, the rate at which the ova are lost increases, and their quality diminishes. In addition, the ova do not always mature properly, and the frequency of ovulation is therefore reduced, which means that the levels of the female hormones drop sharply. Menopause is actually a single event – the final period; ovulation and menstruation, however, usually become erratic before they cease completely, and related physical, emotional, and mental changes may occur in a woman's body over several years. This process is known medically as perimenopause or the climacteric. The average age for menopause to occur is 51.

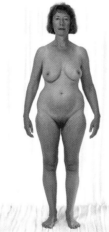

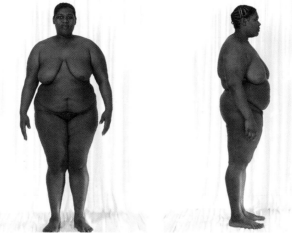

Premenopausal (38 years). Negroid. Large-build mesomorph. Has borne five children.

Perimenopausal (49 years). Caucasoid. Medium-build mesomorph. Has borne two children.

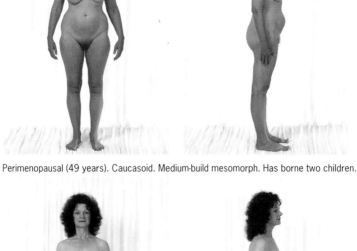
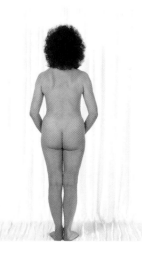

Postmenopausal (59 years). Caucasoid. Small-build endomorph. Has borne three children.

THE PERIMENOPAUSAL BODY

ESTROGEN not only regulates the MENSTRUAL CYCLE but also protects and helps to maintain a woman's bones, joints, reproductive organs, blood vessels and heart; determines mood; and governs fat distribution and the way in which food is metabolized. As ovulation ceases, the production of estrogen declines and the influence of testosterone, which is present in small amounts in all women, increases. This has an impact on every part of the body in the following ways:

REPRODUCTIVE ORGANS

The ENDOMETRIUM (uterine lining) thins, the ovaries gradually become wrinkled and smaller (although they continue to produce ANDROGENS), and the vagina becomes thin, with reduced mucus production.

HEART AND BLOOD VESSELS

Estrogen has a protective effect on the blood vessels. The drop in the level of circulating estrogen throughout the climacteric consequently has a negative effect on the heart and blood vessels. This results in postmenopausal women becoming more prone to coronary HEART DISEASE.

PELVIC FLOOR AND PELVIC ORGANS

The muscles that make up the PELVIC FLOOR lose strength and elasticity. This leads to a tendency for the bladder and uterus to PROLAPSE. Pelvic organs, such as the rectum, bladder, and urethra, lose elasticity and muscle tone. As the urethra becomes less elastic, the possibility that a woman will experience INCONTINENCE increases.

BONES

These become thinner and more fragile, in a process known as OSTEOPOROSIS. If the rate of deterioration is severe, the bones become so weak that they fracture easily.

SKIN

The sebaceous glands gradually stop secreting SEBUM (oil) and the level of the protein COLLAGEN in the skin decreases. Wrinkles appear, or get deeper, and the skin starts to lose its firmness and elasticity.

HAIR

Scalp hair may become thinner, and some woman experience hair loss (usually this is a general thinning, unlike male baldness). Body and facial hair may increase and result in HIRSUTISM. This occurs as a result of the drop in estrogen, which means that the amount of testosterone in a woman's body becomes much more significant.

BODY SHAPE

Owing to the change in the balance between estrogen and testosterone, a woman's waist thickens and her breasts sag and flatten. Her body shape becomes more like a man's.

SYMPTOMS

The reduction in the levels of estrogen can result in many different symptoms. Women vary in the amount and severity of the symptoms that they suffer, and some symptoms are much more common than others. Of the following symptoms associated with the perimenopause, only hot flashes are uniquely menopausal:

- *Headaches*
- *Hot flashes*
- *Insomnia*
- *Sweating*
- *Dizziness*
- *Anxiety*
- *Depression*
- *Irritability*
- *Loss of concentration*
- *Libido changes*
- *Urge INCONTINENCE*
- *Vaginal dryness*
- *Bone aches and pains*

WOMAN VS. ANIMAL

A woman is the only animal to lose the ability to bear offspring during her lifetime; in every other species, the female remains fertile until she dies. All male animals, including human males, also retain the ability to reproduce until they die. Survival beyond the loss of fertility implies, in evolutionary terms, that a woman was necessary to the species even when she had lost her ability to bear children. This is in contrast to many perceived Western ideas about the relative values of young and old women.

The monthly cycle

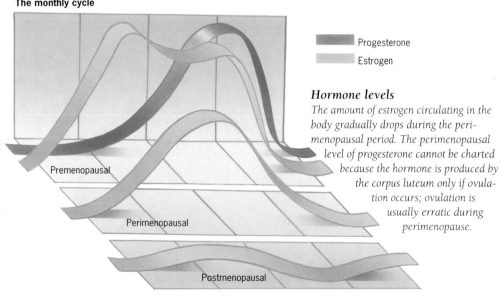

Progesterone
Estrogen

Hormone levels

The amount of estrogen circulating in the body gradually drops during the perimenopausal period. The perimenopausal level of progesterone cannot be charted because the hormone is produced by the corpus luteum only if ovulation occurs; ovulation is usually erratic during perimenopause.

Premenopausal

Perimenopausal

Postmenopausal

MENOPAUSE AND CULTURE

How a woman experiences menopause is greatly influenced by different cultural norms, although the actual symptoms do not differ from society to society.

In the Western world, for example, where youth and sexual attractiveness are highly valued, the perceived image of the menopausal woman is not particularly positive. She is frequently portrayed as irrational, depressed, unstable, unattractive, and as someone who is suffering from an abnormal medical complaint. This is in some ways similar to the medical view of pregnancy that was prevalent until fairly recently. In other cultures, however, the cessation of MENSTRUATION is welcomed as a time when a woman is freed from the physical demands of childbearing. In such cultures, there is quite frequently a ritual celebration of menopause or a clearly defined role for the postmenopausal woman.

In some areas of India and the Middle East, for example, women discard the veil after menopause, whereas in some American Indian societies, menopausal women join

Grandmotherly care
In many African societies, children are supervised predominantly by their grandmothers.

Religious ceremonies
This postmenopausal Balinese woman is offering kuta (religious food) to placate the sea gods.

the "grandmother lodge" where they are encouraged to develop their philosophies and ideas for the good of the nation. In many African cultures, post-menopausal women look after their grand-children while their daughters work. In Bali, they take part in some religious ceremonies (occasionally with the young unmarried women) and are permitted to use obscene language. Where the family is arranged on strongly matriarchal lines, such as in Indian, South American, Italian, Chinese, and some Jewish families, a woman's position (and therefore her power) is usually strengthened following menopause.

MIDLIFE CRISES

During the menopausal years, a number of factors can cause a depressed mood in a woman. These may be directly related to the cessation of menstruation, and thus the ability to reproduce. Other factors that can have an effect are the illness or death of a parent, children seeking their independence, or a husband who is experiencing his own midlife crisis.

In the majority of families, a 20- to 30-year gap between the generations can mean that there is often a period when many problems occur all at once. During such a period, a woman may feel less able to cope than she usually does. This can have a particularly profound effect if a woman has always taken on the primary responsibility for solving family and emotional problems, as many women still do.

Professional counseling can enable such a woman to acknowledge her needs, and deal with them, and with other problems, in a constructive manner.

Counseling can be helpful during menopause if:

- *A woman is depressed or anxious about menopause or about the aging process.*
- *She is suffering from any debilitating menopausal symptoms.*
- *One or more of her parents or parents-in-law dies, or is suffering poor health.*
- *Her partner is experiencing a midlife crisis.*
- *She has been, or is in the process of being, divorced.*
- *She has been widowed recently.*

THE "WISE" WOMAN

In many cultures, past and present, post-menopausal human females have an essential role in the successful functioning of their society. The old are the repositories of the wisdom, information, and skills (women have focused particularly on health, plant cultivation and lore, and childrearing) that enrich their culture. Those groups in which older women reach menopause and survive beyond it consequently are more likely to have a flourishing culture than those groups in which knowledge is lost because women die at a young age.

HORMONE REPLACEMENT THERAPY

The idea that the symptoms of menopause could be treated by hormones instead of surgery dates from the end of the 19th century, but hormone replacement therapy (HRT) became an established treatment only in the 1960s. HRT attempts to return a woman's body to its premenopausal state through the use of ESTROGEN and PROGESTERONE. HRT has helped many women cope with debilitating symptoms, and is known to be protective against OSTEOPOROSIS. Its long-term effects on women are not fully known, although so far they appear to be mainly beneficial. Some women find that HRT has unpleasant side effects, most particularly continuing monthly periods. Other women may not be suitable candidates for HRT due to pre-existing medical conditions.

CONTRAINDICATIONS

There are few contraindications to HRT treatment because it is not greatly different from a woman's natural hormones. With some medical conditions the dose or type of HRT is modified to prevent problems from developing. Estrogen-only HRT may put a woman at greater risk of developing CANCER of the ENDOMETRIUM (uterine lining); other treatments do not appear to carry the same risk. Whereas in the past, HRT was not advised for a woman suffering from liver or gall-bladder disease, venous thrombosis (blood clots in the veins), UTERINE or BREAST CANCER, or DIABETES, this is now not the case.

Tablets Usually contain ESTROGEN and PROGESTERONE.	Creams & Suppositories Contain estrogen.	Skin patches Usually contain only estrogen.	Skin implants Contain only estrogen.
Advantages Widely prescribed by doctors. Woman is in control. Combat most physical symptoms. Protect against OSTEOPOROSIS. Can be stopped immediately. Many different varieties.	**Advantages** Widely prescribed by doctors. Woman is in control. Eliminate vaginal dryness. May help reduce INCONTINENCE caused by atrophy of the urinary tract. Menses (periods) do not restart.	**Advantages** Prescribed by doctors. Woman is in control. Combat most physical symptoms. Offer most women adequate protection against osteoporosis. Can be stopped immediately.	**Advantages** Combat most physical symptoms. Protect against osteoporosis.
Disadvantages May cause breast tenderness, bloating, and nausea. May cause breakthrough bleeding. Will cause menses (periods) to restart if tablets contain both estrogen and progesterone.	**Disadvantages** Do not combat hot flashes and sweats. No protection against osteoporosis.	**Disadvantages** Skin can become red and itchy at the site of a patch. May cause breast tenderness, spotting, and bloating. Will cause menses to restart. Very low doses do not protect against osteoporosis.	**Disadvantages** Procedure (under local anesthetic) to insert implant is invasive. Too high or too low dose can't be modified. May cause breast tenderness, bloating, and nausea. Tolerance or dependency, and early recurrence of symptoms, can occur.

COMPLEMENTARY TREATMENTS

Where HRT (above) is inadvisable or undesirable, alternative therapies can be very helpful, whether used alone, in tandem with one another, or in addition to medical treatments. These therapies may help relieve symptoms such as hot flashes or poor sleeping patterns. However, only HRT will prevent osteoporosis and give protection to the cardiovascular system. There are many different therapies, but the following are probably the most common, although they are unproven. Always consult a qualified and experienced practitioner.

HOMEOPATHY

This works on the basis that like cures like: for example, a dilute, nontoxic solution of the venom of the bushmaster snake (*Lachesis*) is given to relieve hot flashes because the undiluted venom causes severe palpitations and flushing. Homeopathic remedies are matched to both the symptoms and the woman's personality.

HERBALISM

Among the herbs prescribed to treat symptoms of menopause are sage, which may relieve hot flashes; blackberry root, which may be recommended for urinary problems; and elderflower and valerian root, which may help treat INSOMNIA.

ACUPUNCTURE

Skilled practitioners of this Eastern therapy apply very fine needles to specific points on the body, which they believe will rebalance a woman's chi (flow of energy through the body). ACUPUNCTURE is particularly effective in relieving pain.

AROMATHERAPY

The use of diluted essential oils can be effective in invigorating and relaxing a woman, so AROMATHERAPY is particularly good at relieving anxiety and problems related to fatigue.

AGING PROCESS

WHAT IS AGING?

It is generally accepted that the body deteriorates with age. Although some of the aging process is determined biologically, much is the result of a woman's lifestyle. Many women become increasingly sedentary as they get older, while cigarette smoking, alcohol consumption, and atmospheric pollution all take their toll on a woman's body.

Women generally tend to show the aging effects of an unhealthy lifestyle more readily than men do.

HAIR

Approximately half of the total population has GRAY HAIR by the age of 40. The rate at which a woman goes gray is largely determined by her genes. Some women start to go gray in their teens, while others never go gray. Graying can be accelerated by STRESS and a poor diet. Consequently, it is not really a reliable indicator of age, although gray hair is intrinsically associated with the aging process.

Hair loss generally affects women far less than it does men; hair tends to decrease across the whole scalp, resulting in thinner hair overall rather than a noticeable bald patch.

THE OLDER WOMAN'S SKIN

As a woman grows older, a number of physical changes gradually occur that affect the appearance of the skin (right). Her genetic inheritance, the attention her skin receives, and her lifestyle can all accelerate or delay these changes.

As the skin ages, cells are renewed less often and they are shed from the surface of the epidermis less readily. Dryness and pigmentation increase, and the skin loses elasticity and plumpness. The combination of these factors results in a thickened skin that has a coarse and leathery appearance. Patchy pigmentation may also occur. Damage from sunlight, traffic and air pollution, poor diet, and cigarettes, alcohol, and caffeine, moreover greatly increases these biological processes. Specific facial exercises can help to improve the tone of the underlying facial muscles, which can prevent the skin on the face from sagging.

Solar keratoses

Solar keratoses
Also known as "sun" or "liver" spots, these are caused by sun damage. They develop on exposed body parts, such as the hands.

Physical changes

- *Cell renewal in the EPIDERMIS slows down, causing the skin to become rougher.*

- *The interface between the epidermis and DERMIS becomes flatter and some of the COLLAGEN is lost from the dermis, causing loss of elasticity.*

- *Subcutaneous fat begins to be reabsorbed into the body.*

- *Wrinkles appear where the skin is constantly creased, such as when frowning or smiling.*

- *Pigment increases*

- *SEBACEOUS (oil) gland function decreases.*

EYES

PRESBYOPIA (age-related farsightedness) is caused by the lens of the eye gradually hardening and the ciliary muscle weakening. As a result, a woman finds it increasingly difficult to focus on objects nearby, and requires eyeglasses to read and do close work. Although there is a natural deterioration that is age-related, many modern women have occupations that involve close work, which means that their focusing muscles are constantly contracted, which contributes to the problem.

The incidence of CATARACTS (the loss of transparency of the lens), increases with age. By the age of 75, most women have at least a minor deterioration of vision. Excessive exposure to UV LIGHT is thought to increase the likelihood of damage, and cataracts can also be caused by DIABETES MELLITUS (a disease which is often age-related).

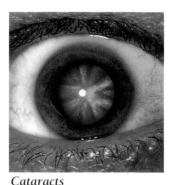

Cataracts
Increasing density of the lens never causes total blindness, but the clarity and detail of the image is progressively lost.

DECLINING BONE MASS

BONE MASS (the density of the bones as measured by the amount of calcium they contain) peaks in women at about the age of 35 and then declines by approximately 1% a year until the age of 65, after which the loss slows by about two-thirds. OSTEOPOROSIS (loss of bone mass) occurs in all women to a certain degree after menopause. Bone mass decreases owing to the loss of the protein matrix tissue from the bone, which causes it to become very brittle. This in turn means that the bones are easily fractured or broken during a fall that would have no effect on a younger woman.

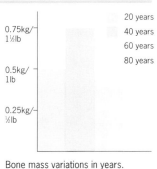

0.75kg/ 1½lb

0.5kg/ 1lb

0.25kg/ ½lb

20 years
40 years
60 years
80 years

Bone mass variations in years.

OLDER FEET

Problems such as calluses, corns, and bunions are common among the elderly, particularly women. During the aging process, renewal of the skin cells tends to decline, which leads to a hard build-up of dead skin; this is known as a callus when on the soles of the feet, and as a corn on the toes. The toenails, too, often become thicker and yellower with age. Vulnerable foot musculature, which is usually an inherited weakness, combined with years of wearing high, pointed-toed shoes, usually results in a bunion forming.

Bunion
The joint at the base of the big toe becomes inflamed and a firm bursa (fluid-filled sac that acts as a cushion) forms. The big toe is forced in toward the other toes.

AGING JOINTS

Some wear and tear to the JOINTS occurs naturally as the body ages, and may lead to OSTEOARTHRITIS. This is more common, however, in women who have subjected their joints to excessive stress (ballet dancers, for example), if the joints are overloaded because a woman is overweight, or if the joints are underused through lack of activity or exercise. The joints can also become painful as a result of RHEUMATOID ARTHRITIS, an inflammation and destruction of joint lining.

SEXUALITY

The idea that the old remain sexual beings is one that many people have problems with, especially in the Western world, where there is an obsession with youth. It can be difficult for an older woman to have her sexuality acknowledged in an open and support-ive way. An aging woman does not lose her desire for, and enjoy-ment of, sensual and sexual love. While there may be some physical problems, such as some thinning of the vaginal walls (which can cause pain during sex) and a decline in production of lubricating mucus, a woman's ability to have an orgasm is not lost.

AGING MOUTH

TEETH
Over time, teeth become worn down, may suffer injury, become decayed or are lost or have to be removed. GUM DISEASE is the biggest cause of tooth loss, even if the tooth itself is healthy. Gum disease is generally caused by excess sugar in the diet rather than age, although it is more common in the elderly.

TASTE BUDS
The renewal process for taste buds on the tongue slows down as a woman ages. This results in fewer tastebuds and a consequent deteriora-tion in the ability to detect subtle flavors.

EARS AND AGING

Human ears evolved in a very quiet world and are ill-equipped to deal with high noise levels, especially noises sustained for any length of time. Harmful noise levels in the indus-trialized world are created by sources such as traffic, trains, factories, construc-tion work, rock concerts, music systems and personal stereos, washing machines, vacuum cleaners, and tele-visions. Noise pollution destroys the hair cells in the inner ear, leading to a grad-ual deterioration in hearing. Studies of pre-industrial tribes, such as the San (Bushmen) of southern Africa, have shown that only a minor loss of hearing occurs naturally with age.

Impaired hearing can be improved by a hearing aid (below). A woman who becomes totally deaf can usually be taught to lip-read or use sign language, and may be able to obtain a "hearing dog," which is trained to alert her to sounds such as a telephone or a doorbell ringing.

Hearing aid
Modern technology has produced a wide variety of barely discernible devices capable of improving sound detection for sufferers of most degrees of hearing loss, such as the "low-profile" hearing aid, above.

OSTEOPOROSIS

This is when the amount of BONE MASS decreases very severely, which causes the bones to become pitted, holey, thin, and brittle. It is a normal part of aging, and it is far more common in women than it is in men. Women are protected throughout their fertile years because they produce ESTROGEN, which helps maintain bone mass. Once estrogen levels start to drop during the PERIMENOPAUSAL period, however, this protection is lost. Osteoporosis is much more common in CAUCASOID women than it is in MONGOLOID or NEGROID women. There appears to be a genetic link, although it can be exacerbated by smoking and alcohol.

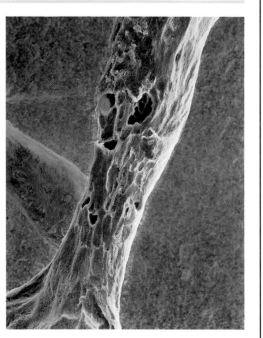

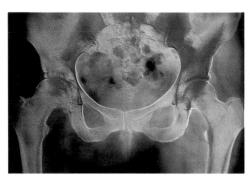

Fragile bones
In osteoporosis, the reduced bone density results in pitted and brittle bones (above). The main supporting joints, such as the knees and hips (left), eventually become extremely fragile and are easily fractured during even a minor fall.

HEART DISEASE

During their fertile years, women are much less likely to suffer from HEART DISEASE than men because ESTROGEN protects arteries from athero-sclerosis (hardening of the arteries).

Following menopause, this protection is lost, and the numbers of women suffering from heart disease comes into line with numbers of male sufferers of the same age.

A woman's heart

- *Heart disease is the most common cause of death in women over the age of 50.*
- *Before menopause, the action of estrogen protects a woman's heart from fat deposits.*
- *Women who were HIRSUTE premenopausally are more prone to heart disease after menopause.*

ARTHRITIS

This is the term generally used to describe inflammation of the joints of the body, whatever the cause.

OSTEOARTHRITIS

Also known as degenerative joint disease, this is most common in joints that have been subjected to high levels of wear and tear, such as the knees and hips. Being overweight is an exacerbating factor. Osteoarthritis is more common in women than men, and occurs most often in those aged over 65.

RHEUMATOID ARTHRITIS

The body's immune system attacks the joints in this disorder. Although no one is certain of the cause as yet, it is thought to be triggered by a viral infection, combined with a genetic susceptibility. Rheumatoid arthritis can cause severe inflammation, pain, and disability, although every case is different. The disease has been known to clear up of its own accord. It is two or three times more common in women than in men, and most cases appear before the age of 50.

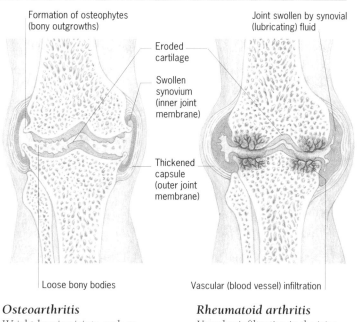

Osteoarthritis
Weight-bearing joints, such as the knee, can suffer erosion.

Rheumatoid arthritis
Vascular infiltration in the joint destroys the bone.

PELVIC PROLAPSE IN WOMAN

When an organ becomes displaced from its normal position within a woman's body, the condition is called a prolapse. The uterus is the most likely organ to suffer prolapse, although the bladder, rectum, and urethra may also be affected. All prolapses become more common following menopause because the decline in the body's level of ESTROGEN reduces tissue elasticity.

Prolapse occurs because a woman's uterine LIGAMENTS have become stretched (typically during pregnancy or childbirth), or because the PELVIC FLOOR MUSCLES have weakened as a result of lack of exercise or following menopause. It is more common in women who have a retroverted uterus (a uterus that is angled backward) or who are overweight. Surgery is required in severe cases.

UTERINE PROLAPSE

Weakening of a woman's pelvic musculature can cause the uterus to drop down into the vagina (below). The degree of displacement varies from slight, which is often described as being a mild sensation of something having "dropped" (known as "first degree," or mild, prolapse), to the point where the uterus can be seen outside the vaginal opening (known as severe prolapse – below).

PROLAPSES IN THE PELVIC AREA

There are other types of prolapse that can occur in the pelvic area. They include urethrocele, when the urethra bulges into the front wall of the vagina; rectocele, when the rectum bulges into the back wall of the vagina; and cystocele, when the bladder sags, causing stress INCONTINENCE (below). These types of prolapse are the result of a lack of muscular tone in the pelvic area.

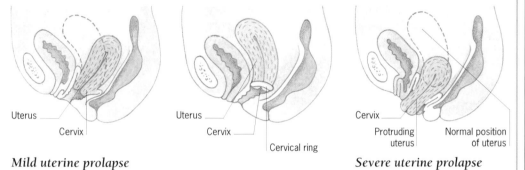

Uterus
Cervix

Uterus
Cervix
Cervical ring

Cervix
Protruding uterus
Normal position of uterus

Mild uterine prolapse
If the uterus drops only a little way into the vagina (above left), it is often possible for the uterus to be held in position with a cervical ring (above).

Severe uterine prolapse
A protruding uterus (above) necessitates a hysterectomy.

INCONTINENCE

This is the term for uncontrollable, involuntary urination, which ranges in degree from mild (stress incontinence, when a small amount of urine is lost, upon coughing or laughing, for example) to debilitating (urge incontinence, when there is an inability to control the need to urinate and the urine flows until the bladder is empty).

Stress incontinence is caused by lack of tone of the sphincter muscles surrounding the urethra, and tends to become more common with age, owing to inactivity. Urge incontinence is caused by factors such as an unstable bladder muscle, which can occur as ESTROGEN levels decline.

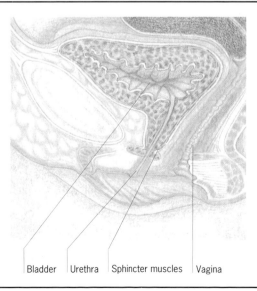

Bladder | Urethra | Sphincter muscles | Vagina

DEMENTIA

Brain cells begin to be lost from the age of 35 onward, although the loss is minimal and in the normal course of things would have very little effect on an older woman's mental ability.

Between 10 and 20% of the population over the age of 65, however, suffer from a decline in mental ability known as dementia. Dementia is often caused by ALZHEIMER'S DISEASE, a stroke, or a head injury, although lifestyle may also play a part. (It is thought that TOXINS contribute to the incidence of Alzheimer's disease, for example.)

Symptoms include loss of short-term memory, confusion, and an inability to recognize people, even close family members. Further degenerative changes can often result in a sufferer becoming aggressive, paranoid, disoriented, untidy, and unclean, with an inability to speak coherently.

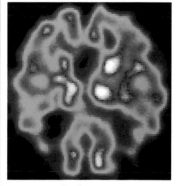

Imaging the brain
The above is a positron emission tomography (PET) scan of the brain of a patient suffering from senile dementia. The scan shows brain activity in the cerebral layer, from low levels (blue) to high levels (yellow). The sparse and patchy appearance of the high activity (yellow) areas in this PET scan indicates advanced degeneration of the brain tissue, as is characteristic of dementia.

AGISM

Society in Canada is agist, particularly so in the case of women. Older women are more likely than men to be portrayed in a negative manner by the media. In addition, the age of a woman is considered a pertinent piece of information that must be given whenever a woman is mentioned in newspapers or magazines, whatever her role or position in society.

In many other cultures, such as in Asia, Africa, India, South America, and southern Europe, growing older is generally seen as a desirable state, and there is much respect for the older "WISE" WOMAN. In Indonesia age and maturity are venerated; this is also the case in China and Japan. In most parts of India, postmenopausal women play an increasingly important part in decision making.

HEALTHY OLD AGE

PHYSICAL HEALTH

Staying active, maintaining fitness, and minimizing destructive behavior such as smoking, drinking alcohol, and eating junk food, all contribute to a healthy old age. Avoiding environmental hazards, such as exposure to sun, pollution, and pesticides, wherever possible, is also beneficial.

MENTAL HEALTH

Studies have shown that those women who remain interested and involved in life, and who continue learning new things and exercising their mental abilities throughout old age, stay mentally agile.

Average life spans worldwide

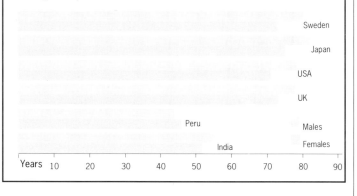

							Sweden	
							Japan	
							USA	
							UK	
					Peru		Males	
						India	Females	

Years 10   20   30   40   50   60   70   80   90

BEREAVEMENT

This is the state of having lost a particularly precious person, such as a spouse or a child, and is more likely to have been experienced by women over the age of 65 than it is by men of a similar age. This is the result of a combination of factors: women live longer than men on average (see chart above) and they tend to marry men who are at least slightly older than themselves. Following bereavement, a period of grieving occurs. Grieving is a very complicated process that encompasses many emotional responses throughout five distinct stages:

LOSS

Feelings of emptiness and shock constitute the first of the recognized stages of grieving that a bereaved woman must go through.

NUMBNESS

The emotions shut down and all response is deadened. This often enables the bereaved woman to cope with funeral practicalities.

ANGER

Indignation, resentment, and self-pity are felt, as well as anger toward the deceased. The bereaved woman may apportion blame (to the hospital, for example) for the death. Revenge may be sought.

DENIAL

Refusal to accept that the death has occurred is experienced. The bereaved woman often searches for the dead person, especially in crowds, and may "see" him or her. If the corpse has not been seen, the belief that the person is still alive "somewhere" may be especially strong.

ACCEPTANCE

Calmness and a rational acceptance of death occurs. The lost person is finally laid to rest, and optimism and hope start to return. The bereaved woman will gradually return to normal, although she may return to earlier stages of grieving periodically.

IT'S A FACT

Georgia O'Keeffe, 1887– 1986 (Wisconsin). An artist who has been recognized as having profound influence. Many of her major paintings were produced in the last decades of her life.

♦

Margaret Thatcher, born 1925 (UK). Prime Minister from May 4, 1979 to November 28, 1990. In 1987 she became the first UK Prime Minister to be elected for a third term.

♦

Dervla Murphy, born 1931 (Ireland). Author of many travel books, reflecting her great resourcefulness and endurance, as well as her insatiable curiosity about the world and its people. One of her longest journeys was a 1,300-mile walk through the Andes.

♦

Mother Teresa, born 1910 (Albania). She became an Indian citizen in 1948 and founded the Missionaries of Charity in Calcutta. She was awarded the Nobel Peace Prize in 1979.

Ageless model
US model Lauren Hutton is still modeling at the age of 50.

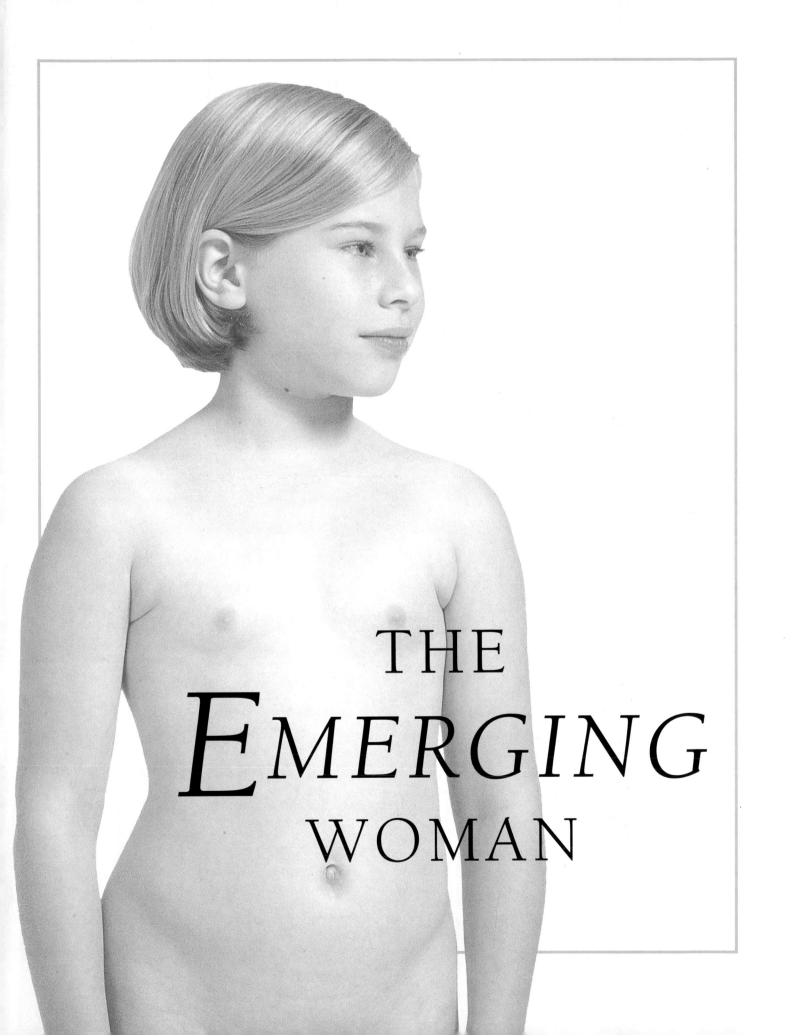

THE
EMERGING
WOMAN

WOMAN
VS. ANIMAL

At the embryonic stage of development, all animals, including women, are surprisingly similar in appearance. This is because all these life forms use the same basic "building blocks" (GENES) to construct their individual characteristics.

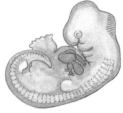

Human embryo

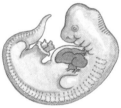

Pig embryo

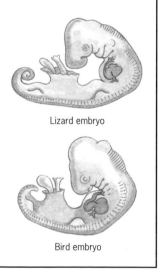

Lizard embryo

Bird embryo

Infant. Three years old. Negroid.

Prepubescent. Nine years old. Caucasoid.

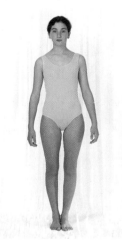

Adolescent. Twelve years old. Caucasoid.

THE DEVELOPING FEMALE FETUS

1 Month
Length: 4mm (⅛in)
Weight: less than 1g (0.03oz)

Cells specialize into three layers and most of the organs start to develop. The inner layer of cells will develop into the lungs, liver, thyroid gland, pancreas, urinary tract, and bladder. The middle layer will become the heart, skeleton, muscles, ovaries, kidneys, spleen, and blood vessels. The outer layer will become skin, sweat glands, nipples, hair, and nails. By the end of the third week, there is a heartbeat and the internal ear has started to form.

2 Months
Length: 2.5cm (1in)
Weight: 3g (0.1oz)

The circulatory system is established. The soft tissue that will harden into the facial bones has formed and is fusing together. Sweat glands start to form. The external ears start to develop. Arm buds lengthen and extend forward; pads form on fingertips and the tips of the toes. Leg buds sprout and toes start to appear. By the seventh week, embryonic movement can be identified, using ultrasound.

3 Months
Length: 9cm (3½in)
Weight: 48g (1½oz)

Bone tissue appears. The heart beats between 110 and 160 times per minute. The basic face is formed: the eyes are completely formed although covered by eyelids; there is a definite nose and chin, and 32 permanent tooth buds. Fingers and toes grow rapidly and nails form. External genital organs can now be identified as female or male. Twitchy movements are made. The sucking reflex is established.

4 Months
Length: 13.5cm (5⅓in)
Weight: 180g (6oz)

The lungs are developing. More bone develops; tiny bones inside the ear harden. The immune system is developing. First facial expressions occur. The fetus is conscious of bright lights from outside the abdominal wall. Eyebrows, lashes, and hair on the head begin to grow. The vaginal plate (precursor to the vagina) is developing. The majority of the connections between nerves and muscles are established; limbs now move properly.

5 Months
Length: 18.5cm (7⅓in)
Weight: 0.5kg (1lb)

The skin is red and wrinkled owing to lack of subcutaneous fat. The fetus is sensitive to touch and moves if there is pressure on the abdomen. The ears are developed and sounds can be heard. The body is covered with LANUGO (fetal hair). Nipples develop. The vagina begins to become hollow. The ovaries contain about seven million ova (eggs). The sebaceous glands become active and produce vernix caseosa (greasy coating on skin).

6 months
Length: 25cm (10in)
Weight: 1kg (2lb)

The body and legs are now more in proportion, and facial features are similar to those of a newborn baby. The centers of the bones harden. The skin is less translucent and more reddish looking. The brain cells used for conscious thought begin to mature – the brainwave patterns begin to resemble those of a newborn baby more closely. Ova (eggs) in the fetus' ovaries begin to be lost – five million will have been lost by the time she is born.

7 Months
Length: 27.5cm (11in)
Weight: 1.5kg (3lb)

The head and body proportions now resemble those of a newborn baby. The skin becomes smoother as subcutaneous fat builds up underneath the skin. Air sacs in the lungs develop. The eyelids separate so that the eyes can now open. Lanugo starts to diminish. Hands and feet are now fully formed; nails grow longer. The brain grows larger and the brainwaves are similar to those of a newborn baby.

8 Months
Length: 30cm (12in)
Weight: 2.5kg (5lb)

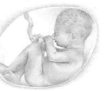

Fat deposits have built up so that the fetus' skin is pink rather than red. Fat will provide energy and regulate body temperature once the baby is born. The organs are almost fully mature, except for the lungs. The face is smooth. The eyes are able to focus within a field of vision of 20–25cm (8–10in) because the irises can now dilate and contract. There is a very thick coating of vernix caseosa on the fetus' skin.

9 Months
Length: 35–37.5cm (14–15in)
Weight: 3–4kg (6–8lb)

The skin is smooth and soft and the last of the fat is laid down, making the fetus chubby. The lungs mature. All the organs are fully formed and working. Usually all the lanugo has been shed from the body, although a few patches may remain. The fingernails are long and may scratch the fetus' face. The ovaries contain only two million ova (eggs) and are still above the pelvic brim; they do not reach their final position until after the baby has been born.

THE NEWBORN GIRL

At birth, a baby's average length is 47.5–50cm (19–20in). Her head appears large in proportion to her body because it comprises about a quarter of her total length. All newborn babies make automatic movements if they are touched or held in a certain way. After about three months, babies can make voluntary responses.

Looking
Images 20–25cm (8–10in) away can be seen. She will look toward sounds and movements.

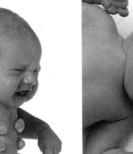
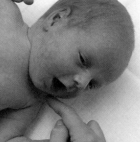

Rooting (left)
She instinctively seeks her mother's breast to feed. If her cheek is gently stroked, she will turn her head and open her mouth.

Grasping (below)
A baby will automatically grip anything that is put into her palm. This is a remnant of the grasping reflex inherited from our ape ancestors.

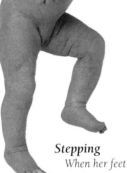

Her grip is strong enough to support her weight

Her soles will automatically curl and try to grip if they are touched

Stepping
When her feet come in contact with a firm surface, she "steps."

Crying (above)
Many babies cry a lot. Crying is her way of communicating feelings and can indicate many things.

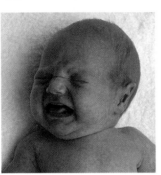

WOMAN VS. MAN

Babies are treated differently depending on their gender. In one study, it was found that babies dressed as, and therefore perceived as, girls (regardless of their actual gender) were treated much more carefully and gently than those babies dressed as, and consequently recognized as, boys. The latter were likely to be jiggled more roughly. In addition, the participants in the study tended to use soothing and reassuring "baby talk" when speaking to a baby that they thought was a girl than they did if they thought the baby was a boy.

All of the adult participants looked, and reported feeling, uncomfortable when handling and speaking to an infant that was dressed in an ambiguous way so that the gender was not apparent. This feeling was resolved as soon as they were told whether the baby was a girl or a boy.

INFANT MORTALITY

In the Western world, infant mortality has fallen over the past 60 years, from about 6% of babies born in 1930 to under 1% in 1990. Of this 1%, about 45% are stillbirths (babies who die before labor begins); about 5% are intrapartum deaths (babies who die during labor); and about 50% are neonatal deaths (babies that die soon after birth; most are premature or handicapped infants). The incidence of infant mortality rises significantly in areas with inadequate prenatal care.

Before labor
During labor
Soon after birth

PHYSICAL DEVELOPMENT

A girl's growth is very rapid during the first few years of her life. Throughout the rest of her childhood, her growth rate slows, although her height will increase gradually. In the prepubescent phase (which begins at about nine years of age), a girl experiences another major period of growth. During this time, she grows very rapidly, with her legs developing at a faster rate than the rest of her body. Her pelvic bones become more developed, and fat builds up on her breasts, hips, and thighs until the characteristic female curves have been acquired.

Changes to female body proportions between birth and adolescence

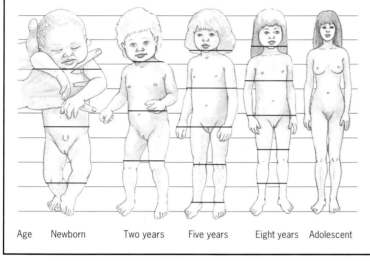

| Age | Newborn | Two years | Five years | Eight years | Adolescent |

Body proportions
The size of the head does not increase much from its newborn size. Consequently, its ratio to the rest of the body can be used to gauge the body's proportions at all stages in a girl's development. By dividing the body into eight equal parts (because the adult head is about one-eighth of the adult body), it is evident that the proportions of the body change radically between birth and adolescence.

WOMAN VS. MAN
Average growth patterns vary between girls and boys. Boys tend to be taller than girls until the age of three, after which girls become slightly taller. When girls reach puberty, (between the ages of 11 and 14), this difference increases, and young teenage girls tend to be taller than their male peers. Once boys reach puberty, however – which occurs a couple of years later in boys than in girls – they begin steadily to outstrip girls in both height and weight. The tallest girls will remain taller than the shortest boys.

BREASTS

The emerging woman's breast development is divided into specific phases: prepubertal, breast budding, enlargement, and areolae formation. The age at which these changes occur varies, but they usually start between nine and 14 years.

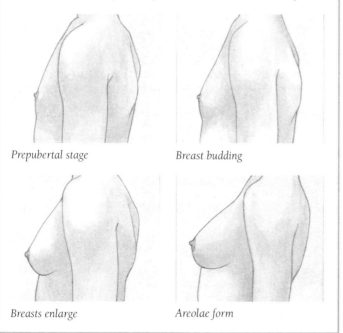

Prepubertal stage

Breast budding

Breasts enlarge

Areolae form

REPRODUCTIVE TRACT

The proportions of the reproductive tract change as a girl matures. At birth, the uterine body is equal in length to the CERVIX because of the presence of ESTROGEN in the mother's (and therefore the fetus') circulation. Soon after birth estrogen levels drop, and the proportions become 1:2 until puberty. At puberty, the girl produces large amounts of estrogen, which changes the size of her uterus.

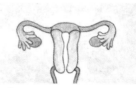

Birth ratio 1:1

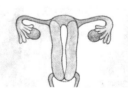

Childhood ratio 1:2

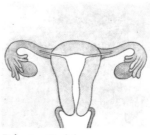

Puberty ratio 1:1

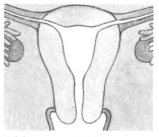

Adolescence ratio 2:1

It is usually a year before a human infant is able to stand and take her first steps. This is very slow in comparison with most animals. Newborn horses are among the fastest to gain their feet after birth (below); they share this ability with other herbivores, such as deer, gazelles, and wildebeest, which rely on speed and agility to stay ahead of their predators.

Ten minutes old
The newborn foal has been thoroughly cleaned.

Thirty minutes old
The foal attempts to stand steadily on its feet.

Sixty minutes old
The foal is relatively steady and can walk and suckle.

AMBULATION SKILLS

Supporting the weight of her own head is the first step a baby girl takes in learning to move independently. After gaining control of her head, she then learns how to sit upright, roll over, use her hands to pull herself forward on her buttocks, crawl, stand upright, toddle, walk, and run. Further coordination, such as that necessary to smoothly climb or descend stairs (climbing is much easier than descending), skip, or ride a tricycle, comes as she matures.

Three months
She is able to hold up her head continually while lying down. She starts to try crawling.

Two years (right)
She can jump up and down and run, although she has trouble slowing down or turning corners.

Four years
She can walk downstairs with one foot on each step.

Thirteen months (right)
She is able to stand independently and may be able to walk.

Five years
She can skip rope, and roller skate.

MOVEMENT WITHIN A CULTURAL CONTEXT

Balancing games
Playing enhances a girl's abilities.

In societies where the members do a lot of walking, such as among the San (Bushmen) of Africa and the nomadic tribes of the Middle East, young children are expected to do far more walking than the majority of their peers in Western cultures. In industrialized nations, many children are habitually ferried about in strollers and cars and given few opportunities to walk any distance.

Skipping, chasing, and leaping games have been popular throughout history, and encourage a girl to become more coordinated and balanced. Many of the chain games that young children play, such as London Bridge, date from the Middle Ages. Studies have shown that although the words may change, the actions remain the same for generation after generation.

MANIPULATION SKILLS

Before she can learn to grasp and hold an object voluntarily, a girl must lose the involuntary grasp reflex she is born with. The reflex is common to all tree-swinging primates; it ensures that the infant ape remains securely attached to its mother. The reflex is said to have been retained throughout the hypothetical AQUATIC PERIOD; the newborn baby's ability to hold on to her mother's hair guaranteed that she would stay afloat. Once a girl is able to hold an object, she then begins to refine her manipulative skills.

Three months (below left)
She is able to hold objects for a few minutes at a time.

Eight months (below)
She is able to hold an object tightly, and will often shake it or bang it against something else.

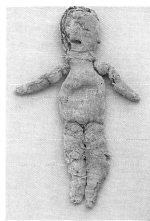

One year (above)
She can deliberately throw objects and will try to hold more than one thing in her hand at a time.

Two years (above)
She is learning to dress and undress herself, and is able to turn doorknobs and take the lids off jars. She can also move a pencil or pen and turn the pages of a book one by one.

Three years (right)
She can draw a picture, thread beads on a string, fasten and unfasten buttons.

WOMAN VS. MAN

Children of the same sex differ more from each other than do girls from boys. Research into the subject has shown, however, that there are a few areas where there is a distinct gender difference.

Girls tend to be quicker to develop physical skills, such as walking and holding, than boys. Girls are also usually better coordinated and, as a result, generally better at skipping, jumping, hopping, dancing, and gymnastics than boys, especially in the preschool years. This difference often continues after childhood, with women generally having greater MOTOR FITNESS than men.

There is little difference in speed and strength between boys and girls until puberty, when boys become both stronger and faster than girls.

PLAY AND LEARNING SKILLS

Learning is the natural result of playing, and children of all cultures use play to find out about their world and make sense of their place within it. The best toys are often very simple, such as a cardboard box, sand, and pebbles, as well as dolls made out of simple materials. Occasionally, dolls are found by archeologists, which suggests that the need to play with a human "model" is ancient. Play that involves complicated physical manipulation, as in weaving grasses and making daisy chains, promotes the dexterity that is necessary for other skills.

Roman doll (left)
This ancient cloth doll was found on an archeological dig; it is Roman and dates from the 3rd century BC.

Tying shoelaces (right)
The ability to tie shoelaces requires a high degree of manipulation.

INTELLECTUAL DEVELOPMENT

The development of INTELLIGENCE is the result of a combination of a child's inherent mental abilities and the environment in which she grows up.

As far as development is concerned, the average girl is thought to be able to smile at about 6–8 weeks (which shows she is able to recognize intimates), begins to show a sense of humor at 16 weeks, makes recognizable sounds at 28 weeks, responds to her name at 36 weeks, forms recognizable words by 48 weeks, understands simple requests at one year old, and speaks by two years old. Most girls learn to read at about four or five years of age and can fully understand abstract concepts, such as democracy, by puberty. Intelligence is notoriously difficult to quantify; IQ (intelligence quotient) tests are the classic measure of intelligence, but are very overrated as indicators of a girl's actual ability and capacity to learn. This is because they are universal assessments that do not take into account cultural or social differences in knowledge.

Gifted girls
Occasionally, a young girl may exhibit an extremely high level of intellectual ability. Ruth Lawrence, above, who took just under two years to gain a first-class degree in mathematics (she was a month short of her 14th birthday when she graduated), is an excellent example of the female capacity for genius.

WOMAN VS. MAN

Boys and girls communicate in different ways from an early age. Girls tend to spend a lot of time talking with their "best friend" and usually talk about personal subjects. Boys tend to play in groups, are usually more restless and physical than girls, interrupt each other constantly, and are combative. Problems are shared by girls as a way of expressing affection and making the sufferer feel normal; boys dismiss problems as a means of expressing affection and respect ("I believe in your ability to cope"). When they are talking, girls usually directly engage with one another, face to face. In contrast, boys rarely sit and talk, and if they do, they tend to sit side by side, seemingly disengaged, although body language is closely mirrored. Looking directly at each other could be interpreted as aggressive. Not looking at each other therefore becomes a friendly act.

Close contact
Girls spend much time in face-to-face conversation.

IT'S A FACT

A girl's position within the family is thought to influence her development and character. First-born girls are often confident high-achievers.

◆

Elizabeth Barrett Browning, born 1806 (UK). The eldest of 11 children, she was a prolific and brilliant poet, whose work has remained justifiably popular.

◆

Margaret Mead, born 1901 (USA). The eldest of five children, she was a highly respected anthropologist, and was one of the pioneers in the research of family relationships worldwide.

ACQUIRING SPEECH

In the theory of the AQUATIC PERIOD, the evolution of speech is thought to have taken place during that time. Communication by body language and posture would have been less effective because a lot of the body would frequently have been hidden under water. Vocalization would then have become an increasingly important tool for communication.

Children learn to speak by listening to and mimicking the speech they hear around them, and those who grow up in a very oral environment are themselves likely to talk a lot, while those with quiet parents usually are unlikely to do so. Girls reared in environments where there is a constant background noise, such as music that is playing continually or a television that is rarely switched off, take longer to learn to speak.

All babies, even those who are deaf, "babble" before the sounds they make become proper language. All babies babble in the same way, regardless of sex, race, culture, or environment. Girls who hear two or more languages during childhood often become bi- or multilingual. Accents are very fluid before the age of eight, although it is usually the parents' accent that is the predominant influence.

EDUCATIONAL DEVELOPMENT

Classroom technology
Western girls are increasingly using computers in the classroom.

Wrestling for the ball
Team sports encourage camaraderie.

Compulsory schooling until the age of at least 14 is the norm in the Western world. In Canada, most girls attend mixed-gender schools, although some are educated in single-sex schools, and a few at home. Difference in the average examination performance between the sexes is very slight, but girls tend to outperform boys in all subjects except mathematics, physics, and chemistry. This was explained for many years as a basic sex difference, but recent research suggests that social expectations and different experiences are actually the major influences on gender difference in performance.

A belief remains that girls do not need mathematical ability as much as boys; boys tend to be given mechanical toys far more often than do girls, which facilitate the learning of physics – a stopwatch, for example, relates movement to time. Girls sometimes do better at single-sex schools. This may be because teachers unconsciously pay more attention to boys in mixed classes; boys use more attention-seeking behavior (so the teacher then becomes more aware of the boys), and are often slower than girls (so the teacher has to spend more time with the boys).

SCHOOLING IN DIFFERENT CULTURES

Historically, girls fared worse than boys when it came to schooling. Educating a boy has usually been seen as necessary to his future life, while a girl was expected only to marry. She therefore needed to become proficient only in those achievements, such as cooking and needlecraft, that would be useful in her married life. This continues to be the case in many parts of the world, such as the Middle East and Africa. In contrast, in imperial Russia during Catherine the Great's reign in the 18th century, women's education was seen as important and intellectualism among women was celebrated.

In modern China, only single children receive free education, in accordance with the government's campaign to reduce the birthrate. In schools, great emphasis is placed upon cooperative behavior, while competitiveness and individualism are discouraged. However, despite the fact that education may cost nothing, in rural China about 20% of schoolgirls under the age of 14 are regularly kept away from school to help at home or on the land.

Indian schoolgirls
School lessons in India usually take place in open-air courtyards. Learning by rote is a central part of an Indian girl's education. For every 100 Indian boys that attend school, approximately 60–65 Indian girls attend.

SOCIAL DEVELOPMENT

A child learns the basic principles of social interaction within the first year of her life – primarily from her parents, although other caregivers will have an influence. She develops these social skills throughout her childhood and adolescence, and other people and influences, such as her siblings, peers, teachers, and the media, especially television and magazines, become important factors in her social development. The more of the world she encounters, the greater is the possibility of extending her skills.

One year old
By this age, a girl has learned many basic social skills.

Three years old
She is now forming friendships and is able to play relatively unselfishly with other children.

Teenage years
Many adolescent girls spend hours socializing on the telephone.

BOWEL AND BLADDER CONTROL

Learning how to control the excretory functions until a convenient, private time is an extremely important social skill in all cultures. By the age of five about 90% of all children are dry night and day and have control of their bowel movements. Girls usually reach these stages quicker than boys do.

Toilet-trained
By two, many girls are happy to use a potty by themselves.

RELATIONSHIP SKILLS

Babies are born with a built-in desire and ability to relate to adults, to ensure their survival. Even very tiny babies have strong likes and dislikes (they prefer looking at their mother's face to anyone else's, and they also prefer looking at new faces to ones they have seen already) and these develop as they grow up. By the age of three, most girls will have at least one close friend. Many girls form particularly close relationships with their grandparents.

To achieve harmonious relationships with other people, girls who grow up in a society where there is little personal space have to learn to modify their behavior to a much greater extent than those girls who grow up in under-populated areas, such as in many parts of Australia.

Chinese children
Growing up in a society where there is little personal space, such as in China and Japan, makes considerate and constrained behavior essential for successful social interaction.

WOMAN VS. MAN

Girls are often expected to be polite and obedient and to obey commands without question, to a far greater extent than are boys. This often has the result of restricting girls' independence and ability to think for themselves. Unquestioning obedience is also likely to put girls at risk of abduction or abuse because such children are likely to obey any adult, even one who is unknown to them, without question. Telling children not to talk to strangers was found by a recent study to have little effect in preventing children from obeying adults who were unknown to them. The reason for this was that children often think of a "stranger" as being some-one who looks weird or acts bizarrely.

◆

A girl who persistently evinces so-called "boyish" behavior, such as running about, shouting, climbing trees, or getting dirty, is often labeled a tomboy.

GIRLS THROUGH THE AGES

Clothes give a clear reflection of the extent to which restraint is exercised on a girl's mind and body by society. Girls are coming into their own toward the end of the 20th century. Independence, the ability to think for themselves, and nonconformity are more likely to be causes for celebration than condemnation.

18th-century girl
The stomacher (a V-shaped bodice of stiff material) and long skirt suggest decorum and restriction.

Victorian girl (above)
Toward the end of this era, clothes began to loosen up — but girls' bodies still remained covered.

Modern African girl
Third World girls, like this one, still face restrictions and poverty.

1920s girl (right)
In the period after World War I, women's clothes became shorter and less structured. This was a reflection of greater female freedom. Girls' clothes, such as those illustrated on the right, followed suit.

1950s girl
Socks and sandals freed the legs and allowed for the rough-and-tumble of play and work.

Modern swaddled baby
This newborn Chinese baby girl, wrapped in swaddling clothes, is protected from contact with the world.

Modern Western girls (above)
Contemporary girls in the West welcome the adventure of individual choice in life. They will grow up with egalitarian expectations.

SEXUAL DEVELOPMENT

The age at which a girl reaches puberty varies between individuals. The majority of girls enter puberty between the ages of nine and 15 years, and it is normal for girls at the midpoint (between the ages of 12 and 13 years) to show obvious differences in their development (below). Sexual maturity is attained with the development of the breasts and genitals, the broadening of the pelvis, and the growth of pubic hair.

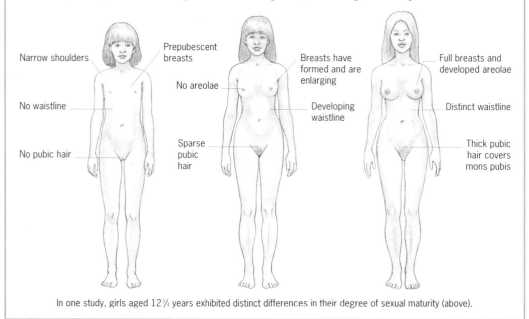

Narrow shoulders
Prepubescent breasts
No areolae
No waistline
No pubic hair

Breasts have formed and are enlarging
Developing waistline
Sparse pubic hair

Full breasts and developed areolae
Distinct waistline
Thick pubic hair covers mons pubis

In one study, girls aged 12¾ years exhibited distinct differences in their degree of sexual maturity (above).

RITES OF PASSAGE

Attitudes about teenagers vary from society to society. In many Western cultures teenagers are generally regarded as children. Countries can vary within this as the different ages of consent within Europe testify. In France, the age of consent is 15, and in Spain, 12. In Canada, in most provinces, the age of consent is 18 years. In some other countries, particularly South America, India, and much of Africa, girls are often married or mothers by the age of 15. In India and the Middle East, betrothal often occurs during childhood.

Courtship (above)
Where marriages are not arranged, as in the West, couples date to determine their compatibility.

Indian child bride
The marriages of prepubescent girls are often not consummated until after puberty.

WOMAN VS. MAN

Western girls and boys are most likely to discover masturbation between the ages of 11 and 13, and to have their first experience of sexual intercourse between 15 to 18 years.

Age when first masturbated

Ages	Man	Woman
By 10 years	19	19
11–13 years	53	25
14–16 years	16	18
17–21 years	5	15
22–30 years	1	7
31+ years	1	5
Never	5	11

Age when first had sex

Ages	Man	Woman
By 10 years	3	2
11–14 years	18	13
15–18 years	70	68
19–25 years	9	16
26 years or over	0	1

All the figures in the above charts are taken from the 1993 Janus study and represent percentages of the respondents.

TEENAGE PREGNANCY

In recent years, teenage pregnancy in the West has risen at an alarming rate. Media and peer pressure contribute to this modern epidemic. In addition, many of these young women are ignorant about contraception and how their bodies work.

INDEX

ACKNOWLEDGMENTS

Carroll & Brown would like to thank

Typesetting:
Deborah Rhodes, Rowena Feeny

Illustration:
Joanna Cameron, John Lang, Joe Lawrence, Annabel Milne, Coral Mula, Howard Pemberton, Emma Whiting, Paul Williams, Lydia Umney

Picture researchers:
Diana Morris, Donna Thynne

Equipment:
Boots Opticians (the Boots Low Profile Hearing Aid, courtesy of Boots Hearing Care at selected Boots Opticians, appears on page 201). Boots The Chemist, Marie Stopes Health Clinics, Timesco

Index:
Anne McCarthy

Models:
Julie Adams, Koreen Aliane, Vivian Austin, Deanne Barnes, Cassie-Ella Bernard, Zoë Carroll, Barbara Cogswell, Kerry Cresswell, Lyndel Donaldson, Hilary Goodman, Joanne Goulbourne, Aideen Jennings, Fiona Johnson, Majorie Johnston, Susi Langridge, Sheena McFarlane, Mira Mehta, Mitch Munroe, Sylvia Newton, Carlena Odumesi, Jenny Reitsema, Gabrielle Roth

Picture credits

7 **bl**: SPL; 13 **tr**: Image Select; 14 **tr**: Rex, **cl**: Rex, **cl**: Natural History Museum Picture Library; 15 **t**: SPL/Manfred Kage, **c**: SPL/Dr Brian Eyden, **b**: SPL/CNRI; 16 **t**: Syndication International, **b**: Allsport/Gray Mortimore; 17 **tl**: TRIP/R. Pomens, **tr**: Mary Evans Picture Library, **bl**: Mary Evans Picture Library; 18 **tl**: Rex, **tc**: Universal Pictorial Press and Agency Ltd, **r**: Hulton Deutsch Collection; **bl**: Image Bank, **bc**: Popperfoto; 19 **t**: Zefa UK, **b**: Zefa UK; 23 **t**: SPL; 26: Brain surgery: SPL/Alexander Tsiaras; 28 **ct**: SPL/Prof P. Motta, **r**: SPL/Dr Ray Clark & M.R.Goff, **cb**: SPL/John Burbidge; 29 **tr**: SPL/CNRI, **br**: Fortean Picture Library, **bc**: SPL/Martin Dohrn; 30 **r**: National Medical Slidebank, Kobal Collection; 31: Sally and Richard Greenhill; 33 **bl**: SPL/P Manazzi, **bc**: National Medical Slidebank, **br**: SPL/James Stevenson; 34 **cl**: Zefa UK, **cr**: SPL/Dr P Manazzi, **crb**: Coleman/John Shaw, **bl**:Coleman/John Caucalosi, **br**: SPL/Dr J Burgess; 35 **c**: SPL/St Bartholomew's Hospital; 37 **b**: SPL/John Burbidge; 38: Robert Harding Picture Library; 39 **tl**: Bridgeman Art Library & Source, **tr**: Hulton Deutsch Collection, **cr**: Hulton Deutsch Collection, **cb**: Popperfoto, **bl**: Hulton Deutsch Collection; 40: Robert Harding Picture Library; 41 **t**: SPL/Manfred Kage, **b**: SPL/CNRI; 43 **cl**: Kobal Collection; 44 **r**: SPL/Prof P Motta, **br**: SPL/Adam Hart-Davis; 46 **cl**: Robert Harding Picture Library/Thierry Mauger, **ct**: Robert Harding Picture Library/Jake Chessum, **c**: Robert Harding Picture Library; 49 **tr**: SPL, **cl**: Zefa UK, **clb**: Zefa UK, **bl**: Zefa UK, **br**: SPL/Dr Goran Bredberg; 50 **tr**: Rex, **c**: Sally & Richard Greenhill, **bl**: Zefa UK, **br**: SPL/Dr Goran Bredberg; 52 **cl**: Coleman/Peter Davey, **clb**: Coleman/J. Caucarlosi, **bl**: Coleman/Jane Burton; 53 **t**: Hulton Deutsch Collection, **c**: Kobal, **bl**: Zefa UK; 55 **tr**: SPL, 56 **cl**: Rex, **c**: Zefa UK; 59 **br**: SPL/CNRI, **br**: SPL/CNRI, 60 **t**: Clive Barda; 61 **c**: Zefa UK, **bl**: Coleman, **br**: Bridgeman Art Library & Source; 63 **tl**: National Medical Slidebank, **bl**: Rex, **br**: Rex; 64 **l**: C.M. Dixon, **br**: SPL/James Stevenson; 63 **cl**: SPL/Alexander Tsiaras, **bl**: National Medical Slidebank; 67 **rb**: Collections/Anthea Sieveking; 68 SPL/Philippe Plailly; 70 **t**: Bridgeman Art Library & Source, **bc**: SPL; 71 **br**: Zefa UK; 73 **br**: Trustees of the British Museum; 75 **tl**: Mr Shepherd, St Bartholomew's Hospital, **tr**: Mr Shepherd, St Bartholomew's Hospital; 77 **br**: Réunion de Musées; 78 **tr**: Alwin H Küchler, **bl**: Mary Evans Picture Library; 79 **bc**: Hutchison Picture Library, **br**: Mansell Collection; 82 **bl**: Mary Evans; 85 **c**: SPL/Frieder Michler; 87 **bl**: Hutchison Picture Library; 93 **t**: SPL/CNRI, **c**: SPL/NIBSC, **b**: SPL/CNRI; 94 **t**: SPL/CNRI, **b**: SPL/CNRI; 95 **tl**: SPL/CNRI, **cb** SPL; 97 **r**, **t** and **b**: SPL/Philippe Plailly, **cr**: SPL/Hank Morgan; 100 **cl**: Jules Selmes, **cb**: Rex, **br**: Mary Evans; 102 **bl**: SPL; 103 **br**: SPL; 105 **cr**: SPL; 106 **c**: SPL; 107 **bc**: S Halliday, **br**: Lucinda Lambton; 108 **c**: SPL/Salisbury District Hospital; 111 **t**: Bridgeman Art Library & Source, **b**: Hulton Deutsch Collection; 112: Hulton; 113 **t**: Hulton, **b**: Hulton; 114 **tl**: Bridgeman Art Library & Source, **tr**: Bridgeman Art Library & Source, **bl**: Mary Evans, **bc**: R Harding; 115 **tr**: Bridgeman Art Library & Source, **c**: Images, **bl**: Rex; 116 **bc** & **br**: Mary Evans; 117 **tl**: Bridgeman, **tc**: Hulton, **cl**: Hulton, **c**: Hulton, **cr**: Hulton, **bl**: Hulton, **br**: Rex; 119 **tr**: Bridgeman Art Library & Source, **c**: Bridgeman Art Library & Source, **b**: Mary Evans; 120 **tr**: SPL, **c**: Zefa UK, **br**: Rex; 121 **c**: Hulton, **cr**: Bruce Coleman Ltd, **bl**: Hulton, **bc**: SPL; 122 **r**: Mary Evans, **c**: Hulton; 125 **cl**: Bridgeman Art Library & Source, **c**: Werner Forman Archive; 129 **r**: Zefa UK; 136 **cl**: Bruce Coleman Ltd, **clb**: Bruce Coleman Ltd, **c**: Bruce Coleman Ltd; 139 **c**: Zefa UK, **br**: Zefa UK; 140 **t**: Rex, **b**: Rex; 141: SPL; 142: Zefa UK; 143 **bc**: Image Bank, **c**: Jules Selmes; 144 **tc**: Zefa UK, **tr**: Zefa UK; 146 **tl**: Zefa UK, **tr**: Zefa UK, **tc**: Zefa UK; 147 **b**: Bubbles/Loisjoy Thurston; 148 **t**: Ancient Art & Architecture, **c**: Worldview/Igho Cuypets/SPL; 149 **b**: Zefa UK, **cl**: Paul Biddle/SPL, **c**: Paul Biddle/SPL, **cr**: Zefa UK; 150 **tr**: Bridgeman Art Library & Source, **c**: Zefa UK, **bl**: Mary Evans, **bc**: Zefa UK; 151 **tr**: Bruce Coleman Ltd, **cr**: Harry Smith, **c**: Francoise Sauze/SPL, **bl**: SPL, **bc**: Francoise Sauze/SPL, **br**: Francoise Sauze/SPL; 152 **tcl**: AFIP, Photo Researchers/SPL, **tcr**: SPL; 154: Manfred Kage/SPL; 155 **r**: SPL; 156 **t**: SPL/David Scharf, **cl**: SPL/Petit Format/CSI, **c**: SPL/Petit Format/CSI, **cr**: SPL/Prof P Motta; 157 **c**: Petit Format/CSI/SPL; 164 **t**: SPL/Neil Brumhall, **b**: SPL; 165 **bc**: Nurture; 166: SPL/Hank Morgan; 173 **b**: SPL/Institut Pasteur/CNRI; 174 **c**: SPL/Marcelo Brodsky/CNRI; 176 **b** SPL/Alexander Tstaras; 177 **r**: SPL; 178: Nancy Durrell McKenna; 180: SPL/Petit Format/Nestle; 184 **tl**: Nancy Durrell McKenna, **tr**: Hutchison Library/Nancy Durrell McKenna, **cl**: SPL/Pascale Roche/Petit Format, **cr**: Janine Wiedel, **b**: TRIP/Bob Turner; 186 **b**: Nancy Durrell McKenna; 189 **ct**: Collections/Anthea Sieveking, **c**: Collections/Anthea Sieveking, **b**: Collections/Anthea Sieveking, **r**: Collections/Anthea Sieveking; 190 **main**: S & R Greenhill, **it**: SPL/Biophoto Ass, **ib**: SPL/James Stevenson; 191 **c**: Collections/Anthea Sieveking, **c**: Collections/Anthea Sieveking, **b**: Collections/Anthea Sieveking, **r**: Sally & Richard Greenhill; 198 **tr**: Zefa UK/Munden, **br**: Hutchison ; 200 **br**: SPL; 201 **br**: Boots Opticians; 202 **tc**: SPL/Prof P Motta, **cl**: SPL/CNRI; 203 **cr**: SPL/Tim Beddow; 204 **br**: Rex; 208 **tr**: Bubbles; 210 **cl**: Bruce Coleman Ltd/Jane Burton, **clb**: Bruce Coleman Ltd/Jane Burton, **bl**: Bruce Coleman Ltd/Jane Burton, **bc**: Barnabys/Ernest R Manewah; 211 **bl**: DK © BM, **br**: Zefa UK; 212 **t**: Rex, **br**: Zefa UK; 213 **tl**: Barnaby, **cl**: Supersport, **b**: R Harding; 214 **cl**: Zefa UK/Stockmarket, **bc**: R Harding/Nigel Blyton, **br**: Zefa UK; 215 **tl**: Bridgeman Art Library, **tc**: Mary Evans, **tr**: Mary Evans, **cr**: Mary Evans, **bl**: R Harding, **bc**: R Harding, **br**: Zefa UK; 216 **bc**: Zefa UK, **br**: Zefa UK